Arthritis Sourcebook

Basic Information about Specific Forms of Arthritis and Related Rheumatic Disorders, Including Rheumatoid Arthritis, Osteoarthritis, Gout, Polymyalgia Rheumatica, Psoriatic Arthritis, Spondyloarthropathies, Juvenile Rheumatoid Arthritis, and Juvenile Ankylosing Spondylitis; Along with Information about Medical, Surgical, and Alternative Treatment Options and Including Strategies for Coping with Pain, Fatigue, and Stress

Edited by Allan R. Cook. 600 pages. 1998. 0-7808-0201-2. $78.

Back & Neck Disorders Sourcebook

Basic Information about Disorders and Injuries of the Spinal Cord and Vertebrae, Including Facts on Chiropractic Treatment, Surgical Interventions, Paralysis, and Rehabilitation, Along with Advice for Preventing Back Trouble

Edited by Karen Bellenir. 548 pages. 1997. 0-7808-0202-0. $78.

"The strength of this work is its basic, easy-to-read format. Recommended."
— *Reference and User Services Quarterly, Winter '97*

Blood & Circulatory Disorders Sourcebook

Basic Information about Blood and Its Components, Anemias, Leukemias, Bleeding Disorders, and Circulatory Disorders, Including Aplastic Anemia, Thalassemia, Sickle-Cell Disease, Hemochromatosis, Hemophilia, Von Willebrand Disease, and Vascular Diseases; Along with a Special Section on Blood Transfusions and Blood Supply Safety, a Glossary, and Source Listings for Further Help and Information

Edited by Karen Bellenir and Linda M. Shin. 575 pages. 1998. 0-7808-0203-9. $78.

Burns Sourcebook

Basic Information about Various Types of Burns and Scalds, Including Flame, Heat, Electrical, Chemical, and Sun; Along with Short- and Long-Term Treatments, Tissue Reconstruction, Plastic Surgery, Prevention Suggestions, and First Aid

Edited by Allan R. Cook. 600 pages. 1998. 0-7808-0204-7. $78.

Cancer Sourcebook, 1st Edition

Basic Information on Cancer Types, Symptoms, Diagnostic Methods, and Treatments, Including Statistics on Cancer Occurrences Worldwide and the Risks Associated with Known Carcinogens and Activities

Edited by Frank E. Bair. 932 pages. 1990. 1-55888-888-8. $78.

"Written in nontechnical language. Useful for patients, their families, medical professionals, and librarians."
— *Guide to Reference Books, '96*

"Designed with the non-medical professional in mind. Libraries and medical facilities interested in patient education should certainly consider adding the *Cancer Sourcebook* to their holdings. This compact collection of reliable information . . . is an invaluable tool for helping patients and patients' families and friends to take the first steps in coping with the many difficulties of cancer."
— *Medical Reference Services Quarterly, Winter '91*

"Specifically created for the nontechnical reader . . . an important resource for the general reader trying to understand the complexities of cancer."
— *American Reference Books Annual, '91*

"This publication's nontechnical nature and very comprehensive format make it useful for both the general public and undergraduate students." — *Choice, Oct '90*

New Cancer Sourcebook, 2nd Edition

Basic Information about Major Forms and Stages of Cancer, Featuring Facts about Primary and Secondary Tumors of the Respiratory, Nervous, Lymphatic, Circulatory, Skeletal, and Gastrointestinal Systems, and Specific Organs; Statistical and Demographic Data; Treatment Options; and Strategies for Coping

Edited by Allan R. Cook. 1,313 pages. 1996. 0-7808-0041-9. $78.

"This book is an excellent resource for patients with newly diagnosed cancer and their families. The dialogue is simple, direct, and comprehensive. Highly recommended for patients and families to aid in their understanding of cancer and its treatment"
— *Booklist Health Sciences Supplement, Oct '97*

"The amount of factual and useful information is extensive. The writing is very clear, geared to general readers. Recommended for all levels." — *Choice, Jan '97*

Cancer Sourcebook for Women

Basic Information about Specific Forms of Cancer That Affect Women, Featuring Facts about Breast Cancer, Cervical Cancer, Ovarian Cancer, Cancer of the Uterus and Uterine Sarcoma, Cancer of the Vagina, and Cancer of the Vulva; Statistical and Demographic Data; Treatments, Self-Help Management Suggestions, and Current Research Initiatives

Edited by Allan R. Cook and Peter D. Dresser. 524 pages. 1996. 0-7808-0076-1. $78.

". . . written in easily understandable, non-technical language. Recommended for public libraries or hospital and academic libraries that collect patient education or consumer health materials."
— *Medical Reference Services Quarterly, Spring '97*

Cancer Sourcebook for Women *(Continued)*

"Would be of value in a consumer health library. . . . written with the health care consumer in mind. Medical jargon is at a minimum, and medical terms are explained in clear, understandable sentences."
— *Bulletin of the MLA, Oct '96*

"The availability under one cover of all these pertinent publications, grouped under cohesive headings, makes this certainly a most useful sourcebook."
— *Choice, Jun '96*

"Presents a comprehensive knowledge base for general readers. Men and women both benefit from the gold mine of information nestled between the two covers of this book. Recommended."
— *Academic Library Book Review, Summer '96*

"This timely book is highly recommended for consumer health and patient education collections in all libraries."
— *Library Journal, Apr '96*

Cardiovascular Diseases & Disorders Sourcebook

Basic Information about Cardiovascular Diseases and Disorders, Featuring Facts about the Cardiovascular System, Demographic and Statistical Data, Descriptions of Pharmacological and Surgical Interventions, Lifestyle Modifications, and a Special Section Focusing on Heart Disorders in Children

Edited by Karen Bellenir and Peter D. Dresser. 683 pages. 1995. 0-7808-0032-X. $78.

". . . comprehensive format provides an extensive overview on this subject."
— *Choice, Jun '96*

". . . an easily understood, complete, up-to-date resource. This well executed public health tool will make valuable information available to those that need it most, patients and their families. The typeface, sturdy non-reflective paper, and library binding add a feel of quality found wanting in other publications. Highly recommended for academic and general libraries. "
— *Academic Library Book Review, Summer '96*

Communication Disorders Sourcebook

Basic Information about Deafness and Hearing Loss, Speech and Language Disorders, Voice Disorders, Balance and Vestibular Disorders, and Disorders of Smell, Taste, and Touch

Edited by Linda M. Ross. 533 pages. 1996. 0-7808-0077-X. $78.

"This is skillfully edited and is a welcome resource for the layperson. It should be found in every public and medical library."
— *Booklist Health Sciences Supplement, Oct '97*

Congenital Disorders Sourcebook

Basic Information about Disorders Acquired during Gestation, Including Spina Bifida, Hydrocephalus, Cerebral Palsy, Heart Defects, Craniofacial Abnormalities, Fetal Alcohol Syndrome, and More, Along with Current Treatment Options and Statistical Data

Edited by Karen Bellenir. 607 pages. 1997. 0-7808-0205-5. $78.

"Recommended reference source." — *Booklist, Oct '97*

Consumer Issues in Health Care Sourcebook

Basic Information about Health Care Fundamentals and Related Consumer Issues, Including Exams and Screening Tests, Physician Specialties, Choosing a Doctor, Using Prescription and Over-the-Counter Medications Safely, Avoiding Health Scams, Managing Common Health Risks in the Home, Care Options for Chronically or Terminally Ill Patients, and a List of Resources for Obtaining Help and Further Information

Edited by Karen Bellenir. 592 pages. 1998. 0-7808-0221-7. $78.

Contagious & Non-Contagious Infectious Diseases Sourcebook

Basic Information about Contagious Diseases like Measles, Polio, Hepatitis B, and Infectious Mononucleosis, and Non-Contagious Infectious Diseases like Tetanus and Toxic Shock Syndrome, and Diseases Occurring as Secondary Infections Such as Shingles and Reye Syndrome, Along with Vaccination, Prevention, and Treatment Information, and a Section Describing Emerging Infectious Disease Threats

Edited by Karen Bellenir and Peter D. Dresser. 566 pages. 1996. 0-7808-0075-3. $78.

Diabetes Sourcebook, 1st Edition

Basic Information about Insulin-Dependent and Noninsulin-Dependent Diabetes Mellitus, Gestational Diabetes, and Diabetic Complications, Symptoms, Treatment, and Research Results, Including Statistics on Prevalence, Morbidity, and Mortality, Along with Source Listings for Further Help and Information

Edited by Karen Bellenir and Peter D. Dresser. 827 pages. 1994. 1-55888-751-2. $78.

. . . very informative and understandable for the layperson without being simplistic. It provides a comprehensive overview for laypersons who want a general understanding of the disease or who want to focus on various aspects of the disease." — *Bulletin of the MLA, Jan '96*

DISABILITIES
SOURCEBOOK

Health Reference Series

AIDS Sourcebook, 1st Edition
AIDS Sourcebook, 2nd Edition
Allergies Sourcebook
Alternative Medicine Sourcebook
Alzheimer's, Stroke & 29 Other Neurological Disorders Sourcebook
Alzheimer's Disease Sourcebook, 2nd Edition
Arthritis Sourcebook
Back & Neck Disorders Sourcebook
Blood & Circulatory Disorders Sourcebook
Burns Sourcebook
Cancer Sourcebook, 1st Edition
New Cancer Sourcebook, 2nd Edition
Cancer Sourcebook for Women
Cardiovascular Diseases & Disorders Sourcebook
Communication Disorders Sourcebook
Congenital Disorders Sourcebook
Consumer Issues in Health Care Sourcebook
Contagious & Non-Contagious Infectious Diseases Sourcebook
Diabetes Sourcebook, 1st Edition
Diabetes Sourcebook, 2nd Edition
Diet & Nutrition Sourcebook, 1st Edition
Diet & Nutrition Sourcebook, 2nd Edition
Ear, Nose & Throat Disorders Sourcebook
Endocrine & Metabolic Disorders Sourcebook
Environmentally Induced Disorders Sourcebook
Fitness & Exercise Sourcebook
Food & Animal Borne Diseases Sourcebook
Gastrointestinal Diseases & Disorders Sourcebook
Genetic Disorders Sourcebook
Head Trauma Sourcebook
Health Insurance Sourcebook
Immune System Disorders Sourcebook
Kidney & Urinary Tract Diseases & Disorders Sourcebook
Learning Disabilities Sourcebook
Men's Health Concerns Sourcebook
Mental Health Disorders Sourcebook
Ophthalmic Disorders Sourcebook
Oral Health Sourcebook
Pain Sourcebook
Pregnancy & Birth Sourcebook
Public Health Sourcebook
Rehabilitation Sourcebook
Respiratory Diseases & Disorders Sourcebook
Sexually Transmitted Diseases Sourcebook
Skin Disorders Sourcebook
Sleep Disorders Sourcebook
Sports Injuries Sourcebook
Substance Abuse Sourcebook
Women's Health Concerns Sourcebook

Health Reference Series

Volume Thirty-three

LEARNING DISABILITIES
SOURCEBOOK

*Basic Information about Disorders
Such as Dyslexia, Visual and Auditory
Processing Deficits, Attention Deficit/
Hyperactivity Disorder, and Autism, along
with Statistical and Demographic Data,
Reports on Current Research Initiatives,
an Explanation of the Assessment Process,
and a Special Section for Adults with
Learning Disabilities*

Edited by
Linda M. Shin

Omnigraphics, Inc.

Penobscot Building / Detroit, MI 48226

BIBLIOGRAPHIC NOTE

This book contains information from publications issued by the National Institutes of Health (NIH) and its subagencies including the National Institute of Child Health and Human Development (NICHD) and the National Institute of Mental Health (NIMH); the U.S. Department of Education (DOE); National Information Center for Children and Youth with Disabilities (NICHCY); ERIC (Educational Resources Information Center); Heath Resource Center; and the American Council on Education. Copyrighted information is reprinted with permission of the following copyright holders: the American Speech-Language-Hearing Association, COPE (Creating Opportunities for Parent Empowerment), the International Center for the Disabled, Learning Disabilities Association of America, the Learning Disabilities Network Exchange, the National Center for Learning Disabilities, the Orton Dyslexia Society, the University of Michigan, *Journal of Learning Disabilities*, *Parent Journal*, and *Scientific American*. Full citation information is provided on the first page of each chapter.

Edited by Linda M. Shin

Laurie DiMauro, Associate Editor
Karen Bellenir, Series Editor, *Health Reference Series*
Peter D. Dresser, Managing Editor, *Health Reference Series*

Omnigraphics, Inc.

Matthew P. Barbour, *Manager, Production and Fulfillment*
Laurie Lanzen Harris, *Vice President, Editorial Director*
Peter E. Ruffner, *Vice President, Administration*
James A. Sellgren, *Vice President, Operations and Finance*
Jane J. Steele, *Marketing Consultant*

Frederick G. Ruffner, Jr., Publisher

Copyright ©1998, Omnigraphics, Inc.

Library of Congress Cataloging-in-Publication Data

Learning disabilities sourcebook : basic information about disorders such as
   dyslexia, visual and auditory processing deficits, attention deficit/hyperac-
   tivity disorder, and autism, along with statistical and demographic data,
   reports on current research initiatives, an explanation of the assessment
   process, and a special section for adults with learning disabilities / edited by
   Linda M. Shin.
      p.   cm. — (Health reference series ; v. 33)
      Includes bibliographical references and index.
      ISBN 0-7808-0210-1 (Lib. bdg. : alk. paper)
      1. Learning disabilities—United States. 2. Learning disabled children—
   Education—United States. 3. Learning disabled—Education—United States.
   4. Learning disabilities—United States—Diagnosis. I. Shin, Linda M.
   II. Series.
   LC4705/L434   1998   97-52049
   371.92'6—dc21   CIP

∞

This book is printed on acid-free paper meeting the ANSI Z39.48 Standard. The infinity symbol that appears above indicates that the paper in this book meets that standard.

Printed in the United States of America

Table of Contents

Part IV: Sensory and Communication Disorders

Part V: Other Neurological Disorders that Impede Learning

Part VI: Legal and Social Information for Parents of Learning Disabled Children

Part VII: Special Information for Older Students and Adults with Learning Disabilities

Appendix

Preface

About This Book

The diagnosis of "learning disability" is not a diagnosis in the same sense as a disease with a single, known cause and predictable set of symptoms. Instead, it is a broad term that encompasses a wide range of disorders in reading, writing, mathematics, listening, and speaking. Deficits in attention and social behavior often accompany specific learning disabilities. Learning disabilities affect people's ability to either interpret what they see and hear or to link information from different parts of the brain. Although often associated with childhood and classroom activities, learning disabilities can manifest themselves as life-long conditions that affect multiple aspects of a person's life, including work, daily routines, and social interactions.

According to estimates made by the National Institute of Child Health and Human Development, children with learning disabilities constitute between seven and 10 percent of the school-aged population and represent over half of the children who receive special education services in the United States. Despite this frequency of occurrence, learning disabilities remain poorly understood. This book is designed to give parents and other concerned individuals the information they need to understand the underlying medical theories about learning disabilities, current diagnostic methods, and approaches to treatment.

How to Use This Book

This book is divided into parts and chapters. Parts focus on broad areas of interest; individual chapters look at specific topics within those areas.

Part I: Introduction to Learning Disabilities presents an overview of the current state of knowledge about learning disabilities and provides information about on-going and projected future research strategies. Selected statistics from the U.S. Department of Education help define the scope of the problem and document progress made in the education of children with learning disabilities.

Part II: Assessment is designed to help parents navigate through the complex process of diagnosing and assessing a specific learning disability. A glossary of terms and a list of some of the tests that are commonly used will help parents communicate effectively with educators and other evaluators.

Part III: Dyslexia and Other Academic Skills Disorders looks at some of the most common types of learning disabilities: disorders of reading, writing, movement, and calculation.

Part IV: Sensory and Communication Disorders provides information and intervention strategies for students struggling with disorders that affect their ability to understand what is seen or heard. These include speech, receptive language, and sensory processing disorders.

Part V: Other Neurological Disorders that Impede Learning includes information about Attention Deficit/Hyperactivity Disorder (AD/HD), autism, and pervasive developmental disorder.

Part VI: Legal and Social Information for Parents of Learning Disabled Children outlines legal provisions designed to assist in securing an appropriate education for children diagnosed with learning disabilities. In addition, it gives practical suggestions for helping children make the necessary social adjustments to maximize their learning potential.

Part VII: Special Information for Older Students and Adults with Learning Disabilities offers information about postsecondary school adjustment and help in overcoming potential long-term negative effects of learning disabilities such as poor peer relationships, diminished self-esteem, and limited occupational opportunities.

Acknowledgements

Many people and organizations have contributed the material in this volume. The editors gratefully acknowledge the assistance and cooperation of the American Speech-Language-Hearing Association, COPE (Creating Opportunities for Parent Empowerment), the International Center for the Disabled, Learning Disabilities Association of America, the Learning Disabilities Network Exchange, the National Center for Learning Disabilities, the Orton Dyslexia Society, and the University of Michigan.

Note from the Editor

This book is part of Omnigraphics' *Health Reference Series*. The series provides basic information about a broad range of medical concerns. It is not intended to serve as a tool for diagnosing illness, in prescribing treatments, or as a substitute for the physician/patient relationship. All persons concerned about medical symptoms or the possibility of disease are encouraged to seek professional care from an appropriate health care provider.

Part One

Introduction to Learning Disabilities

Chapter 1

Understanding Learning Disabilities

Imagine having important needs and ideas to communicate, but being unable to express them. Perhaps feeling bombarded by sights and sounds, unable to focus your attention. Or trying to read or add but not being able to make sense of the letters or numbers.

You may not need to imagine. You may be the parent or teacher of a child experiencing academic problems, or have someone in your family diagnosed as learning disabled. Or possibly as a child you were told you had a reading problem called dyslexia or some other learning handicap.

Although different from person to person, these difficulties make up the common daily experiences of many learning disabled children, adolescents, and adults. A person with a learning disability may experience a cycle of academic failure and lowered self-esteem. Having these handicaps—or living with someone who has them—can bring overwhelming frustration.

But the prospects are hopeful. It is important to remember that a person with a learning disability can learn. The disability usually only affects certain limited areas of a child's development. In fact, rarely are learning disabilities severe enough to impair a person's potential to live a happy, normal life.

The test in this chapter is provided by the National Institute of Mental Health (NIMH), the Federal agency that supports research nationwide on the brain, mental illnesses, and mental health. Scientists supported by NIMH are dedicated to understanding the workings and

National Institutes of Mental Health, NIH Pub. No. 93–3611, September 1993.

3

interrelationships of the various regions of the brain, and to finding preventions and treatments to overcome brain dysfunctions that handicap people in school, work, and play. The chapter provides up-to-date information on learning disabilities and the role of NIMH sponsored research in discovering underlying causes and effective treatments. It describes treatment options, strategies for coping, and sources of information and support. Among these sources are doctors, special education teachers, and mental health professionals who can help identify learning disabilities and recommend the right combination of medical, psychosocial, and educational treatment.

In this chapter, you'll also read the stories of Susan, Wallace, and Dennis, three people who have learning disabilities. Although each had a rough start, with help they learned to cope with their handicaps. You'll see their early frustrations, their steps toward getting help, and their hopes for the future.

The stories of Susan, Wallace, and Dennis are representative of people with learning disabilities, but the characters are not real. Of course, people with learning disabilities are not all alike, so these stories may not fit any particular individual.

Understanding the Problem

Susan

At age 14, Susan still tends to be quiet. Even when she was a child, she was so withdrawn that people sometimes forgot she was there. She seemed to drift into a world of her own. When she did talk, she often called objects by the wrong names. She had few friends and mostly played with dolls or her little sister. In school, Susan hated reading and math because none of the letters, numbers or "+" and "-" signs made any sense. She felt awful about herself. She'd been told—and was convinced—that she was retarded.

Wallace

Wallace has lived 46 years, and still has trouble understanding what people say. Even as a boy, many words sounded alike. His father patiently said things over and over. But whenever his mother was drunk, she flew into a rage and spanked him for not listening. Wallace's speech also came out funny. He had such problems saying words that in school his teacher sometimes couldn't understand him. When classmates called him a "dummy," his fists just seemed to take over.

Dennis

Dennis is 23 years old and still seems to have so much energy. But he had always been an overactive boy, sometimes jumping on the sofa for hours until he collapsed with exhaustion. In grade school, he never sat still. He interrupted lessons. But he was a friendly, well-meaning kid, so adults didn't get too angry. His academic problems became evident in third grade, when his teacher realized that Dennis could only recognize a few words and wrote like a first grader. She recommended that Dennis repeat third grade, to give him time to "catch up." After another full year, his behavior was still out of control, and his reading and writing had not improved.

What Is a Learning Disability?

Unlike other disabilities, such as paralysis or blindness, a learning disability (LD) is a hidden handicap. A learning disability doesn't disfigure or leave visible signs that would invite others to be understanding or offer support. A woman once blurted to Wallace, "You seem so intelligent—you don't look handicapped!"

LD is a disorder that affects people's ability to either interpret what they see and hear or to link information from different parts of the brain. These limitations can show up in many ways—as specific difficulties with spoken and written language, coordination, self-control, or attention. Such difficulties extend to schoolwork and can impede learning to read or write, or to do math.

Learning disabilities can be lifelong conditions that, in some cases, affect many parts of a person's life: school or work, daily routines, family life, and sometimes even friendships and play. In some people, many overlapping learning disabilities may be apparent. Other people may have a single, isolated learning problem that has little impact on other areas of their lives.

What Are the Types of Learning Disabilities?

"Learning disability" is not a diagnosis in the same sense as "chickenpox" or "mumps." Chickenpox and mumps imply a single, known cause with a predictable set of symptoms. Rather, LD is a broad term that covers a pool of possible causes, symptoms, treatments, and outcomes. Partly because learning disabilities can show up in so many forms, it is difficult to diagnose or to pinpoint the causes. And no one knows of a pill or remedy that will cure them.

Not all learning problems are necessarily learning disabilities. Many children are simply slower in developing certain skills. Because children show natural differences in their rate of development, sometimes what seems to be a learning disability may simply be a delay in maturation. To be diagnosed as a learning disability, specific criteria must be met.

The criteria and characteristics for diagnosing learning disabilities appear in a reference book called the DSM (short for the Diagnostic and Statistical Manual of Mental Disorders). The DSM diagnosis is commonly used when applying for health insurance coverage of diagnostic and treatment services.

Learning disabilities can be divided into three broad categories:

- Developmental speech and language disorders.
- Academic skills disorders.
- "Other," a catch-all that includes certain coordination disorders and learning handicaps not covered by the other terms.

Each of these categories includes a number of more specific disorders.

Developmental Speech and Language Disorders

Speech and language problems are often the earliest indicators of a learning disability. People with developmental speech and language disorders have difficulty producing speech sounds, using spoken language to communicate, or understanding what other people say. Depending on the problem, the specific diagnosis may be:

- Developmental articulation disorder
- Developmental expressive language disorder
- Developmental receptive language disorder

Developmental articulation disorder. Children with this disorder may have trouble controlling their rate of speech. Or they may lag behind playmates in learning to make speech sounds. For example, Wallace at age 6 still said "wabbit" instead of "rabbit" and "thwim" for "swim." Developmental articulation disorders are common. They appear in at least 10 percent of children younger than age 8. Fortunately, articulation disorders can often be outgrown or successfully treated with speech therapy.

Developmental expressive language disorder. Some children with language impairments have problems expressing themselves in

6

speech. Their disorder is called, therefore, a developmental expressive language disorder. Susan, who often calls objects by the wrong names, has an expressive language disorder. Of course, an expressive language disorder can take other forms. A 4-year-old who speaks only in two-word phrases and a 6-year-old who can't answer simple questions also have an expressive language disability.

Developmental receptive language disorder. Some people have trouble understanding certain aspects of speech. It's as if their brains are set to a different frequency and the reception is poor. There's the toddler who doesn't respond to his name, a preschooler who hands you a bell when you asked for a ball, or the worker who consistently can't follow simple directions. Their hearing is fine, but they can't make sense of certain sounds, words, or sentences they hear. They may even seem inattentive. These people have a receptive language disorder. Because using and understanding speech are strongly related, many people with receptive language disorders also have an expressive language disability.

Of course, in preschoolers, some misuse of sounds, words, or grammar is a normal part of learning to speak. It's only when these problems persist that there is any cause for concern.

Academic Skills Disorders

Students with academic skills disorders are often years behind their classmates in developing reading, writing, or arithmetic skills. The diagnoses in this category include:

- Developmental reading disorder
- Developmental writing disorder
- Developmental arithmetic disorder

Developmental reading disorder. This type of disorder, also known as dyslexia, is quite widespread. In fact, reading disabilities affect 2 to 8 percent of elementary school children.

When you think of what is involved in the "three R's"—reading, 'riting, and 'rithmetic—it's astounding that most of us do learn them. Consider that to read, you must simultaneously:

- Focus attention on the printed marks and control eye movements across the page
- Recognize the sounds associated with letters

7

- Understand words and grammar
- Build ideas and images
- Compare new ideas to what you already know
- Store ideas in memory

Such mental juggling requires a rich, intact network of nerve cells that connect the brain's centers of vision, language, and memory.

A person can have problems in any of the tasks involved in reading. However, scientists found that a significant number of people with dyslexia share an inability to distinguish or separate the sounds in spoken words. Dennis, for example, can't identify the word "bat" by sounding out the individual letters, b-a-t. Other children with dyslexia may have trouble with rhyming games, such as rhyming "cat" with "bat." Yet scientists have found these skills fundamental to learning to read. Fortunately, remedial reading specialists have developed techniques that can help many children with dyslexia acquire these skills.

However, there is more to reading than recognizing words. If the brain is unable to form images or relate new ideas to those stored in memory, the reader can't understand or remember the new concepts. So other types of reading disabilities can appear in the upper grades when the focus of reading shifts from word identification to comprehension.

Developmental writing disorder. Writing, too, involves several brain areas and functions. The brain networks for vocabulary, grammar, hand movement, and memory must all be in good working order. So a developmental writing disorder may result from problems in any of these areas. For example, Dennis, who was unable to distinguish the sequence of sounds in a word, had problems with spelling. A child with a writing disability, particularly an expressive language disorder, might be unable to compose complete, grammatical sentences.

Developmental arithmetic disorder. If you doubt that arithmetic is a complex process, think of the steps you take to solve this simple problem: 23 divided by 3 = ?.

Arithmetic involves recognizing numbers and symbols, memorizing facts such as the multiplication table, aligning numbers, and understanding abstract concepts like place value and fractions. Any of these may be difficult for children with developmental arithmetic disorders. Problems with numbers or basic concepts are likely to show up early. Disabilities that appear in the later grades are more often tied to problems in reasoning.

Many aspects of speaking, listening, reading, writing, and arithmetic overlap and build on the same brain capabilities. So it's not surprising that people can be diagnosed as having more than one area of learning disability. For example, the ability to understand language underlies learning to speak. Therefore, any disorder that hinders the ability to understand language will also interfere with the development of speech, which in turn hinders learning to read and write. A single gap in the brain's operation can disrupt many types of activity.

"Other" Learning Disabilities

The DSM also lists additional categories, such as "motor skills disorders" and "specific developmental disorders not otherwise specified." These diagnoses include delays in acquiring language, academic, and motor skills that can affect the ability to learn, but do not meet the criteria for a specific learning disability. Also included are coordination disorders that can lead to poor penmanship, as well as certain spelling and memory disorders.

Attention Disorders

Nearly 4 million school-age children have learning disabilities. Of these, at least 20 percent have a type of disorder that leaves them unable to focus their attention.

Some children and adults who have attention disorders appear to daydream excessively. And once you get their attention, they're often easily distracted. Susan, for example, tends to mentally drift off into a world of her own. Children like Susan may have a number of learning difficulties. If, like Susan, they are quiet and don't cause problems, their problems may go unnoticed. They may be passed along from grade to grade, without getting the special assistance they need.

In a large proportion of affected children—mostly boys—the attention deficit is accompanied by hyperactivity. Dennis is an example of a person with attention deficit hyperactivity disorder—ADHD. Like young Dennis, who jumped on the sofa to exhaustion, hyperactive children can't sit still. They act impulsively, running into traffic or toppling desks. They blurt out answers and interrupt. In games, they can't wait their turn. These children's problems are usually hard to miss. Because of their constant motion and explosive energy, hyperactive children often get into trouble with parents, teachers, and peers.

9

By adolescence, physical hyperactivity usually subsides into fidgeting and restlessness. But the problems with attention and concentration often continue into adulthood. At work, adults with ADHD often have trouble organizing tasks or completing their work. They don't seem to listen to or follow directions. Their work may be messy and appear careless. Attention disorders, with or without hyperactivity, are not considered learning disabilities in themselves. However, because attention problems can seriously interfere with school performance, they often accompany academic skills disorders.

What Causes Learning Disabilities?

Understandably, one of the first questions parents ask when they learn their child has a learning disorder is "Why? What went wrong?"

Mental health professionals stress that since no one knows what causes learning disabilities, it doesn't help parents to look backward to search for possible reasons. There are too many possibilities to pin down the cause of the disability with certainty. It is far more important for the family to move forward in finding ways to get the right help.

Scientists, however, do need to study causes in an effort to identify ways to prevent learning disabilities.

Once, scientists thought that all learning disabilities were caused by a single neurological problem. But research supported by NIMH has helped us see that the causes are more diverse and complex. New evidence seems to show that most learning disabilities do not stem from a single, specific area of the brain, but from difficulties in bringing together information from various brain regions.

Today, a leading theory is that learning disabilities stem from subtle disturbances in brain structures and functions. Some scientists believe that, in many cases, the disturbance begins before birth.

Errors in Fetal Brain Development

Throughout pregnancy, the fetal brain develops from a few all-purpose cells into a complex organ made of billions of specialized, interconnected nerve cells called neurons. During this amazing evolution, things can go wrong that may alter how the neurons form or interconnect.

In the early stages of pregnancy, the brain stem forms. It controls basic life functions such as breathing and digestion. Later, a deep ridge divides the cerebrum—the thinking part of the brain—into two halves, a right and left hemisphere. Finally, the areas involved with processing sight, sound, and other senses develop, as well as the areas associated with attention, thinking, and emotion.

As new cells form, they move into place to create various brain structures. Nerve cells rapidly grow to form networks with other parts of the brain. These networks are what allow information to be shared among various regions of the brain.

Throughout pregnancy, this brain development is vulnerable to disruptions. If the disruption occurs early, the fetus may die, or the infant may be born with widespread disabilities and possibly mental retardation. If the disruption occurs later, when the cells are becoming specialized and moving into place, it may leave errors in the cell makeup, location, or connections. Some scientists believe that these errors may later show up as learning disorders.

Other Factors that Affect Brain Development

Through experiments with animals, scientists at NIMH and other research facilities are tracking clues to determine what disrupts brain development. By studying the normal processes of brain development, scientists can better understand what can go wrong. Some of these studies are examining how genes, substance abuse, pregnancy problems, and toxins may affect the developing brain.

Genetic factors. The fact that learning disabilities tend to run in families indicates that there may be a genetic link. For example, children who lack some of the skills needed for reading, such as hearing the separate sounds of words, are likely to have a parent with a related problem. However, a parent's learning disability may take a slightly different form in the child. A parent who has a writing disorder may have a child with an expressive language disorder. For this reason, it seems unlikely that specific learning disorders are inherited directly. Possibly, what is inherited is a subtle brain dysfunction that can in turn lead to a learning disability.

There may be an alternative explanation for why LD might seem to run in families. Some learning difficulties may actually stem from the family environment. For example, parents who have expressive language disorders might talk less to their children, or the language they use may be distorted. In such cases, the child lacks a good model for acquiring language and therefore, may seem to be learning disabled.

Tobacco, alcohol, and other drug use. Many drugs taken by the mother pass directly to the fetus. Research shows that a mother's use of cigarettes, alcohol, or other drugs during pregnancy may have damaging effects on the unborn child. Therefore, to prevent potential harm to developing babies, the U.S. Public Health Service supports efforts to make people aware of the possible dangers of smoking, drinking, and using drugs.

Scientists have found that mothers who smoke during pregnancy may be more likely to bear smaller babies. This is a concern because small newborns, usually those weighing less than 5 pounds, tend to be at risk for a variety of problems, including learning disorders.

Alcohol also may be dangerous to the fetus' developing brain. It appears that alcohol may distort the developing neurons. Heavy alcohol use during pregnancy has been linked to fetal alcohol syndrome, a condition that can lead to low birth weight, intellectual impairment, hyperactivity, and certain physical defects. Any alcohol use during pregnancy, however, may influence the child's development and lead to problems with learning, attention, memory, or problem solving. Because scientists have not yet identified "safe" levels, alcohol should be used cautiously by women who are pregnant or who may soon become pregnant. Drugs such as cocaine—especially in its smokable form known as crack—seem to affect the normal development of brain receptors. These brain cell parts help to transmit incoming signals from our skin, eyes, and ears, and help regulate our physical response to the environment. Because children with certain learning disabilities have difficulty understanding speech sounds or letters, some researchers believe that learning disabilities, as well as ADHD, may be related to faulty receptors. Current research points to drug abuse as a possible cause of receptor damage.

Problems during pregnancy or delivery. Other possible causes of learning disabilities involve complications during pregnancy. In some cases, the mother's immune system reacts to the fetus and attacks it as if it were an infection. This type of disruption seems to cause newly formed brain cells to settle in the wrong part of the brain. Or during delivery, the umbilical cord may become twisted and temporarily cut off oxygen to the fetus. This, too, can impair brain functions and lead to LD.

Toxins in the child's environment. New brain cells and neural networks continue to be produced for a year or so after the child is born. These cells are vulnerable to certain disruptions, also.

Researchers are looking into environmental toxins that may lead to learning disabilities, possibly by disrupting childhood brain development or brain processes. Cadmium and lead, both prevalent in the environment, are becoming a leading focus of neurological research. Cadmium, used in making some steel products, can get into the soil, then into the foods we eat. Lead was once common in paint and gasoline, and is still present in some water pipes. A study of animals sponsored by the National Institutes of Health showed a connection between exposure to lead and learning difficulties. In the study, rats exposed to lead experienced changes in their brain waves, slowing their ability to learn. The learning problems lasted for weeks, long after the rats were no longer exposed to lead.

In addition, there is growing evidence that learning problems may develop in children with cancer who had been treated with chemotherapy or radiation at an early age. This seems particularly true of children with brain tumors who received radiation to the skull.

Are Learning Disabilities Related to Differences in the Brain?

In comparing people with and without learning disabilities, scientists have observed certain differences in the structure and functioning of the brain. For example, new research indicates that there may be variations in the brain structure called the planum temporale, a language-related area found in both sides of the brain. In people with dyslexia, the two structures were found to be equal in size. In people who are not dyslexic, however, the left planum temporale was noticeably larger. Some scientists believe reading problems may be related to such differences.

With more research, scientists hope to learn precisely how differences in the structures and processes of the brain contribute to learning disabilities, and how these differences might be treated or prevented.

Getting Help

Susan

Susan was promoted to the sixth grade but still couldn't do basic math. So, her mother brought her to a private clinic for testing. The clinician observed that Susan had trouble associating symbols with their meaning, and this was holding back her language, reading, and math development. Susan called objects by the wrong words and she could not associate sounds with letters or recognize math symbols.

However, an IQ of 100 meant that Susan was quite bright. In addition to developing an Individualized Education Plan, the clinician recommended that Susan receive counseling for her low self-esteem and depression.

Wallace

In the early 1960s, at the request of his ninth grade teacher, Wallace was examined by a doctor to see why he didn't speak or listen well. The doctor tested his vocal cords, vision, and hearing. They were all fine. The teacher concluded that Wallace must have "brain damage," so not much could be done. Wallace kept failing in school and was suspended several times for fighting. He finally dropped out after tenth grade. He spent the next 25 years working as a janitor. Because LD frequently went undiagnosed at the time when Wallace was young, the needed help was not available to him.

Dennis

In fifth grade, Dennis' teacher sent him to the school psychologist for testing. Dennis was diagnosed as having developmental reading and developmental writing disorders. He was also identified as having an attention disorder with hyperactivity. He was placed in an all-day special education program, where he could work on his particular deficits and get individual attention. His family doctor prescribed the medication Ritalin to reduce his hyperactivity and distractibility. Along with working to improve his reading, the special education teacher helped him improve his listening skills. Since his hand-writing was still poor, he learned to type homework and reports on a computer. At age 19, Dennis graduated from high school and was accepted b a college that gives special assistance to students with learning disabilities.

How Are Learning Disabilities First Identified?

The first step in solving any problem is realizing there is one. Wallace, sadly, was a product of his time, when learning disabilities were more of a mystery and often went unrecognized. Today, professionals would know how to help Wallace. Dennis and Susan were able to get help because someone saw the problem and referred them for help.

When a baby is born, the parents eagerly wait for the baby's first step, first word, a myriad of other "firsts." During routine checkups, the pediatrician, too, watches for more subtle signs of development. The parents and doctor are watching for the child to achieve developmental milestones.

Parents are usually the first to notice obvious delays in their child reaching early milestones. The pediatrician may observe more subtle signs of minor neurological damage, such as a lack of coordination. But the classroom teacher, in fact, may be the first to notice the child's persistent difficulties in reading, writing, or arithmetic. As school tasks become more complex, a child with a learning disability may have problems mentally juggling more information.

The learning problems of children who are quiet and polite in school may go unnoticed. Children with above average intelligence, who manage to maintain passing grades despite their disability, are even less likely to be identified. Children with hyperactivity, on the other hand, will be identified quickly by their impulsive behavior and excessive movement. Hyperactivity usually begins before age 4 but may not be recognized until the child enters school.

What should parents, doctors, and teachers do if critical developmental milestones haven't appeared by the usual age? Sometimes it's best to allow a little more time, simply for the brain to mature a bit. But if a milestone is already long delayed, if there's a history of learning disabilities in the family, or if there are several delayed skills, the child should be professionally evaluated as soon as possible. An educator or a doctor who treats children can suggest where to go for help.

How Are Learning Disabilities Formally Diagnosed?

By law, learning disability is defined as a significant gap between a person's intelligence and the skills the person has achieved at each age. This means that a severely retarded 10-year-old who speaks like a 6-year-old probably doesn't have a language or speech disability. He has mastered language up to the limits of his intelligence. On the other hand, a fifth grader with an IQ of 100 who can't write a simple sentence probably does have LD.

Learning disorders may be informally flagged by observing significant delays in the child's skill development. A 2-year delay in the primary grades is usually considered significant. For older students, such a delay is not as debilitating, so learning disabilities aren't usually suspected unless there is more than a 2-year delay. Actual diagnosis of learning disabilities, however, is made using standardized tests that compare the child's level of ability to what is considered normal development for a person of that age and intelligence.

15

For example, as late as fifth grade, Susan couldn't add two numbers, even though she rarely missed school and was good in other subjects. Her mother took her to a clinician, who observed Susan's behavior and administered standardized math and intelligence tests. The test results showed that Susan's math skills were several years behind, given her mental capacity for learning. Once other possible causes like lack of motivation and vision problems were ruled out, Susan's math problem was formally diagnosed as a specific learning disability.

Test outcomes depend not only on the child's actual abilities, but on the reliability of the test and the child's ability to pay attention and understand the questions. Children like Dennis, with poor attention or hyperactivity, may score several points below their true level of ability. Testing a child in an isolated room can sometimes help the child concentrate and score higher.

Each type of LD is diagnosed in slightly different ways. To diagnose speech and language disorders, a speech therapist tests the child's pronunciation, vocabulary, and grammar and compares them to the developmental abilities seen in most children that age. A psychologist tests the child's intelligence. A physician checks for any ear infections, and an audiologist may be consulted to rule out auditory problems. If the problem involves articulation, a doctor examines the child's vocal cords and throat.

In the case of academic skills disorders, academic development in reading, writing, and math is evaluated using standardized tests. In addition, vision and hearing are tested to be sure the student can see words clearly and can hear adequately. The specialist also checks if the child has missed much school. It's important to rule out these other possible factors. After all, treatment for a learning disability is very different from the remedy for poor vision or missing school.

ADHD is diagnosed by checking for the long-term presence of specific behaviors, such as considerable fidgeting, losing things, interrupting, and talking excessively. Other signs include an inability to remain seated, stay on task, or take turns. A diagnosis of ADHD is made only if the child shows such behaviors substantially more than other children of the same age.

If the school fails to notice a learning delay, parents can request an outside evaluation. In Susan's case, her mother chose to bring Susan to a clinic for testing. She then brought documentation of the disability back to the school. After confirming the diagnosis, the public school was obligated to provide the kind of instructional program that Susan needed.

Parents should stay abreast of each step of the school's evaluation. Parents also need to know that they may appeal the school's decision if they disagree with the findings of the diagnostic team. And like Susan's mother, who brought Susan to a clinic, parents always have the option of getting a second opinion.

Some parents feel alone and confused when talking to learning specialists. Such parents may find it helpful to ask someone they like and trust to go with them to school meetings. The person may be the child's clinician or caseworker, or even a neighbor. It can help to have someone along who knows the child and can help understand the child's test scores or learning problems.

What Are the Education Options?

Although obtaining a diagnosis is important, even more important is creating a plan for getting the right help. Because LD can affect the child and family in so many ways, help may be needed on a variety of fronts: educational, medical, emotional, and practical.

In most ways, children with learning disabilities are no different from children without these disabilities. At school, they eat together and share sports, games, and after-school activities. But since children with learning disabilities do have specific learning needs, most public schools provide special programs.

Schools typically provide special education programs either in a separate all-day classroom or as a special education class that the student attends for several hours each week. Some parents hire trained tutors to work with their child after school. If the problems are severe, some parents choose to place their child in a special school for the learning disabled.

If parents choose to get help outside the public schools, they should select a learning specialist carefully. The specialist should be able to explain things in terms that the parents can understand. Whenever possible, the specialist should have professional certification and experience with the learner's specific age group and type of disability. Some of the support groups listed at the end of this chapter can provide references to qualified special education programs.

Planning a special education program begins with systematically identifying what the student can and cannot do. The specialist looks for patterns in the child's gaps. For example, if the child fails to hear the separate sounds in words, are there other sound discrimination problems? If there's a problem with handwriting, are there other motor delays? Are there any consistent problems with memory?

17

Special education teachers also identify the types of tasks the child can do and the senses that function well. By using the senses that are intact and bypassing the disabilities, many children can develop needed skills. These strengths offer alternative ways the child can learn.

After assessing the child's strengths and weaknesses, the special education teacher designs an Individualized Educational Program (IEP). The IEP outlines the specific skills the child needs to develop as well as appropriate learning activities that build on the child's strengths. Many effective learning activities engage several skills and senses. For example, in learning to spell and recognize words, a student may be asked to see, say, write, and spell each new word. The student may also write the words in sand, which engages the sense of touch. Many experts believe that the more senses children use in learning a skill, the more likely they are to retain it.

An individualized, skill-based approach—like the approach used by speech and language therapists—often succeeds in helping where regular classroom instruction fails. Therapy for speech and language disorders focuses on providing a stimulating but structured environment for hearing and practicing language patterns. For example, the therapist may help a child who has an articulation disorder to produce specific speech sounds. During an engaging activity, the therapist may talk about the toys, then encourage the child to use the same sounds or words. In addition, the child may watch the therapist make the sound, feel the vibration in the therapist's throat, then practice making the sounds before a mirror.

Researchers are also investigating nonstandard teaching methods. Some create artificial learning conditions that may help the brain receive information in nonstandard ways. For example, in some language disorders, the brain seems abnormally slow to process verbal information. Scientists are testing whether computers that talk can help teach children to process spoken sounds more quickly. The computer starts slowly, pronouncing one sound at a time. As the child gets better at recognizing the sounds and hearing them as words, the sounds are gradually speeded up to a normal rate of speech.

Is Medication Available?

For nearly six decades, many children with attention disorders have benefited from being treated with medication. Three drugs, Ritalin (methylphenidate), Dexedrine (dextroamphetamine), and

Cylert (pemoline), have been used successfully. Although these drugs are stimulants in the same category as "speed" and "diet pills," they seldom make children "high" or more jittery. Rather, they temporarily improve children's attention and ability to focus. They also help children control their impulsiveness and other hyperactive behaviors.

The effects of medication are most dramatic in children with ADHD. Shortly after taking the medication, they become more able to focus their attention. They become more ready to learn. Studies by NIMH scientists and other researchers have shown that at least 90 percent of hyperactive children can be helped by either Ritalin or Dexedrine. If one medication does not help a hyperactive child to calm down and pay attention in school, the other medication might.

The drugs are effective for 3 to 4 hours and move out of the body within 12 hours. The child's doctor or a psychiatrist works closely with the family and child to carefully adjust the dosage and medication schedule for the best effect. Typically, the child takes the medication so that the drug is active during peak school hours, such as when reading and math are taught.

In the past few years, researchers have tested these drugs on adults who have attention disorders. Just as in children, the results show that low doses of these medications can help reduce distractibility and impulsivity in adults. Use of these medications has made it possible for many severely disordered adults to organize their lives, hold jobs, and care for themselves. In trying to do everything possible to help their children, many parents have been quick to try new treatments. Most of these treatments sound scientific and reasonable, but a few are pure quackery. Many are developed by reputable doctors or specialists—but when tested scientifically, cannot be proven to help. Following are types of therapy that have not proven effective in treating the majority of children with learning disabilities or attention disorders:

- Megavitamins
- Colored lenses
- Special diets
- Sugar-free diets
- Body stimulation or manipulation

Although scientists hope that brain research will lead to new medical interventions and drugs, at present there are no medicines for speech, language, or academic disabilities.

19

How Do Families Learn to Cope?

The effects of learning disabilities can ripple outward from the disabled child or adult to family, friends, and peers at school or work.

Children with LD often absorb what others thoughtlessly say about them. They may define themselves in light of their disabilities, as "behind," "slow," or "different."

Sometimes they don't know how they're different, but they know how awful they feel. Their tension or shame can lead them to act out in various ways—from withdrawal to belligerence. Like Wallace, they may get into fights. They may stop trying to learn and achieve and eventually drop out of school. Or, like Susan, they may become isolated and depressed.

Children with learning disabilities and attention disorders may have trouble making friends with peers. For children with ADHD, this may be due to their impulsive, hostile, or withdrawn behavior. Some children with delays may be more comfortable with younger children who play at their level. Social problems may also be a product of their disability. Some people with LD seem unable to interpret tone of voice or facial expressions. Misunderstanding the situation, they act inappropriately, turning people away.

Without professional help, the situation can spiral out of control. The more that children or teenagers fail, the more they may act out their frustration and damage their self-esteem. The more they act out, the more trouble and punishment it brings, further lowering their self-esteem. Wallace, who lashed out when teased about his poor pronunciation and was repeatedly suspended from school, shows how harmful this cycle can be.

Having a child with a learning disability may also be an emotional burden for the family. Parents often sweep through a range of emotions: denial, guilt, blame, frustration, anger, and despair. Brothers and sisters may be annoyed or embarrassed by their sibling, or jealous of all the attention the child with LD gets.

Counseling can be very helpful to people with LD and their families. Counseling can help affected children, teenagers, and adults develop greater self-control and a more positive attitude toward their own abilities. Talking with a counselor or psychologist also allows family members to air their feelings as well as get support and reassurance.

Many parents find that joining a support group also makes a difference. Support groups can be a source of information, practical suggestions, and mutual understanding. Self-help books written by educators and mental health professionals can also be helpful. A number of references and support groups are listed at the end of this chapter.

Behavior modification also seems to help many children with hyperactivity and LD. In behavior modification, children receive immediate, tangible rewards when they act appropriately. Receiving an immediate reward can help children learn to control their own actions, both at home and in class. A school or private counselor can explain behavior modification and help parents and teachers set up appropriate rewards for the child. Parents and teachers can help by structuring tasks and environments for the child in ways that allow the child to succeed. They can find ways to help children build on their strengths and work around their disabilities. This may mean deliberately making eye contact before speaking to a child with an attention disorder. For a teenager with a language problem, it may mean providing pictures and diagrams for performing a task. For students like Dennis with handwriting or spelling problems, a solution may be to provide a word processor and software that checks spelling. A counselor or school psychologist can help identify practical solutions that make it easier for the child and family to cope day by day.

Every child needs to grow up feeling competent and loved. When children have learning disabilities, parents may need to work harder at developing their children's self-esteem and relationship-building skills. But self-esteem and good relationships are as worth developing as any academic skill.

Sustaining Hope

Susan

Susan is now in ninth grade and enjoys learning. She no longer believes she's retarded, and her use of words has improved. Susan has become a talented craftsperson and loves making clothes and furniture for her sister's dolls. Although she's still in a special education program, she is making slow but steady progress in reading and math.

Wallace

Over the years, Wallace found he liked tinkering with cars and singing in the church choir. At church, he met a woman who knew about learning disabilities. She told him he could get help through his county social services office. Since then, Wallace has been working with a speech therapist, learning to articulate and notice differences in speech sounds.

When he complains that he's too old to learn, his therapist reminds him, "It's never too late to work your good brain!" His state vocational rehabilitation office recently referred him to a job-training program. Today, at age 46, Wallace is starting night school to become an auto mechanic. He likes it because it's a hands-on program where he can learn by doing.

Dennis

Dennis is now age 23. As he walks into the college job placement office, he smiles and shakes hands confidently. After shuffling through a messy stack of papers, he finally hands his counselor a neatly typed resume. Although Dennis jiggles his foot and interrupts occasionally, he's clearly enthusiastic. He explains that because tape-recorded books and lectures got him through college, he'd like to sell electronics. Dennis says he'll also be getting married next year. He and his fiancée are concerned that their children also will have LD. "But we'll just have to watch and get help early—a lot earlier than I did!"

Can Learning Disabilities Be Outgrown or Cured?

Even though most people don't outgrow their brain dysfunction, people do learn to adapt and live fulfilling lives. Dennis, Susan, and Wallace made a life for themselves—not by being cured, but by developing their personal strengths. Like Dennis' tape-recorded books and lectures, or Wallace's hands-on auto mechanics class, they found alternative ways to learn. And like Susan's crafts or Wallace's singing, they found ways to enjoy their other talents.

Even though a learning disability doesn't disappear, given the right types of educational experiences, people have a remarkable ability to learn. The brain's flexibility to learn new skills is probably greatest in young children and may diminish somewhat after puberty. This is why early intervention is so important. Nevertheless, we retain the ability to learn throughout our lives.

Even though learning disabilities can't be cured, there is still cause for hope. Because certain learning problems reflect delayed development, many children do eventually catch up. Of the speech and language disorders, children who have an articulation or an expressive language disorder are the least likely to have long-term problems. Despite initial delays, most children do learn to speak.

For people with dyslexia, the outlook is mixed. But an appropriate remedial reading program can help learners make great strides.

With age, and appropriate help from parents and clinicians, children with ADHD become better able to suppress their hyperactivity and to channel it into more socially acceptable behaviors. As with Dennis, the problem may take less disruptive forms, such as fidgeting.

Can an adult be helped? For example, can an adult with dyslexia still learn to read? In many cases, the answer is yes. It may not come as easily as for a child. It may take more time and more repetition, and it may even take more diverse teaching methods. But we know more about reading and about adult learning than ever before. We know that adults have a wealth of life experience to build on as they learn. And because adults choose to learn, they do so with a determination that most children don't have. A variety of literacy and adult education programs sponsored by libraries, public schools, and community colleges are available to help adults develop skills in reading, writing, and math. Some of these programs, as well as private and nonprofit tutoring and learning centers, provide appropriate programs for adults with LD.

What Aid Does the Government Offer?

As of 1981, people with learning disabilities came under the protection of laws originally designed to protect the rights of people with mobility handicaps. More recent Federal laws specifically guarantee equal opportunity and raise the level of services to people with disabilities. Once a learning disability is identified, children are guaranteed a free public education specifically designed around their individual needs. Adolescents with disabilities can receive practical assistance and extra training to help make the transition to jobs and independent living. Adults have access to job training and technology that open new doors of opportunity.

Increased Services, Equal Opportunity

The Individuals with Disabilities Education Act of 1990 (IDEA) assures a public education to school-aged children with diagnosed learning disabilities. Under this act, public schools are required to design and implement an Individualized Educational Program tailored to each child's specific needs. The 1991 Individuals with Disabilities Education Act extended services to developmentally delayed children down to age 5. This law makes it possible for young children to receive help even before they begin school.

Another law, the Americans with Disabilities Act of 1990, guarantees equal employment opportunity for people with learning disabilities and protects disabled workers against job discrimination. Employers may not consider the learning disability when selecting among job applicants. Employers must also make "reasonable accommodations" to help workers who have handicaps do their job. Such accommodations may include shifting job responsibilities, modifying equipment, or adjusting work schedules.

By law, publicly funded colleges and universities must also remove barriers that keep out disabled students. As a result, many colleges now recruit and work with students with learning disabilities to make it possible for them to attend. Depending on the student's areas of difficulty, this help may include providing recorded books and lectures, providing an isolated area to take tests, or allowing a student to tape record rather than write reports. Students with learning disabilities can arrange to take college entrance exams orally or in isolated rooms free from distraction. Many colleges are creating special programs to specifically accommodate these students.

Programs like these made it possible for Dennis to attend and succeed in college. The HEATH Resource Center, sponsored by the American Council on Education, assists students with learning disabilities to identify appropriate colleges and universities. Information on the HEATH center and related organizations appears at the end of this chapter.

Public Agency Support

Effective service agencies are also in place to assist people of all ages. Each state department of education can help parents identify the requirements and the process for getting special education services for their child. Other agencies serve disabled infants and preschool children. Still others offer mental health and counseling services. The National Information Center for Children and Youth can provide referrals to appropriate local resources and state agencies.

Counselors at each state department of vocational rehabilitation serve the employment needs of adolescents and adults with learning disabilities. They can refer adults to free or subsidized health care, counseling, and high school equivalence (GED) programs. They can assist in arranging for job training that sidesteps the disability. For example, a vocational counselor helped Wallace identify his aptitude for car repair. To work around Wallace's language problems, the counselor helped locate a job-training program that teaches through demonstrations and active practice rather than lectures.

State departments of vocational rehabilitation can also assist in finding special equipment that can make it possible for disabled individuals to receive training, retain a job, or live on their own. For example, because Dennis couldn't read the electronics manuals in his new job, a vocational rehabilitation counselor helped him locate and purchase a special computer that reads books aloud.

Finally, state-run protection and advocacy agencies and client assistance programs serve to protect these rights. As experts on the laws, they offer legal assistance, as well as information about local health, housing, and social services.

What Hope Does Research Offer?

Sophisticated brain imaging technology is now making it possible to directly observe the brain at work and to detect subtle malfunctions that could never be seen before. Other techniques allow scientists to study the points of contact among brain cells and the ways signals are transmitted from cell to cell.

With this array of technology, NIMH is conducting research to identify which parts of the brain are used during certain activities, such as reading. For example, researchers are comparing the brain processes of people with and without dyslexia as they read. Research of this kind may eventually associate portions of the brain with different reading problems.

Clinical research also continues to amass data on the causes of learning disorders. NIMH grantees at Yale are examining the brain structures of children with different combinations of learning disabilities. Such research will help identify differences in the nervous system of children with these related disorders. Eventually, scientists will know, for example, whether children who have both dyslexia and an attention disorder will benefit from the same treatment as dyslexic children without an attention disorder.

Studies of identical and fraternal twins are also being conducted. Identical twins have the same genetic makeup, while fraternal twins do not. By studying if learning disabilities are more likely to be shared by identical twins than fraternal twins, researchers hope to determine whether these disorders are influenced more by genetic or by environmental factors. One such study is being conducted by scientists funded by the National Institute of Child Health and Human Development. So far, the research indicates that genes may, in fact, influence the ability to sound out words.

25

Animal studies also are adding to our knowledge of learning disabilities in humans. Animal subjects make it possible to study some of the possible causes of LD in ways that can't be studied in humans. One NIMH grantee is researching the effects of barbiturates and other drugs that are sometimes prescribed during pregnancy. Another researcher discovered through animal studies that certain prenatal viruses can affect future learning. Research of this kind may someday pinpoint prenatal problems that can trigger specific disabilities and tell us how they can be prevented.

Animal research also allows the safety and effectiveness of experimental new drugs to be tested long before they can be tried on humans. One NIH-sponsored team is studying dogs to learn how new stimulant drugs that are similar to Ritalin act on the brain. Another is using mice to test a chemical that may counter memory loss.

This accumulation of data sets the stage for applied research. In the coming years, NIMH-sponsored research will focus on identifying the conditions that are required for learning and the best combination of instructional approaches for each child.

Piece by piece, using a myriad of research techniques and technologies, scientists are beginning to solve the puzzle. As research deepens our understanding, we approach a future where we can prevent certain brain and mental disorders, make valid diagnoses, and treat each effectively. This is the hope, mission, and vision of the National Institute of Mental Health.

What Are Sources of Information and Support?

Several publications, organizations, and support groups exist to help individuals, teachers, and families to understand and cope with learning disabilities. The following resources provide a good starting point for gaining insight, practical solutions, and support. Further information can be found at libraries and book stores.

Publications

Books for Children and Teens with Learning Disabilities

Fisher, G., and Cummings, R., *The Survival Guide for Kids with LD*. Minneapolis: Free Spirit Publishing, 1990. (Also available on cassette)

Gehret, J. *Learning Disabilities and the Don't-Give-Up-Kid*. Fairport, NY: Verbal Images Press, 1990.

Janover, C. *Josh: A Boy with Dyslexia*. Burlington, VT: Waterfront Books 1988.

Landau, E. *Dyslexia*. New York: Franklin Watts Publishing Co., 1991.

Marek, M. *Different, Not Dumb*. New York: Franklin Watts Publishing Co., 1985.

Levine, M. *Keeping A Head in School: A Student's Book about Learning Abilities and Learning Disorders*. Cambridge, MA: Educators Publishing Services, Inc., 1990.

Books for Adults with Learning Disabilities

Adelman, P., and Wren, C. *Learning Disabilities, Graduate School, and Careers: The Student's Perspective*. Lake Forest, IL: Learning Opportunities Program, Barat College, 1990.

Cordoni, B. *Living with a Learning Disability*. Carbondale, IL: Southern Illinois University Press, 1987.

Kravets, M., and Wax, I. *The K&W Guide: Colleges and the Learning Disabled Student*. New York: Harper Collins Publishers, 1992.

Magnum, C., and Strichard, S., eds. *Colleges with Programs for Students with Learning Disabilities*. Princeton, NJ: Petersons Guides, 1992.

Books for Parents

Greene, L. *Learning Disabilities and Your Child: A Survival Handbook*. New York: Fawcett Columbine, 1987.

Novick, B., and Arnold, M. *Why Is My Child Having Trouble in School?* New York: Villard Books, 1991.

Silver, L. *The Misunderstood Child: A Guide for Parents of Children with Learning Disabilities*. 2d ed. Blue Ridge Summit, PA: Tab Books, 1992.

Silver, L. *Dr. Silver's Advice to Parents on Attention-Deficit Hyperactivity Disorder*. Washington, DC: American Psychiatric Press, 1993.

Vail, P. *Smart Kids with School Problems*. New York: EP Dutton, 1987.

Weiss, E. *Mothers Talk About Learning Disabilities*. New York: Prentice Hall Press, 1989.

<u>Books and Pamphlets for Teachers and Specialists</u>

Adelman, P., and Wren, C. *Learning Disabilities, Graduate School, and Careers*. Lake Forest, Learning Opportunities Program, Barat College, 1990.

Silver, L. *ADHD: Attention Deficit-Hyperactivity Disorder, Booklet for Teachers*. Summit, NJ: CIBA-GEIGY, 1989.

Smith, S. *Success Against the Odds: Strategies and Insights from the Learning Disabled*. Los Angeles: Jeremy Tarcher, Inc., 1991.

Wender, P. *The Hyperactive Child, Adolescent, and Adult. Attention Disorder through the Lifespan*. New York: Oxford University Press, 1987.

<u>Related Pamphlets Available from NIH</u>

Facts About Dyslexia
National Institute of Child Health and Human Development
Building 31, Room 2A32
9000 Rockville Pike
Bethesda, MD 20892
(301) 496-5133

Developmental Speech and Language Disorders—Hope through Research
National Institute on Deafness and Other Communicative Disorders
P.O. Box 37777
Washington, DC 20013
(800) 241-1044

Support Groups and Organizations

American Speech-Language-Hearing Association
10801 Rockville Pike
Rockville, MD 20852
(800) 638-8255

Provides information on speech and language disorders, as well as referrals to certified speech-language therapists.

Attention Deficit Information Network
475 Hillside Avenue
Needham, MA 02194
(617) 455-9895

Provides up-to-date information on current research, regional meetings. Offers aid in finding solutions to practical problems faced by adults and children with an attention disorder.

Candlelighters Childhood Cancer Foundation
7910 Woodmont Avenue, Suite 460
Bethesda, MD 20814
(800) 366-2223

Provides information and support for children treated for cancer who later experience learning disabilities.

Center for Mental Health Services
Office of Consumer, Family, and Public Information
5600 Fishers Lane, Room 15-81
Rockville, MD 20857
(301) 443-2792

This new national center, a component of the U.S. Public Health Service, provides a range of information on mental health, treatment, and support services.

Children with Attention Deficit Disorders (CHADD)
499 NW 70th Avenue, Suite 308
Plantation, FL 33317
(305) 587-3700

Runs support groups and publishes two newsletters concerning attention disorders for parents and professionals.

Council for Exceptional Children
11920 Association Drive
Reston, VA 22091
(703) 620-3660

Provides publications for educators. Can also provide referral to ERIC Clearinghouse for Handicapped and Gifted Children.

Federation of Families for Children's Mental Health
1021 Prince Street
Alexandria, VA 22314
(703) 684-7710

Provides information, support, and referrals through federation chapters throughout the country. This national parent-run organization focuses on the needs of children with broad mental health problems.

HEATH Resource Center
American Council on Education
One Dupont Circle, Suite 800
Washington, DC 20036
(800) 544-3284

A national clearinghouse on post-high school education for people with disabilities.

Learning Disabilities Association of America
4156 Library Road
Pittsburgh, PA 15234
(412) 341-8077

Provides information and referral to state chapters, parent resources, and local support groups. Publishes news briefs and a professional journal.

Library of Congress National Library Service for the Blind and Physically Handicapped
1291 Taylor Street, NW
Washington, DC 20542
(202) 707-5100

Publishes *Talking Books and Reading Disabilities*, a factsheet outlining eligibility requirements for borrowing talking books.

National Alliance for the Mentally Ill Children and Adolescents Network (NAMICAN)
2101 Wilson Boulevard, Suite 302
Arlington, VA 22201
(800) 950-NAMI

Provides support to families through personal contact and support meetings. Provides education regarding coping strategies; reading material; and information about what works—and what doesn't.

National Association of Private Schools for Exceptional Children
1522 K Street, NW Suite 1032
Washington, DC 20005
(202) 408-3338

Provides referrals to private special education programs.

National Center for Learning Disabilities
381 Park Avenue South, Suite 1420
New York, NY 10016
(212) 687-7211

Provides referrals and resources. Publishes *Their World* magazine describing true stories on ways children and adults cope with LD.

National Information Center for Children and Youth with Disabilities
P.O. Box 1492
Washington, DC 20013
(800) 999-5599

Publishes newsletter, arranges workshops. Advises parents on the laws entitling children with disabilities to special education and other services.

Orton Dyslexia Society
Chester Building, Suite 382
8600 LaSalle Road
Baltimore, MD 21286-2044
(410) 296-0232

Answers individual questions on reading disability. Provides information and referrals to local resources.

To Arrange for Special College Entrance Testing for LD Adults

- ACT Special Testing: (319) 337-1332
- SAT Scholastic Aptitude Test: (609) 771-7137
- GED: (202) 939-9490

Chapter 2

Brain Development and Implications for Learning

An alliance between the fields of neuroscience and education holds great promise for the education of children with learning difficulties. While few neurologists are making definitive claims about the exact nature of the dyslexic brain, the research is thought-provoking and frequently inspiring. At the very least, teacher attention to the research has the potential to improve instruction, giving practitioners the information they need to make more informed choices about teaching techniques and activities. There are many reasons for teachers to avoid thinking about brain research: the research is tentative; the conclusions may be wrong; the distance from medical research to traditional classrooms is enormous. Yet, there are compelling reasons to ponder and search. This quest is the soul of finding solutions for students who learn differently.

Here are synopses of several important neuroscientific studies. They are ordered from those with obvious teaching implications to those with more complex connotations. [A brief glossary of the technical terms used in this discussion is included at the end of this chapter.]

Plasticity—Use It or Lose It

Marian Diamond, UCLA

If a young rat is placed in an environment with toys and playmates, its cortex will begin to thicken after just a few days. Young rats placed

Reprinted with permission from "A Teacher's Guide to the Brain," *The Network Exchange*, Vol. 13 No.1. (1995). *The Exchange* is published by The Learning Disabilities Network, 72 Sharpe Street, Suite A-2, Hingham, MA 02043.

in impoverished environments experience much less neural development. The cortex can be up to 16 times thicker in the enriched rats. Rats with enlarged cortices out perform other rats on the ultimate test of intelligence—the maze.

Implications for children with LD. This study suggests that our students will prosper in learning environments that are stimulating. Teachers and parents are crucial in creating enriched learning experiences such as field trips and active lifestyles. Teachers need to activate the full range of human functioning, so that classrooms are rich with visual, experiential, and language opportunities, especially for children who struggle with language. Oral and receptive language activities are essential at early ages to develop oral and aural language skills that may later support the weaker visual memory for words that plague most dyslexics. Lots of visual support needs to accompany all this language. This study also speaks to the importance on nurturing, close human contact, and positive interchange.

Arborization

Jean-Pierre Changeux, Pasteur Institute

Neurons are perfectly capable of surviving in a laboratory dish for long periods of time, given the proper aqueous solution. But they do not grow, change, or connect with other neurons. However, when substances from muscle tissues are added to the solution, the neurons develop axon-dendrite connections and build networks within a day. Like trees, branches keep on developing as muscle tissue extracts are added to the solution.

Implications for children with LD. The kinesthetic channel is the great forgotten learning channel in American classrooms. Most children learn best when there are tangible, concrete manipulatives that help explain an abstract or complex concept. Further, the human neurological system is designed to place potent entrails in our memory systems when we experience multimodal, tactile, kinesthetic, and haptic routines. Whenever possible, it is best to have students "doing"—talking, moving, acting, responding, building, rehearsing, gesturing, and creating. We need additional research to broadcast more widely the notion that human movement is a powerful learning channel.

Novice Verses Competent Learners

Richard Haier, UC Irvine

PET Scans show that more energy is expended by people learning a task than those who have mastered the task. That is, we become more efficient as we gain competence.

Implications for children with LD. It makes little sense to allow children to continue to employ excessive amounts of brain energy to do tasks that should be so routine as to require minimal neurological expense. For example, what do we do with children who decode very poorly but seem to comprehend adequately? Many teachers say that if the child comprehends well, we don't need to worry about the decoding. Yet Haier's research suggests that ignoring the weak decoding skills will leave the child with a life-long handicap. Too much energy is being wasted in the inefficient decoding system. The same argument can be made in favor of drill, repetition, and master of mathematics facts, keyboarding, organizational patterns, sentence structure, note taking, and any number of other basic skills. We need to help children become nearly automatic in their use of essential skills whenever possible.

Neuroanatomical Dyslexia Findings

Albert Galaburda, et al., Beth Israel Hospital

Postmortem research accomplished in the Dyslexia Brain Laboratory at Beth Israel Hospital has identified four central anatomical differences in the brains of dyslexics:

- planum temporale symmetry;
- focal abnormalities in cerebral areas;
- larger right hemispheres; and
- high inner-hemispheric connectivity.

Implications for children with LD. There is insufficient space in this article to explain each of these findings. What is worth exploring here, though, is that the research tells us that dyslexia is real. No longer can teachers dismiss dyslexia as fiction. The differences in the dyslexic brains appear in crucial language centers. Therefore, it seems logical that language instruction for these students should be delivered in ways that dignify these differences. We need to find ways to teach differently and to teach better. The finding of larger right hemispheres might offer teachers confidence that there will be a series of notable strengths in the learning profiles of these children who struggle so mightily with reading, writing, spelling, and computation. We simply cannot rely on traditional teaching practices that fail with these children. We need to employ a truly diagnostic-prescriptive teaching methodology:

- determine the student's strengths and weaknesses,
- decide which weaknesses deserve priority for remediation,
- select a remedial approach,
- test often to determine the effectiveness of the intervention,
- choose alternative strategies should the intervention not work, and
- move on to students' other needs if the intervention works and maintains.

Magno Cellular Defects

Margaret Livingstone, et al., Harvard

Research in the visual system suggests that there is a defect in the fast processing system in dyslexics. Neuronal size in the LGN may be up to 27% smaller than normal. This may contribute to a delay in early (fast) processing when reading. That is, the faster magno cellular system may interfere with the more refined parvo cellular system to impede visual perception while reading.

Implications for children with LD. This elegant study provides a plausible explanation for why reading is so difficult for children with dyslexia. It also addresses the perplexity that so many dyslexics are so smart and so facile with spoken language. Livingstone's work offers the explanation that a perceptual problem is responsible for dyslexic decoding problems. This is interesting for several reasons: (a) dyslexia is not, at its roots, a cognitive defect; thinking ability and intelligence deficits are not causal; (b) dyslexia as a decoding problem is very real; and (c) once we teach our students to read effectively, many of them are then ready to benefit fully from mainstream schooling.

If this research proves correct, the teaching implications are profound and champion the reasons for teaching the structure of the language. We need to use a multimodal approach to teaching decoding so that the visual problem is not alone trying to unravel the mystery of sound/sound associations. Teachers need to show their students that the printed word follows a structured series of rules, generalizations, and patterns. We need to employ the strengths of our students' language experiences, their sense of language, and their enjoyment of learning through words. Teachers need to strengthen their students' receptive and expressive oral language skills to support the syntactic and semantic patterns of language. It seems unlikely that effective reading will occur through mere exposure to books. Whole-word approaches that rely largely on visual perception and visual memory are unlikely to be effective or efficient with these children.

Auditory Processing Defects

Paul Tallal, Rutgers

As early as 1973, Tallal identified a delay in the auditory processing rate of subjects with dyslexia. Children had difficulty separating closely timed, similar sounds (such as short vowels or voiced/unvoiced pairs). The later work of Livingstone identifies a similar difficulty in the visual system. Perhaps there are magno/parvo cellular interferences in the MGN auditory system as well. This may contribute to difficulty with rapidly changing auditory stimuli, such as phonology.

Thus, a child born without full representation capabilities in the auditory system has difficulty when learning to read because the weak auditory system seeks help from the weak visual system. Then two inefficient systems try to support one another in the attempt to decode complex, symbolic, phonological information.

Implications for children with LD. The implications of this research are similar to those of Livingstone's, yet, by combining the research in the visual and auditory systems, we face interacting obstacles. In the previous section, teachers may have hoped that a strong auditory system would support a student's weak visual processor. Indeed, often students succeed in precisely this manner. Combining Tallal's research with Livingstone's, educators may understand the likelihood that many dyslexics will experience perceptual difficulties in the two most important sensory channels for academic work. How can we expect to teach essential skills if both the visual and auditory systems are ill-prepared for such work?

Perhaps teachers will find direction in solving this challenge by reviewing the research cited. Teachers must enrich the experience for these children. Learning occurs through more than visual and auditory channels. Repetition is necessary to ensure the memories are indelibly stored. A spiraling approach to teaching ensures that students return to familiar locations (skills) as the curriculum moves upward. Reading, writing, memorization, expression, and evaluation must be thought of within a new perspective.

If dyslexia is primarily a perceptual problem, then teachers can also expect good thinking from their students who have dyslexic learning styles. Therefore, students can master rule-based instruction, and they can develop clever self-instructional strategies to improve academic performance.

Conclusion

This brief chapter can only serve to introduce teachers to the educational implications of neurological research. There is nothing magical or unique in the implications sections. The implications are only the musings of a teacher who is looking for better ways to help children who learn language differently.

Schools, teachers, and students are in great peril when we follow arbitrary, often whimsical educational movements. Economics and politics seem to dictate so much of our educational programming. These are false idols. Well-educated teachers should be the policy makers. By informing ourselves regarding human learning capacity (neuropsychology), educators can build a formidable force that will shape instruction for the benefit of all children, including those who learn differently.

Glossary

Arborization—a term referring to the tree-like dendrites that form as the human brain develops.

Axon—the information sending end of a neuron.

Cortex—the part of the brain devoted to uniquely primate tasks (language planning, reasoning).

Cortices—plural of cortex.

Dendrites—the information receiving end of neuron.

Haptic—related to or based on the sense of touch.

LGN (lateral geniculate nucleus)—a collection of neurons essential in the visual system.

Magno Cellular System—the quick, color blind part of the visual system that must work in synchronization with the slower, high resolution, color system called the parvo cellular system.

MGN (medial geniculate nucleus)—a collection of neurons essential in the auditory system.

Neuron—brain cells.

PET Scans (positron emissions tomography)—a sort of MRI method of observing where the greatest neurological activity occurs during different types of activity.

Phonology—the sound system of a language.

Plasticity—a term referring to the malleable and changeable quality of the human brain, especially early in life.

—by Steve Wilkins

Chapter 3

Research in Learning Disabilities

Introduction

Learning disabilities (LD) encompass a wide range of disorders is listening, speaking, reading, writing, and mathematics that are frequently accompanied by comorbid deficits in attention and social behavior. Current estimates indicate that children with LD compose between seven to 10 percent of the school-aged population and represent over half of the children who receive special education services in the United States.[1] Despite this frequency of occurrence, LD remains one of the least understood yet most disabling conditions that affect both children and adults. This is unfortunate since learning disabilities are extremely deleterious to the development of children in general, and the negative effects of LD go well beyond school failure. For example, poor peer relationships, decrements in self-concept, poor post-school adjustment, and limited placed occupational opportunities are some of the known outcomes of LD.

A number of influences have contributed to the persistent difficulties in diagnosing and treating. In fact, until research supported by the National Institute of Child Health and Human Development (NICHD) and the Natural Sciences and Engineering Council of Canada to study learning disabilities began to lead to major discoveries during the past decade, the consensus in the biological and behavioral sciences field was that the field of LD lacked scientific validity

National Institute of Child Health and Human Development (NICHD), National Institutes of Health, 1995.

and clinical utility.[2,3] To better understand the difficulties that have plagued the LD field and the NICHD's programmatic response to alleviate them, a brief review of both problems and progress in the field is presented in this chapter.

Impediments of Scientific Developments in Learning Disabilities: An Historical Perspective

Historically, a number of influences have contributed to difficulties in validating scientifically the construct of LD.[1,3] First, the field's limitations as a clinical science can be related to its brief tenure as a recognized category of disability. Specifically, LD as a federally designated condition, has been in existence only since 1968.[6] Thus, there has not been time to collect and consolidate the necessary observations under experimental conditions that could lead to a better understanding of the critical diagnostic markers and treatment interventions that have a known probability of success.

Second, many different theoretical and conceptual views are offered to explain LD and these views clearly reflect the multidisciplinary nature of the field.[2] Learning disabilities are considered the legitimate concern of many disciplines and professions, including education, psychology, neurology, neuropsychology, optometry, psychiatry, and speech and language pathology, to name a few. Each of these professions has focused on different aspects of the child or adult with LD, so that there exist highly divergent ideas, and frequently contentious disagreements about the importance of etiology, diagnostic methods, intervention methods, and professional roles and responsibilities. Unfortunately, from the perspective of developing a valid definition and classification system for LD, such variation in views and beliefs results in differences in the numbers of children identified and their characteristics. In turn, conducting research on samples of children with ostensible LD who vary widely in diagnostic and demographic characteristics provides little opportunity for the replication and generalization of findings—the cornerstones of scientific inquiry.

Third, many diagnostic and treatment decisions about individuals with LD have been based on technically inadequate tests and measures. Recent comprehensive reviews[4] suggest that fewer than one-third of the psychometric tools used in the diagnosis of LD meet criteria for adequate norms, reliability, and validity. As important, the valid assessment of change over time, and change as a function of treatment, is very difficult to accomplish at present because few instruments have the scaling properties to satisfy conditions for the measurement of individual growth curves.[4]

Fourth and by far the most significant and persistent problem impeding progress in the field of LD has been the difficulty in establishing a precise inclusionary definition and a theoretically based classification system that provides (1) a framework for the identification of different types of LD, and (2) a framework for recognizing distinctions and interrelationships (comorbidities) between LD and other learning disorders to include attention deficit disorders, general academic underachievement, mental retardation, and emotional disturbance. The precise characterization of LD has been hindered on the one hand by associating learning disabilities with the concept of aptitude achievement discrepancy, and on the other hand by conducting "single-shot" studies on "school-identified" or "clinic-referred" samples of children.[1,2,3,4] The assumption that an aptitude (typically assessed using intelligence tests) achievement discrepancy is a clear diagnostic marker for LD or can be considered a pathognomonic sign is at best premature, and at worst invalid.[2,3,7] Such an assumption is based on the premise that individuals who display an IQ-achievement discrepancy are indeed different from individuals who do not with respect to phenotypic variables such as information processing characteristics and response to intervention, and genotypic features such as differences in the heritability of the disorder or its neurophysiological signature. As will be pointed out later, a major thrust of the NICHD efforts in the study of LD has been to evaluate the efficacy of discrepancy in defining learning disabilities by systematically comparing "discrepant" versus "non-discrepant" low achieving children on both phenotypic and genotypic variables.

The study of individuals identified a priori as LD by school or clinic criteria within the context of single investigations or cross-sectional designs have also significantly hampered efforts to develop a valid definition and classification system for learning disabilities. It has been pointed out many times that schools and clinics lack consistency in the way in which LD is diagnosed. A child can literally be "cured" of an LD condition simply by moving across state boundaries or by changing schools within the same community.[1,2] Such variability in sample characteristics prohibits replication and generalization of findings—a severe impediment to the development of any clinical science. Moreover, "singleshot" investigations that compare children achieving normally with children with LD on one or more dependent variables of interest at one point in time ignores the developmental nature of learning and change over time, and how such change interacts with information processing characteristics, teacher characteristics, different interventions, and classroom climates. As such, limited information is available on the developmental course of LD, and how children may display different characteristics at different points in time.

The foregoing brief review provides the rationale for the development of the NICHD research programs in learning disabilities. Prior to the initiation of the programs, much of our research-based thinking about LD was predicated on information obtained from ambiguously defined school-identified samples of children who were administered technically inadequate tests. Frequently the research problem was further confounded by the tendency to interpret these test data in the context of invalid theoretical and conceptual frameworks. Finally, the majority of studies carried out with individuals with LD were not informed by a longitudinal, developmental perspective. It has been within this context of scientific need that the NICHD has systematically developed a portfolio of individual research initiatives, program projects, and Learning Disability Research Centers (LDRCs) to define and classify LD, and to obtain new knowledge related to etiologies, developmental trajectories, and interventions for learning disabilities. The following sections provide a review and analysis of the major findings of the NICHD-supported research projects with an eye toward identifying additional future research needs and directions.

The Role of the NICHD in the Planning and Conduct of Research in Learning Disabilities

By way of background, the Health Research Extension Act of 1985 (P.L. 99–158) mandated the establishment of an Interagency Committee on Learning Disabilities (ICLD) for the express purpose of addressing the persistent problems in identifying a valid classification system and a definition for LD. More specifically, the ICLD was charged with the task of reviewing and assessing Federal research priorities, activities, and findings regarding LD. The NICHD was designated the lead agency for this congressional initiative. With respect to legislative and administrative action, the ICLD was required to make recommendations to increase the effectiveness of research on LD and to improve the dissemination of findings, and to prioritize research efforts in the causes, diagnosis, treatment, and prevention of learning disabilities. Following a comprehensive review of extant data and information related to the study of LD,[8] the ICLD concluded that:

> "...collaborative, integrated, and coordinated multidisciplinary approaches to research questions, such as could be undertaken on university campuses in large program projects and in specialized research centers of excellence, would be the most appropriate way to increase the effectiveness of this research...A major goal of this research should be the development of a classification system that more clearly defines and diagnoses LD, conduct disorders, and attention deficit disorders, and their interrelationships. Such information is prerequisite to the delineation of homogeneous subgroups and the delineation of more precise and reliable strategies for treatment, remediation, and prevention that will increase the effectiveness of both research and therapy."[8]

Within this context, the NICHD proceeded to develop Requests for Applications (RFAs) for Program Projects in 1985, Learning Disability Research Centers (LDRCs) in 1987,[9] and treatment/intervention research projects in 1993. By way of background, the Program Project research award is an NIH funding mechanism that can support at least three discrete, yet closely related and synergistic projects. The LDRCs are funded via Specialized Research Center Grants that provide support for both the synergistic research projects and supporting core service projects. This type of mechanism is used to stimulate research in a given field by encouraging collaborative, interdisciplinary research.

In response to the Program Project RFA, five program Projects were awarded by the NICHD. The recipients were Dr. John DeFries and his research group at the University of Colorado, Dr. Frank Wood and his team at the Bowman Gray School of Medicine, Dr. Herbert Lubs and his colleagues at the University of Miami, Dr. Bennett Shaywitz and his collaborators at Yale University and the University of Houston (led by Dr. Jack Fletcher), and Dr. Albert Galaburda and his group at Beth Israel Hospital and Harvard University. In response to the LDRC RFA, three centers were established; one at Johns Hopkins University under the leadership of Dr. Martha Denckla, another at Yale University (also directed by Shaywitz) and one at University of Colorado (also directed by DeFries). In response to the treatment/intervention research RFA, one research program was established at Florida State University under the direction of Dr. Joseph Torgesen, and one at The University of Houston lead by Dr. Barbara Foorman. These longitudinal intervention studies are in the beginning phases and data are not yet available.

A brief overview of the major goals and objectives of the NICHD Program Projects and LDRCs is provided in the following sections. Individual Program Projects (Bowman Gray, Miami, Beth Israel/Harvard) will be summarized first followed by a review of the research programs that have been awarded an LDRC (Johns Hopkins) and both a Program Project and an LDRC (Colorado, Yale). This overview will be followed by sections which provide a synthesis of the major discoveries made by the research programs in targeted areas of inquiry (i.e., classification/definition, reading and language related processes, attention, genetics, neurophysiology/neuroimaging, and treatment/intervention). Readers should note that comprehensive reviews of the goals and findings from each of the projects and centers, written by each of the principle investigators and their research teams, can be found in Duane and Gray (1991),[5] Lyon et al.,[1] Fletcher et al.,[7] and Lyon.[4]

The NICHD Research Programs in Learning Disabilities Program Projects

The Bowman Gray Program Project. This project is designed to study childhood reading disability with an eye toward developing a definition and subtyping system for dyslexia.[5] Within this context, research studies have been, and continue to be, conducted to (1) identify an appropriate combination of measures in the first grade that can define dyslexia and predict reading performance throughout the later grades, (2) determine whether Attention Deficit Disorder (ADD) has an independent impact on reading development and disorders, (3) develop the most powerful combination of linguistic (e.g., phonological, naming) tasks that can be used to chart the developmental course of reading and reading disability, (4) identify the efficacy of code-emphasis reading approaches versus context-based reading approaches with well-defined groups of reading disabled children, (5) study regional cerebral blood flow and positron emission tomographic activation signatures that are correlated with specific linguistic and cognitive parameters in a unique sample of adult dyslexics, first seen as children by Mrs. June Orton, and (6) externally validate distinctions between dyslexia and ADD using event-related potential electrophysiology.

46

The University of Miami Program Project. This project has completed its first five years of investigations to identify inherited subtypes of specific dyslexia via both behavioral genetic studies and genetic linkage analyses, and to further characterize these subtypes by psychophysical, behavioral, and neuroimaging studies. More specifically, Dr. Lubs and his group have attempted to define the chromosomal location of the several genes that produce autosomal dominantly inherited dyslexia. Project goals were addressed through scientific experiments in three major areas.[4] In the first area, the Miami group designed and conducted linkage studies to delineate the location of chromosomes and chromosome bands of several genes that could be specifically related to a different phenotypic expressions of dyslexia. In the second area of investigation, psychophysical and neuropsychological tasks were administered to dyslexic subjects to delineate information processing and cognitive profiles that could be used to validate genetically different subtypes. In the third area, Magnetic Resonance Imaging and Positron Emission Tomography studies were carried out in an attempt to identify unique neurophysicalogical signatures for dyslexic subtypes.

The Beth Israel/Harvard Program Project. This study has as a primary goal the development of an understanding of the relationships between subtle abnormalities of brain development and specific childhood learning disabilities to include dyslexia. The ultimate goal of the research is to identify the causes of such neural anomalies, and thus the neurobiological causes of LD and dyslexia.[5] Within this context, Dr. Galaburda and his colleagues have sought to develop an animal model of brain development that provides a window on how cortical abnormalities occur during ontogenesis and how such abnormalities affect behavior. Major efforts have also been deployed to delineate the cytoarchitectonic organization and the chemoarchitectonics of those brain regions implicated in developmental dyslexia. In addition, several investigations are underway to specify immunological variables responsible for anatomical and behavioral anomalies in human and animal brain.

The Johns Hopkins LDRC. This group represents a multidisciplinary research effort designed to understand the neurodevelopmental bases of LD. Dr. Denckla and her associates pursue this complex research task through four major lines of research.[4,9] In one project, the Johns Hopkins group is attempting to discover the causes of nonverbal LD via behavioral, neuropsychological and neuroimaging studies of LD individuals and individuals with neurofibromatosis. A second project is designed to examine the spectrum and severity of social deficits in female children who are heterozygous for the Fragile X genetic anomaly and to investigate the relationship of these deficits to specific cognitive, linguistic, and neuropsychological problems observed in LD individuals without Fragile X. A third line of research is designed to investigate the relationship between Tourette Syndrome and ADD using both genetic and neuropsychological procedures. The fourth project is designed to develop assessment methods to differentiate between hard to remediate dyslexic children versus children who respond to intervention. This project is also designed to identify the most powerful predictors of dyslexia and intervention approaches that have a high probability of success with disabled readers.

The Colorado Program Project and LDRC. The Colorado Program Project has been composed of four interrelated projects designed (1) to assess the genetic etiology of reading disability, and, in particular, the heritability of phonological and orthographic skills, (2) to identify the specific language and perceptual skills that are critical for the development of fluent reading skills, (3) to determine whether reading disability is correlated with deficiencies in the immunological system, and (4) to conduct genetic linkage analyses to localize, if possible, specific genes implicated in the expression of reading disability.[4,5,9]

With the Colorado LDRC, Dr. DeFries and his group extend the research carried out in the Program Project by increasing sample sizes and developing creative behavioral genetic analytic methodologies to assess the genetic and environmental etiologies of deficient component phonological, orthographic, reading skills in reading disability. Within this context, genetic linkage analysis is being employed to search for major genes and quantitative trait loci that influence learning disabilities. In addition, a treatment/intervention project is being conducted with 100 twin pairs of disabled readers in an effort to discover reading subtype/dimension by treatment interactions.

The Yale University Program Project and LDRC. The Yale University Program Project is designed to address major questions related to the definition, etiology, developmental course, and biological/neurophysiological bases for dyslexia.[4,5,9] The Yale studies are unique in that they are being carried out with the largest longitudinal cohort of reading disabled children in North America. As such, Dr. Shaywitz and his associates are continuing to obtain major findings that are not biased by the vagaries of studying school-identified or clinic-referred samples. In Project 1 of the Program Project, the longitudinal cohort is studied to identify (1) whether distinct subtypes of dyslexia exist, (2) whether subtypes are stable over time, (3) whether dyslexia constitutes a developmental lag versus a fixed deficit in reading, neurolinguistic, and cognitive skills, (4) whether deficits in single word reading are attributable to a combination of deficits in phonological and orthographic processes, and (5) whether positive or negative outcomes of dyslexia are associated with sociodemographic factors, the nature and severity of the reading disability, co-morbidity, and self-esteem.

In Project 2, a well defined group of children with early language disorders is studied to assess the development of reading-related language skills (e.g., phonological awareness) and to determine how particular early language impairments relate to the emergence of different types of reading disability. In Project 3, dyslexic, math disabled, and nondisabled boys and girls are followed and studied as they pass through puberty in order to assess the effects of specific endocrinological influences on reading, cognitive, and neuro–linguistic skills. Finally in Project 4 of the Program Project, the Yale group is employing state-of-the-art Functional Magnetic Resonance neuroimaging technology to examine brain structures and brain functions in well defined groups of dyslexic children as the children carry out tasks designed to assess reading, phonological awareness, orthographic decision making, and phonological decision making skills.

The Yale University LDRC has been charged with the complex task of developing a comprehensive classification system for the range of common disorders that can influence school performance. A major focus of the Center is the development of a classification system for children with attention and oppositional/conduct disorders with and without learning disabilities. In addition, one large project within the Center is tasked with the continued in-depth epidemiological study of 414 reading disabled children, now entering the ninth grade, who were originally identified during kindergarten. This ongoing investigation continues to provide data relevant to the stability and generalizability of learning disability subtypes over time.

Major Findings and Conclusions

A number of independent and replicated discoveries relevant to learning disabilities in general, and dyslexia in particular, have been obtained through the research efforts at each of the NICHD Program Projects and Larch's, as well as through the Stanovich and Siegel research programs funded by the Canadian government. Selected important discoveries will be highlighted here according to major domains of study, and those programs obtaining the findings will be indicated in parentheses. Due to limitations on the number of references that could be used for this paper, readers are encouraged to peruse the edited sources cited for both an overview of the research, an analysis of other important discoveries, and citations for specific studies.

Classification/Definition

- The definition and classification of learning disabilities and dyslexia must be accomplished within a longitudinal developmental framework that does not require adherence to a priori assumptions reflected in current definitions. Further a valid definition can best be developed by studies that investigate representative groups of children over time and that document how differences among children emerge, change, and influence further development (Bowman Gray,[5] Yale[1,4,5,7]).

- Current exclusionary definitions of learning disabilities appear to be invalid, particularly in the area of reading disabilities and particularly when discrepancy formulae are used (Yale[7]).

Reading and Language Related Processes

- Reading disabilities (dyslexia) affect at least 10 million children, or approximately 1 child in 5 (Yale[9,10]).

- While schools identify approximately four times as many boys as girls as reading disabled, longitudinal and epidemiological studies show that as many girls are affected as boys (Bowman Gray,[5,9] Colorado,[4,9,11] Miami,[5,9] Yale[2,5,7,12]).

- Reading disability reflects a persistent deficit rather than a developmental lag in linguistic and reading skills. Longitudinal

50

studies show that of the children who are reading disabled in the third grade, 74 percent remain disabled in the ninth grade (Yale,[1,4,7,10] Stanovich & Siegel[3]).

- The practice of distinguishing between disabled readers with an IQ-Achievement discrepancy and those without a discrepancy appears invalid.[3,7] More specifically, children with and without a discrepancy do not differ in the information processing subskills (phonological and orthographic coding) that are necessary for the reading of single words.[3] Likewise genetic and neurophysiological studies have not indicated differential etiologies for reading disabled children with and without discrepancies.[1,3,4,7] It remains to be seen whether a discrepancy between achievement and IQ is a worthwhile predictor of choice of, or response to, intervention.

- Children with reading disability differ from one another and from other readers along a continuous distribution, and do not aggregate together in a distinct "hump" at the tail of the distribution as once thought (Bowman Gray,[5] Colorado,[4,5] Yale,[1,4,7,10] Stanovich & Siegel[3]).

- The ability to read and comprehend depends upon rapid and automatic recognition and decoding of single words and slow and inaccurate decoding are the best predictors of difficulties in reading comprehension (Bowman Gray,[5] Colorado,[5,11] Johns Hopkins,[4] Yale[1,3,5,7]).

- The ability to decode single words accurately and fluently is dependent upon the ability to segment words and syllables into abstract constituent sound units (phonemes). Deficits in phonological awareness reflect the core deficit in dyslexia (Bowman Gray,[5] Colorado,[4,5,11] Johns Hopkins,[4] Miami,[5] Yale[4,7]).

- The best predictor of reading ability/disability from kindergarten and first grade test performance is phoneme segmentation ability (Bowman Grays[5]). However there may be different predictors for different component reading skills. For example, rapid naming ability may predict word identification while tasks assessing phonological awareness best predicts word attack skills (Bowman Grays[5]).

Attention

- A precise classification of ADD with and without hyperactivity is not yet available. A classification methodology that assesses internal and external validity of dimensional and categorical models must be applied to the issue (Yale[1,4]).

- ADD and reading disability often co-exist, but the two disorders are distinct and separable (Bowman Gray,[5,9] Yale[4,5,9]).

- ADD occurs more frequently in males and ADD exacerbates the severity and cognitive morbidity of reading deficits. Since ADD and reading deficits often co-occur, more males are typically identified as reading disabled, spuriously inflating the gender ratio in favor of males (Bowman Gray,[5,9] Miami[9]).

- The effects of ADD on cognitive functioning are variable with primary deficits in rote verbal learning and memory. ADD appears relatively unrelated to naming and phonemic awareness tasks (Bowman Grays[5,9]).

Genetics

- A multiple regression analytic procedure has been developed by DeFries and his colleagues that allows for the analysis of the genetic etiology of individual differences in component language and reading skills. This is a unique and flexible methodology that can be used to assess differential genetic and environmental effects (Colorado[4,5,9,13]).

- There is strong evidence for genetic etiology of reading disability, with deficits in phonological awareness reflecting the greatest degree of heritability (Colorado[4,5,13]).

- There appears to be at least one type of reading disability that can be linked to the HLA region of Chromosome 6 reflecting an association with autoimmune disorders (Colorado,[5,9] Miami[9]). Recent evidence obtained from twin and kindred siblings with severe deficits in reading performance show strong evidence for a Quantitative Trait Locus on chromosome 6 (Colorado[13]).

Neuroanatomy, Neurophysiology, and Neuroimaging

- Several types of brain pathology, including microdysgenesis (Ectopias), cell loss, and abnormalities of the corpus callosum are present in a number of strains of immune defective mice. There is a similarity between the brain lesions seen in the mouse model and in humans with dyslexia (Beth Israel/Harvard[5,9]).

- At the macroscopic level, atypical neural organization in dyslexic individuals is suggested by absence of the normal left-greater-than-right asymmetry in the posterior temporal planum (Beth Israel/Harvard[5,9]).

- There is converging evidence from anatomical microstructure studies, gross morphology studies, and neuroimaging studies that the phenotypic expression in dyslexia is related to anomalous organization of tissue and processing systems subserved within the posterior left hemisphere (Beth Israel/Harvard,[5,9] Bowman Grays[9]).

- Regional Blood Flow studies indicate that the poor reading development in dyslexics is associated with less activation than normal in the left temporal region with atypically increased activation in the region of the angular gyrus (Bowman Grays[5,9]).

- Positron Emission Tomographic studies indicate that dyslexic adults have greater than normal activation in regional metabolic values in the occipital (lingual) and pre-frontal regions of the cortex (Miami[9]).

Treatment/Intervention

- Disabled readers do not readily acquire the alphabetic code when learning to read due to deficiencies in the processing of phonological processing. As such, disabled readers must be presented highly structured, explicit and intensive instruction in phonics rules and the application of the rules to print (Bowman Grays[9]).

- Longitudinal data indicate that systematic structured phonics instruction results in more favorable outcomes in reading than does a context-emphasis (Whole Language) approach (Bowman Grays[9]).

- Dyslexic readers who have been remediated and who are at normal to near normal reading levels in adulthood continue to display atypical neural processing as assessed by regional cerebral blood flow studies. This finding suggests that initial neuropathology remains stable over time, despite remediation, and that compensatory mechanisms may be developed (Bowman Grays[9]).

Future Research Directions in LD

In addition to the research initiatives and programs described above, the NICHD is developing and expanding programs and plans in area of treatment/intervention for LD children and in the area of cognitive neuroscience and neuroimaging. Each of these areas of inquiry are described briefly.

Treatments/Intervention

Review of the literature related to reading disabilities and other learning disabilities indicates that no single treatment/intervention approach or method is likely to yield clinically significant, long-term, therapeutic gains with children diagnosed with LD.[1,2] Unfortunately, to date, there exists scant scientific support for the use of particular interventions or combinations of interventions with different types of learning disabilities. Because of this, the NICHD has recently launched a major research effort to determine which treatment methods or combinations of methods, provided in which setting, have the most effective impact on well defined domains of child functioning, for how long, and for what reasons. Within this context, two highly controlled and well designed longitudinal prospective intervention studies with LD children are now being supported at the Florida State University under the direction of Dr. Joseph Torgesen and the University of Houston under the direction of Dr. Barbara Foorman. Additional treatment/intervention initiatives are being planned at this time.

Cognitive Neuroscience and Neuroimaging

There exists a critical need to understand how the human brain is organized for complex behaviors, and to know more specifically how the child with LD and the normal learner differ with respect to central nervous system functioning. In addition, it is important for us to understand how such physiological and neuroanatomical differences are related to indices of heritability and environmental influences. Our ability to assess brain behavior relationships in an accurate, yet noninvasive manner, is improving significantly as we begin to employ dramatic new advances in neuroimaging technology. For instance, The Shaywitz group at Yale is moving forward with the application of Functional Magnetic Resonance Imaging studies with reading disabled and normal children. In addition, Dr. Allen Reiss and his colleagues at Johns Hopkins are designing imaging software that will allow different sites to compare neuroimaging data and how best to register functional brain information with structural brain information. These projects, as well as initiatives being planned, should serve to provide the empirical foundation necessary to not only understand the limits of individual variability in brain structure and function, but to identify the neurobiological underpinnings of learning disabilities.

Summary

The NICHD has been, and will continue to be responsive to the critical research needs in LD and related disorders. As an index of the heightened research activity in this arena, consider that NICHD support for projects related to learning and language disabilities has increased from $1.75 million in 1975 to over $15 million in 1993—a cumulative total of approximately $80 million. Given the significant discoveries made by the Program Projects, LDRCs and individual research grants supported through these increases, the money clearly has been well spent. Within the past 10 years, NICHD research has identified the major cognitive mechanisms underlying dyslexia and other learning disabilities and how the assessment of these mechanisms can help to predict the onset, developmental course, and outcomes of such disorders. Moreover, NICHD scientists have contributed substantially to an understanding of how the genome, the brain, and the environment interact to produce individual variations in learning. Given this knowledge, we are hopeful that the newly funded treatment/ intervention projects will provide guidance with respect to ameliorating the devastating effects of learning disabilities on both children and adults.

References

1. Lyon GR, Gray DB, Kavanagh, JF, et al (Eds): *Better Understanding Learning Disabilities: New Views from Research and Their Implications for Education and Public Policies*. Baltimore, Brookes, 1993.

2. Moats, LC, Lyon GR: Learning disabilities in the United States: Advocacy, science, and the future of the field. *J Learn Disab* 1993; 26:282–294.

3. Stanovich KE, Siegel LS: Phenotypic performance profile of children with reading disabilities: A regression-based test of the phonological-core variable-difference model. *J Ed Psych* 1994; 86:24–53.

4. Lyon GR (Ed): *Frames of Reference for the Assessment of Learning Disabilities: New Views on Measurement Issues*. Baltimore, Brookes, 1994.

5. Duane DD, Gray DB (Eds): *The Reading Brain: The Biological Basis of Dyslexia*. Parkton, MD: York, 1991.

6. National Advisory Committee on Handicapped Children: *Special Education for Handicapped Children*. Washington, D.C., Department of Health, Education, and Welfare, 1968.

7. Fletcher JM, Shaywitz SE, Shankweiler DP, et al: Cognitive profiles of reading disability: Comparisons of discrepancy and low achievement definitions. *J Ed Psych* 1994; 86:6–23.

8. Kavanagh JF, Truss TJ (Eds): *Learning Disabilities: Proceedings of the National Conference*. Parkton, MD: York, 1988.

9. Lyon GR: *Research in Learning Disabilities* (Tech. Rep.). Bethesda MD: National Institute of Child Health and Human Development. 1991.

10. Shaywitz SE, Escobar MD, Shaywitz, BA et al.: Evidence that dyslexia may represent the lower tail of a normal distribution of reading disability. *N Engl J Med* 1992; 326:145–150.

11. Olson R. Forsberg H. Wise B et al.: Measurement of word recognition, orthographic, and phonological skills, in Lyon GR (Ed): *Frames of Reference for the Assessment of Learning Disabilities: New Views on Measurement Issues*. Baltimore, Brookes, 1994, pp 243–278.

12. Shaywitz SE, Shaywitz, BA, Fletcher, JM et al.: Prevalence of reading disability in boys and girls: Results of the Connecticut longitudinal study. *JAMA* 1990; 264:998–1002.

13. Cardon LR, DeFries JC, Fulker DW et al.: Quantitative trait locus on chromosome 6 predisposing to reading disability. *Science* (in press).

14. Gray DB, Kavanagh JF (Eds): *Biobehavioral Measures of Dyslexia*. Parkton, MD: York.

Chapter 4

Learning Disabilities in the United States: Advocacy, Science, and the Future of the Field

In the United States the field of learning disabilities (LD) has grown, since its recognition as a federally designated handicapping condition in 1968, to represent almost one-half of all students receiving special education services nationally (United States Department of Education, 1989). At the same time, it remains one of the least understood yet most debated disabling conditions that affect children in the United States. Indeed, even a cursory perusal of the literature relevant to the history and current status of LD as conceptualized in this country reveals that the field has been, and continues to be, beset by pervasive and, at times, contentious disagreements about definitions, diagnostic criteria, assessment practices, teaching or intervention procedures, and educational policy (see Lyon, 1987, Lyon; Gray, Kavanagh, & Krasnegor, 1993).

Is this state of affairs endemic only to the United States, or are other countries grappling with similar issues? This question is difficult to answer, because literature relevant to descriptions of LD programs, practices, and policies in other countries has been virtually nonexistent. Yet, one can assume that schools in other countries are also confronted with the very real dilemma of understanding how best to educate youngsters who fail to learn despite generally robust intellectual capability and adequate opportunity to learn.

Should they want to emulate our policies or practices, we would urge caution and patience until better resolution of our basic questions

From "Learning Disabilities in the United States," by Louisa Cook Moats and G. Reid Lyon, May 1993, Volume 26, Number 5, *Journal of Learning Disabilities*, pp. 282-294. © 1993 by PRO-ED, Inc. Reprinted with permission.

regarding definition, identification, and instruction is achieved. Twenty-five years ago, children in American schools who displayed unusual learning characteristics were disenfranchised from any formal special education services because their cognitive and educational features did not correspond to any of the recognized categories of handicap. This disenfranchisement has successfully driven a social, political, and educational movement designed to protect children from being under-served by our educational system. The strength and success of this advocacy movement may well distinguish LD in the United States from LD in other countries, far more than any scientific underpinning that is generalizable from one nation to another.

But can a movement born of fierce and well-intentioned advocacy continue to prosper if its growth has preceded, rather than followed, scientific development and examination of its basic constructs, concepts, and operating principles? We do not think so. Although the initial political and social forces that led to the recognition of LD as a handicapping condition were indeed necessary at the time of the field's birth, they will not continue unchallenged unless we establish credible scientific and clinical validation of learning disabilities. To be blunt, the field courts its own destruction until it can respond systematically and objectively to pressures to overstate our knowledge for social, political, and educational purposes. More specifically, LD in the United States is at a critical juncture where, if we are ever to understand this tremendously heterogeneous array of disorders, we must establish precise definitions for research purposes and a theoretically based classification system that is open to empirical scrutiny. Such a classification system must not only provide a valid framework for clinical scientists to identify different types of learning disabilities, but also be robust enough to recognize the distinctions and interrelationships (comorbidities) between LD and other childhood disorders and include general academic underachievement, attention deficit disorder, mental retardation, and emotional disturbance (Fletcher & Morris, 1986; Lyon et al., 1993; Morris, 1988, 1993).

In the context of this challenge, we will attempt to trace, albeit briefly, the growth and emergence of LD in the United States, its basis in advocacy, its political and social roots, and the field's current responses to legitimate charges that it lacks scientific validity and clinical utility. However, given a topic that is so impossibly broad, we must prioritize our efforts. Thus, we have chosen to discuss some aspects of the dialectical interchange between advocacy and science, summarize some of what we know, and speculate about what the future might hold. Readers should note that we have relied heavily on a number of works detailing the field's social, political, and scientific development (Coles, 1987; Fletcher & Morris, 1986; Kavale & Forness, 1985; Kavanagh & Truss, 1988; Vaughn & Bos, 1987) to accomplish our goal. These are fine resources and they should be read to achieve a fuller understanding of the complexity we will attempt to represent in this article.

The Past and the Present

A Brief History of LD

The concept of LD was generated in the United States about 30 years ago to gain educational leverage for a group of children who were overlooked or excluded from basic educational services (Doris, 1986, 1993; Kirk & Bateman, 1962). Children with presumed neurological dysfunction and perceptual-motor difficulties were the focus of the first meeting of the Association for Children with Learning Disabilities in 1963, convened by frustrated parents and educators. The new field, with leaders such as Samuel Kirk, William Cruickshank, Helmer Myklebust, Barbara Bateman, and Marianne Frostig, was born at the convergence of several disciplines that shared, historically, an interest in learning problems—neurology, psychology, remedial education, and speech-language pathology. The pioneers promoted theories of disability, designed tests presumed to measure processing dysfunctions, and developed remedial techniques that were appealing because they were logically designed to repair learning breakdowns.

The field progressed rapidly through many developmental stages after its conception, including, but not limited to, infatuation with ideas such as perceptual-motor training (e.g., Ayres, 1972; Cratty, 1973; Frostig & Maslow, 1973; Kephart, 1971); psycholinguistic prescription based on the Illinois Test of Psycholinguistic Abilities (e.g., Bush & Giles, 1969; Kirk & Kirk, 1971); interactional analysis (e.g., Bryan & Bryan, 1978; Kronick, 1976); criterion-referenced testing and task analysis (e.g., Bateman, 1971; Frank, 1973; Siegel, 1972); holism (Heshusius, 1989, Poplin, 1984); and constructivism (Reid & Stone, 1991). Each of these approaches was zealously promoted, summarily attacked, and sometimes discredited for failing to produce miracle cures. Nevertheless, the LD enterprise became an enormous machine—indeed, a factory—with attending cottage industries, fueled by legal, sociopolitical, educational, and entrepreneurial energy (Coles, 1987; Senf, 1987). Historically, there has been no logical blueprint for this machine that could provide objective knowledge about who and how many children were at issue, why they could not learn, or how they might be helped. It is important to understand, albeit with hindsight, how we could have gotten so far ahead of ourselves.

Will the Real LD Please Stand Up?

Defining Who Is LD. How can we be writing laws, categorizing children, certifying teachers, consuming tests, and promoting special education practices before we know clearly who should be receiving services and what interventions are efficacious? On the other hand, how can critics (e.g., Coles, 1987) question the very existence of LD? Certainly our persistent use of vague, ambiguous, exclusionary, and nonvalidated definitions of LD continue to get us into trouble in this regard. Consider the following past and current definitions, which serve to frame diagnostic and eligibility criteria.

The Education for All Handicapped Children Act (Public Law 94–142) incorporated the following definition, originally proposed by the National Advisory Committee on Handicapped Children (1968):

> The term "specific learning disability" means a disorder in one or more basic psychological processes involved in understanding or in using language, spoken or written, which may manifest itself in an imperfect ability to listen, speak, read, write, spell, or do mathematical calculations. The term includes such conditions as perceptual handicaps, brain injury, minimal brain dysfunction, dyslexia, and developmental aphasia. Such terms do not include children who have learning disabilities which are primarily the result of visual, hearing, or motor handicaps, of mental retardation, of emotional disturbance, or of environmental, cultural, or economic disadvantage. (United States Office of Education, 1977, p. 65083)

Say what? It does not take an expert in nosological science to see that this early definition is impotent with respect to providing objective guidelines and criteria for distinguishing individuals with LD from those with other primary handicaps or generalized learning difficulties. Indeed, many papers have been written bemoaning the use of this vague definition in driving educational policy and practice (e.g., Fletcher & Morris, 1986; Kavale & Forness, 1985; Kavale & Nye, 1981; Lyon, 1987; Senf, 1981, 1986, 1987; Ysseldyke & Algozzine, 1983).

Unfortunately, recent attempts to tighten the definition have not fared appreciably better, as can be seen in the revised definition produced by the National Joint Committee On Learning Disabilities (see Hammill, Leigh, McNutt, & Larsen, 1981, NJCLD, 1988). This version states the following:

> Learning disabilities is a general term that refers to a heterogeneous group of disorders manifested by significant difficulties in the acquisition and use of listening, speaking, reading, writing, reasoning, or mathematical abilities. These disorders are intrinsic to the individual, presumed to be due to central nervous system dysfunction, and may occur across the life span. Problems in self-regulatory behaviors, social perception, and social interaction may exist with learning disabilities but do not by themselves constitute a learning disability. Although learning disabilities may occur concomitantly with other handicapping conditions (for example, sensory impairment, mental retardation, social and emotional disturbance) or with extrinsic influences (such as cultural differences, insufficient or inappropriate instruction), they are not the result of these conditions or influences. (NJCLD, 1988, p. 1)

Although the NJCLD definition reflects consensus on the concept of LD in clinical, educational, and political arenas (Hammill, 1990), it too falls short of providing inclusionary criteria for classification. However, it eliminates the word "children" and adopts a "life-span" perspective that is more consistent with the wide age range of individuals in need of identification and services in adult basic education, vocational education, job training, and higher education (Ryan & Price, 1992). Yet, the broader definitional umbrella simply exacerbates the problem of vagueness. It is obvious that to this date, the field lacks logically consistent, easily operationalized, and empirically valid definitions. There is scant evidence that these current definitions and the classification systems predicated on them provide teachers and researchers useful information to enhance communication or improve predictions—the two primary reasons for developing definitions and classifications (Morris, 1988). Nevertheless, many individuals have been identified as LD using such definitions. How many are there? What are their characteristics? Why were they identified?

Identification in Practice. The first year that records were kept after the passage of P.L. 94–142 (1976–77), 1.8% of school-age students were served under this label (U.S. Department of Education, 1989). At present, almost 2 million school children in the United States are classified as LD in public schools before 12th grade, totaling about 5% of school enrollment and almost 50% of the children receiving special education services (U.S. Department of Education, 1989). [Updated statistical information is included in the next chapter.] The category was described derogatorily by Senf (1987) as an ever-expanding "sociological sponge" to soak up educational misfits.

Each state has been left to operationalize its definition of LD, and each has done so with widely varying standards and procedures (Mercer, Hughes, & Mercer, 1985; Mercer, King-Sears, & Mercer, 1990). It is not uncommon for a student to be considered to have LD in one state but not in its neighbor. In spite of efforts to refine formulas to measure true aptitude-achievement discrepancies reliably (Reynolds, 1984–85), eligibility decisions made by educators in the field have been shown to be based more on contextual and subjective criteria than on objective ones (Ysseldyke & Algozzine, 1983).

In practice, teachers refer children for special education assessment based on the teacher's need for additional help with that student at that point in time, rather than on any objective characteristic of the student (Gerber & Semmel, 1985; Zigmond, 1993). Teachers tolerate academic failure, learning difficulties, and low achievement in just as many children whom they never refer for evaluation or supplementary service (Bryan, Bay, & Donahue, 1988; Zigmond, 1993), when they believe they are still capable of teaching them. In schools where teachers are optimistic about the likelihood that children will succeed without special education, referral rates for special education are low (Zigmond & Baker, 1990). Thus, LD in the United States appears to be a systemic problem: It is an educational category into which children are channeled when the learning-teaching interaction is no longer productive or rewarding for one or both parties. The reality of LD in schools is thus removed from the abstract issues of definition, classification, and experimental criteria that might provide the cornerstones of a science of developmental learning disorders.

These concerns and issues are not new. They have been discussed ad nauseam throughout the United States for years. Thus, a fundamental question is, how can the LD population continue to proliferate despite the lack of accepted theoretical frameworks and, most important, reliable and valid diagnostic criteria? One answer clearly lies in the examination of advocacy, the political response to such advocacy, and the efforts of parents and professionals on behalf of students who are not getting competent, fair treatment in their classrooms.

The Advocacy Movement in Learning Disabilities

Although descriptions of educational reality have repeatedly cast doubt on the efficacy of the LD classification and the clinical utility of the category, organized advocacy continues to score successes at the legislative level in the United States, even though advocates are sometimes scorned in some scientific circles and feared in some public schools. This is not surprising. In the United States, the majority of advances in the public health domain have not occurred serendipitously: They have been stimulated, and sometimes forced, by vocal critics of the status quo. In fact, no disease or significant public health problem (e.g., AIDS, mental retardation, autism, or posttraumatic stress disorder) in this country is given much attention until political forces are motivated by parents, patients, or victims expressing their very real and heartfelt concerns about their quality of life. The force of advocacy in creating positive change is undeniable.

The continued success of the LD movement in the United States is primarily the result of such advocacy efforts. Science has taken a back seat (and more accurately, the rumble seat). Individuals with LD are represented jointly and separately by the Learning Disabilities Association of America, the Orton Dyslexia Society, the American Speech-Language-Hearing Association, the Council for Exceptional Children's Division of Learning Disabilities, the Council for Learning Disabilities, the National Center for Learning Disabilities, the National Clearinghouse for Postsecondary Education for the Handicapped, and others. Individually, these organizations pursue somewhat different agendas and serve quite different constituencies; collectively, however, these organizations and their members have lobbied Congress successfully since the late 1960s.

There are currently four federal laws under which a range of education and related services are mandated for individuals with learning disabilities: The Individuals with Disabilities Act (IDEA, formerly the Education for All Handicapped Children Act, or P.L. 94–142); Section 504 of the Rehabilitation Act and interpretations of that by federal agencies; letters of findings issued by the Office of Civil Rights and similar policy clarifications by the U.S. Office of Education; and the Americans with Disabilities Act of 1992. Together, these laws mandate provision of a comprehensive Individualized Education Program for students with disabilities through their graduation from high school. In addition, they mandate accommodations in every aspect of the regular education environment that might be needed for a student to have equal access to the total educational experience and to have equal opportunity to benefit from education. A learning disability is characterized by law as a type of barrier, akin to a sensory limitation, that can be compensated for with the right combination of prostheses. Mandated modifications for identified students with disabilities include the use of special technology; change of the environment; provision of note takers and proofreaders; curricular changes; and testing accommodations, such as extra time, scribes, readers, and altered testing formats. Imagine the deluge of petitions, complaints, lawsuits, and student policy changes that these rules have wrought on college campuses—all in the absence of a clear definition as to who is LD in the first place!

Why Advocacy Has Been Necessary

Why have such strong advocacy and extensive legal safeguards been needed in the United States? We are not sociologists but will venture to speculate. First, although the policies of American schools reflect the intent to accommodate individual differences, classroom groupings are heterogeneous, and most curriculum and teaching in graded classrooms are aimed at the common denominator. We have no system like Germany's (Opp, 1992), whereby children are tracked early according to their academic ability and taught in relatively homogeneous groups. Thus, academic failure does not lead to a qualitatively different instructional program, unless it is provided through special education supplements. American teachers are responsible for ever-increasing diversity in their classrooms and are clearly poorly trained to handle the demands (Lyon, Vaasen, & Toomey, 1989).

Second, as Katz (1987) argued, American schools are committed to purposes rooted in social inequality and infused with the frontier mentality of independence and self-reliance. Children and their parents tend to be blamed when educational or social failure occurs. The system reacts to school failure as if individuals with disabilities are less worthy morally and less deserving of public resources. The responsibility of schools is to provide equality of opportunity, not equality of condition; therefore, in the sifting process that occurs in school, those who sink to the bottom are not automatically buoyed by a safety net of services. Until parents demand protection and programs for their children, those children are often allowed to fail without concerted community response. What conscientious parents would willingly allow their child to sink into the abyss of limited economic opportunity that comes with educational disadvantage in this country?

Third, we typically finance our schools through local property taxes, and there are enormous inequities in per-pupil expenditures from district to district—a range of about $2,000 to $10,000 (Kozol, 1991). When resources are scarce, communities simply do not voluntarily allocate funds for minority children, whether they are gifted, have mental retardation, have LD, or are disadvantaged, racially different, or bilingual. State and federal governments alleviate some of these inequities, but federal funding for education constitutes only 6% of the total spent (Kozol, 1991). State aid is declining in most states, and local property owners will not voluntarily accept the burden of education that benefits a few.

Fourth, education reform movements in this country, and there have been many (Sarason, 1990), typically have not focused on public responsibility for educating all students. The Bush administration's America 2000 initiatives emphasized parental choice of schools, academic excellence, higher and more uniform standards of performance, and model programs. Students with differences must organize defensively into voting blocks to secure recognition if their needs are not actively and specifically promoted by political leadership. Put up and fight, or be ignored.

Finally, social, medical and educational services to children in this country have never been a national priority, as they are in many other industrialized nations. The Children's Defense Fund has recently shown that while investment in elderly care continues to increase, investment in programs for children continues to decline. Why? Children do not vote or contribute to campaigns. If large groups, such as individuals with disabilities, can be organized as a voting block, the larger the block, the more likely that funding and programs will be secured. Thus, vague, inclusionary definitions of disability are an advantage in advocacy.

Policy Ambivalence. Hard-won legal mandates have not been issued without a significant degree of political ambivalence, however. Although P.L. 94–142 was passed in 1975 with an original entitlement that would have reimbursed states for 40% of the cost of serving children with disabilities, at the present time our national budget provides for only 6% federal reimbursement for special education costs to the states. Over the last 12 years, military spending rose 43% (adjusting for inflation), while funding for elementary education in toto decreased by 15% and for postsecondary education decreased by 24% (Kozol, 1991). Present budget projections include a 3% increase in special education funding, to 2.9 billion dollars, which is less than the rate of inflation (Learning Disabilities Association, 1991). State grants for special education would be increased by 5% but would be financed by a 10% decrease in funds for students with disabilities receiving compensatory Chapter 1 programs. Funding levels are, in essence, still decreasing and are far lower than Congress originally intended.

Federal ambivalence toward the concept of LD is also expressed in the recent reform movement, the Regular Education Initiative (REI), generated from the U.S. Office of Education (Will, 1986). The initiative, which called for a return to mainstreaming and a reduction of pull-out services for students with mild handicaps was designed to counteract service delivery problems: a dual system of education (regular and special); an increasing number of children assigned to special education; fragmented educational services provided under categorical programs; segregation of students and resultant poor self-esteem and negative attitudes toward learning; evidence that pull-out services were ineffective; expensive placement procedures; burdensome paperwork that prevented trained teachers from teaching; and territorial conflict fostered among concerned professionals. A number of solutions to these dilemmas were proposed, including instructional support teams for teachers, prereferral intervention, cooperative learning, curriculum-based assessment, employment of consulting teachers, and peer tutoring (see Idol, 1989–90, for a fuller discussion of these alternatives).

The professional special education community has been, for the most part, cautious of, critical of, and dismayed by this sudden policy shift (Carnine & Kameenui, 1990; Keogh, 1988; Kronick, 1990). Having witnessed the historical failure by noncategorical education to benefit children with learning problems and provide professional expertise and resources to this deserving minority, many have argued that the proposed REI cure was perhaps worse than the illness (Hallahan, Keller, McKinney, Lloyd, & Bryan, 1988; Kauffman, Gerber, & Semmel, 1988). The REI seemed based on shortsighted budgetary concerns more than research-based policy or consideration of educational history, which has repeatedly demonstrated the ineffectiveness of conventional classrooms in educating children with learning difficulties—which is why LD advocacy was needed in the first place. Critics of the REI have questioned whether, in fact, students with LD were overidentified, whether categorization was, in fact, harmful, and whether it was realistic to expect classroom teachers (who did not initiate the REI) to have the energy, expertise, commitment, tolerance, and time to be all things to all students. In fact, a majority of teachers who are expected to address a range of individual differences in their classrooms report that they have not received adequate training in their content, much less in how to teach it to those who do not understand and do not learn it (Lyon et al., 1989).

To review, the field of LD was born from a genuine social and educational need and, for the time being, is robust and viable in law, policy, and practice. Parents and advocates have successfully negotiated a category of problem as a means to educational protection (Keogh, in press). Only in passing did they and the research community also define an arena for scientific inquiry, in which persistent and complex questions were entertained with less than satisfactory results. Who has entered that arena, and why has science not been taken seriously until recently?

Why the Field of LD Lacks Scientific Validity

Contributing Influences

A number of influences contribute to difficulties in validating the LD construct in the United States (see Lyon, 1987). First, the field's limitations as a clinical science can be related to its young chronological age. Learning disabilities as a federally designated handicapping condition has been in existence only since 1968 (National Advisory Committee on Handicapped Children, 1968). Thus, there simply may not have been time to collect and consolidate all the necessary information that could lead to a better understanding of the nature of LD and to identify teaching methodologies that have a predictable probability of success.

Second, and more significant than the field's limited history, are the many different theoretical and conceptual views that reflect the multidisciplinary nature of the field. As Torgesen (1986, in press) pointed out, learning disabilities are considered the proper and legitimate concern of many disciplines and professions, including education, psychology, neuropsychology, speech and language pathology, neurology, psychiatry, ophthalmology, optometry, and occupational therapy. Each of these professions has traditionally focused on different aspects of the child with LD, so that there are sometimes extremely divergent ideas, and sometimes contentious disagreements, about the importance of etiology, diagnostic methods, the importance of different characteristics, instructional content and teaching methodologies, and professional roles and responsibilities. Such variation results in differences in the numbers of children identified and their characteristics, leading to, as Torgesen (1993) states, an "eye of the beholder" effect. In turn, conducting research on samples of children with LD who vary widely with respect to diagnostic and demographic characteristics provides little opportunity for the replication and generalization of findings—the cornerstones of scientific inquiry.

Third, although a discrepancy between aptitude (as measured, e.g., by standard intelligence tests) and academic achievement has been a widely accepted criterion for the identification of LD, there is considerable variation in how that discrepancy is operationalized (see Siegel, 1989) and concern about whether it constitutes a valid marker (see Fletcher & Morris, 1986; Stanovich, 1991, 1993). Federal regulations and extant clinical criteria (e.g., DSM-III-R) do not specify particular formulas or numerical values to objectively assess discrepancy. These different approaches to discrepancy measurement lead to different research sample characteristics and different prevalence estimates. Moreover, until recently, no well-designed research had been conducted to compare youngsters identified according to different discrepancy criteria on external validation measures (Fletcher & Moms, 1986; Morris, 1988).

A fourth threat to the internal and external validation of the construct of LD is linked to the discrepancy issue but relates more specifically to measurement practices. Many diagnostic and identification decisions about LD are based on technically inadequate tests and measures. Recent reviews (e.g., Lyon, in press) suggest that fewer than one third of the psychometric tools used in the diagnosis of LD meet criteria for adequate norms reliability, and validity. In addition, the valid measurement of changes in academic skill level over time, and as a function of intervention, is literally impossible at present, because few instruments have the necessary scaling properties to satisfy conditions for longitudinal measurement (Frances, Fletcher, Stuebing, Davidson, Thompson, 1991).

Fifth, until recently, classification research conducted with children with LD has not included comparisons with children who manifest other learning disorders. As Morris (1988, 1993) pointed out, this isolation of disorders has created substantial debate in the field and has led to the use of exclusionary criteria to select samples for study. Unfortunately, the scientific validity and clinical utility of exclusionary criteria has rarely been validated. Furthermore, separating children into possibly artificial categories precludes our understanding of how multiple and comorbid difficulties influence learning and response to instruction. Such isolation of groups in research limits the ecological validity of any findings, in that teachers and clinicians are constantly attempting to instruct youngsters with a range and multiplicity of individual differences.

Finally, a significant amount of what is known or believed about LD has been based on data collected on "school-identified" or "clinic-referred" samples (Lyon, 1987). Unfortunately, such sampling practices undermine the reliability and validity of any information obtained on the youngsters because of the lack of consistency in the way in which school and clinic professionals identify youngsters as LD. As we pointed out earlier, a child can be "cured" of an LD condition simply by moving across state lines (or even by changing schools within the same community). As we have also pointed out, such variability in sample characteristics prohibits replication and generalization of findings—a severe impediment to the development of any clinical science.

In summary, much of our research based thinking about learning disabilities in the United States is predicated on information that is obtained from ambiguously defined school-identified samples of children who have been administered technically inadequate measurement instruments and tests. Frequently, the research problem is further confounded by our tendency to interpret these test data in the context of theoretical and conceptual frameworks that have not been scientifically or clinically validated. What is surprising and unfortunate is that while these problems have been noted in detail for more than a decade, they persist and continue to have a negative effect on research practice (and thus on the validation of the LD construct). New exclusionary definitions of LD are offered up every 5 years or so without empirical validation and provide little in terms of logical consistency, communicative power, or predictive capability. Journal editors continue to accept and publish manuscripts describing theoretical research with poorly defined samples, inadequate measurement instruments, and ill-conceived and poorly described interventions. Indeed, research practices are slow to change; but in the United States we have the right to advocate for more rapid change, and in the field of learning disabilities, where there is advocacy, there is hope, even for better research.

The Relationship Between Research and Advocacy

Given the present state of research in the field, it is not surprising that so many educators and scientists have abandoned the concept of LD to explain individual differences, or that parental advocacy remains its strongest voice amidst the cacophony of nay-sayers. Parents do not require empirical validation for their intuitions and concerns about their children. They know something is not right for their youngster in a particular classroom in a particular school, and the most vocal parents know they have the right to ask for explanations and solutions to the very real difficulties confronting their children on a daily basis. Despite years of less than productive research practices, parental advocates have remained the strongest force in keeping alive the concept of learning disabilities and the need for basic research. The question is, has advocacy-driven research produced anything of recent value?

We have attempted to make the point that what might distinguish the LD movement in the United States from how learning disabilities are conceptualized and supported in other countries is the role advocacy plays in the field's growth and direction. In addition, national health policy driven by advocacy, rather than educational policy driven by political forces, has been an important contributor to the development of a research base for LD in this country. In particular, both advocacy and scientific initiatives developed by the National Institutes of Health have had a major impact on the development of systematic research efforts in LD. By systematic, we mean research that has at its core a firm grounding in classification methodology to include the construction of theory-driven hypotheses, the selection and or development of tasks and measures to test the hypotheses, a determination of the reliability and replicability of the findings, and an external validation of the findings. By systematic, we are also referring to research that is conducted within a developmental, longitudinal framework. In this context the same children are repeatedly observed and studied, without the need for any a priori assumptions about who is LD (as in school-identified LD), particularly if children are studied during the preschool years and then followed with consistent probes for several years.

Until the National Institute of Child Health and Human Development (NICHD) began to initiate and sponsor programmatic research in dyslexia in 1979 (University of Colorado), with continued support of the Dyslexia Program Projects in 1986 (Bowman Gray School of Medicine; Beth Israel Hospital) and 1987 (University of Miami; Yale), a substantial number of research efforts in the United States consisted primarily of single investigations that compared children with LD with normally achieving persons on one or more dependent variables of interest (Lyon, 1987). Unfortunately, this "single-shot" research was typically carried out without any understanding of what constituted the independent variables—namely, who would be called LD and who would not. Keep in mind that this practice continues in earnest. Many recent studies cannot be replicated because youngsters are selected on the basis of meeting vague criteria associated with the exclusionary definitions we described earlier. In the United States it has taken us quite a while to understand that youngsters labeled LD via exclusionary criteria are more different than alike and can range significantly in IQ, socioeconomic status, age, gender, and educational history. Surprisingly, few studies have accounted for the influence these variables have on the individual expression of learning differences, and, not surprisingly, few studies have provided solid information on the nature or needs of individuals with learning disabilities.

Although the educational research community may not have noticed the scientific futility of conducting research with school-identified samples, advocacy groups certainly have. As a result of parental recognition that educational policy for LD was being formulated with little scientific basis, individuals from the Foundation for Children with Learning Disabilities (now NCLD), the Learning Disabilities Association of America (LDA), the Orton Dyslexia Society, the Division for Children with Learning Disabilities of the Council for Exceptional Children, the American Speech-Hearing-Language Association (ASHA), and many others began an intensive dialogue with members of Congress to voice their concerns. As a result of this interaction, the Health Research Extension Act of 1985 (P.L. 99–158) was passed, mandating that the director of the National Institutes of Health establish an Interagency Committee on Learning Disabilities (ICLD) to review and assess federal research priorities, activities, and findings concerning learning disabilities. The mandate further required that the ICLD report to Congress (a) the number of persons affected by learning disabilities and the demographic data describing such persons; (b) a description of the current research findings on the cause, diagnosis, treatment, and prevention of learning disabilities; and (c) recommendations to increase the effectiveness of research on learning disabilities and the dissemination of findings (Interagency Committee on Learning Disabilities, 1987).

A clear recommendation made by the ICLD to Congress was to establish multidisciplinary research centers that could carry out prospective, longitudinal investigations to illuminate the causes, developmental course, outcomes, and treatment possibilities for individuals with learning and attention disorders. In response to this recommendation, the

NICHD was charged with the responsibility of developing a scientific initiative and accompanying guidelines for the conduct of such research. By 1989, Learning Disability Research Centers (LDRC) had been established at Yale University under the direction of Bennett Shaywitz and at Johns Hopkins University under the direction of Martha Denckla, and a third LDRC was established at the University of Colorado under the direction of John DeFries in 1990. These three Centers were established following peer review accomplished by the NIH. However, the impetus for the research and the fund set aside by Congress for the Centers' development were clearly a function of advocacy and the ability of citizens to make known their concerns about the scientific status quo in learning disabilities research. The efforts being carried out at the three LDRCs are now extending the work carried out at the Dyslexia Program Projects in developing a reliable and valid classification system for a range of learning and attention disorders, and in attempting to identify causes, map developmental courses, and identify efficacious interventions. To date, a number of findings have been reported from the five Dyslexia Program Projects and the three LDRCs and a few of these are summarized below. A number of published and unpublished sources review these research efforts in detail; the reader is referred to Duane and Gray (1991) and Lyon (1991) for more specific information.

The Future of LD: Reaping the Benefits of Research

A Brief Synthesis of Recent Research Findings

As the findings from prospective, longitudinal, and multidisciplinary research accumulate, the necessity for such efforts is also being confirmed. Some of our most basic assumptions about learning disabilities are apparently in error and need to be revised. For example, researchers at Yale and Colorado have confirmed that children with dyslexia differ from one another along a continuous distribution and do not "clump" together in syndromes marked by distinctive diagnostic boundaries (DeFries, Olson, Pennington, & Smith, 1991; Shaywitz, Escobar, Shaywitz, Fletcher, & Makuch, 1992). However, Yale researchers have shown that children can be assigned to subtypes for research purposes, and that the subtypes will be somewhat arbitrary depending on where the cutoff points for group inclusion are set on the distribution.

Furthermore, converging evidence from researchers at Yale, Bowman Gray, Colorado, and Johns Hopkins is confirming that accurate, fluent reading ability is dependent on rapid and automatic recognition and decoding of words (Felton & Wood, 1989; Rack, Snowling, & Olson, 1991; Shaywitz, Shaywitz, Fletcher, & Escobar, 1990; Vellutino & Scanlon, 1987). The decoding deficit is related primarily to phonological processing skills, especially the ability to abstract and manipulate constituent phonemes in words (Felton & Wood, 1989; Shaywitz et al., 1991). Decoding ability and phonological processing have been found to be highly heritable (DeFries et al., 1991). Phonological deficits appear to impede the development of reading ability regardless of level of intelligence: Poor readers with and without IQ-achievement discrepancies demonstrate impairments in linguistic awareness (Francis, Shaywitz, Steubing, Shaywitz, & Fletcher, 1993). In other words, individuals with dyslexia are distinguished by their phonologically based decoding disability, not by the presence or absence of a significant discrepancy between IQ and reading. Ultimately, the presence or absence of a discrepancy may have no relevance to the definition of reading disability, although it may have relevance as a secondary characteristic that predicts such things as psychological response to disability, response to instruction, or long-term outcomes (Lyon, 1989).

Contrary to popular belief, researchers at Yale, Colorado, Bowman Gray, and Miami have all found that boys and girls are represented equally in the reading disabled population, if reading disability is defined as a specific deficit in decoding skills. However, boys are identified as having disorders of attention more frequently than girls (Felton & Wood, 1989; Lubs et al., 1991). Disorders of reading and attention may coexist, but the two disorders are distinct and separable and have different effects on reading and linguistic processing (Felton & Wood, 1989). The predisposition of males to attention disorders, as well as their predisposition to more severe forms of reading disability (Lubs et al., 1991), may in part account for their higher rate of identification for special education in public schools.

Substantial progress is being made, especially with the problem of classification and definition of dyslexia and related disorders. These and other findings will provide a stable context for additional epidemiological studies on various learning disorders (math, written language, etc.) and allow better data to be gathered on their prevalence, developmental course, and response to various interventions. How might such information influence the efforts of researchers and advocates in the future? Requests for funds, requests for programs, and legal exercise of due process rights under our various laws will be far more successful if they are made in reference to both what we already know and what we have yet to learn.

Implications for the Future

Preventive Intervention. It is conceivable that in the future, practitioners will argue with good cause that a child with a family history of reading disability and/or attention difficulties can be identified before he or she encounters school failure and placed in preventive intervention programs designed to strengthen the child's learning weaknesses. Just as we advise preventive monitoring and prophylactic treatment for children with heritable diseases, we could advise early placement of at-risk children in validated programs and monitor their progress before disability becomes severe.

Adoption of New Measurement Practices. Disability could be reconceptualized as failure to learn a specific skill or set of skills during or after validated intervention (Berninger, Hart, Abbott, & Karovsky, 1992). The identification of various disorders of attention, reading, spelling, written language, mathematics, nonverbal reasoning, and oral language might thus be based on repeated measures of performance over time (Francis et al., 1991). Measurement of performance in each domain of learning could be conducted with static and dynamic measures that had appropriate scaling properties and that sampled the target domain appropriately (see Lyon, in press). Researchers, test makers, and practitioners need incentives to design and use valid assessment strategies so that studies can be replicated from one setting to another and so that individuals can be observed over time.

Differentiation of Science and Public Policy. The field's leaders might endeavor to clarify the difference between public policy and scientific priorities. Whereas for policy or program funding purposes, the use of the umbrella term LD might still have merit, for scientific or research purposes, a variety of specific disorders need to be precisely defined for a valid classification system (Stanovich, 1993). Research on the developmental course and individual expression of each disorder needs to be carried out, as well as research on the efficacy of various interventions over time. If this research is systematic and conducted in accordance with standards already discussed, it will require long-term planning and funding. Leadership will be necessary to sustain public patience and commitment for this long-term effort.

Research in Treatment Effectiveness. A science of learning disabilities will ultimately rest on our ability to show that once a disorder is identified, we know what to do to help the individual. Building a foundation of validated interventions will be a very complex and challenging task, one that will not be accomplished even in a few years. Before us is an extremely complex agenda: How do nondisabled learners acquire information in each domain? How do well-defined groups of children with disabilities respond to instruction and/or instructional context? What teacher knowledge and skills are essential to get results? Which combination of approaches and conditions for instruction have the most impact on which types of students, at which developmental stage, for how long? Directly put, what are the instructional conditions that must be in place for a child to learn, retain, and generalize concepts? Only when these conditions are identified and defined will the preparation of teachers in the United States become systematic, productive, and accountable. Moreover, if we do not succeed in establishing a legitimate clinical science, the field will continue to be vulnerable to criticism and capricious policy shifts (Lyon & Moats, 1988). Likewise, until there is a validated science of intervention for well-defined learning disorders, quack therapies (see Worrall, 1990) will continue to proliferate like mushrooms on a rainy day—and we will continue to waste our intellectual energy picking them off.

Such basic research is painstaking and will be accomplished in stages according to a well-conceived set of priorities over many years. In the meantime, teachers are being trained for tomorrow's jobs as remedial and consulting teachers, and children must be educated. Regular education teachers are increasingly being asked to serve diverse needs in their classes. Are they prepared to do so? Not if one looks at current program requirements, training practices, and certification standards in states across the United States.

Teacher Training. As mentioned in the previous section, the successful preparation of teachers and clinicians to address the needs of individuals with learning disabilities is dependent to a large extent on our ability to identify and define the declarative and procedural knowledge required of practitioners for producing learning and generalization in children. Unfortunately, even when such conditions are relatively well known and understood for specific content areas (e.g., reading and spelling), teachers continue to be trained in a superficial manner and often remain unprepared to provide competent intervention. The lack of responsible preparation in reading education for special educators is disheartening, because we have learned a substantial amount about the cognitive and linguistic characteristics of reading disability (Liberman, Shankweiler, & Liberman, 1989; Rack, Snowling, & Olson, 1991) and spelling disabilities (Moats, in press-a, in press-b). What good is it to affirm in basic research that reading disability has a phonological core and that "code emphasis" approaches should constitute at least part of an intervention, if those who will be responsible for teaching children have only a cursory knowledge of phonetics, phonology, the alphabetic correspondence system, and the reasons why children have trouble learning orthography? Moreover, such concerns are exacerbated when one considers that approximately 80% of children identified as LD manifest their primary difficulties in reading and related language functions. Who is qualified to address their needs?

Only 29 states require elementary teachers in training to have coursework specific to reading instruction, and even in those states only about 12 hours of graduate training is mandated (Nolen, McCutchen, & Berninger, 1990). In addition, over half of our states have noncategorical teacher preparation programs in special education. During and after minimal coursework, in which, teachers report, they are typically given a "smattering of everything" and nothing in depth (Anderson, Hiebert, Scott, & Wilkinson, 1985), there are few opportunities for them to obtain supervision and guidance in the actual practice of teaching (Lyon et al., 1989). Equally distressing are the results of a recent survey of special and regular educators, in which a majority of teachers of exceptional children, responding to questions about their preparation, reported (a) significant grade inflation in superficial undergraduate and graduate content courses; (b) a tendency for professors of education to teach primarily through lecture rather than modeling and demonstrating teaching practices in applied settings; and (c) limited, inconsistent, and fragmentary feedback during practice and student teaching (Lyon et al., 1989).

Not surprisingly, a disturbing number of regular and special education teachers report that the bulk of their real education and preparation to teach occurs after they have entered the classroom (Lyon et al., 1989). No doubt, experience is an essential ingredient to the development of teaching expertise; however, if such experience does not accrue in the context of adequate content and pedagogical preparation, less than informed teaching practices can result—and, as a matter of fact, do (Drucker, 1989; Graham, 1988; Kennedy, 1987). A major question that continues to confront us is whether teacher preparation practices will improve as a function of time, or whether some external force will need to be applied to bolster training effectiveness. As Graham pointed out, bringing about changes in colleges of education will be difficult. In American colleges of education, many professors have only limited experience in the classroom setting, obviously limiting their own content expertise and application of pedagogical principles. Moreover, the inherent tension that exists between the need to conduct and publish research and the need to teach and supervise students in a university setting typically forces education professors to emulate the practices of faculty members in the arts and sciences. Thus, scholarship, usually and unfortunately decontextualized from the act of teaching in classrooms, becomes the major pursuit of professors of education. No doubt, scholarship should be valued, but such scholarship should bear forcefully and directly on the principles and practices of teaching (Lyon et al., 1989). Because history has not indicated that such changes are likely to occur, it may take the force of advocacy to stimulate colleges of education to integrate theory and practice into teacher preparation, and to do so in school settings and under the conditions that teachers will ultimately be faced with as they engage in the complex activities of their profession.

To conclude, we note that our nation is changing rapidly. Children in the United States are no longer typically white, affluent, or necessarily English-speaking, according to the U.S. Census Bureau's most recent report (Barringer, 1992). One in five are poor; 14% live in non-English speaking households; 25% are black, Hispanic, or Asian. In the last 10 years, 9 million people emigrated to the United States. The gulf between rich and poor is increasing: The percentage of those living in poverty has increased in the last decade. In this sociological context, the problems of individuals with learning disabilities may begin to seem unimportant in comparison to the overwhelming needs of this country's entire population.

If advocates, clinicians, and researchers press for validated theories, definitions, and methods, the field might possibly thrive. To preserve the gains we have made in public recognition of LD, program funding, and legal safeguards, we need to redouble our efforts to put science in the driver's seat.

—by Louisa Cook Moats
and G. Reid Lyon

References

Anderson, R.C., Hiebert, E.H., Scott, J. A., & Wilkinson, I.A.G. (1985). *Becoming a nation of readers: The report of the Commission on Reading*. Washington, DC: The National Institute of Education, U.S. Department of Education.

Ayres, A.J. (1972). *Sensory integration and learning disorders*. Los Angeles: Western Psychological Services.

Barringer, F. (1992, May 29). New census data reveal redistribution of poverty. *New York Times*, p. A14.

Bateman, B. (1971). *The essentials of teaching*. San Rafael, CA: Dimensions.

Berninger, V., Hart, T., Abbott, R., & Karovsky, P. (1992). Defining reading and writing disabilities with and without IQ: A flexible, developmental perspective. *Learning Disability Quarterly, 15*, 103–118.

Bryan, T., Bay, M., & Donahue, M. (1988). Implications of the learning disabilities definition for the regular education initiative. *Journal of Learning Disabilities, 21*, 23–28.

Bryan, T., & Bryan, J. (1978). *Understanding learning disabilities*. Sherman Oaks, CA: Alfred.

Bush, W., & Giles, W. (1969). *Aids to psycholinguistic teaching*. Columbus, OH: Merrill.

Carnine, D.W., & Kameenui, E.J. (1990). The General Education Initiative and children with special needs: A fake dilemma in the face of true problems. *Journal of Learning Disabilities, 23*, 141–144.

Coles, G. (1987). *The learning mystique: A critical look at "learning disabilities."* New York: Pantheon Books.

Cratty, B. (1973). *Intelligence in action*. Englewood Cliffs, NJ: Prentice-Hall.

DeFries, J.C., Olson, K., Pennington, B.F., & Smith, S.D. (1991). The Colorado Reading Project: An update. In D.D. Duane & D.B. Gray

(Eds.), *The reading brain: The biological basis of dyslexia* (pp. 53–87). Parkton, MD: York Press.

Doris, J. (1986). Learning disabilities. In S. Ceci (Ed.), *Handbook of cognitive, social and neuropsychological aspects of learning disabilities* (Vol. 1, pp. 3–53). Hillsdale, NJ: Erlbaum.

Doris, J. (in press). Some historical notes on the definition and prevalence of learning disabilities. In G.R. Lyon, D.B. Gray, J. Kavanagh, & N. Krasnegor (Eds.), *Better understanding of learning disabilities: New views from research and their implications for education and public policy*. Baltimore: Brookes.

Drucker, P.F. (1989, May). How schools must change. *Psychology Today*, pp. 18–20.

Duane, D.D., & Gray, D.B. (1991). *The reading brain: The biological basis of dyslexia*. Parkton, MD: York Press.

Felton, R.H., & Wood, F.B. (1989). Cognitive deficits in reading disability and attention deficit disorder. *Journal of Learning Disabilities*, 22, 3–13.

Fletcher, J.M., & Morris, R. (1986). Classification of disabled learners: Beyond exclusionary definitions. In S. Ceci (Ed.), *Handbook of cognitive, social and neuropsychological aspects of learning disabilities* (Vol. 1, pp. 55–80). Hillsdale, NJ: Erlbaum.

Foley, L. (1992). Washington Update. *LDA Newsbriefs*, 27, 1.

Francis, D.J., Fletcher, J.M., Steubing, K.K., Davidson, K.C., & Thompson, N.M. (1991). Analysis of change: Modeling individual growth. *Journal of Consulting and Clinical Psychology*, 59, 27–37.

Francis, D.J., Shaywitz, S.E., Steubing, K.K., Shaywitz, B.A., & Fletcher, J.M. (in press). The measurement of change: Assessing behavior over time and within a developmental context. In G.R. Lyon (Ed.), *Frames of reference for the assessment of learning disabilities: New views on measurement issues*. Baltimore: Brookes.

Frank, A.R., (1973). Breaking down learning tasks: A sequence approach. *Teaching Exceptional Children*, 6, 16–19.

Frostig, M., & Maslow, P. (1973). *Learning problems in the classroom.* New York: Grune & Stratton.

Gerber, M., & Semmel, M.I. (1985). The microeconomics of referral and reintegration: A paradigm for evaluation of special education. *Studies in Educational Evaluation*, 11, 13–29.

Graham, P.A. (1988, March). *Revolution in pedagogy.* Paper presented at the Wisconsin Symposium on Higher Education, LaCrosse, WI.

Hallahan, D.P., Keller, C.E., McKinney, J.D., Lloyd, J.W., & Bryan, T. (1988). Examining the research base of the Regular Education Initiative: Efficacy studies and the Adaptive Learning Environments Model. *Journal of Learning Disabilities*, 21, 29–35.

Hammill, D.D. (1990). On defining learning disabilities: An emerging consensus. *Journal of Learning Disabilities*, 23, 74–84.

Hammill, D.D., Leigh, J., McNutt, G., & Larsen, S. (1981). A new definition of learning disabilities. *Learning Disabilities Quarterly*, 4, 336–342.

Heshusius, L. (1989). The Newtonian mechanistic paradigm, special education, and contours of alternatives: An overview. *Journal of Learning Disabilities*, 22, 403–415.

Idol, L. (Ed.). (1989-90). Alternative service delivery models [Special series]. *Remedial and Special Education*, 10(6); 11(1).

Interagency Committee on Learning Disabilities. (1987). *Learning disabilities: A report to the U.S. Congress.* Bethesda, MD: National Institutes of Heath.

Katz, M.B. (1987). *Restructuring American education.* Cambridge, MA: Harvard University Press.

Kauffman, J.M., Gerber, M.M., & Semmel, M.I. (1988). Arguable assumptions underlying the Regular Education Initiative. *Journal of Learning Disabilities*, 21, 6–18.

Kavale, K., & Forness, S.R. (1985). *The science of learning disabilities.* San Diego: College-Hill.

Kavale, K., & Nye, C. (1981). Identification criteria for learning disabilities: A Survey of the research literature. *Learning Disability Quarterly*, 4, 383–388.

Kavanagh, J.F., & Truss, T.J. (Eds.). (1988). *Learning disabilities: Proceedings of the national conference*. Parkton, MD: York Press.

Kennedy, M.M. (1987). *Inexact sciences: Professional education and the development of expertise* (Issue Paper 87-2). East Lansing, MI: The National Center for Research on Teacher Education.

Keogh, B. (1988). Improving services for problem learners: Rethinking and restructuring. *Journal of Learning Disabilities*, 21, 19–22.

Keogh, B. (1993). Linking purpose and practice: Social/political and developmental perspectives on classification. In G.R. Lyon, D.B. Gray, J. Kavanagh, & N. Krasnegor (Eds.), *Better understanding of learning disabilities: New views from research and their implications for education and public policy* (pp. 311–323). Baltimore: Brookes.

Kephart, N. (1971). *The slow learner in the classroom*. Columbus, OH: Merrill.

Kirk, S., & Bateman, B. (1962). Diagnosis and remediation of learning disabilities. *Exceptional Children*, 29, 73–78.

Kirk, S., & Kirk, W.D. (1971). *Psycholinguistic learning disabilities: Diagnosis and remediation*. Chicago: University of Chicago Press.

Kozol, J.K. (1991). *Savage inequalities: Children in America's schools*. New York: Crown.

Kronick, D. (1976). *Three families*. San Rafael, CA: Academic Therapy Publications.

Kronick, D. (1990). Holism and empiricism as complementary paradigms. *Journal of Learning Disabilities*, 23, 5–10.

Learning Disabilities Association. (1991). *LDA Newsbriefs (Special Legislative Issue)* 26, 5–19.

Liberman, I.Y., Shankweiler, D., & Liberman, A. (1989). The alphabetic principle and learning to read. In D. Shankweiler and I.Y. Liberman (Eds.), *Phonology and reading disability: Solving the reading puzzle* (pp.1–33). Ann Arbor: University of Michigan Press.

Lubs, H.A., Duara, R., Levin, B., Jallad, B., Lubs, M., Rabin, M., Kushch, A., & Gross-Glenn, K. (1991). Dyslexia subtypes: Genetics, behavior, and brain imaging. In D.D. Duane & D.B. Gray (Eds.), *The reading brain: The biological basis of dyslexia* (pp. 89–117). Parkton, MD: York Press.

Lyon, G.R. (1987). Learning disabilities research: False starts and broken promises. In S. Vaughn & C. Bos (Eds.), *Research in learning disabilities: Issues and future directions* (pp. 69–85). Austin, TX: PRO-ED.

Lyon, G.R. (1989). IQ is irrelevant to the definition of learning disabilities: A position in search of logic and data. *Journal of Learning Disabilities, 22,* 504–506, 512.

Lyon, G.R. (1991). *Research in learning disabilities* (Tech. Rep.). Bethesda, MD: National Institutes of Child Health and Human Development.

Lyon, G.R. (in press). *Frames of reference for the assessment of learning disabilities: New views on measurement issues.* Baltimore: Brookes.

Lyon, G.R., Gray, D.B., Kavanagh, J., & Krasnegor, N. (Eds.). (1993). *Better understanding of learning disabilities: New view from research and their implications for education and public policy.* Baltimore: Brookes.

Lyon, G.R., & Moats, L.C. (1988). Critical conditions in instruction of the learning disabled. *Journal of Consulting and Clinical Psychology, 56,* 830-835.

Lyon, G.R., Vaasen, M., & Toomey, F. (1989). Teachers' perceptions of their undergraduate and graduate preparation. *Teacher Education and Special Education, 12,* 164–169.

Mercer, C.D., Hughes, C., & Mercer, A.R. (1985). Learning disabilities definitions used by state education departments. *Learning Disability Quarterly*, 8, 45–55.

Mercer, C.D., King-Sears, P., & Mercer, A.R. (1990). Learning disabilities definitions and criteria used by state education departments. *Learning Disability Quarterly*, 13, 141–152.

Moats, L.C. (in press-a). Assessment of spelling in learning disabilities research. In G.R. Lyon (Ed.), *Frames of reference for the assessment of learning disabilities: New views on measurement issues*. Baltimore: Brookes.

Moats, L.C. (in press-b). *Spelling development and spelling disability*. Parkton, MD: York Press.

Morris, R. (1988). Classification of learning disabilities: Old problems and new approaches. *Journal of Consulting and Clinical Psychology*, 56, 789–794.

Morris, R. (1993). Issues in empirical versus clinical identification of learning disabilities. In G.R. Lyon, D.B. Gray, J. Kavanagh, & N. Krasnegor (Eds.), *Better understanding learning disabilities: New views from research and their implications for education and public policy* (pp.73–93). Baltimore: Brookes.

National Advisory Committee on Handicapped Children. (1968). *Special education for handicapped children* (First Annual Report). Washington, DC: Department of Health, Education & Welfare.

National Joint Committee on Learning Disabilities. (1988). [Letter to NJCLD member organizations].

Nolen, P.A., McCutchen, D., & Berninger, V. (1990). Ensuring tomorrow's literacy: A shared responsibility. *Journal of Teacher Education*, 41, 63–72.

Opp, G. (1992). A German perspective on learning disabilities. *Journal of Learning Disabilities*, 25, 351–360.

Poplin, M.S. (1984). Toward a holistic view of persons with learning disabilities. *Learning Disability Quarterly*, 7, 290–294.

Rack, J.P., Snowling, M.J., & Olson, R.K. (1991). The nonword reading deficit in developmental dyslexia: A review. *Reading Research Quarterly*, 27, 28–53.

Reid, D.K., & Stone, A. (1991). Why is cognitive instruction effective? Underlying learning mechanisms. *Remedial and Special Education*, 12(3), 8–19.

Reynolds, C.R. (1984–85). Critical measurement issues in learning disabilities. *The Journal of Special Education*, 18, 451–475.

Ryan, A.G., & Price, L. (1992). Adults with LD in the 1990s. Intervention in School and Clinic, 28, 6–20.

Sarason, S.B. (1990). *The predictable failure of education reform*. San Francisco: Jossey-Bass.

Senf, G.M. (1981). Issues surrounding the diagnosis of learning disabilities: Child handicap vs. The failure of the child-school interaction. In T.R. Kratochwill (Ed.), *Advances in school psychology* (Vol. 1, pp. 88–131). Hillsdale, NJ: Erlbaum.

Senf, G.M. (1986). Learning disabilities research in sociological and scientific perspective. In J.K. Torgesen & B.Y.L. Wong (Eds.), *Psychological and educational perspectives on learning disabilities* (pp. 27–53). Orlando, FL: Academic Press.

Senf, G.M. (1987). Learning disabilities as a sociological sponge: Wiping up life's spills. In S. Vaughn & C.S. Bos (Eds.), *Research in learning disabilities: Issues and future directions* (pp. 87–101). Austin, TX: PRO-ED.

Shaywitz, B., Shaywitz, S., Liberman, I., Fletcher, J., Shankweiler, D., Duncan, J., Katz, L., Liberman, A., Francis, D., Dreyer, L., Crain, S., Brady, S., Fowler, A., Kier, L., Rosenfield, N., Gore, J., & Makuch, R. (1991). Neurolinguistic and biological mechanisms in dyslexia. In D.D. Duane & D.B. Gray (Eds.), *The reading brains: The biological basis of dyslexia* (pp. 27–52). Parkton, MD: York Press.

Shaywitz, S.E., Escobar, M.D., Shaywitz, B.A., Fletcher, J.M. & Makuch, R. (1992). Evidence that dyslexia may represent the lower tail of a normal distribution or reading ability. *New England Journal of Medicine*, 326, 145–150.

Shaywitz, S.E., Shaywitz, B.A., Fletcher, J.M., & Escobar, M.D. (1990). Prevalence of reading disability in boys and girls: Results of the Connecticut longitudinal study. *Journal of the American Medical Association*, 264, 998–1002.

Siegel, E. (1972). Task analysis and effective teaching. *Journal of Learning Disabilities*, 5, 519–532.

Siegel, L.S. (1989). IQ is irrelevant to the definition of learning disabilities. *Journal of Learning Disabilities*, 22, 469–478.

Stanovich, K. (1991). Discrepancy definitions of reading disability: Has intelligence led us astray? *Reading Research Quarterly*, 26, 7–29.

Stanovich, K. (1993). The construct validity of discrepancy definitions of reading disability. In G.R. Lyon, D.B. Gray, J. Kavanagh, & N. Krasnegor (Eds.), *Better understanding learning disabilities: New views from research and their implications for education and public policy* (pp. 273–307). Baltimore: Brookes.

Torgesen, J. (1986). Learning disabilities theory: Its current state and future prospects. *Journal of Learning Disabilities*, 19, 385–448.

U.S. Department of Education. (1989). *To assure the free appropriate public education of all handicapped children: Eleventh report to Congress on the implementation of the Education of the Handicapped Act.* Washington, DC: Department of Education.

U.S. Office of Education. (1977). Definition and criteria for defining students as learning disabled. *Federal Register*, 42:250, p. 65083. Washington, DC: U.S. Government Printing Office.

Vaughn, S. & Bos, C. (1987) *Research in learning disabilities: Issues and future directions.* Austin, TX: PRO-ED.

Vellutino, F. & Scanlon, D.M. (1987). Phonological coding, phonological awareness, and reading ability: Evidence from a longitudinal and experimental study. *Merrill-Palmer Quarterly*, 33, 321–363.

Will, M.C. (1986). Educating children with learning problems: A shared responsibility. *Exceptional Children*, 52, 411–415.

Worral, R.S. (1990). Detecting health fraud in the field of learning disabilities. *Journal of Learning Disabilities*, 23, 207–212.

Ysseldyke, J.E. & Algozzine, B. (1993). LD or Not LD: That's not the question! *Journal of Learning Disabilities*, 16: 29–31.

Zigmond, N. (1993). Learning Disabilities from an educational perspective. In G.R. Lyon, D.B. Gray, J. Kavanagh, & N. Krasnegor (Eds.). *Better understanding learning disabilities: New views from research and their implications for education and public policy* (pp. 251–272). Baltimore: Brookes.

Zigmond, N. & Baker J. (1990). Mainstreaming experiences for learning disabled students: A preliminary report. *Exceptional Children*, 57, 176–185.

Chapter 5

Selected Special Education Statistics

The Individuals with Disabilities Education Act (IDEA) requires that all children and youth with disabilities have access to a free appropriate public education (FAPE) that is determined on an individual basis and designed to meet their unique needs. This education must be provided in the least restrictive environment (LRE), and the rights of the child and family are protected through procedural safeguards.

Age Groups of Students Served under IDEA, Part B

The two largest age groups served under IDEA, Part B in 1994-95 were ages 6-11 (2,520,863) and 12-17 (2,154,963). The remaining age groups, ages 3-5 (524,458) and 18-21 (239,342) comprised less than 15 percent of all students served under IDEA, Part B. Analyzing the growth in the number of children by age range provides some insights into the dynamics of the 3.2 percent increase (from 5,271,847 to 5,439,626) in the number of children ages 3-21 served under IDEA, Part B. Students ages 6-21 comprised about 90 percent of the special education population. However, they accounted for only 80 percent of the increase in total number of children served. Preschool children ages 3-5, who were only 9.6 percent of all children receiving special education, accounted for about 20 percent of the growth in the number of students served. Preschool children also had the largest growth

Information in this chapter was taken from *To Assure the Free Appropriate Public Education of all Children with Disabilities: Eighteenth Annual Report to Congress on the Implementation of The Individuals with Disabilities Education Act*, U.S. Department of Education, 1996.

Table 5.1. Number and Percentage Change of Students Ages 6-21 Served: School Years 1993-94 through 1994-95

Disability	Total		Change		% of Total 6-21
	1993-94	1994-95	Number	Percent	
Specific learning disabilities	2,428,062	2,513,977	85,915	3.5	51.1
Speech or language impairments	1,018,208	1,023,665	5,457	0.5	20.8
Mental retardation	553,869	570,855	16,986	3.1	11.6
Serious emotional disturbance	415,071	428,168	13,097	3.2	8.7
Multiple disabilities	109,730	89,646	-20,084	-18.3	-1.8
Hearing impairments	64,667	65,568	901	1.4	1.3
Orthopedic impairments	56,842	60,604	3,762	6.6	1.2
Other health impairments	83,080	106,509	23,429	28.2	2.2
Visual impairments	24,813	24,877	64	0.3	0.5
Autism	19,058	22,780	3,722	19.5	0.5
Deaf-blindness	1,367	1,331	-36	-2.6	0.0
Traumatic brain injury	5,395	7,188	1,793	33.2	0.1
All disabilities	**4,780,162**	**4,915,168**	**135,006**	**2.8**	**100.0**

Note: For 1993-94, funding for children and youth with disabilities included children counted under IDEA, Part B and the Chapter 1 Handicapped Program. For 1994-95, all children were counted under IDEA, Part B.

Source: U.S. Department of Education, Office of Special Education Programs, Data Analysis System (DANS).

rate of all age groups served with a 6.7 percent increase (from 491,685 to 524,458), followed by students ages 12-17 with a 3.6 percent increase (from 2,079,094 to 2,154,963). The number of students ages 18-21 served decreased by 1.2 percent (from 242,144 to 239,342). This decrease may be attributable to the 1.8 percent decrease in the 18-21 resident population between 1993-94 and 1994-95.

Dicabilitioo of Studonto Scrvcd Undcr IDEA, Part B

IDEA, Part B served 4,915,168 students ages 6-21 during the 1994-95 school year. The information in this section refers only to children ages 6-21 because the 1986 Amendments to EHA, P.L. 99-457 (now IDEA) ended the practice of collecting disability category data on children less than 6 years old.

Students with specific learning disabilities continue to account for more than half of all students with disabilities (51.1 percent). During the 1994-95 school year, 2,513,977 students with specific learning disabilities were served under IDEA, Part B, 3.5 percent (85,915) more than in 1993-94 under the Part B and Chapter 1 Handicapped Programs. However, the 1994-95 percentage of students with learning disabilities in the resident population ages 6-21 is identical to the 1993-94 percentage. Students with speech or language impairments (20.8 percent), mental retardation (11.6 percent), and serious emotional disturbance (8.7 percent) made up an additional 41.1 percent of all students ages 6-21 with disabilities. Again, these percentage distributions are similar to the 199394 distributions.

The increases within several disability categories were proportionately greater than the 2.8 percent increase across all categories. The largest increase occurred in the traumatic brain injury category, which increased by 33.2 percent (from 5,395 to 7,188). Significant increases also occurred in the categories of other health impairments (28.2 percent from 83,080 to 106,509) and autism (19.5 percent from 19,058 to 22,780). There was a significant decrease in the category of students with multiple disabilities (from 109,730 to 89,646, or -18.3 percent).

The increases in the number of students with autism and traumatic brain injury are probably due to the relative newness of those reporting categories. The 1994-95 school year was the third year States were required to report the number of students in those categories (reporting was optional for those categories in 1991-92). Many States attributed these increases to the provision of technical assistance to districts on the identification and evaluation of students with autism and traumatic brain injury. States also indicated that during triennial review and evaluations, these relatively new categories were likely used for students who previously were reported under other disability categories.

The increase in the number of students with other health impairments appears to be the result of an expansion of the service population. Many States indicated that the increase was primarily due to increased service provision to students with attention deficit disorder. This is the third year several States have reported increases in the number of students identified as having other health impairments because of increased services to students with attention deficit disorder. The decrease in the number of students with multiple disabilities was primarily due to Wisconsin's decision to stop using the category and report all students under their primary disability condition. In 1993-94, over 20 percent of all students with multiple disabilities were served in Wisconsin.

Five-Year Trends in Number of Students Served

The number of students ages 6-21 served increased by 12.7 percent (553,417) from 199091 through 1994-95. The increases within several disability categories were proportionately greater than the 12.7 percent increase across all categories. The largest increase occurred in the number of students with other health impairments, which increased by 89 percent (from 56,349 to 106,509). As noted earlier, much of the increase may be related to students with attention deficit disorder. A large increase also occurred in the category of students with orthopedic impairments (22.8 percent from 49,340 to 60,604). The increase in the percentage of students with orthopedic impairments and other health impairments is partly related to the relatively small number of students served in these categories. For a number of years, Michigan has combined the orthopedic impairments category with the other health impairments category. Students in both of these categories are reported under students with orthopedic impairments. Specific learning disabilities increased by 17.3 percent (from 2,144,017 to 2,513,977). There were also increases in the new categories of autism over a 4-year period (from 5,415 to 22,780) and traumatic brain injury (from 245 to 7,188). (Autism and traumatic brain injury were introduced as separate reporting categories in the 1991-92 school year as a result of P.L. 101-476, the 1990 Amendments to IDEA.) Two categories have decreased since 1990-91: deaf-blindness (-12.7 percent from 1,524 to 1,331) and multiple disabilities (-8.2 percent from 97,629 to 89,646). The decrease in the multiple disability category occurred in 1994-95 as a result of a decision by the Wisconsin SEA to report all students by their primary disability condition.

Table 5.2. Number of Students Ages 6-21 Served[a]/ During the 1990-91 through 1994-95 School Years.

Disability Condition	School Year					Change from 1990-91 through 1994-95	
	1990-91	1991-92	1992-93	1993-94	1994-95	Number	Percent
Specific learning disabilities	2,144,017	2,247,004	2,366,487	2,428,112	2,513,977	369,960	17.3
Speech or language impairments	987,778	998,904	998,049	1,018,208	1,023,665	35,887	3.6
Mental retardation	551,457	553,262	532,362	553,869	570,855	19,398	3.5
Serious emotional disturbance	390,764	400,211	401,652	415,071	428,168	37,404	9.6
Multiple disabilities	97,629	98,408	103,279	109,730	89,646	-7,983	-8.2
Hearing impairments	59,211	60,727	60,616	64,667	65,568	6,357	10.7
Orthopedic impairments	49,340	51,389	52,588	56,842	60,604	11,264	22.8
Other health impairments	56,349	58,749	66,063	83,080	106,509	50,160	89.0
Visual impairments	23,682	24,083	23,544	24,813	24,877	1,195	5.0
Autism	NA	5,415	15,580	19,058	22,780	22,780	--
Deaf-blindness	1,524	1,427	1,394	1,367	1,331	-193	-12.7
Traumatic brain injury	NA	245	3,960	5,395	7,188	7,188	--
All disabilities	4,361,751	4,499,824	4,625,574	4,780,212	4,915,168	553,417	12.7

a/   The data for 1990-91 through 1993-94 include children 6 through 21 years of age served under IDEA, Part B and Chapter 1 Handicapped Program. For 1994-95 all children ages 6-21 are served under Part B, which includes children previously counted under the Chapter 1 Handicapped Program. Autism and traumatic brain injury were introduced as separate reporting categories in the 1991-92 school year as a result of P.L. 101-476, the 1990 Amendments to IDEA.

Source: U.S. Department of Education, Office of Special Education Programs, Data Analysis System (DANS).

93

Students with Disabilities Exiting Special Education

Research indicates that the school exit status of students with disabilities is an important predictor of postschool success. High school graduates with disabilities are significantly more likely to be engaged in productive activities outside the home, such as employment, postsecondary education, or volunteer work, than high school dropouts. Due to requirements in IDEA, OSEP has been collecting these data since 1984-85. However, the data have changed somewhat over the years, and 1993-94 was the first year for which all States reported data on students exiting special education using revised OSEP data categories. These exit categories include:

- graduated with diploma,
- graduated with certificate,
- reached the maximum age for services,
- returned to regular education,
- died,
- moved, known to be continuing
- moved, not known to be continuing, and
- dropped out

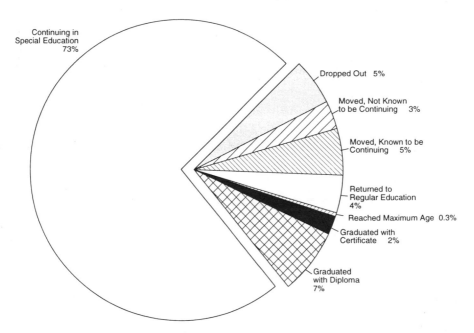

Figure 5.3. *Enrollment and Exit Status of Students with Disabilities Ages 14-21: 1993-94. Note: The figure does not include students who died (.1 percent). Source: Department of Education, Office of Special Education Programs, Data Analysis Systems (DANS).*

In addition to collecting data in new exit categories, the method of analyzing these data has also changed. Rather than calculating percentages based on the number of total exiters with disabilities as in the past, percentages are now calculated based on total child count for students ages 14 and older. This revision was made primarily to make OSEP dropout rates comparable with rates used by other Federal agencies. Readers must keep in mind that not all students ages 14-21 will exit special education each year, and, as a consequence, percentages of exiting students will not sum to 100 percent. The new rates indicate the annual rate at which students with disabilities 14 and older continue to be enrolled in and exit special education through the various bases.

Students Who Graduated with a Diploma or Certificate

Graduation with a standard high school diploma was the most common basis of exit for students with disabilities; 7.5 percent of all students ages 14-21 graduated with a diploma. That graduation rate varied by disability category. Of all students ages 14-21 in special education in 1993-94, the students most likely to graduate with a diploma were those with visual impairments (10.3 percent of all students with visual impairments ages 14-21), hearing impairments (9.7 percent), orthopedic impairments (9.0 percent), and traumatic brain injury (9.5 percent). Those students least likely to graduate with a diploma were those with multiple disabilities (3.2 percent) and autism (2.9 percent).

Among the 1.6 percent of students who graduated with a certificate of completion or modified diploma, students with mental retardation (3.8 percent of all students with mental retardation ages 14-21) and deaf-blindness (4.6 percent) were most likely to graduate in this manner. Graduation with a certificate of completion or modified diploma was also common for students beyond the typical age for secondary school students; during the year, almost one-fourth of all students ages 21 and older received a certificate or modified diploma.

During the past 5 years, the percentage of all students with disabilities ages 14 and older graduating with a diploma or certificate has remained fairly constant, although the percentage decreased slightly in 1993-94. The decline in the percentage of students graduating in 1993-94 reflects a smaller proportion of students receiving certificates of completion and modified diplomas. Some of this decline may be accounted for by policy changes in the States. For example, Texas no longer offers students with disabilities a modified diploma.

95

Table 5.4. Number and Percentage of Students with Disabilities 14 and Older Exiting Special Education by Disability and Basis of Exit: 1993-94. (Source: U.S. Department of Education, Office of Special Education Programs, Data Analysis System (DANS).

	Graduated with Diploma	Graduated with Certificate	Reached Maximum Age	Returned to Regular Education	Moved, Known to Be Continuing	Moved, Not Known to Be Continuing	Died	Dropped Out	Total
Specific learning disabilities	76,735 8.4	10,871 1.2	891 0.1	34,229 3.8	45,447 5.0	22,944 2.5	438 0.1	44,244 4.9	235,799 25.9%
Speech or language impairments	3,423 7.0	473 1.0	121 0.2	8,358 17.0	2,377 4.9	2,059 4.2	31 0.1	1,875 3.8	18,717 38.2%
Mental retardation	13,900 5.8	9,117 3.8	2,307 1.0	2,273 0.9	9,899 4.1	4,739 2.0	361 0.2	10,270 4.2	52,866 21.9%
Serious emotional disturbance	11,251 6.0	1,649 0.9	331 0.2	8,041 4.3	20,170 10.7	10,905 5.8	184 0.1	17,370 9.2	69,901 37.0%
Multiple disabilities	1,254 3.2	675 1.7	553 1.4	330 0.8	1,192 3.1	324 0.8	133 0.3	531 1.4	4,992 12.8%
Hearing impairments	2,209 9.7	391 1.7	48 0.2	518 2.3	896 3.9	370 1.6	11 0.1	570 2.5	5,013 22.0%
Orthopedic impairments	1,557 9.0	285 1.7	133 0.8	1,259 7.3	635 3.7	280 1.6	82 0.5	412 2.4	4,643 26.9%
Other health impairments	2,250 8.5	191 0.7	44 0.2	4,733 17.9	1,528 5.8	536 2.0	97 0.4	1,005 3.8	10,384 39.8%
Visual impairments	931 10.3	105 1.2	53 0.6	218 2.4	324 3.6	164 1.8	19 0.2	195 2.2	2,009 22.2%
Autism	169 2.9	120 2.1	80 1.4	51 0.9	148 2.6	75 1.3	3 0.1	55 1.0	701 12.1%
Deaf-blindness	34 6.0	26 4.6	8 1.4	11 1.9	32 5.6	17 3.0	6 1.1	8 1.4	142 24.9%
Traumatic brain injury	232 9.5	45 1.8	25 1.0	73 3.0	157 6.4	47 1.9	3 0.1	73 3.0	655 26.7%
All disabilities	113,945 7.5	23,948 1.6	4,594 0.3	60,094 4.0	82,805 5.5	42,460 2.8	1,368 0.1	76,608 5.1	405,822 26.8%

Educational Placements for Students with Disabilities

The Office of Special Education Programs (OSEP) uses several approaches to promote appropriate placements for students with disabilities in the least restrictive environment, including funded research, technical assistance, targeted grant awards for statewide systems change, and compliance monitoring. To examine State and national trends in educational placements for students with disabilities, each year OSEP collects data from States and Outlying Areas on the number of students with disabilities served in each of six different educational environments: regular class, resource room, separate class, public or private separate school, public or private residential facility, and homebound/hospital placements. The data are collected by age group for students ages 3-21. Data for students ages 6-21 are collected by disability.

The purpose of this data collection is to describe how States and the nation are meeting the LRE mandate as expressed in IDEA and its implementing regulations. During the past several years, the percentage of students with disabilities served in regular classes has increased considerably, while the percentage of students in resource rooms has gradually decreased. Other placement percentages have remained stable. During the past 5 years, not only have States and local school districts worked to meet the needs of students with disabilities within the general education classroom, but they have also improved their data collection and reporting procedures. As a result, for 1993-94, States reported serving 43.4 percent of students with disabilities ages 6-21 in regular classroom placements, 29.5 percent in resource rooms, 22.7 percent in separate classes, 3.1 percent in separate schools, 0.7 percent in residential facilities, and 0.6 percent in homebound/hospital placements.

Placement Patterns by Age

States report a tendency to serve a larger percentage of students with disabilities ages 6-11 in regular classrooms; that percentage decreases for students ages 12-17 and 18-21. This pattern holds across the disability groups. The only exception is for students with learning disabilities. In that case, the percentage of students ages 18-21 in regular class placements is larger than the percentage of students ages 12-17 in regular class placements. Field-based research confirms that efforts to integrate younger students have generally been more successful than efforts with older students. This may be attributed, in part, to the departmentalized structure of secondary schools, the academic demands of the secondary curriculum, or the competitive culture that exists in many secondary schools. Furthermore, a substantial proportion of elementary school students with disabilities have speech or language impairments, which are often addressed in regular classes or resource rooms; many of these students do not require special education and related services in secondary school.

A relatively large percentage of students ages 18-21 are served in separate classes and schools. Because general education students typically graduate at age 18, students with disabilities ages 18-21 who are still in school do not have same-age peers with whom to interact. Some educators assert that the most natural environments for these students are colleges and universities, work sites, postsecondary vocational training programs, or community-based instructional settings other than secondary schools.

Table 5.5. Educational Environments for Students with Disabilities

Regular class includes students who receive the majority of their education program in a regular classroom and receive special education and related services outside the regular classroom for less than 21 percent of the school day.

Resource room includes students who receive special education and related services outside of the regular classroom for at least 21 percent but no more than 60 percent of the school day.

Separate class includes students who receive special education and related services outside the regular class for more than 60 percent of the school day.

Separate school includes students who receive special education and related services in a public or private separate day school for students with disabilities, at public expense, for more than 50 percent of the school day.

Residential facility includes students who receive special education in a public or private residential facility, at public expense, for more than 50 percent of the school day.

Homebound/hospital environment includes students placed in and receiving special education in a hospital or homebound program.

Source: OSEP Data Dictionary, Office of Special Education Programs, U.S. Department of Education.

Placement Patterns by Disability

Placement patterns also vary considerably by disability. The majority of students with speech and language impairments (87.5 percent) are served in regular classes, and an additional 7.6 percent are served in resource rooms. Students with speech and language impairments are more likely than students with any other disability to spend the majority of their day with peers who do not have disabilities.

Students with learning disabilities, orthopedic impairments, other health impairments, serious emotional disturbance, and traumatic brain injury are generally placed within the regular school building, but then students are spread across regular classes, resource rooms, and separate classes. It is likely that many of these students spend a portion of their day in classes with peers who do not have disabilities, but are "pulled out" for extended resource room support or alternative academic courses.

Separate classroom placements are most prevalent for students with mental retardation (57.0 percent), autism (54.5 percent), and multiple disabilities (44.1 percent), although resource room placements are also commonly used to serve students with mental retardation and multiple disabilities. By definition, those in separate classroom placements may spend up to 40 percent of the school day in a regular classroom.

This section has presented data on educational placements for students with disabilities. The percentage of students with disabilities served in regular classes has increased considerably over the past 5 years, although, on a national level, regular classroom placements are still primarily used with elementary-aged students and those with speech or language impairments and learning disabilities.

Meeting the Needs of Students with Disabilities in the Inner Cities

Anecdotal information suggests that special education programs in inner cities face unique challenges, and differ from nationally representative data on special education students, personnel, and services. Despite a keen interest in exploring issues of inner city needs and services, due to the scarcity of data, OSEP must rely on information collected by the Office for Civil Rights (OCR), the National Longitudinal Transition Study of Special Education Students (NLTS), and secondary data sources. This section synthesizes information from a variety of those sources to provide a profile of

Table 5.6. Percentage of Students with Disabilities Ages 6-21 Served in Different Educational Environments, by Disability: School Year 1993-94 (Source: Department of Education, Office of Special Education Programs, Data Analysis Sytems—DANS).

Disability	Regular Class	Resource Room	Separate Class	Separate School	Residential Facility	Home-bound/ Hospital
Specific learning disabilities	39.3	41.0	18.8	0.6	0.1	0.1
Speech or language impairments	87.5	7.6	4.5	0.3	0.04	0.05
Mental retardation	8.6	26.1	57.0	7.0	0.7	0.5
Serious emotional disturbance	20.5	25.8	35.3	13.4	3.2	1.8
Multiple disabilities	9.1	19.8	44.1	21.8	3.2	2.0
Hearing impairments	30.6	20.0	30.6	7.0	11.6	0.2
Orthopedic impairments	37.4	20.7	33.3	5.3	0.5	2.9
Other health impairments	40.0	27.0	21.3	1.8	0.4	9.4
Visual impairments	45.2	21.3	18.3	4.1	10.6	0.5
Autism	9.6	8.1	54.5	23.4	3.9	0.5
Deaf-blindness	7.7	8.0	34.6	24.3	23.2	2.2
Traumatic brain injury	22.3	23.5	30.2	18.3	2.6	3.0
U.S. and Outlying Areas	43.4	29.5	22.7	3.1	0.7	0.6
50 States, D.C., & P.R.	43.4	29.4	22.7	3.1	0.7	0.6

special education in the nation's inner cities. The section addresses the following specific questions.

- What are the characteristics and needs of inner city students with disabilities as compared to students with disabilities in suburban and rural areas?

- How do special education services in inner city areas compare to special education in suburban and rural areas?

- How do poverty and race/ethnicity affect the need for and the nature of special education services in inner cities?

- How do outcomes for youth with disabilities in urban areas compare with outcomes for youth in suburban and rural areas?

Table 5.7. Estimated Number and Percentage of Students with Disabilities in Inner-City and Non-Inner-City School Districts in the 1992-93 School Year.

Disability	Inner-city		Non-inner-city	
	Number	Percent	Number	Percent
Specific learning disabilities	554,044	5.1%	1,684,256	5.4%
Speech or language impairments	232,949	2.1	847,552	2.7
Mental retardation	147,819	1.4	403,450	1.3
Serious emotional disturbance	89,342	0.8	205,314	0.7
Multiple impairments	29,625	0.3	45,570	0.2
Hearing impairments	16,209	0.2	36,614	0.1
Orthopedic impairments	13,964	0.1	27,768	0.1
Other health impairments	23,268	0.2	58,041	0.2
Visual impairments	6,135	0.1	15,118	0.1
Autism	7,001	0.1	8,202	0.0
Deaf-blindness	713	0.0	1,115	0.0
Traumatic brain injury	463	0.0	2,661	0.0
All disabilities	**1,121,532**	**10.4%**	**3,335,661**	**10.8%**

Percentage in "All disabilities" row may not equal sum of other rows due to rounding.

Source: The 1992 Office for Civil Rights Elementary and Secondary School Survey and the 1992 Common Core of Data Public School Universe File.

Table 5.8. Estimated Number and Percentage of Students in Special Education in Inner-City and Non-Inner-City School Districts, by Ethnicity and Disability, 1992-93 School Year

Race and Disability Catetory	Inner-City		Non-Inner-City		Total	
	Number	%	Number	%	Number	%
White, non-Hispanic						
Mental retardation	58,772	1.3	269,010	1.1	327,782	1.1
Serious emotional disburbance	40,409	.9	157,934	.7	198,343	.7
Specific learning disability	241,678	5.2	1,280,875	5.4	1,522,553	5.3
African American, non-Hispanic						
Mental retardation	65,535	2.0	103,947	2.8	169,482	2.5
Serious emotional disburbance	35,433	1.1	34,645	.9	70,078	1.0
Specific learning disability	176,107	5.5	222,730	6.1	398,837	5.8
Hispanic						
Mental retardation	20,339	.8	20,278	.8	40,617	.8
Serious emotional disburbance	12,362	.5	8,043	.3	20,405	.4
Specific learning disability	124,042	5.0	138,289	5.5	262,331	5.3
Total[a]						
Mental retardation	147,820	1.4	403,451	1.3	551,271	1.3
Serious emotional disburbance	89,342	.8	205,314	.7	294,656	.7
Specific learning disability	554,045	5.1	1,684,257	5.4	2,238,302	5.3
All Students with Disabilities[b]	1,121,532	10.3	3,335,661	10.6	4,457,193	10.5

a/ Also includes Asian and American Indian students (not shown).

b/ consists of all students with an IEP (Individualized Education Program).

Source: The 1992 Office for Civil Rights Elementary and Secondary School Survey and the 1992 Common Core of Data Public School Universe File.

Table 5.9. Estimated Percentage of Students with Disabilities in Full-Time and Part-Time Special Education Placements for Inner-City and Non-Inner-City Districts, 1992-93 School Year.

Disability	Inner-city		Non-inner-city	
	Part-Time	Full-Time	Part-Time	Full-Time
Specific learning disabilities	64.3%	36.4%	81.2%	19.0%
Speech or language impairments	86.2	13.8	93.9	6.2
Mental retardation	19.9	81.5	39.0	60.9
Serious emotional disturbance	33.0	67.7	57.9	42.1
Multiple impairments	40.0	60.0	32.9	67.2
Hearing impairments	48.2	51.8	71.5	28.5
Orthopedic impairments	43.2	57.1	66.1	33.9
Other health impairments	66.3	33.7	73.4	26.6
Visual impairments	57.4	42.5	81.0	19.0
Autism	18.1	82.0	25.9	74.2
Deaf-blindness	27.6	72.4	49.5	50.5
Traumatic brain injury	40.7	58.9	58.1	42.1
All disabilities	**58.7%**	**41.3%**	**76.6%**	**23.4%**

Source: The 1992 Office for Civil Rights Elementary and Secondary School Survey and the 1992 Common Core of Data Public School Universe File.

Table 5.10. Parental Reports of Disability Status of Children by Race and Hispanic Origin: 1992. (Source: Current Population Survey, 1992 Supplement on School Enrollment.)

	White Non-Hispanic		Black Non-Hispanic		Hispanic[a]		Other		Total	
	Number	Percent Distribution	Number	Percent Distribution	Number	Percent Distribution	Number	Percent Distribution	Number	Percent Distribution
Current Population Survey: Ages 5 to 17										
Learning disability	3,606,564	11.1%	635,115	8.6%	304,928	5.7%	105,592	5.2%	4,651,740	9.9%
Mental retardation	1,568,023	4.8	305,832	4.2	111,043	2.1	38,619	1.9	2,023,046	4.3
Speech impairment	235,296	0.7	58,957	0.8	29,857	0.6	7,631	0.4	331,270	0.7
Serious emotional disturbance	912,231	2.8	185,312	2.5	61,615	1.2	27,387	1.4	1,186,074	2.5
Deafness	328,719	1.0	71,376	1.0	35,280	0.7	6,894	0.3	441,798	0.9
Other hearing impairment	130,082	0.4	34,867	0.5	12,934	0.2	3,117	0.2	180,529	0.4
Blindness	449,921	1.4	64,312	0.9	38,486	0.7	15,898	0.8	568,146	1.2
Other visual impairment	87,743	0.3	26,302	0.4	7,376	0.1	157	0.0	121,107	0.3
Orthopedic impairment	654,257	2.0	114,751	1.6	68,986	1.3	14,082	0.7	851,605	1.8
Other health impairment	343,199	1.1	55,886	0.8	37,142	0.7	15,143	0.7	450,899	1.0
	676,905	2.1	141,830	1.9	62,291	1.2	17,713	0.9	898,268	1.9
Total	1,818,532	5.6%	341,534	4.6%	139,378	2.6%	72,612	3.6%	2,371,585	5.0%

a/ Hispanics can be of any race.

Table 5.11. Secondary School Completion for Youth with Disabilities, by Community Type

	Urban	Suburban	Rural
Graduated	50.8	66.9	60.8
	(4.3)	(3.6)	(3.5)
Dropped Out	36.6	24.6	31.4
	(4.2)	(3.3)	(3.4)
Suspended/Expelled	5.5	3.4	3.0
	(2.0)	(1.4)	(1.2)
Reached Maxiumum Age	7.1	5.1	4.9
	(2.2)	(1.7)	(1.6)

Note: Standard errors are in parenthesis.

Source: Valdés, K.A., Williamson, C.L. and Wagner, M. (1990). The National Longitudinal Transition Study of Special Education Students, Statistical Almanac, Volume 1. Menlo Park, CA: SRI International.

Summary and Implications

Analysis of available data results in a complex picture of students with disabilities in inner cities. The interrelationships among urbanicity, race/ethnicity, and socioeconomic status and their impact on placement in special education are difficult to untangle.

Several findings from the data analyses are clear, however. Students in inner cities are identified as eligible for special education at approximately the same rate as non-inner-city students. A larger percentage of families living in the inner cities live in poverty, and this pattern applies to families of students with disabilities as well. Furthermore, public schools in the inner cities enroll large percentages of students from racial and ethnic minority groups. Less clear are the relative influences of poverty and race/ethnicity on the disproportionate representation of racial and ethnic minorities in special education. Disability rates reported by parents differ by income and race, and also differ from disability rates reported by schools and school districts. Why this occurs is not clear.

Data on special education services for secondary students with disabilities in inner cities and other areas indicate similar course-taking and service patterns, with some exceptions. Fewer secondary students with disabilities in inner cities are enrolled in vocational education classes compared to students in rural and suburban areas. Data also suggest that students with disabilities in inner cities are more likely than students in non-inner-city districts to be placed in more restrictive learning environments.

Data from the NLTS suggest that urban youth with disabilities have a particularly difficult time adjusting to postsecondary roles. High dropout rates, low levels of enrollment in postsecondary education, and high rates of unemployment are indicative of the problems experienced by many of these youth.

In response to perceived needs, OSEP recently established a priority to train scholars in historically black colleges and universities (HBCUs) and other minority institutions (OMIs) to conduct research in special education and urban issues. This will help focus attention on a much-needed area of study. OSEP also uses its compliance monitoring to ensure that all students with disabilities, including those in inner cities, are receiving a free appropriate public education as guaranteed under IDEA. OSEP is committed to working with States and local education agencies continuously to improve programs and meet the changing needs of inner-city students.

Part Two

Assessment

Chapter 6

Understanding Assessment Jargon

Jargon Dictionary

The language used by professionals in doing the work that they do is often not understood by families and persons who do not do the same work. The words and phrases selected here are part of a special vocabulary often used by service providers who do assessments. This is not an extensive listing.

Adaptive Behavior Scale measures the individual's ability to perform adaptive or self-help behaviors such as eating, dressing, bathing, etc. The information is usually obtained from a parent, teacher, or person who knows the individual well.

Aptitude Test measures capacity, capability, or talent for learning a thing.

At Risk is a term used with children who have or could have problems with their development that may affect later learning.

Auditory Discrimination is the ability to detect subtle differences among sounds in words; i.e., tap/cap, cap/cop.

Excerpted from *COPING: Creating Opportunities of Parent Empowerment*, April 1996; reprinted with permission. For more information contact: COPE (Creating Opportunities for Parent Empowerment), 300 I Street ND, Suite 112, Washington, DC 20002.

Auditory Memory is the ability to remember what is heard (words, numbers, stories). This includes short and long term memory.

Auditory Perception is the ability to receive sounds accurately and to understand what they mean.

Behavior Modification is a process based on the belief that all behavior can be changed. The specific behavior to be changed must be pinpointed, and a plan for accomplishing that goal must be decided.

Cognitive refers to the act or process of knowing. Analytical or logical thinking.

Congenital refers to a condition existing at birth.

Coordination, Fine Motor refers to the use of small muscle groups; i.e., writing, using scissors.

Coordination, Gross Motor refers to the use of large muscle groups; i.e. running, jumping.

Coordination, Visual/Motor is the ability to pair vision with movements of the body or parts of the body.

Developmental History is the developmental progress of a child/ student (ages 0-18 years) in such skills as sitting, walking, or talking.

Developmental Tests are standardized tests that measure a child's development as it compares to the development of all other children at that age.

Echolalia is repeating what others say.

Expressive Language refers to the ability to express oneself in words.

Receptive Language refers to processing and understanding spoken or written communication.

Assessment Tests

The following list was taken from *The Special Education Handbook*, a publication of the Information Protection and Advocacy Center for Individuals with Disabilities (IPACHI). The chart lists assessment measures or tests which may be used to evaluate a child, adolescent, or adult.

Key

NT   Name of Test
AR   Age Range
GB   Given By
PP   Purpose

Tests

NT   Weschler Adult Intelligence Scale Revised (WAIS-R)
AR   16 years to adult
GB   Psychologist

NT   Weschler Intelligence Scale for Children Revised (WISC-R)
AR   5 to 15 years
GB   Psychologist

NT   Weschler Preschool and Primary Scale of Intelligence
AR   4 to 6.5
GB   Psychologist
PP   The above tests assess specific mental abilities and processes including general fund of knowledge, practical and social judgement, attention and concentration, visual/auditory perception, numerical ability, abstract reasoning, and memory. Verbal and nonverbal skills are also assessed.

NT   McCarthy Scales of Children's Abilities
AR   2.5 years to 8.5 years
GB   Psychologist or Special Educator
PP   Assesses visual perceptual performance, quantitative motor skills, memory, and general knowledge.

NT   Bayley Scales of Infant Development
AR   0 to 30 months

GB Psychologist
PP Assesses physical and social development.

NT Peabody Picture Vocabulary Revised (PPVT-R)
AR 39 months to 18 years
GB Psychologist, Special Educator or Speech Therapist
PP Uses a finger-pointing response: assesses a child's auditory receptive vocabulary.

NT Leiter International Performance Scale
AR 2 to 18 years
GB Psychologist
PP May be administered to nonverbal students. Assesses mental capabilities.

NT Columbia Mental Maturity Scale
AR 2 to 10 years
GB Psychologist
PP May be administered to nonverbal students. Assesses mental capabilities.

NT Illinois Test of Psycholinguistic Abilities (ITPA)
AR 28 months to 10.3 years
GB Psychologist or Special Educator
PP Provides a differential assessment of language skills.

NT Peabody Individual Achievement Test (PIAT)
AR Kindergarten to Grade 12
GB Psychologist or Special Educator
PP Provides a diagnostic assessment of a student's current academic level. Evaluates skills in math, reading recognition, reading comprehension, spelling, and general information.

NT Keymath Diagnostic Arithmetic Test
AR Grades 1 to 6 and Grade 12
GB Psychologist or Special Educator
PP Assesses basic computation abilities in addition, subtraction, multiplication and division.

NT Wide Range Achievement Test (WRAT)
AR 5 years to adult

GB Psychologist or Special Educator
PP Assesses academic achievement in word recognition, pronunciation, written spelling, and math computation.

NT **Woodcock Johnson Psychoeducational Battery**
AR 3 years to adult
GB Psychologist
PP Tests cognitive ability and achievement.

NT **Berry Test of Visual/Motor Integration**
AR 5 years to adult
GB Psychologist
PP Assesses visual perception abilities and motor behavior which are essential to the development of basic skills.

NT **Draw A Person (DAP) Test**
AR 5 years to adult
GB Psychologist
PP Provides insight into the individual's personality structure and awareness of self/body. Situations structured upon personality dynamics.

NT **House/Tree/Person (HTP)**
AR 3 years to adult
GB Psychologist
PP Provides insight into the individual's personality, self/body awareness, and level of socioemotional adjustment.

NT **Bender Visual/Motor Gestalt**
AR 5 to 10.5 years
GB Psychologist
PP Measures visual acuity, visual interpretation, and motor ability.

Chapter 7

The Assessment Process

The Individuals with Disabilities Education Act (IDEA), Public Law 101–476, lists 13 separate categories of disabilities under which children may be eligible for special education and related services. To determine if a child is eligible for classification under one of these areas of exceptionality, an evaluation, or assessment, of the child must be conducted. Every year, millions of children, ages 3 and up, are assessed for the presence of a disability and are found eligible for special education and related services because they are in need of support in order to achieve success in school.

This chapter and the two following focus upon the assessment process—the ways and primary skill areas in which school systems collect information in order to determine if a child is eligible for special education and related services and to make informed decisions about that child's educational placement and instruction. By law, this process must involve much more than just giving the student a standardized test in the area of his or her suspected disability. Valuable information about the student's skills and needs can come from many sources, including parents, teachers, and specialists, and by using a variety of assessment approaches, such as observations, interviews, testing, and methods such as dynamic assessment or ecological assessment. In this way, a comprehensive picture of the student can be obtained and used to guide eligibility decisions and educational programming.

Excerpted from National Information Center for Children and Youth with Disabilities (NICHCY) *News Digest*, Vol. 4, No.1, 1994.

In this text, we describe what federal law requires in terms of assessing school-aged children with disabilities and explore what thorough assessment involves. The various skill areas in which children are often assessed—intelligence, language, perception, achievement, and behavioral and emotional/social development—are described, so that readers may gain an understanding of how a child's abilities and disabilities in each skill area contribute to his or her learning and education performance. The chapter concludes with an extensive reference list and a brief list of organizations that may be able to provide information on the assessment of specific disabilities. Two more extensive bibliographies of additional resources on assessment—one for families and one for schools—are available separately from NICHCY upon request.

Introduction to Assessment

Stacey is in danger of failing second grade again. She appears to have difficulty; following directions, completing assignments on time, progressing in reading and spelling, and interacting with her peers. Her teacher believes that Stacey may have a learning disability and has made a referral to the Committee on Special Education.

Joe has spina bifida and uses a wheelchair. He has recently moved into the community and enrolled in the local high school. His parents are concerned that Joe is not developing the mobility and daily living skills that he needs now and in the future. They request that the new school system evaluate Joe to identify his special needs.

Bob has become severely withdrawn in the last year. His grades have been declining steadily, he is starting to skip school, and when the teacher calls on him in class he responds rudely or not at all. The teacher is worried that Bob may have an emotional disorder. She makes a referral to the special education department.

While these children are different from each other in very many ways, they may also share something in common. Each may be a student who has a disability that will require special education services in the school setting. Before decisions may be made about what those special education services will be, each child will require an evaluation conducted by specially trained educational personnel, which may include a school psychologist, a speech/language pathologist, special education and regular education teachers, social workers, and, when appropriate, medical personnel. This is true for any child suspected of having a disability.

Assessment in educational settings serves five primary purposes:

- *Screening and identification:* to screen children and identify those who may be experiencing delays or learning problems

- *Eligibility and diagnosis:* to determine whether a child has a disability and is eligible for special education services, and to diagnose the specific nature of the student's problems or disability

- *IEP development and placement:* to provide detailed information so that an Individualized Education Program (IEP) may be developed and appropriate decisions may be made about the child's educational placement

- *Instructional planning:* to develop and plan instruction appropriate to the child's special needs; and

- *Evaluation:* to evaluate student progress. (Berdine & Meyer, 1987, p. 5)

This chapter and the two following focus upon the assessment process for determining if a child is eligible for special education and related services and for diagnosing the nature of his or her special needs. In this chapter, a definition of assessment is presented, along with a brief discussion of what the IDEA mandates in terms of assessment, the parents' role in the assessment process, an overview to the issues associated with assessing students who are culturally or linguistically diverse, and interpretation of results. This chapter concludes with a reference listing of readings on assessment and additional resources. More extensive NICHCY bibliographies on assessment are available separately upon request. Chapter Eight provides an overview of some of the methods used to gather information about a child with a suspected disability (e.g., reviewing school records, observations, interviews, standardized tests, curriculum based assessment). In Chapter Nine the various skill areas that are typically the focus of assessment are highlighted. These are: intelligence, language, perception, achievement, and behavioral and emotional/social development.

Defining Assessment

There is sometimes confusion regarding the terms "assessment" and "testing." While they are related, they are not synonymous. Testing is the administration of specifically designed and often standardized educational and psychological measures of behavior and is a part of the assessment process. Assessment, also known as evaluation, can be seen as a problem-solving process (Swanson & Watson, 1989) that involves many ways of collecting information about the student. Roth-Smith (1991) suggests that this information-gathering process involves:

- observing the student's interactions with parents, teachers, and peers;

- interviewing the student and significant others in his or her life;

- examining school records and past evaluation results;

- evaluating developmental and medical histories;

- using information from checklists completed by parents, teachers, or the student;

- evaluating curriculum requirements and options;

- evaluating the student's type and rate of learning during trial teaching periods;

- using task analysis to identify which task components already have been mastered and in what order unmastered skills need to be taught;

- and collecting ratings on teacher attitude towards students with disabilities, peer acceptance, and classroom climate (Roth-Smith, 1991, p. 307).

Clearly, gathering information about the student using such a variety of techniques and information sources can be expected to shed considerable light upon the student's strengths and needs, the nature of his or her disability and how it affects educational performance, and what type of instructional goals and objectives should be established for the student. More detail about many of these methods of collecting information about the student will be presented in the next chapter.

How Students Are Identified for Assessment

There are at least two ways in which a student may be identified for assessment. The first is that the school suspects the presence of a learning or behavior problem and asks the student's parents for permission to evaluate the student individually. Schools routinely give tests to all students in a particular grade; when a student scores too far below his or her peers, this alerts the school to a potential problem. Alternatively, the student's classroom teacher may identify that a problem exists—perhaps the student's work is below expectations for his or her grade or age, or the student's behavior is disrupting learning—and so the teacher refers the student for assessment.

The student's parents may also call or write to the school or to the director of special education and request that their child be evaluated. They may feel that the child is not progressing as he or she should be, or notice particular problems in how the child learns. If the school suspects that the child, indeed, may have a disability, then the school must conduct an assessment.

If school personnel do not feel that the child has a disability, they may refuse to assess the child, but must inform the parents in writing as to their reasons for refusing. If parents feel strongly that their child does, indeed, have a disability that requires special education, they may request a due process hearing, where they will have the opportunity to show why they feel their child should be evaluated. Due process proceedings are beyond the scope of this chapter; more information about parents' due process rights is available in another NICHCY publication: *Questions and Answers About the Individuals with Disabilities Education Act*.

Assessment and Federal Law

The Individuals with Disabilities Education Act (IDEA), Public Law 101–476, lists 13 separate categories of disabilities under which children may be eligible for special education and related services. These are presented below. To determine if a child is eligible for classification under one of these areas of exceptionality, an individualized evaluation, or assessment, of the child must be conducted.

The IDEA specifies a number of requirements regarding evaluations of children suspected of having a disability. While a more complete description of these requirements is available in NICHCY's *Questions and Answers About the Individuals with Disabilities Education Act*, these requirements are briefly summarized as follows:

- Before a child is evaluated for the first time, the school district must notify parents in writing. Parents must give written permission for the school system to conduct this first evaluation (known as a preplacement evaluation).

- Evaluations must be conducted by a multidisciplinary team (e.g., speech and language pathologist, occupational or physical therapist, medical specialists, school psychologist) and must include at least one teacher or specialist who is knowledgeable about the area of the child's suspected disability.

- The assessment must thoroughly investigate all areas related to the child's suspected disability.

- No single procedure may be used as the sole criterion for determining a child's eligibility for special services or for determining his or her appropriate educational placement. Rather, the evaluation process must utilize a variety of valid assessment instruments and observational data.

- All testing must be done individually.

- Tests and other evaluation materials must be provided in the child's primary language or mode of communication, unless it is clearly not feasible to do so.

- All tests and other evaluation materials must be validated for the specific purpose for which they are used. This means that a test may not be used to assess a student in a particular area (e.g., intelligence) unless the test has been designed and validated through research as measuring that specific area.

- Assessments must be conducted in a nondiscriminatory way. This means that the tests and evaluation materials and procedures that are used may not be racially or culturally discriminatory (biased) against the child.

- The evaluation team must ensure that any test used is administered appropriately by a person trained to do so, that the test is being used for the purposes for which it was designed, and that the child's disability does not interfere with the child's ability to take any test measuring specific abilities (e.g., the child's visual impairment affects his or her ability to read and correctly answer the questions on an achievement test). [34 CFR §§300.530–300.532]

Appropriately, comprehensively, and accurately assessing a child with a suspected disability clearly presents a significant challenge to the assessment team.

Federal Disability Categories

Autism: a developmental disability significantly affecting verbal and nonverbal communication and social interaction, generally evident before age 3.

Deafness: a hearing impairment that is so severe that the child is impaired in processing linguistic information, with or without amplification.

Deaf-blindness: simultaneous hearing and visual impairments.

Hearing impairment: an impairment in hearing, whether permanent or fluctuating.

Mental retardation: significantly subaverage general intellectual functioning existing concurrently with deficits in adaptive behavior.

Multiple disabilities: the manifestation of two or more disabilities (such as mental retardation-blindness), the combination of which requires special accommodation for maximal learning.

Orthopedic impairment: physical disabilities, including congenital impairments, impairments caused by disease, and impairments from other causes.

Other health impairment: having limited strength, vitality, or alertness due to chronic or acute health problems.

Serious emotional disturbance: a disability where a child of typical intelligence has difficulty, over time and to a marked degree, building satisfactory interpersonal relationships; responds inappropriately behaviorally or emotionally under normal circumstances;

demonstrates a pervasive mood of unhappiness; or has a tendency to develop physical symptoms or fears.

Specific learning disability: a disorder in one or more of the basic psychological processes involved in understanding or in using language, spoken or written, which may manifest itself in an imperfect ability to listen, think, speak, read, write, spell, or do mathematical calculations.

Speech or language impairment: a communication disorder such as stuttering, impaired articulation, a language impairment, or a voice impairment.

Traumatic brain injury: an acquired injury to the brain caused by an external physical force, resulting in total or partial functional disability or psychosocial impairment, or both.

Visual impairment: a visual difficulty (including blindness) that, even with correction, adversely affects a child's educational performance.

The Parents' Role in the Assessment Process

While designing, conducting, interpreting, and paying for the assessment are the school system's responsibilities, parents have an important part to play before, during, and after the evaluation. The purpose of this section is to provide parents with suggestions for the range of ways in which they might involve themselves in the assessment of their child. The extent to which parents involve themselves, however, is a personal decision and will vary from family to family.

Before the evaluation, parents:

- May initiate the evaluation process by requesting that the school system evaluate their child for the presence of a disability and the need for special education.

- Must be notified by the school, and give their consent, before any initial evaluation of the child may be conducted.

- May wish to talk with the person responsible for conducting the evaluation to find out what the evaluation will involve.

- May find it very useful to become informed about assessment issues in general and any specific issues relevant to their child (e.g., assessment of minority children, use of specific tests or assessment techniques with a specific disability).

- May need to advocate for a comprehensive evaluation—one that investigates all skill areas apparently affected by the suspected disability and that uses multiple means of collecting information (e.g., observations, interviews, alternative approaches).

- May suggest specific questions they would like to see addressed through the evaluation (see "Other Assessment Questions").

- Should inform the school of any accommodations the child will need (e.g., removing time limits from tests, conducting interviews/testing in the child's native language, adapting testing environment to child's specific physical and other needs).

- Should inform the school if they themselves need an interpreter or other accommodations during any of their discussions with the school.

- May prepare their child for the evaluation process, explaining what will happen and, where necessary, reducing the child's anxiety. It may help the child to know that he or she will not be receiving a "grade" on the tests he or she will be taking but that the purpose behind any testing is to gather information to help the student succeed in school.

During the evaluation process, parents:

- Need to share with the school their insights into the child's background (developmental, medical, and academic) and past and present school performance.

- May wish to share with the school any prior school records, reports, tests, or evaluation information available on their child.

- May need to share information about cultural differences that can illuminate the educational team's understanding of the student.

- Need to make every effort to attend interviews the school may set up with them and provide information about their child.

After the evaluation, parents:

- Need to carefully consider the results that emerge from their child's evaluation, in light of their own observation and knowledge of the child. Do the results make sense in terms of the behaviors, skills, needs, and attitudes they have observed in their child? Are there gaps, inconsistencies, or unexpected findings in the results that parents feel are important to address, if a comprehensive picture of the student's strengths and needs is to be developed?

- May share their insights and concerns about the evaluation results with the school and suggest areas where additional information may be needed. Schools may or may not act upon parents' suggestions, and parents have certain recourses under law, should they feel strongly about pursuing the matter.

- Participate fully in the development of their child's Individualized Education Program (IEP), using information from the evaluation.

Assessing Students Who Are Culturally and Linguistically Diverse

It is a well-known fact that the demographics of American schools are changing. Many students come from ethnic, racial, or linguistic backgrounds that are different from the dominant culture, and this number is steadily increasing (National Center for Education Statistics, 1992). Much concern has been expressed in recent years about the overrepresentation of minority students in special education programs, particularly in programs for students with mild disabilities, and a great deal of research has been conducted to identify the reasons why. Many factors appear to contribute, including considerable bias against children from different cultural and linguistic backgrounds, particularly those who are poor (Harry, 1992). The style and emphasis of the school may also be very different from those found in the cultures of students who are racially or linguistically diverse. Because culture and language affect learning and behavior (Franklin, 1992), the school system may misinterpret what students know, how they behave, or how they learn. Students may appear less competent than they are, leading educators to inappropriately refer them for assessment. Once referred, inappropriate methods may then be used to assess the students, leading to inappropriate conclusions and placement into special education.

There is also a great deal of research and numerous court decisions (e.g., *Larry P. v. Riles* 1979; *Guadalupe v. Tempe Elementary District*, 1972) to support the fact that standardized tests (particularly intelligence and achievement tests) are often culturally and linguistically biased against students from backgrounds different from the majority culture. On many tests, being able to answer questions correctly too often depends upon having specific culturally based information or knowledge. If students have not been exposed to that information through their culture, or have not had the experiences that lead to gaining specific knowledge, then they will not be able to answer certain questions at all or will answer them in a way that is considered "incorrect" within the majority culture. This can lead to inappropriate conclusions about students' ability to function within the school setting.

Therefore, when students come from a nondominant culture or speak a native language other than English, care must be taken in how they are evaluated. "All professionals involved in the assessment process need to be aware that their beliefs and perceptions may not match those of the population they serve" (Hoy & Gregg, 1994, p. 65). Because most cognitive, language, and academic measures are developed using standards of the majority English-speaking culture, their use with students who are not from that culture may be inappropriate. It is, therefore, imperative that the evaluation team collect the majority of their information about the student in other ways, such as through interviews, observations, and approaches such as dynamic assessment, which has shown promise for use with minority students (Lidz, 1987). "Professionals must attend carefully to the overall picture of a child's background and performance," states Harry (1992), and adds that "assessment cannot be complete without an understanding of whether prior instruction has been adequate and appropriate" (p. 87).

To this end, Ortiz (1986) recommends that such students first undergo the prereferral process mentioned earlier. Many schools are moving toward requiring a prereferral process before any individualized evaluation is done. The purpose of the prereferral process is "to determine if appropriate and sufficient approaches have been attempted" (Wallace, Larsen, & Elksnin, 1992, p. 467). This allows the school to adjust instruction or make other classroom modifications and see if these changes address the problem being noted. The prereferral process includes:

- direct observation of the student in the regular classroom;
- analyzing how the student behaves and interacts verbally in different settings; and
- reviewing the methods of instruction that are used in the regular classroom.

It is also important to interview people who are familiar with the student, for these individuals can provide a wealth of information about his or her intents, adaptive behavior, how he or she processes information and approaches learning, language ability, and (in the case of students who are not native speakers of English) language dominance. Interviewers should be aware, however, that the differing culture and/or language of those being interviewed can seriously affect the nature and interpretation of information gathered. Some understanding of how individuals within that culture view disability, the educational system, and authority figures will be helpful in designing, conducting, and interpreting a culturally sensitive interview. [See Harry, 1992, for an interesting discussion of the traditional worldviews of the African American, Hispanic, Native American, and Asian cultures; she defines a group's "worldview" as its members' "underlying beliefs about humanity's purpose and place in the universe, beliefs that affect codes of personal and interpersonal behavior as well as attitudes to the health, life, and death of human beings" (p. 25).] It may be particularly useful to gather information from the home environment, which will help the assessment team develop an understanding of the student within his or her own culture. To facilitate this, parents need to communicate openly with the school and share their insight into their child's behaviors, attitudes, successes and needs, and, when appropriate, information about the minority culture.

Before conducting any formal testing of a student who is a nonnative speaker of English, it is vital to determine the student's preferred language and to conduct a comprehensive language assessment in both English and the native language. Examiners need to be aware that it is highly inappropriate to evaluate students in English when that is not their dominant language (unless the purpose of the testing is to assess the student's English language proficiency). Translation tests from English is not an acceptable practice either; the IDEA states that tests and other evaluation materials must be provided and administered in the child's primary language or mode of communication unless it is clearly not feasible to do so [34 CFR § 300.532(a)(1)]. If possible, the evaluator in any testing situation or interview should be familiar to the child and speak the child's language.

When tests or evaluation materials are not available in the student's native language, examiners may find it necessary to use English-language instruments. Because this is a practice fraught with the possibility of misinterpretation, examiners need to be cautious in how they administer the test and interpret results. Alterations may need to be made to the standardized procedures used to administer tests; these can include paraphrasing instructions, providing a demonstration of how test tasks are to be performed, reading test items to the student rather than having him or her read them, allowing the student to respond verbally rather than in writing, or allowing the student to use a dictionary (Wallace, Larsen, & Elksnin, 1992, p. 471). However, if any such alterations are made, it is important to recognize that standardization has been broken, limiting the usefulness and applicability of test norms. Results should be cautiously interpreted, and all alterations made to the testing procedures should be fully detailed in the report describing the student's test performance. As mentioned earlier, it is also essential that other assessment approaches be an integral part of collecting information about the student.

A full discussion of the recommended procedures for evaluating students from culturally or linguistically diverse backgrounds is beyond the scope of this text, yet it is a topic of great importance. The reader is urged to view the resource section at the end of this chapter.

Putting It All Together—Interpreting Results

Clearly, a vast quantity of information can be collected about many aspects—virtually every aspect—of a student's functioning. How is all this information put together and utilized to make eligibility and educational decisions about and for the student?

The interpretation of assessment results relies greatly upon the skills and experience of the individuals involved in the assessment process and the degree to which they work together as a team, pooling findings and discussing implications in a multidisciplinary way. All professionals responsible for any aspect of the assessment should prepare a written report on their findings or be prepared to present this information orally at the meeting where eligibility is determined or the student's Individualized Education Program (IEP) is developed.

The report should not merely state the student's raw or derived test scores or the statistical quantification of observed behavior (e.g., x number of "out-of-seats" in y minutes), but should extend to the implications that can be drawn from the scores or behavior. The educational recommendations and insights of the professional should also be included. It is very important that each report be stated in a way that allows others on the team, including parents and teachers, to understand what was found, what the results mean, and what the professional recommends. The use of specialized, technical vocabulary—jargon—often obscures meaning and should be avoided or explained in lay terms.

Data gathered from all assessment procedures then need to be related and synthesized. When the team looks individually and globally at information gathered from observations, previous school experiences, review of prior records, tests, interviews, daily work assignments, and so on, what picture emerges of the student's areas of strength and need? What information appears to be contradictory? Where is more information or detail needed about the student to assist either in diagnosis or in instructional planning?

It is important to remember that all assessment involves error. What emerges from the assessment process is not a "true" picture of the student but, rather, a patchwork of pictures that have captured the student at various moments in time. The more comprehensively the assessment was conducted—sampling or observing student behavior in different settings at different times, consultation with the family, interviewing those involved with the student, administering tests, ecologically assessing the student's environments, and so on—the more comprehensive the picture of the student should be and the more informed decision-making will be as well.

Interpretation of results, then, should not end with the statement, "No, this student is not eligible for special education" or "Yes, he or she is eligible." The data need to be directly useful to the educational team in identifying the specific areas in which the student needs special instruction or accommodation (or, at the least, the areas in which additional evaluation or diagnosis is necessary) and in suggesting what type of instruction or educational program might be appropriate.

Independent Educational Evaluation (IEE)

Parents may disagree with the results of the school's evaluation or feel that the school did not conduct the evaluation appropriately (e.g., tested a language minority student solely in English or based eligibility decisions upon the use of only one test). The IDEA gives parents the right to obtain an independent educational evaluation. Parents may ask the school to pay for the IEE; the school may do so willingly, or they may request a due process hearing to show that their evaluation was, indeed, appropriate. If the hearing officer's decision is that the school system's evaluation was inappropriate, then the IEE will be at public expense (the school system pays). If, however, the evaluation was appropriate, then the parents may still obtain an IEE but they must pay for it. Regardless of who pays for the IEE, the school is obligated to consider the results of the evaluation at the eligibility or IEP development meeting. (For more information on the IDEA's stipulations regarding IEEs, request a copy of NICHCY's *Questions and Answers About the IDEA.*)

Individual Education Program (IEP) Meeting

The student's educational program is planned and developed by a multidisciplinary team of individuals and specified in the Individualized Education Program (IEP). Just as parents can contribute to the assessment process, they have much to share during the meeting where the IEP is developed, including their own perceptions and preferences as to the skill areas that might best be emphasized with their child. Therefore, when the assessment team and parents sit down to discuss assessment results and plan the student's educational program, it is vital that the parents participate fully. Parent Training and Information Centers (PTIs), which exist in every state, may be able to assist parents in regards to the IEP process and strategies for effective participation. For parents who are not native speakers of English, it may be essential for the school to provide an interpreter, so that parents can understand what is being discussed and offer their own insights and suggestions.

It is beyond the scope of this chapter to discuss the IEP process in any depth (if you need information on this topic, you may contact NICHCY and talk to one of the information specialists). Briefly, however, the evaluation team, or at least one individual knowledgeable about how the student was evaluated and what results were obtained, will attend the meeting to present and explain what has been learned through assessing the student. Using this information, the team will then discuss what type of educational program would be appropriate for the student and begin specifying this in the IEP.

Summary

Assessment is a complex process that needs to be conducted by a multi-disciplinary team of trained professionals and involve both formal and informal methods of collecting information about the student. While the team may choose to administer a series of tests to the student, by law assessment must involve much more than standardized tests. Interviews of all key participants in the student's education and observations of student behaviors in the classroom or in other sites should be included as well. To develop a comprehensive picture of the student and to develop practical intervention strategies to address that student's special needs, the team must ask questions and use assessment techniques that will help them determine the factors that are facilitating—and interfering with—the child's learning. Ecological assessment, dynamic assessment, curriculum-based assessment, learning styles inventories, and other less traditional approaches may be particularly helpful in answering such questions.

It is also important that assessment be an ongoing process. The process begins even before the student is referred for formal evaluation; his or her teacher or parent may have noticed that some aspect of the student's performance or behavior is below expectations and, so, requests an official assessment. After eligibility has been established and the IEP developed for the student, assessment should continue, through teacher-made tests, through ongoing behavioral assessment, or through incorporating curriculum-based assessment or task analysis into the classroom. This allows teachers and parents to monitor the student's progress towards the goals and objectives stated in his or her IEP. Thus, assessment should not end when the eligibility decision is made or the IEP is developed; it has great value to contribute to the daily, weekly, and monthly instructional decision-making that accompanies the provision of special education and related services.

References

Alley, C.R., & Deshler, D. (1979). *Teaching the learning disabled adolescent: Strategies and methods*. Denver, CO: London Publishing Company. (This book is no longer available from the publisher, but may be available in your local public library.)

American Association on Mental Retardation. (1992). *Mental retardation: Definition, classification, and systems of support* (9th ed.). Washington, DC: Author.

Berdine, W.H., & Meyer, S.A. (1987). *Assessment in special education*. Boston: Little, Brown and Company. (Available from Harper-Collins.)

Bigge, J.L. (1990). *Teaching individuals with physical and multiple disabilities* (3rd ed.). Columbus, OH: Merrill.

Bloom, L., & Lahey, M. (1978). *Language development and language disorders*. New York: Wiley.

Campione, J.C., & Brown, A.L. (1987). Linking dynamic assessment with school achievement. In C.S. Lidz (Ed.), *Dynamic assessment: An interactional approach to evaluating learning potential* (pp. 82–115). New York: Guilford.

Carlson, J.S., & Wiedl, K.H. (1978). Use of testing-the-limits procedures in the assessment of intellectual capabilities of children with learning difficulties. *American Journal of Mental Deficiency*, 82, 559–564.

Carlson, J.S., & Wiedl, K.H. (1979). Toward a differential testing approach: Testing-the-limits employing the Raven Matrices. *Intelligence*, 3, 323–344.

Code of Federal Regulations (CFR); Title 34; Parts 300 to 399, July 1, 1993. (Available from the U.S. Government Printing Office.)

Conoley, J.C., & Kramer, J.J. (Eds.). (1992). *Eleventh mental measurement yearbook*. Lincoln: University of Nebraska Press.

Covarrubias v. San Diego Unified School District (Southern California), No. 70-394-T, (S.D., Cal. February, 1971).

Diana v. California State Board of Education. No. C-70 37 RFP, District Court of Northern California (February, 1970).

Elliot; R. (1987). *Litigating intelligence: IQ tests, special education, and social science in the courtroom*. Dover, MA: Auburn House.

Franklin, M.E. (1992, October/November). Culturally sensitive instructional practices for African-America learners with disabilities. *Exceptional Children*, 59(2), 115–122.

Grossman, H.J. (Ed.). (1983). *Manual on terminology and classification in mental retardation* (3rd ed. rev.). Washington, DC: American Association on Mental Deficiency. (No longer available from the publisher.)

Guadalupe Organization Inc. v. Tempe Elementary School District. No. CIV 71-435, Phoenix (D. Arizona, January 24, 1972).

Hamill, D.D., Brown, L., & Bryant, B.R. (1992). *A consumer's guide to tests in print.* Austin: Pro-Ed.

Harry, B. (1992). *Cultural diversity, families, and the special education system: Communication and empowerment.* New York: Teachers College Press.

Henderson, E. (1985). *Teaching spelling.* Boston, MA: Houghton Mifflin. (This book is no longer available from the publisher, but a 1990 update is.)

Heward, W.L., & Orlansky, M.D. (1992). *Exceptional children: An introductory survey of special education* (4th ed.). New York: Merrill.

Hodgkinson, L. (1985). *All one system: Demographics of education.* Washington, DC: Institute for Educational Leadership.

Hoy, C., & Gregg, N. (1994). *Assessment: The special educator's role.* Pacific Grove, CA: Brooks/Cole.

Individuals with Disabilities Education Act (P.L. 101–476), 20 U.S.C. Chapter 33, Sections 1400–1485, 1990.

Jitendra, A.K., & Kameenui, E.J. (1993, September/October). Dynamic assessment as a compensatory assessment approach: A description and analysis. *Remedial and Special Education*, 14(5), 6–18.

Kamphaus, R.W. (1993). *Clinical assessment of children's intelligence.* Boston: Allyn & Bacon.

Keogh, B., & Margolis, T. (1976). Learn to labor and wait: Attentional problems of children with learning disorders. *Journal of Learning Disabilities*, 9, 276–286.

Kozloff, M. (1994). *Improving educational outcomes for children with disabilities: Principles for assessment, program planning, and evaluation*. Baltimore, MD: Paul H. Brookes.

Larry P. v. Riles, C-71-2270 RFP, Opinion, October 10, 1979.

Lerner, J. (1988). *Learning disabilities: Theories, diagnosis, and teaching strategies* (3rd ed.). Boston: Houghton Mifflin. (This book is no longer available from the publisher, but the 6th edition, published in 1993, is available.)

Liberman, I., & Shankweiler, D. (1987). Phonology and the problems of learning to read and write. In H.L. Swanson (Ed.), *Advances in learning and behavioral disabilities*. Greenwich, CT: Jai Press. (This book is no longer available, but the 8th edition, published in 1994, is available.)

Lidz, C.S. (Ed.). (1987). *Dynamic assessment: An interactional approach to evaluating learning potential*. New York: Guilford.

National Center for Education Statistics. (1992). *American education at a glance*. Washington, DC: Author.

Ortiz, A. (1986). Characteristics of limited English proficient Hispanic students served in programs for the learning disabled: Implications for policy and practice (Part 11). *Bilingual Special Education Newsletter*, University of Texas at Austin, Vol. IV.

Overton, T. (1992). *Assessment in special education: An applied approach*. New York: Macmillan.

Reid, D.K., & Hresko, W.P. (1981). *A cognitive approach to learning disabilities*. New York McGraw-Hill. (This book is no longer available from the publisher.)

Roth-Smith, C. (1991). *Learning disabilities: The interaction of learner, task, and setting*. Boston: Allyn & Bacon. (This book is no longer available from the publisher.)

Salvia, J., & Ysseldyke, J. (1991). *Assessment in special education and remedial education* (5th ed.). Boston, MA: Houghton Mifflin.

Sewell, T.E. (1987). Dynamic assessment as a non-discriminatory procedure. In C.S. Lidz (Ed.), *Dynamic assessment: An interactional approach to evaluating learning potential* (pp. 426–443). New York: Guilford.

Shapiro, E.S. (1989). *Academic skills problems: Direct assessment and intervention*. New York: Guilford.

Stanovich, K. (1982). Individual differences in the cognitive processes of reading. I: Word decoding. *Journal of Learning Disabilities*, 15, 485–493.

Swanson, H.C., & Watson, B.L. (1989). *Educational and psychological assessment of exceptional children* (2nd ed.). Columbus, OH: Merrill Publishing Company.

Sweetland, R.C., & Keyser, D.J. (Eds.). (1991). *Tests: A comprehensive reference for assessments in psychology, education, and business* (3rd ed.). Austin, TX: Pro-Ed.

Taylor, R.L. (1993). *Assessment of exceptional children: Educational and psychological procedures* (3rd ed.). Boston: Allyn & Bacon.

Terrell, S.L. (Ed.). (1983, June). Nonbiased assessment of language differences [Special issue]. *Topics in Language Disorders*, 3(3).

Vellutino, F.R. (1979). *Dyslexia: Theory and research*. Cambridge, MA: MIT Press.

Wallace, G., Larsen, S.C., & Elksnin, L.K. (1992). *Educational assessment of learning problems: Testing for teaching*. Boston: Allyn and Bacon.

Wechsler, D. (1958). *The measurement and appraisal of adult intelligence* (4th ed.). Baltimore, MD: Williams & Wilkins.

Wiederhold, J.L., Hammill, D.D., & Brown, V.L. (1978). *The resource teacher*. Boston: Allyn & Bacon.

Wodrich, D.L., & Joy, J.E. (1986). *Multidisciplinary assessment of children with learning disabilities and mental retardation*. Baltimore, MD: Paul H. Brookes. (This book is no longer available from the publisher.)

Organizations

The organizations listed below are only a few of the many that provide services and information about disability issues to families and professionals. These organizations have been selected because they may be able to respond to questions about the assessment of specific disabilities or provide guidance about the IEP development process. When calling or writing an organization, it is always a good idea to be as specific as you can in stating your needs and concerns. This helps organizations provide you with information that is truly helpful and on target.

Clearinghouse and Information Centers

DB-Link, National Information Clearinghouse on Children Who are Deaf-Blind, 345 N. Monmouth Avenue, Monmouth, OR 97361. Telephone: (800) 438-9376; (800) 854-7013 (TTY).

ERIC Clearinghouse on Disabilities & Gifted Education, Council for Exceptional Children (CEC), 1920 Association Drive, Reston, VA 22091-1589. Telephone: (703) 620-3660; (800) 328-0272.

National Health Information Center, P.O. Box 1133, Washington, D.C. 20013-1133. Telephone: (301) 565-4167; (800) 336-4797.

National Information Center on Deafness (NICD), 800 Florida Avenue, NE, Washington, D.C. 20002. Telephone: (202) 651-5051 (Voice); (202) 651-5052 (TT).

National Organization on Rare Disorders (NORD), 100 Route 37, P.O. Box 8923, New Farfield, CT 06812-1783. Telephone: (800) 999-6673; (203) 746-6518; (203) 746-6927 (TT).

Other Organizations

American Association on Mental Retardation, 1719 Kalorama Road, NW, Washington, DC 20009. Telephone: (800) 424-3688; (202) 387-1968.

American Foundation for the Blind (AFB), 15 West 16th Street, New York, NY 10011. Telephone: (800) 232-5463: (212) 620-2000 (Voice); (212) 620-2158 (TT).

American Occupational Therapy Association (AOTA), P.O. Box 1725, 1383 Piccard Drive, Rockville, MD 20849-1725. Telephone: (301) 948-9626; (301) 948-9626 (TT).

American Physical Therapy Association (APTA), 1111 North Fairfax Street, Alexandria, VA 22314. Telephone: (703) 684-2782.

American Psychological Association, 750 First Street NE, Washington, DC 20002-4242. Telephone: (202) 336-5500.

American Speech-Language-Hearing Association (ASHA), 10801 Rockville Pike, Rockville, MD 20852. Telephone: (800) 638-8255; (301) 897-5700 (Voice/TT).

The Arc (formerly the Association for Retarded Citizens of the U.S.), 500 East Border St., Suite 300, Arlington. TX 76010. Telephone: (817) 261-6003; (817) 277-0553 (TT).

Association for Persons with Severe Handicaps (TASH), 11201 Greenwood Avenue North, Seattle, WA 98133. Telephone: (206) 361-8870; (206) 361-0113 (TT).

Autism Society of America, 7910 Woodmont Avenue, Suite 650, Bethesda, MD 20814. Telephone: (800) 3-AUTISM; (301) 657-0881.

Children and Adults with Attention Deficit Disorder (CH.A.D.D.), 499 NW 70th Avenue, Suite 308, Plantation, FL 33317. Telephone: (305) 587-3700.

Council for Exceptional Children (CEC), 1920 Association Drive, Reston, VA 22091. Telephone: (703) 620-3660.

Epilepsy Foundation of America (EFA), 4351 Garden City Drive, Suite 406, Landover, MD 20785. Telephone: (800) 332-1000; (301) 459-3700.

Family Resource Center on Disabilities, 20 East Jackson Boulevard, Room 900, Chicago, IL 60604. Telephone: (800) 952-4199; (312) 939-3513; (312) 939-3519 (TT).

International Rett Syndrome Association, 8511 Rose Marie Drive, Fort Washington, MD 20744. Telephone: (301) 248-7031.

Learning Disabilities Association of America (LDA), 4156 Library Road, Pittsburgh, PA 15234. Telephone: (412) 341-1515; (412) 341-8077.

Muscular Dystrophy Association (MDA), 3561 East Sunrise Drive, Tucson, AZ 85718. Telephone: (800) 223-6666; (602) 529-2000.

National Alliance for the Mentally Ill (NAMI), 2101 Wilson Boulevard, Suite 302, Arlington, VA 22201. Telephone: (800) 950-NAMI; (703) 524-7600.

National Association of School Psychologists, 8455 Colesville Road, Silver Spring, MD 20910. Telephone: (301) 608-0500.

National Association of State Directors of Education, 1800 Diagonal Road, Suite 320, Alexandria, VA 22314. Telephone: (703) 519-3800; (703) 519-7008 (TT).

National Down Syndrome Congress, 1605 Chantilly Drive, Suite 250, Atlanta, GA 30324. Telephone: (800) 232<6372; (404) 633-1555.

National Down Syndrome Society, 666 Broadway, New York, NY 10012. Telephone: (800) 221-4602; (212) 460-9330.

National Easter Seal Society, 230 West Monroe Street, Suite 1800, Chicago, IL 60606. Telephone: (800) 221-6827; (312) 726-6200; (312) 726-4258 (TT).

National Head Injury Foundation, Inc., 1140 Connecticut Avenue, NW, Suite 812, Washington, DC 20036. Telephone: (202) 296-6443.

National Spinal Cord Injury Association, 600 West Cummings Park, Suite 2000, Woburn, MA 01801. Telephone: (800) 962-9629; (617) 935-2722.

Orton Dyslexia Society, Chester Building #382, 8600 LaSalle Road, Baltimore, MD 21204. Telephone: (800) 222-3123; (410) 296-0232.

PACER Center, 4826 Chicago Avenue South, Minneapolis, MN 55417. Telephone: Outside of MN, (612) 827-2966; in MN, 1-800-537-2237.

Spina Bifida Association of America, 4590 MacArthur Boulevard, NW, Suite 250, Washington, DC 20007. Telephone: (800) 621-3141; (202) 944-3285.

United Cerebral Palsy Associations, Inc., 1522 K Street, NW, Suite 1112, Washington, D.C. 20005. Telephone: (800) 872-5827; (202) 842-1266.

List of Publishers

The publishers listed below (in alphabetical order) are presented to help readers obtain the resources listed throughout this and the two following chapters. If you are interested in obtaining any of the resources we've listed, it's a good idea to contact the publisher and find out the latest payment and ordering procedures. These addresses and phone numbers are, of course, subject to change without notice.

Allyn & Bacon, Order Processing Center, P.O. Box 11071, Des Moines, IA 50336-1071. 1-800-947-7700.

American Association on Mental Retardation, Publications Center, P.O. Box 25, Annapolis Junction, MD 20701-0025. Telephone: (301) 604-1340.

Auburn House: Contact Greenwood Publishing, 88 Post Road W., Box 5007, Westport, CT 06881. Telephone: 1-800-225-5800; (203) 226-3571.

Brooks/Cole, Wadsworth, Inc. Distribution Center, Customer Service, 7625 Empire Drive, Florence, KY 41042. Telephone: 1-800-354-9706.

Guilford Press, 72 Spring Street, New York, NY 10012. Telephone: 1-800-365-7006.

Harper Collins, 1160 Battery Street, San Francisco, CA 94111. Telephone: 1-800-328-5125.

Harvard University Press, Attention: Customer Service, 79 Garden Street, Cambridge, MA 02138. Telephone: 1-800-448-2242; (617) 495-2600.

Houghton Mifflin, Wayside Road, Burlington, MA 01803. Telephone: 1-800-225-1464.

Jai Press, 55 Old Post Road, No. 2. P.O. Box 1678. Greenwich, CT 06836. Telephone: (203) 661-7602.

John Wiley and Sons, Orders to: Eastern Distribution Center, 1 Wiley Drive, Somerset, NJ 08875-1272. Telephone: 1-800-225-5945.

Macmillan Publishing Company, 100 Front Street, Box 500, Riverside, NJ 08075-7500. Telephone: 1-800-257-5755.

Merrill, see Macmillan.

MIT Press, 55 Hayward Street. Cambridge, MA 02142. Telephone: (617) 625-8569; 1-800-356-0343.

Paul H. Brookes Publishing Company, P.O. Box 10624, Baltimore, MD 21285-0624. Telephone: 1-800-638-3775.

Pro-Ed, 8700 Shoal Creek Boulevard, Austin, TX 78758. Telephone: 1-800-397-7633; (512) 451-3246.

Teachers College Press, P.O. Box 20, Williston, VT 05495. Telephone: 1-800-488-2665.

University of Nebraska Press, 901 N. 17th Street, Room 327, Lincoln, NE 68588-0520. Telephone: (402) 472-3581; 1-800-755-1105.

Wiley, see John Wiley and Sons, above.

— by Betsy W. Waterman, Ph.D.
State University of New York
at Oswego

Chapter 8

Methods of Gathering Assessment Information

One of the cornerstones of the IDEA's evaluation requirements is that it is inappropriate and unacceptable to base any eligibility or placement decision upon the results of only one procedure [34 *Code of Federal Regulations* (CFR) §300.532(d)]. The child must be assessed "in all areas related to the suspected disability, including, if appropriate, health, vision, hearing, social and emotional status, general intelligence, academic performance, communicative status, and motor abilities" [34 CFR §300.532(f)].

Because of the convenient and plentiful nature of standardized tests, it is perhaps tempting to administer a battery (group) of tests to a student and make an eligibility or placement determination based upon the results. However, tests alone will not give a comprehensive picture of how a child performs or what he or she knows or does not know. Evaluators need to use a variety of tools and approaches to assess a child, including observing the child in different settings to see how he or she functions in those environments, interviewing individuals who know the child to gain their insights, and testing the child to evaluate his or her competence in whatever skill areas appear affected by the suspected disability, as well as those that may be areas of strength. There are, recently, a number of other approaches being used to collect information about students as well; these include curriculum-based assessment, ecological assessment, task analysis, dynamic assessment, and assessment of learning style. These

Excerpted from National Information Center for Children and Youth with Disabilities (NICHCY) *News Digest*, Vol. 4, No.1, 1994.

approaches yield rich information about students, are especially important when assessing students who are from culturally or linguistically diverse backgrounds, and, therefore, are critical methods in the overall approach to assessment. Students possessing medical or mental health problems may also have assessment information from sources outside of the school. Such information would need to be considered along with assessment information from the school's evaluation team in making appropriate diagnoses, placement decisions, and instructional plans.

Only through collecting data through a variety of approaches (observations, interviews, tests, curriculum-based assessment, and so on) and from a variety of sources (parents, teachers, specialists, peers, student) can an adequate picture be obtained of the child's strengths and weaknesses. Synthesized, this information can be used to determine the specific nature of the child's special needs, whether the child needs special services and, if so, to design an appropriate program.

Reviewing School Records

School records can be a rich source of information about the student and his or her background. The number of times the student has changed schools may be of interest; frequent *school changes* can be disruptive emotionally as well as academically and may be a factor in the problems that have resulted in the student's being referred for assessment. *Attendance* is another area to note; are there patterns in absences (e.g., during a specific part of the year, as is the case with some students who have respiratory problems or allergies), or is there a noticeable pattern of declining attendance, which may be linked to a decline in motivation, an undiagnosed health problem, or a change within the family?

The student's past history of *grades* is usually of interest to the assessment team as well. Is the student's current performance in a particular subject typical of the student, or is the problem being observed something new? Are patterns noticeable in the student's grades? For example, many students begin the year with poor grades and then show gradual improvement as they get back into the swing of school. For others, the reverse may be true: During the early part of the year, when prior school material is being reviewed, they may do well, with declines in their grades coming as new material is introduced. Also, transition points such as beginning the fourth grade or middle school may cause students problems; the nature and purpose of reading, for example, tends to change when students enter the fourth grade, where reading to learn content becomes more central. Similarly, middle school requires students to assume more responsibility for long-term projects (Hoy & Gregg, 1994). These shifts may bring about a noticeable decline in grades for some students.

Test scores are also important to review. Comparing these scores to a student's current classroom performance can indicate that the student's difficulties are new ones, perhaps resulting from some environmental change that needs to be investigated more fully, or the comparison may show that the student has always found a particular skill area to be problematic. "In this situation, the current problems the student is experiencing indicate that the classroom demands have reached a point that the student requires more support to be successful" (Hoy & Gregg, 1994, p. 37).

Looking at Student Work

Often, an initial part of the assessment process includes examining a student's work, either by selecting *work samples* that can be analyzed to identify academic skills and deficits, or by conducting a *portfolio assessment*, where folders of the student's work are examined.

When collecting work samples, the teacher selects work from the areas where the student is experiencing difficulty and systematically examines them. The teacher might identify such elements as how the student was directed to do the activity (e.g., orally, in writing), how long it took the student to complete the activity, the pattern of errors (e.g., reversals when writing, etc.), and the pattern of correct answers. Analyzing the student's work in this way can yield valuable insight into the nature of his or her difficulties and suggest possible solutions.

Maintaining portfolios of student work has become a popular way for teachers to track student progress. By assembling in one place the body of a student's work, teachers can see how a student is progressing over time, what problems seem to be re-occurring, what concepts are being grasped or not grasped, and what skills are being developed. The portfolio can be analyzed in much the same way as selective work samples, and can form the basis for discussions with the student or other teachers about difficulties and successes and for determining what modifications teachers might make in their instruction.

Prereferral Procedures

Many school systems recommend or require that, before an individualized evaluation of a student is conducted, his or her teacher meet with an assistance team to discuss the nature of the problem and what possible modifications to instruction or the classroom might be made. These procedures are known as prereferral. Prereferral procedures have arisen out of a number of research studies documenting faulty referral practices, including, among other practices, the overreferral of students who come from backgrounds that are culturally or linguistically different from the majority culture, those who are hard to teach, or those who are felt to have behavioral problems. According to Overton (1992), "the more frequent use of better prereferral intervention strategies is a step forward in the prevention of unnecessary evaluation and the possibility of misdiagnosis and overidentification of special education students" (p. 6).

This process recognizes that many variables affect learning; rather than first assuming that the difficulty lies within the student, the assistance team and the teacher will look specifically at what variables (e.g., classroom, teacher, student, or an interaction of these) might be affecting this particular student. Examining student records and work samples and conducting interviews and observations are part of the assistance team's efforts. These data gathering approaches are intended to specify the problem more precisely and to document its severity. Modifications to the teacher's approach, to the classroom, or to student activities may then be suggested, attempted, and documented; if no progress is made within a specific amount of time, then the student is referred for an individualized evaluation. It is important for teachers to keep track of the specific modifications they attempt with a student who is having trouble learning or behaving, because these can provide valuable information to the assessment team at the point the student is referred for evaluation.

Observation

Observing the student and his or her environment is an important part of any assessment process. Observations in the classroom and in other settings where the student operates can provide valuable information about his or her academic, motor, communication, or social skills; behaviors that contribute to or detract from learning; and overall attitude or demeanor. Observing the student's environment(s) and his or her behavior within those environments can identify the factors that are influencing the student. For the information from observations to be useful, the team must first define the purpose for the observation and specify:

144

- Who will make the observation;
- Who or what will be observed;
- Where the observation will take place (observing a range of situations where the student operates is recommended);
- When the observation will take place (a number of observations at different times is also important); and
- How the observations will be recorded. (Wallace, Larsen, & Elkonin, 1992, p. 12).

Observations are a key part of some of the assessment methods that will be discussed later in this section, including curriculum-based assessment, ecological assessment, and task analysis. There are many ways in which to record what is observed; a future section lists and briefly describes the more common observational methods.

While observations can yield useful information about the student and his or her environments, there are a number of errors that can occur during observations and distort or invalidate the information collected. One source of error may come from the observer—he or she must record accurately, systematically, and without bias. If his or her general impression of the student influences how he or she rates that student in regards to specific characteristics, the data will be misleading and inaccurate. This can be especially true if the student comes from a background that is different from the majority culture. In such cases, it is important that the observer have an understanding of, and a lack of bias regarding, the student's cultural or language group. Often, multiple observers are used to increase the reliability of the observational information collected. All observers should be fully trained in how to collect information using the specific method chosen (e.g., time sampling using a checklist) and how to remain unobtrusive while observing and recording, so as not to influence the student's behavior. It is also important to observe more than once, in a number of situations or locations, and at various times, and to integrate these data with information gathered through other assessment procedures. Decisions should not be made based upon a narrow range of observational samples.

Common Observational Techniques

Anecdotal Records. The observer describes incidents or behaviors observed in a particular setting in concrete, narrative terms (as opposed to drawing inferences about feelings or motives). This type of record allows insight into cause and effect by detailing what occurred before a behavior took place, the behavior itself, and consequences or events that occurred after the behavior.

Event Recording. The observer is interested in recording specific behavioral events (such as how many times the student hits or gets out of his or her seat). A tally sheet listing the behaviors to be observed and counted is useful; when the observer sees the behavior of interest, he or she can simply make a tick mark on the sheet.

Duration Recording. This method usually requires a watch or clock, so that a precise measurement of how much time a student spends doing something of concern to the teacher or assessment team (e.g., talking to others, tapping, rocking) can be recorded.

Time-sampling Recording. With this technique observers count the number of times a behavior occurs during a specific time interval. Rather than observe for long periods of time and tally all incidences of the behavior causing concern, the observer divides the observation period into equal time units and observes and tallies behavior only during short periods of time. Based upon the time sampling, predictions can then be made about the student's total behavior.

Checklists and Rating Scales. A checklist usually requires the observer to note whether a particular characteristic is present or absent, while a rating scale typically asks the observer to note the degree to which a characteristic is present or how often a behavior occurs. There are many commercially available checklists and rating scales, but they may be developed locally as well.

Sources: Swanson & Watson, 1989, pp. 273–277; Wallace, Larsen, & Elksnin, 1992, pp. 12–13.

Interviews

Interviewing the student in question, his or her parents, teachers, and other adults or peers can provide a great deal of useful information about the student. Ultimately, "an interview should be a conversation with a purpose" (Wallace, Larsen, & Elksnin, 1992, p. 16), with questions designed to collect information that "relates to the observed or suspected disability of the child" (p. 260). Preparing for the interview may involve a careful review of the student's school records or work samples, for these may help the assessment team identify patterns or areas of specific concern that can help determine who should be interviewed and some of the questions to be asked. Parents, for example, may be able to provide detailed information about the child's academic or medical background. It is especially important that they contribute their unique, "insider" perspective on their child's functioning, interests, motivation, difficulties, and behavior in the home or community. They may have valuable information to share about possible solutions to the problems being noted. Teachers can provide insight into the types of situations or tasks that the child finds demanding or easy, what factors appear to contribute to the child's difficulties, and what has produced positive results (e.g., specific activities, types of rewards) (Wodrich & Joy, 1986). The student, too, may have much to say to illuminate the problem. "All persons interviewed should be asked if they know of information important to the solution of the academic or behavior problem that was not covered during the interview" (Hoy & Gregg, 1994, p.44).

Organizing interview results is essential. Hoy and Gregg (1994) suggest that the interviewer might summarize the "perceptions of each person interviewed in a way that conveys similarities and differences in viewpoints" (p. 46), including:

- perceptions of the primary problem and its cause,
- what attempts have been made to solve or address the problem,
- any recent changes in the problem's severity, and
- student strengths and weaknesses.

Testing

Most assessments include tests, although this has become increasingly controversial. Many educators question the usefulness of the information gained from tests, for reasons that will be discussed in a moment. However controversial testing may be, this chapter will nonetheless present a basic overview of the issues, because testing so often forms a part of the assessment process. Parents, teachers, and other professionals may find this basic information helpful (a) for understanding some of the controversy surrounding testing and, thus, what principles schools need to consider when using standardized tests, and (b) for identifying what resources of information about tests are available and what alternatives to testing exist.

Standardized tests are very much a part of the education scene, as we all know. Most of us have taken many such tests in our lifetime. Tests may be informal—meaning a measure developed locally—or they may be commercially developed, formal measures, commonly called standardized tests. Unlike informal tests, standardized tests have detailed procedures for administration, timing, and scoring. There is a wide variety of tests available to assess the different skill areas.

Some tests are known as *criterion-referenced tests*. This means that they are scored according to a standard, or criterion, that the teacher, school, or test publisher decides represents an acceptable level of mastery. An example of a criterion-referenced test might be a teacher-made spelling test where there are 20 words to be spelled and where the teacher has defined an "acceptable level of mastery" as 16 correct (or 80%). These tests, sometimes called content-referenced tests, are concerned with the mastery of specific, defined skills; the student's performance on the test indicates whether or not he or she has mastered those skills.

Other tests are known as *norm-referenced tests*. Scores on these tests are not interpreted according to an absolute standard or criterion (i.e., 8 out of 10 correct) but, rather, according to how the student's performance compares with that of a particular group of individuals. In order for this comparison to be meaningful, a valid comparison group—called a norm group—must be defined. A norm group is a large number of children who are representative of all the children in that age group. Such a group can be obtained by selecting a group of children that have the characteristics of children across the United States—that is, a certain percentage must be from each gender, from various ethnic backgrounds (e.g., Caucasian, African American, American Indian, Asian, Hispanic), from each geographic area (e.g., Southeast, Midwest), and from each socioeconomic class. By having all types of children take the test, the test publisher can provide information about how various types of children perform on the test. (This information—what type of students comprised the norm group and how each type performed on the test—is generally given in the manuals that accompany the test.) The school will compare the scores of the child being evaluated to the scores obtained by the norm group. This helps evaluators determine whether the child is performing at a level typical for, below, or above that expected for children of a given ethnicity, socioeconomic status, age, or grade.

Not all tests use large, representative norm groups. This means that such tests were normed using a group of individuals who were *not* representative of the population in general. For example, on one such test, the norm group may have included few or no African American, Hispanic, or Asian students. Because it is not known how such students typically perform on the test, there is nothing to which an individual student's scores can be compared, which has serious implications for interpretation of results.

Thus, before making assumptions about a child's abilities based upon test results, it is important to know something about the group to which the child is being compared—particularly whether or not the student is being compared to children who are similar in ethnicity, socioeconomic status, and so on. The more unlike the child the norm group is, the less valuable the results of testing will generally be. This is one of the areas in which standardized testing has fallen under considerable criticism. Often, test administrators do not use the norm group information appropriately, or there may not be children in the norm group who are similar to the child being tested. Furthermore, many tests were originally developed some time ago, and the norm groups reported in the test manual are not similar at all to the children being tested today.

Selecting an Appropriate Instrument. The similarity of the norm group to the student being tested is just one area to be carefully considered by the professionals who select and administer standardized tests. Choosing which test is appropriate for a given student requires investigation; it is extremely important that those responsible for test selection do not just use what is available to or "always used by" the school district or school. The child's test results will certainly influence eligibility decisions, instructional decisions, and placement decisions, all of which have enormous consequences for the child. If the child is assessed with an instrument that is not appropriate for him or her, the data gathered are likely to be inaccurate and misleading, which in turn results in faulty decisions regarding that child's educational program. This is one of the reasons that many educators object vehemently to standardized testing as a means of making decisions about a student's strengths, weaknesses, and educational needs.

Therefore, selecting instruments with care is vital, as is the need to combine any information gathered through testing with information gathered through other approaches (e.g., interviews, observations, dynamic assessment).

Given the number of standardized tests available today, how does the individual charged with testing select an appropriate test for a given student? Here are some suggestions.

1. Consider the student's skill areas to be assessed, and identify a range of tests that measure those skill areas. There are a variety of books that can help evaluators identify what tests

are available; one useful reference book is Tests: *A Comprehensive Reference for Assessments in Psychology, Education, and Business* (3rd edition) by Sweetland and Keyser (1991). Another is *A Consumer's Guide to Tests in Print* (Hamill, Brown, & Bryant, 1992). Both books describe what each available test claims to measure, the age groups for which it is appropriate, whether it is group- and individually-administered (all testing of children with suspected disabilities must be individualized), how long it takes to administer the test, and much more. Additionally, the reference section at the end of the previous lists many books and resources on assessment which describe and critique a subset of the tests available in any given skill area. Taking advantage of the review information available on tests is a critical responsibility of all those charged with assessing students and making decisions about their education.

2. Investigate how suitable each test identified is for the student to be assessed and select those that are most appropriate. A particularly valuable resource for evaluating tests is the *Mental Measurements Yearbook* (Conoley & Kramer, 1992), which describes tests in detail and includes expert reviews of many tests. This yearbook is typically available in professional libraries for teachers, university libraries, and in the reference section of many public libraries. Publishers of tests generally also make literature available to help professionals determine whether a test is suitable for a specific student. This literature typically includes sample test questions; information on how the test was developed; a description of what groups of individuals (e.g., ethnic groups, ages, grade levels) were included in the "norm" group; and general guidelines for administration and interpretation.

Some questions professionals consider when reviewing a test are:

*   According to the publisher or expert reviewers, what, specifically, is the test supposed to measure? Is its focus directly relevant to the skill area(s) to be assessed? Will student results on the test address the educational questions being asked? (In other words, will the test provide the type of educational information that is needed?) If not, the test is not appropriate for that student and should not be used.

- Is the test reliable and valid? These are two critical issues in assessment. Reliability refers to the degree to which a child's results on the test are the same or similar over repeated testing. If a test is not reliable or if its reliability is uncertain—meaning that it does not yield similar results when the student takes the test again—then it should not be used. Validity refers to the degree to which the test measures what it claims to measure. For example, if a test claims to measure anxiety, a person's scores should be higher under a stressful situation than under a non-stressful situation. Test publishers make available specimen sets that will typically report the reliability and validity of the test. This information may also be reported in books describing the test, in the *Mental Measurement Yearbook* (Conoley & Kramer, 1992), or in many of the books listed in the reference section at the end of the previous chapter.

- Is the content/skill area being assessed by the test appropriate for the student, given his or her age and grade? (Scope and sequence charts that identify the specific hierarchy of skills for different academic areas are useful here.) If not, there is no reason to use the test.

- If the test is norm-referenced, does the norm group resemble the student? This point was mentioned above and is important for interpretation of results.

- Is the test intended to evaluate students, to diagnose the specific nature of a student's disability or academic difficulty, to inform instructional decisions, or to be used for research purposes? Many tests will indicate that a student has a disability or specific problem academically, but results will not be useful for instructional planning purposes. Additional testing may then be needed, in order to fully understand what type of instruction is necessary for the student.

- Is the test administered in a group or individually? By law, group tests are not appropriate when assessing a child for the presence of a disability or to determine his or her eligibility for special education.

- Does the examiner need specialized training in order to administer the test, record student responses, score the test, or interpret results? In most, if not all, cases, the answer to this question is yes. If the school has no one trained to administer or interpret the specific test, then it should not be used unless the school arranges for the student to be assessed by a qualified evaluator outside of the school system.

- Will the student's suspected disability impact upon his or her taking of the test? For example, many tests are timed tests, which means that students are given a certain amount of time to complete items. If a student has weak hand strength or dexterity, his or her performance on a timed test that requires holding a pencil or writing will be negatively affected by the disability. Using a timed test would only be appropriate for determining how speed affects performance. To determine the student's actual knowledge of a certain area, a nontimed test would be more appropriate. It may also be possible to make accommodations for the student (e.g., removing time restrictions from a timed test). If an accommodation is made, however, results must be interpreted with caution. Standardized tests are designed to be administered in an unvarying manner; when accommodations are made, standardization is broken, and the norms reported for the test no longer apply.

- How similar to actual classroom tasks are the tasks the child is asked to complete on the test? For example, measuring spelling ability by asking a child to recognize a misspelled word may be very different from how spelling is usually measured in a class situation (reproducing words from memory). If test tasks differ significantly from classroom tasks, information gathered by the test may do little to predict classroom ability or provide information useful for instruction.

Limitations of Testing. Even when all of the above considerations have been observed, there are those who question the usefulness of traditional testing in making good educational decisions for children. Many educators see traditional tests as offering little in the way of information useful for understanding the abilities and special needs of an individual child. Martin Kozloff (1994) offers the following example to illustrate how rigid use and interpretation of tests can result in useful information being overlooked or misinterpreted.

Ms. Adams: (Holding up a picture of a potato.) And this one?

Indra: You eat it.

Ms. Adams: No. It's a potato. Let's try another. (Holds up a picture of a duck.) What is this?

Indra: Swimming.

Ms. Adams: No. It's a duck. Say, "duck."

Indra: Duck.

Ms. Adams: Very good. (Still showing picture of a duck.) Now, what is this?

Indra: Swimming! (p. 16)

Kozloff notes that: There are many competent ways to respond to "What is this?". Indra said what potatoes are for and what the duck was doing. Ms. Adams scores Indra's answers incorrect because the test Ms. Adams is using narrowly defines as correct those answers with an object-naming function. Thus, Ms. Adams underestimates the size of Indra's object-naming repertoire and does not notice the other functions of Indra's vocabulary (Kozloff, 1994, pp. 16–17).

Another concern about the overuse of testing in assessment is its lack of usefulness in designing interventions. Historically, it has seemed as if tests have not been interpreted in ways that allow for many specific strategies to be developed. While scores help to define the areas in which a student may be performing below his or her peers, they may offer little to determine particular instruction or curricular changes that may benefit the child. Traditional tests often seem to overlap very little with the curriculum being taught. This suggests that scores may not reflect what the child really knows in terms of what is taught in the actual classroom. Other concerns include overfamiliarity with a test that is repeated regularly, inability to apply test findings in any practical way (i.e., generating specific recommendations based on test results), and difficulty in using such measures to monitor short-term achievement gains.

The sometimes circular journey from the referral to the outcome of the assessment process is frustrating. The teacher or parent requests help because the student is having problems, and the assessment results in information that more or less states, "The student is having problems."

It may be, however, that it is not that the tests themselves offer little relevant information but, rather, that the evaluators may fail to interpret them in ways that are useful. If we only ask questions related to eligibility (e.g., does this child meet the criteria as an individual with mental disabilities?) or about global ability (e.g., what is this child's intellectual potential?), then those are the questions that will be answered. Such information is not enough, if the goal is to develop an effective and appropriate educational program for the student.

Other Assessment Questions

During the assessment process, we often ask questions such as:

- How can we help the child to do his or her work?
- How can we manage the child's behavior, or teach the child to manage his or her own behavior?
- How can we help the child to be neater, faster, quieter, more motivated?

As alluded to a moment ago, it may be that a different set of questions needs to be asked, questions that may be more effective in eliciting practical and useful information that can be readily applied toward intervention. Such questions might include:

- In what physical environment does the child learn best?
- What is useful, debilitating, or neutral about the way the child approaches the task?
- Can the student hold multiple pieces of information in memory and then act upon them?
- How does increasing or slowing the speed of instruction impact upon the child's accuracy?
- What processing mechanisms are being taxed in any given task?
- How does this student interact with a certain teacher style?
- With whom has the child been successful? What about the person seems to have contributed to the child's success?
- What is encouraging to the child? What is discouraging?
- How does manipulating the mode of teaching (e.g., visual or auditory presentation) affect the child's performance?

The two sets of questions above differ from each other in two important ways. Within the first set, there is a subtle assumption that the problem is known (e.g., we "know" that the child is not trying hard

154

enough) and that the solution to the problem is all that is needed. The second set of questions, in contrast, is seeking information about the problem. The assessment is designed to find out what is keeping the child from trying harder or producing readable work. Also, the first set of questions tends to be more "child-blaming," while the other set attempts to understand more about the child's experience. Assuming one already "knows" the problem may result in fewer and less effective interventions. On the other hand, if we seek to understand "why" the child is having difficulty succeeding in school (e.g., he or she has trouble remembering and integrating information; fear of failure results in reduced classroom effort), we engage in an assessment process that seeks information about the problem and results in the identification of specific strategies to reduce the problem's negative impact on learning. To this end, assessment that goes beyond administering standardized tests and includes other evaluation methods is essential. In the remainder of this section, several valuable assessment methods will be briefly described.

Ecological Assessment

Ecological assessment basically involves directly observing and assessing the child in the many environments in which he or she routinely operates. The purpose of conducting such an assessment is to probe how the different environments influence the student and his or her school performance. Where does the student manifest difficulties? Are there places where he or she appears to function appropriately? What is expected of the student academically and behaviorally in each type of environment? What differences exist in the environments where the student manifests the greatest and the least difficulty? What implications do these differences have for instructional planning? As Wallace, Larsen, and Elksnin (1992) remark: "An evaluation that fails to consider a student's ecology as a potential causative factor in reported academic or behavioral disorders may be ignoring the very elements that require modification before we can realistically expect changes in that student's behavior" (p. 19).

Direct Assessment

Direct assessment of academic skills is one alternative that has recently gained in popularity. While there are a number of direct assessment models that exist (Shapiro, 1989), they are similar in that they all suggest that assessment needs to be directly tied to instructional curriculum. Curriculum-based assessment (CBA) is one type of direct evaluation. "Tests" of performance in this case come directly from the curriculum. For example, a child may be asked to read from his or her reading book for one minute. Information about the accuracy and the speed of reading can then be obtained and compared with other students in the class, building, or district. CBA is quick and offers specific information about how a student may differ from peers.

> Because the assessment is tied to curriculum content, it allows the teacher to match instruction to a student's current abilities and pinpoints areas where curriculum adaptations or modifications are needed. Unlike many other types of educational assessment, such as I.Q. tests, CBA provides information that is immediately relevant to instructional programming. (Berdine & Meyer, 1987, p. 33)

CBA also offers information about the accuracy and efficiency (speed) of performance. The latter is often overlooked when assessing a child's performance but is an important piece of information when designing intervention strategies. CBA is also useful in evaluating short-term academic progress.

Dynamic Assessment

Dynamic assessment refers to several different, but similar approaches to evaluating student learning. Although these approaches have been in use for some time, only recently has dynamic assessment been acknowledged as a valuable means of gathering information about students (Lidz, 1987). The goal of this type of assessment "is to explore the nature of learning, with the objective of collecting information to bring about cognitive change and to enhance instruction" (Sewell, 1987, p. 436).

One of the chief characteristics of dynamic assessment is that it includes a dialogue or interaction between the examiner and the student. Depending on the specific dynamic assessment approach used, this interaction may include modeling the task for the student, giving the student prompts or cues as he or she tries to solve a given problem, asking what the student is thinking while working on the problem, sharing on the part of the examiner to establish the task's relevance to experience and concepts beyond the test situation, and giving praise or encouragement (Hoy & Gregg, 1994). The interaction allows the examiner to draw conclusions about the student's thinking processes (e.g., why he or she answers a question in a particular way) and his or her response to a learning situation (i.e., whether, with prompting, feedback, or modeling, the student can produce a correct response, and what specific means of instruction produce and maintain positive change in the student's cognitive functioning.

Typically, dynamic assessment involves a test-train-retest approach. The examiner begins by testing the student's ability to perform a task or solve a problem without help. Then, a similar task or problem is given the student, and the examiner models how the task or problem is solved or gives the student cues to assist his or her performance. In Feuerstein's (1979) model of dynamic assessment, the examiner is encouraged to interact constantly with the student, an interaction that is called mediation which is felt to maximize the probability that the student will solve the problem. Other approaches to dynamic assessment use what is called graduated prompting (Campione & Brown, 1987) where "a series of behavioral hints are used to teach the rules needed for task completion" (Hoy & Gregg, 1994, p. 151). These hints do not evolve from the student's responses, as in Feuerstein's model, but, rather, are scripted and preset, a standardization which allows for comparison across students. The prompts are given only if the student needs help in order to solve the problem. In both these approaches, the "teaching" phase is followed by a retesting of the student with a similar task but with no assistance from the examiner. The results indicate the student's "gains" or responsiveness to instruction—whether he or she learned and could apply the earlier instructions of the examiner and the prior experience of solving the problem.

An approach known as "testing the limits" incorporates the classic training and interactional components of dynamic assessment but can be used with many traditional tests, particularly tests of personality or cognitive ability (Carlson & Wiedl, 1978, 1979, as cited in Jitendra & Kameenui, 1993). Modifications are simply included in the testing situation—while taking a particular standardized test, for example, the, student may be encouraged to verbalize before and after solving a problem. Feedback, either simple or elaborated, may be provided by the examiner as well.

Of course, dynamic assessment is not without its limitations or critics. One particular concern is the amount of training needed by the examiner to both conduct the assessment and interpret results. Another is a lack of operational procedures or "instruments" for assessing a student's performance or ability in the different content areas (Jitendra & Kameenui, 1993). Further, conducting a dynamic assessment is undeniably labor intensive.

Even with these limitations, dynamic assessment is a promising addition to current evaluation techniques. Because it incorporates a teaching component into the assessment process, this type of assessment may be particularly useful with students from minority backgrounds who may not have been exposed to the types of problems or tasks found on standardized tests. The interactional aspect of dynamic assessment also can contribute substantially to developing an understanding of the student's thinking process and problem-solving approaches and skills. Certainly, having detailed information about how a student approaches performing a task and how he or she responds to various instructional techniques can be highly relevant to instructional planning.

Task Analysis

Task analysis is very detailed; it involves breaking down a particular task into the basic sequential steps, component parts, or skills necessary to accomplish the task. The degree to which a task is broken down into steps depends upon the student in question; "it is only necessary to break the task down finely enough so that the student can succeed at each step" (Wallace, Larsen, & Elksnin, 1992, p. 14).

Taking this approach to assessment offers several advantages to the teacher. For one, the process identifies what is necessary for accomplishing a particular task. It also tells the teacher whether or not the student can do the task, which part or skill causes the student to falter, and the order in which skills must be taught to help the student learn to perform the task.

According to Bigge (1990), task analysis is a process that can be used to guide the decisions made regarding:

- what to teach next;
- where students encounter problems when they are attempting but are not able to complete a task;
- the steps necessary to complete an entire task;
- what adaptations can be made to help the student accomplish a task;
- options for those students for whom learning a task is not a possible goal (as described in Wallace, Larsen, & Elksnin, 1992, p. 14).

Task analysis is an approach to assessment that goes far beyond the need to make an eligibility or program placement decision regarding a student. It can become an integral part of classroom planning and instructional decision-making.

Outcome-Based Assessment

Outcome-based assessment is another approach to gathering in formation about a student's performance. This type of assessment has been developed, at least in part, to respond to concerns that education, to be meaningful, must be directly related to what educators and parents want the child to have gained in the end. Outcome-based assessment involves considering, teaching, and evaluating the skills that are important in real-life situations. Learning such skills will result in the student becoming an effective adult. Assessment, from this point of view, starts by identifying what outcomes are desired for the student (e.g., being able to use public transportation). In steps similar to what is used with task analysis, the team then determines what competencies are necessary for the outcomes to take place (e.g., the steps or subskills the student needs to have mastered in order to achieve the outcome desired) and identifies which subskills the student has mastered and which he or she still needs to learn. The instruction that is needed can then be pinpointed and undertaken.

Learning Styles

The notion of learning styles is not new, but seems to have revived in the past few years. Learning styles theory suggests that students may learn and problem solve in different ways and that some ways are more natural for them than others. When they are taught or asked to perform in ways that deviate from their natural style, they are thought to learn or perform less well. A learning style assessment, then, would attempt to determine those elements that impact on a child's learning and "ought to be an integral part of the individualized prescriptive process all special education teachers use for instructing pupils" (Berdine & Meyer, 1987, p. 27).

Some of the common elements that may be included here would be the way in which material is typically presented (visually, auditorily, tactilely) in the classroom, the environmental conditions of the classroom (hot, cold, noisy, light, dark), the child's personality characteristics, the expectations for success that are held by the child and others, the response the child receives while engaging in the learning process (e.g., praise or criticism), and the type of thinking the child generally utilizes in solving problems (e.g., trial and error, analyzing). Identifying the factors that positively impact the child's learning may be very valuable in developing effective intervention strategies.

— by Betsy W. Waterman, Ph.D.
State University of New York
at Oswego

Chapter 9

Primary Areas of Assessment

In this chapter, we will look in detail at the primary areas in which students are assessed, which are: intelligence, language, perceptual abilities, academic achievement, behavior, and emotional/ social development. When the disability is related to a medically related condition (e.g., sensory deficit, orthopedic impairment, arthritis), assessment information from physicians or other medical practitioners needs to be included as well. More than one assessment technique should be used in any given area, and the assessment team should clearly understand that each area encompasses more than one ability.

In this chapter, we will look at what skills are involved in these traditional areas of assessment (e.g., intelligence, language, and so on) and how schools may collect information about how a student performs in each area. While standardized testing is often the default means of gathering information about a student, it is highly recommended that other methods be used as well, including interviews, observations, and methodologies such as ecological or dynamic assessment.

Intelligence

While a person's intelligence is typically measured by an intelligence test, there is considerable controversy over what, precisely, is meant by the term "intelligence." Binet, who was largely responsible for the development of the first intelligence test, viewed intelligence

Excerpted from National Information Center for Children and Youth with Disabilities (NICHCY) *News Digest*, Vol. 4, No.1, 1994.

as a collection of faculties, including judgment, practical sense, initiative, and the ability to adapt to circumstances (Wallace, Larsen, & Elksnin, 1992). Thurman, in contrast, developed a multifactor theory of intelligence, which included such mental abilities as verbal, number, perceptual speed, reasoning, memory, word fluency, and spatial visualization. Wechsler, on the other hand, believed that intelligence was the ability of the person "to act purposefully, to think rationally, and to deal effectively with his environment" (Wechsler, 1958, p. 7, as cited in Wallace, Larsen, & Elksnin, 1992, p. 105).

It is important to know that different intelligence tests are based upon different definitions of what constitutes intelligence. As a result, different tests may measure different skills and abilities. It is critical, therefore, that administrators of such tests "be completely aware of an author's definition of intelligence when selecting and interpreting an intelligence test" and "to view the scores as highly tentative estimates of learning ability that must be verified by other evidence" (Wallace, Larsen, & Elksnin, 1992, p. 106).

The theory underlying intelligence tests (e.g., how does one define intelligence or develop tests of intelligence?) is not the only controversy surrounding their use. How fairly they assess certain populations (e.g., minority children, persons with limited experience, children with severe language deficits), and whether or not such tests are reliable and valid (Elliott, 1987) are also areas of hot debate. In the past, intelligence measures have been misused, particularly with African American children, Native Americans, and non-English speaking children, who, based upon their scores, were placed in classes for those with mental retardation or with learning disabilities. However, given the many court cases involving standardized intelligence testing as a means of assessing minority children (e.g., *Diana v. State Board of Education*, 1970; *Covarrubias v. San Diego Unified School District*, 1971; *Larry P. v. Riles*, 1979; *Guadalupe v. Tempe Elementary District*, 1972), and given the strength and volume of advocates' protests, evaluators are now becoming more sensitive to issues of test bias, the importance of testing in a child's native language, the need for specialized training when administering and interpreting standardized tests, and the importance of combining any test scores with information gathered in other ways.

Issues related to the definition of "intelligence" and the "fairness" of using measures of intelligence also become less concerning if one knows the purpose for which the test is being used. Intelligence tests are most helpful (and probably most appropriate) when they are used to determine specific skills, abilities, and knowledge that the child either has or does not have and when such information is combined with other evaluation data and then directly applied to school programming.

There are a number of skills that an intelligence test appears to measure—social judgment, level of thinking, language skill, perceptual organization, processing speed, and spatial abilities. Questions that attempt to measure social judgment and common sense, numerical reasoning, concrete and abstract thinking, the ability to recognize similarities and differences between objects or concepts, and vocabulary and language skill (e.g., the ease with which a person can find words in memory) appear very dependent on experience, training, and intact verbal abilities. Perceptual organization, processing speed, and spatial abilities seem less dependent on experience and verbal skill.

Intelligence tests can also yield valuable information about a student's ability to process information. In order to learn, every person must take in, make sense of, store, and retrieve information from memory in an efficient and accurate way. Each of us can process certain kinds of information more easily than other kinds. The artist sees and reproduces accurate depictions of the world, while others struggle to produce stick figures. The musician creates beautiful sounds from a mixture of separate tones. The writer crafts words to create a mood. Others of us do none of these things well. In school, children need certain skills to function effectively. They must be able to listen attentively so that other movements, sounds, or sights do not distract them. They must be able to understand the words spoken to them. This often requires children to hold multiple pieces of information in memory (e.g., page number, questions to answer) and to act upon them. They must be able to find the words they need to express themselves and, ultimately, commit these words to paper. This involves another whole series of processing skills— holding a writing implement, coordinating visual and motor actions, holding information in memory until it can be transferred to paper, transforming sounds into written symbols, and understanding syntax, punctuation, and capitalization rules. They also must be able to interpret the nonverbal messages of others, such as a frown, a smile, a shake of the head. Equally important, they must do all of these things quickly and accurately and often in a setting with many distractions.

A thorough interpretation of an intelligence test can yield information about how effectively a child processes and retrieves information. Most individually administered intelligence tests can determine, at least to some degree, a child's ability to attend, process information quickly, distinguish relevant from less relevant details, put events in sequence, and retrieve words from memory.

Kamphaus (1993) summarizes a number of research findings related to he use of intelligence tests:

1. Intelligence test scores are more stable for school-aged children than for preschoolers and more stable among individuals with disabilities than those without disabilities;

2. Intelligence test scores can change from childhood to adulthood;

3. It is likely that environmental factors, socioeconomic status, values, family structure, and genetic factors all play a role in determining intelligence test scores;

4. Factors such as low birth weight, malnutrition, anoxia (lack of oxygen), and fetal alcohol exposure have a negative impact on intelligence test scores; and

5. Intelligence and academic achievement appear to be highly related.

This last finding supports the notion that intelligence and achievement tests may not be so different from each other and that "intelligence tests may be interpreted as specialized types of achievement measures" (Kamphaus, 1993, p. 65). This is consistent with the suggestion that intelligence tests may be best used to determine specific skills, abilities, and knowledge.

Language

Language provides the foundation upon which communication, problem solving, and expanding, integrating, analyzing, and synthesizing knowledge take place. Deficits in language, therefore, can have a profound impact on the ability of an individual to learn and function competently and confidently as he or she interacts in the world.

Language is complex and involves multiple domains—nonverbal language, oral language (i.e., listening and speaking), written language (i.e., reading and writing), pragmatic language (e.g., using language for a specific purpose such as asking for help), phonology, and audiology. How quickly a person can access words or ideas in memory further influences his or her use of language. A child who must struggle to find an appropriate term is at a great disadvantage in a learning and social environment. As he or she grapples to retrieve a word, others have moved on. The student may miss critical pieces of knowledge, connect incorrect bits of information in memory, and have an ineffective means of showing others all that he or she knows. Such problems can result in lowered levels of achievement and in feelings of confusion, helplessness, and frustration.

It is clear how important language processing can be to a child's successful adaptation to the school environment and, therefore, it is an important area to be considered in the assessment process. Speech and language pathologists are specially trained professionals who, working with school psychologists and classroom teachers, are frequently the primary individuals gathering data related to a child's language functioning.

Bloom and Lahey (1978) divide language processes into three general categories: form, content, and use. Phonology, morphology, and syntax are all considered to be components of form. The first of these processes, phonology, refers to the knowledge a person has of the sounds in the language. While the number of sounds that exist are limited, a nearly endless number of words can be constructed from these sounds. Awareness of the basic sound units of language appears important to a child's ability to quickly and accurately locate words in memory when speaking, comprehend oral sentences, and learn to read (Liberman & Shankweiler, 1987). It is important to note that the ability to blend or separate sounds (i.e., phonological processing ability) is often overlooked in the assessment process. This may be an unfortunate oversight, given its apparent importance to the reading process.

Morphology, the second form element, refers to the smallest meaningful unit of language. Morphology involves the stringing together of sounds (phonemes) and includes such structures as prefixes, suffixes, word endings that describe number (e.g., dog vs. dogs), and tense (e.g., walk vs. walked). Syntax refers to the rules used in combining words to make a sentence. As with the sounds of language (phonology), the rules of language are finite. The acquisition of syntax is also developmental.

While syntax determines the rules that guide how sentences are put together, such knowledge alone is not sufficient for constructing sentences. The meaning of words constrains what words may or may not be used together. For example, the sentence "I saw the house fly-ing over the orchard" would make little sense, although it is syntac-tically correct. It is this aspect of language, the importance of meaning, that Bloom and Lahey (1978) refer to as content. Content involves knowledge of vocabulary, the relationships between words, and "time-and-event" relationships (Swanson & Watson, 1989). The child must also be able to associate words with the correct environmental expe-rience. It is generally expected that a child understands the mean-ing of more words than he or she can express at any point in time. As Swanson and Watson (1989) point out, when an individual appears able to express more information than he or she is able to receive and comprehend, it may suggest that he or she has difficulty in auditory input and processing.

Use, the final component in the Bloom and Lahey model, refers to "the pragmatic functions of language in varying contexts" (Swanson & Watson, 1989, p. 151). It views the child as an active "communica-tor" whose words and sentences are intentionally selected in relation to the effect the speaker wishes to have on a listener. The speaker needs to be able to (a) change what is said in some way when it is apparent that he or she is not being understood, (b) vary language use when talking with different groups (e.g., peers or adults), and (c) use language in a variety of functional ways (e.g., to begin or end a conversation). Thus, use (or pragmatics, as it is sometimes called) is a vital area to assess in language; to ignore how a student uses lan-guage is to ignore a basic element of language—that we communicate in a context, for a particular purpose or reason (Heward & Orlansky, 1992).

Assessing a Child's Language Abilities. The IDEA's regulations provide a definition of speech-language impairment as "a communi-cation disorder such as stuttering, impaired articulation, a language impairment, or a voice impairment that adversely affects" a child's educational performance [34 CFR 300.7(b)(11)]. In more specific terms, a child with a speech disorder may have difficulty in produc-ing sounds properly, speaking in a normal flow or rhythm, or using his or her voice in an effective way. A child with a language disorder would have problems using or understanding the rules, sounds, or symbols that we use to communicate with each other. This relates to language form, content, and/or use, as discussed above (Heward & Orlansky, 1992). A child with a speech impairment, a language im-pairment, or both, would be eligible for services under the IDEA.

There are many standardized measures of speech and language ability. Some "provide a comprehensive view of all language functioning," while others "measure specific components of linguistic performance (for example, phonology, linguistic structure, or semantics)" (Wallace, Larsen, & Elksnin, 1992, p. 252). The range of tests and what they measure may be identified through consulting resource books on speech/language assessment or more general test references such as *Tests* (Sweetland & Keyser, 1991), or by contacting organizations such as the American Speech-Language-Hearing Association (ASHA) (see the references at the end of Chapter Seven).

It is important to realize, however, that "standardized diagnostic tests are generally insensitive to the subtleties of ongoing functional communication" (Swanson & Watson, 1989, p. 155). Therefore, in addition to or in place of standardized tests, a typical speech/language evaluation should include obtaining a language sample that seeks to capture how the student performs in an actual communication situation. Language samples can be obtained through checklists or observational recording systems, or through informally conversing with the student. Great care must be taken to ensure that assessment of students is culture-free and dialect-sensitive, as many children will speak nonstandard English or another language entirely. [The issue of cultural bias in language assessment is considered in *Topics in Language Disorders* (Terrell, 1983)]. Obtaining such a language sample from the student is often the responsibility of the speech-language pathologist.

Through interviews, observations, and teaching, teachers can also gather valuable information about a student's language use. By engaging in what is known as diagnostic teaching, the teacher can become an invaluable participant in the ongoing assessment and remediation of a child's language deficiencies. It is important, however, for teachers to be thoroughly familiar with the developmental milestone of normal language functioning.

Obtaining a case history of the child (in most cases, from the parents) can also be valuable in the initial stages of assessment. Knowing in detail how the child's language has developed can yield information relevant to the problem and includes gaining an understanding of the early stages of the disorder, any physical or emotional condition that may have been or be involved, whether the disorder occurs in other settings and, if so, how it manifests itself, and any insights the parents may have into how best to assess and work with their child (Wallace, Larsen, & Elksnin, 1992, p. 260).

167

It is also important to realize that the ability to receive and understand language, and to use language verbally, is in part dependent upon how well the body performs physically. Before embarking upon an extensive (and expensive) battery of tests, examiners should ensure that any apparent speech or language impairment is not actually the result of a hearing impairment which, in effect, prevents the child from hearing words clearly and learning to use or understand them. Similarly, many children with physical disabilities may not be able to speak clearly enough to be understood but, when provided with assistive technology (e.g., speech synthesizers, computers), may show themselves to be competent users of language.

Perceptual Abilities

Perceptual abilities determine how individuals perceive information and how they respond. These abilities can be subdivided into at least four general areas: visual-perceptual, auditory-perceptual, perceptual-motor skill, and attention. Assessing a student in these areas is intended to determine strengths and weaknesses in information and sensory processing and can help the assessment team gain an understanding of how the child learns best.

The idea of "perceptual deficits" has long been linked to learning disabilities. It is important to realize that research results in this area have been mixed and controversial, and offer only small support for including evaluation of perceptual abilities in any assessment battery or approach (Overton, 1992). Linguistic issues, rather than perceptual abilities, may more often explain learning deficits. Nevertheless, since assessing perceptual abilities continues to be part of the evaluation process at present, it will be briefly discussed below.

Visual-Perceptual Ability. Visual perception includes the ability to discriminate between two or more visual stimuli, locate a particular figure within a larger scene, and understand position in space. Perceptual skills include detecting specific colors, shapes, and sizes. In reading, it requires the ability to detect the visual features of a letter or word so that the 26 letters of the alphabet can be distinguished from each other. The student must also discriminate between ten written digits.

Auditory-Perceptual Ability. Auditory perception includes the ability to detect certain auditory features such as changes in volume, discrimination of vowel or consonant sounds, and nonphonemic sound discrimination (e.g., the sound of a bell from the sound of a buzzer). In a school setting, then, the student would need the ability to discriminate between different sounds, identify spoken words that are the same or different, and hear sounds in order.

Perceptual-Motor Ability. Most assessments include one or more measures of perceptual-motor ability. It has been an assumption of many educators that perceptual-motor or visual-motor problems are often associated with learning problems and, therefore, should be included in most assessment batteries (Salvia & Ysseldyke, 1991). Historically, tests of perceptual motor skill have been second only to intelligence tests in terms of use in the assessment of school-aged children. Tests of perceptual-motor skill or perceptual motor integration most often ask students to copy geometric designs that are placed in front of them. This requires the child to see the design, attend to and remember the relevant features, and then carry out the motor actions necessary to reproduce the design on paper.

Attention. The ability to focus on a given activity for extended periods is important if a student is to take in information or complete the day-to-day tasks in school. Keogh and Margolis (1976) have suggested three phases of attention: the ability to (a) come to attention; (b) focus attention; and (c) maintain attention. The issue of "selective" attention must also be considered here. Students must be able to attend, and they must be able to sustain attention on the most relevant stimuli. For example, a student must be able to attend to the teacher's words rather than to his or her clothing. Difficulties in any of the three phases of attention can interfere with a student's ability to learn or share what he or she knows in a consistent fashion. While the ability to attend effectively is seldom assessed through a formalized instrument, information related to attention can be gathered through classroom observations and observations of test behaviors.

Assessing Perceptual Ability. As was mentioned above, assessing perceptual abilities is not without its controversies. There are certainly a number of issues that need to be considered when addressing this area.

The first issue relates to the importance of ensuring that a student's apparent perceptual difficulties are not actually the result of a lack of visual or auditory acuity (as opposed to a difficulty with processing stimuli). Before beginning an assessment of perceptual ability, then, the student's eyesight and hearing should be tested (Overton, 1992; Swanson & Watson, 1989). This can be part of the assessment process, with the school referring the student to the appropriate facilities for such screenings.

The second issue is related to the relevance of such measures to the goals of assessment. There has been little to suggest that direct training in perceptual skills improves academic performance (Salvia & Ysseldyke, 1991; Vellutino, 1979). If there is little applicability, then seems reasonable to question whether formal tests of perceptual skill are necessary as part of the assessment battery.

The third issue is related to the validity and reliability of the perceptual test measures. There is some suggestion that tests purported to measure perceptual abilities may actually measure other facts such as language or verbal memory skill (Vellutino, 1979). Information gained from tests thought to measure perceptual processing may actually result in incorrect explanations for learning problems. This may lead those working with the child towards strategies that are not useful (perceptual training such as copying designs) and away from ones that may be helpful, such as training in phonological processing. There are also concerns that many of the instruments currently available do not meet acceptable standards of reliability and validity (Swanson & Wats 1989, p. 217), making their use of questionable value.

Academic Achievement

Academic achievement refers to how well the child is performing in core skill areas such as reading, mathematics, and writing. Assessment batteries typically include an individual measure of academic achievement, although it is important to realize that standardized achievement tests may be inappropriate for use with immigrant or minority group children. Information about the child's placement (i.e., below, at, or above) in his or her peer group and knowledge about the specific skills the child possesses are important both for the planning and evaluation of instruction.

Reading. Reading is an extension of the language process. It provides a way for individuals to exchange information. Reading also represents the means by which much of the information presented in school is learned and is the academic area most often implicated in school failure.

Reading, like language, is an extremely complex process, a process that is, for many, so natural or fluent that many of the subskills are not recognized or identified as a part of the process. Identifying these subskills is important, however, if an adequate assessment in this area is to occur.

Prereading skills include:

- general language competence;
- understanding that reading is a means of exchanging ideas (e.g., the ability to "read" pictures);
- the ability to complete rhymes and identify words that do not rhyme;
- the ability to distinguish between verbal and nonverbal sounds, recognize when words are the same or different, and segment and blend language sounds; and
- the ability to store and retrieve sounds one has heard.

Having opportunities for abundant language experiences, while not a skill, is also important to the development of prereading and later reading ability.

Reading skills can be divided into two general categories: word recognition and comprehension. A number of skills are used when attempting to identify, pronounce, or retrieve a word. Four types of analyses can be used by the child: visual analysis (i.e., the use of visual features), contextual analysis (i.e., using the surrounding words for clues about a given word), phonological analysis (i.e., using information about the sounds in the word), and structural analysis (i.e., recognizing and giving meaning to specific word parts such as prefixes, suffixes, or syllables). Phonological analysis appears particularly important as children attempt to gain reading skill. It allows the child to decode (i.e., read) a word he or she has never seen before, either in isolation or in context. This is not possible with visual, contextual, or structural analysis alone. The ability, then, to engage in phonemic analysis is important to becoming a proficient reader and, therefore, is an area that should be considered in any assessment of any child who is struggling with reading.

Gaining meaning from text (comprehension) is the most common goal of reading. The general approach of the reader (active or passive), use of prior knowledge, and contextual analysis are all skills that appear related to comprehension. The ability to grasp literal information and to predict, interpret, critically analyze, or create new ideas

171

in response to a paragraph are examples of the use of context at the comprehension level. Listening comprehension also appears to be related to reading comprehension, particularly at the higher reading skill levels (Stanovich, 1982).

The assessment of reading, then, needs to address the ability of the child to recognize individual words and to comprehend text. Assessment instruments should be selected that assure that test content and test tasks are as similar as possible to school reading tasks. Both formal and informal assessment may be useful here. Informal measures may include asking the student to:

- read aloud, which permits the teacher to identify errors in decoding and to determine the student's fluency and accuracy when reading;
- answer questions after reading, to determine the student's ability to understand the main idea of the story, capture its details, or place events in sequence;
- paraphrase or re-tell the story in his or her own words;
- fill in missing words in a passage he or she has not read;
- identify which sentence out of several means the same thing as a sentence supplied by the teacher;
- and provide synonyms of selected words.

Mathematics. Another critical area of school achievement is that of mathematics. The terms "mathematics" and "arithmetic" are often used interchangeably but actually mean different things. Mathematics refers to the study of numbers and their relationships to time, space, volume, and geometry, while arithmetic refers to the operations or computations performed. Subskills related to mathematics include:

- problem-solving,
- the ability to perform mathematics in practical situations, performance of appropriate computational skills,
- use of mathematics to predict,
- understanding and use of concepts related to measurement, interpretation and construction of charts or graphs,
- ability to estimate,
- understanding and application of geometric concepts, ability to recognize the reasonableness of results, and computer knowledge (for more information, see Lerner, 1988; Reid & Hresko, 1981; Roth-Smith, 1991).

For a student to learn and act on knowledge of mathematics, he or she must understand terms regarding amount or direction (i.e., language-based knowledge), understand that numbers stand for a quantity, hold multiple pieces of mathematical information in memory and perform mathematical operations (e.g., add, multiply) on them, and know that numbers can be manipulated in meaningful ways.

The assessment of mathematics should measure a student's ability in both calculation and reasoning (application). Like reading, an evaluation of mathematical understanding and performance should also be structured so that it closely matches the demands made on the child in the actual classroom situation. Assessment might begin by analyzing actual samples of the student's work and identifying specific errors and any apparent pattern to those errors. Curriculum-based assessment techniques are also useful, and can be combined with task analysis and error analysis to identify where, specifically, the student is having problems. Interviewing can be useful as well, and may include asking the student to solve a problem and explain the steps used in the process" (Overton, 1992, p. 257). Such an approach can be invaluable in providing insight into a student's mathematical reasoning. Conducting several such interviews is important, however, to avoid drawing hasty conclusions about the nature of a student's difficulties. Observations can also provide productive information to the assessment team and should focus on student behavior during—and his or her approach to—written assignments, working at the chalkboard, and classroom discussions.

Written Language. Written language is a complex form of communicating that consists of three general areas: spelling, handwriting, and written expression or composition. Like reading, writing tasks are an important part of the school curriculum and are often utilized in evaluating a student's understanding of a given concept. Written language is directly tied to reading, listening, and speaking, and skills in all of these areas overlap.

Spelling has often been considered a difficult task (Henderson, 1985). In English, the difficulty arises because there is no one-to-one correspondence between letters and their representative sounds. This can cause problems for the reader and may cause even greater problems for the speller. In spelling there are even fewer cues to aid in recreating a spoken word in print. As Lerner (1988) explains:

173

Several clues aid the reader in recognizing a word in print: context, phonics, structural analysis, and configuration. There is no opportunity, however, to draw on peripheral clues in reproducing a word (p. 105).

Both language and reading experience appear to be important to the development of connections between letters and their sounds. Thus, knowledge of spelling patterns, analysis of word parts, and knowledge of syllable rules all need to be measured.

It is important to consider that any approach that does not require a child to independently reconstruct a word (e.g., one that simply asks a child to select a misspelled word from among a group of words) does little to give information about the child's ability to recreate accurate spelling in a sentence he or she is writing. Assessment of spelling is particularly well given to informal approaches such as curriculum-based measurement or interviews. A number of standardized, commercially available spelling tests are available as well.

Handwriting refers to the actual motor activity that is involved in writing. Most students are taught manuscript (printing) initially and then move to cursive writing. There are those who advocate that only manuscript or only cursive should be taught (Reid & Hresko, 1981). In truth, problems may appear among students in either system. Wiederhold et al. (1978) have suggested a number of areas which may be assessed related to both manuscript and cursive writing. The assessment of manuscript includes evaluating the position of the hand and paper, size of letters and the proportion of letters to each other, quality of the actual pencil lines, the amount and regularity of the slant of the letters, letter formation and alignment, letter or word spacing, and speed of production. Cursive writing can be considered according to many of the same qualities but should also include an evaluation of the way in which letters are connected.

Composition refers to the more creative parts of written expression. Alley and Deshler (1979) suggest three general areas that need to be addressed in any assessment of written expression:

- the student's attitude toward writing;
- ability of the individual to express content (e.g., skill in describing or reporting events, or in expressing views or feelings); and
- the student's ability to "craft" a paragraph (e.g., the student's ability to organize, sequence, choose effective words, use punctuation and capitalization, or take notes).

Both formal and informal measures of assessment of written expression are available and should be considered in a thorough evaluation. Analyzing work samples produced by the student can be particularly useful, as can interviewing the student regarding his or her perceptions of the writing process.

Behavior and Emotional and Social Development

Behavior—how a student conducts himself or herself in school—is often a key factor in educational performance. Certainly, behavior that is off-target academically or socially—inattention, being out of seat, talking too much, hitting or biting, skipping school—can detract from learning. When a student's behavior appears to be interfering with school performance and relationships with others, or when that behavior is maladaptive, bizarre, or dangerous, it becomes important to assess the student's behavior (when the behavior occurs, how often, and for what reasons) as well as his or her emotional and social development. Wallace, Larsen, and Elksnin (1992) "stress the need to take an ecological perspective when assessing a student's nonacademic behaviors in order to obtain a complete picture and examine the relationship between the behavior and the environment" (pp. 164–165).

Negative or inappropriate behaviors may occur for different reasons. One child may be disruptive in class because of attention deficit disorder. A second child may exhibit similar behaviors due to a mental illness, while another's inappropriate behavior may be linked to environmental factors such as his or her parents' recent divorce. Still another child may be disruptive only in one or two classes, for reasons associated with the way instruction is organized (e.g., a predominance of small group, large group, or self-paced activities) or something in that environment which the student finds disturbing. Thus, identifying why a child is exhibiting certain behaviors is an important part of the assessment process. The reasons why, if they can be determined, will influence whether or not the child is determined eligible for special education services and, if so, will certainly affect the nature of decisions made regarding educational and other interventions.

Assessing Problem Behavior. For children exhibiting signs of emotional, social, or behavioral problems, the assessment team will generally conduct a behavioral assessment. The goal of behavioral assessment is to gain an increased understanding of how environmental factors may be influencing the child's behavior. This includes identifying (a) what expectations and rules are established by significant others in the settings where the problem behavior occurs, and (b) what "specific variables in a particular situation . . . may be maintaining problem behaviors" (Berdine & Meyer, 1987, p. 151). This knowledge will then be used directly in designing intervention strategies. "Behavioral assessment depends on keen observation and precise measurement" (Swanson & Watson, 1989, p. 246). Assessment is tied to observing a specific situation (e.g., how the child responds during lunch or reading) at a particular point in time. It is important that a behavioral assessment involve multiple measures and take place in various settings (e.g., the classroom, school playground, chorus, home) and at different times during the day (e.g., morning, afternoon, and night). The ability to observe and record behavior, select the most appropriate places to observe the child, and find efficient and clear means of interpreting results are all critical in behavioral assessment. Collectively, the observations should provide information which:

- pinpoints and quantifies the nature of the behavior problem (including what variables in the environment are contributing to or maintaining the behavior);
- allows eligibility and placement decisions to be made;
- illuminates what type of instruction is needed; and
- provides baseline information against which progress can be measured once intervention begins.

Interviews are also a useful means of gathering information about a child's behavior. Parents and significant others may be able to offer insight into the nature and history of the child's difficulties. The child may also be an excellent source of information. Of primary interest here is determining the child's "awareness of the problem behaviors and their controlling variables, degree of motivation to change, and skill at behavioral self-control" (Berdine & Meyer, 1987, p. 174).

Assessing Adaptive Behavior. Other aspects of behavior may be important to assess as well. Adaptive behavior is a frequent focus of assessment, and is a required area of assessment when a classification of mental retardation is being considered for a student. Adaptive behavior refers to "the effectiveness or degree with which individuals meet the standards of personal independence and social responsibility expected for age and cultural groups" (Grossman, 1983,

p. 1). When assessing a person's adaptive behavior, examiners may investigate his or her strengths and weaknesses in a variety of different skill areas, such as: communication, self-care, home living, social skills, community use, self-direction, health and safety, functional academics, leisure, and work. According to the American Association on Mental Retardation (1992), these are the skills with which individuals most often require assistance or some specialized support.

The IDEA specifies "deficits in adaptive behavior" as one of the two characteristics necessary for a student to be classified as having mental retardation (the other characteristic being "significantly subaverage general intellectual functioning" [34 CFR §300.7(b)(5)]. Measuring a student's adaptive behavior, however, should not be limited to only those students suspected of having mental retardation; this type of assessment has much to offer the decision-making associated with students with other disabilities as well, particularly in regards to IEP development and instructional and transition planning.

Many commercially-developed adaptive behavior instruments exist to help educators evaluate a student's adaptive skills. Using these instruments typically does not require the student to be involved directly; rather, examiners record information collected from a third person who is familiar with the student (e.g., parent, teacher, direct service provider) and who can report what types of adaptive skills the student has mastered and which he or she has not. Unfortunately, there is some concern that many of the available adaptive behavior scales do not meet the technical requirements of good instrumentation [for example, reliability and validity may not be reported by the publisher (Berdine & Meyer, 1987; AAMR, 1992)] and that there may be bias inherent in assessing the behavior of children who are culturally or linguistically different from the majority culture. Therefore, care must be taken with the selection of the adaptive behavior scale to be used. It is also a good idea to use other methods to collect information about the student's skills, such as direct observation and interviewing the student. For minority students, it is imperative to develop an understanding of what types of behavior are considered adaptive (and, thus, appropriate) in the minority culture, before making judgments about the particular functioning of a student.

Assessing Emotional and Social Development. No child lives in a vacuum. His or her relative freedom from internal and external stressors, ability to interact with others comfortably, and ability to respond consistently and positively in the learning environment all are important for the child to benefit maximally from school experiences. In assessing a child's emotional and social adjustment, questions need to be answered related to the child's intrapersonal and interpersonal experience. Assessment of the child's intrapersonal world involves knowledge about how the child views him or herself, how the child responds emotionally, how much conflict or anxiety he or she is currently experiencing, the degree to which the individual believes that personal behaviors can actually make a difference in his or her own life, his or her tolerance for frustration, and general activity level. Interpersonal characteristics are related to how the individual views the world and other people. Such characteristics are developed in response to the child's experiences within the environment. If the child sees the world as a hostile place and views people as untrustworthy, negative interactive patterns and behaviors may emerge.

The development of the child's intrapersonal experience and interpersonal behaviors is, at least in part, related to the way basic physiological and psychological needs (e.g., to be fed, feel safe, belong, be productive, unique, empowered) are being met. If a child is abused, ignored, or neglected, there are often negative behavioral, cognitive, and emotional outcomes. Problem behaviors such as tantrums, aggression toward others, or withdrawal may result from the child's emotional and social turmoil. However, as was mentioned above, it is important to remember that negative behaviors may arise from vastly different reasons than experiences of abuse or neglect (e.g., biochemical or physiological factors).

There are many instruments available to assess a child's emotional and social functioning. Salvia and Ysseldyke (1991) suggest several ways in which personality variables may be measured. The use of Rating Scales was discussed above under "Behavioral Assessment" and is applicable here as well. A second approach, using projective techniques, asks students to respond to vague or ambiguous stimuli such as inkblots or pictures, draw pictures, or express themselves through the use of puppets or dolls. The responses are then interpreted by a person trained in such procedures. A third approach is to administer personality inventories or questionnaires that vary in their focus. Some may measure self-concept or learning style, while others are intended to indicate the possible presence of mental illness. These latter instruments are generally lengthy and present the individual taking them with a substantial reading load, both in terms of how much there is to read and in terms of how complex and abstract many of the ideas are. Thus, many such inventories are not suitable for individuals with low literacy. Furthermore, as Berdine and Meyer (1987) remark, "Many of these measures suffer from technical inadequacies and yield esoteric results that are difficult to translate into treatment goals" (p. 144). For this reason, while information gathered through these instruments may help the assessment team understand the student more fully, information collected through approaches such as direct observation and interviews may be more useful and reliable.

— by Betsy W. Waterman, Ph.D.
State University of New York
at Oswego

Part Three

Dyslexia and
Other Academic Skills
Disorders

Chapter 10

Facts about Dyslexia

Developmental dyslexia is a specific learning disability characterized by difficulty in learning to read. Some dyslexics also may have difficulty learning to write, to spell, and, sometimes, to speak or to work with numbers. We do not know for sure what causes dyslexia, but we do know that it affects children who are physically and emotionally healthy, academically capable, and who come from good home environments. In fact, many dyslexics have the advantages of excellent schools, high mental ability, and parents who are well-educated and value learning.

School children are subject to a broad range of reading problems and researchers have discovered the causes of many problems. Today, most teachers accept these research findings and use them in planning their instruction, but there remains a small group of children who have difficulty in learning to read for no apparent reason. These children are called dyslexic. Although estimates of the prevalence of dyslexia are hard to find, some researchers estimate that as many as 15 percent of American students may be classified as dyslexic.

Defining Dyslexia

Over the years, the term dyslexia has been given a variety of definitions, and for this reason, many teachers have resisted using the

This chapter contains text excerpted from National Institute of Child Health and Human Development, NIH Pub No. 93-3534, April 1993, and a bibliography compiled by the Orton Dyslexia Society, © 1993, reprinted with permission.

term at all. Instead, they have used such terms as "reading disability" or "learning disability" to describe conditions more correctly designated as dyslexia. Although there is no universally recognized definition of dyslexia, the one presented by the World Federation of Neurology has won broad respect: "A disorder manifested by difficulty in learning to read despite conventional instruction, adequate intelligence and sociocultural opportunity."

Symptoms

Children with dyslexia are not all alike. The only trait they share is that they read at levels significantly lower than is typical for children of their age and intelligence. This reading lag usually is described in terms of grade level. For example, a fourth grader who is reading at a second grade level is said to be two years behind in reading. (Such a child may or may not be dyslexic; there are many nondyslexic children who experience problems in reading.)

Referring to grade level as a measure of reading is convenient but it can be misleading. A student who has a two year lag when he is in fourth grade has a much more serious problem than a tenth grader with a two-year lag. The fourth grader has learned few of the reading skills which have been taught in the early grades, while the tenth grader, by this measure, has mastered eight years or 80 percent of the skills needed to be a successful reader.

Samuel T. Orton, a neurologist who became interested in the problems of learning to read in the 1920s, was one of the first scientific investigators of dyslexia. In his work with students in Iowa and New York, he found that dyslexics commonly have one or more of the following problems:

- difficulty in learning and remembering printed words;
- letter reversal (b for d, p for q) and number reversals (6 for 9) and changed order of letters in words (tar for rat, quite for quiet) or numbers (12 for 21);
- leaving out or inserting words while reading;
- confusing vowel sounds or substituting one consonant for another;
- persistent spelling errors;
- difficulty in writing.

Orton noted that many dyslexics are left-handed or ambidextrous and that they often have trouble telling left from right. Other symptoms he observed include: (a) delayed or inadequate speech; (b) trouble with picking the right word to fit the meaning desired when speaking; (c) problems with direction (up and down) and time (before and after, yesterday and tomorrow); and (d) clumsiness, awkwardness in using hands, and illegible handwriting. Orton also found that more boys than girls show these symptoms and that dyslexia often runs in families. Fortunately, most dyslexics have only a few of these problems, but the presence of even one is sufficient to create unique educational needs.

Possible Causes

When researchers first began searching for the cause of dyslexia, they looked for one factor as the exclusive source of the problem. Now most experts agree that a number of factors probably work in combination to produce the disorder. Possible causes of dyslexia may be grouped under three broad categories: educational, psychological, and biological.

Educational Causes

Teaching Methods. Some experts believe that dyslexia is caused by the methods used to teach reading. In particular, they blame the whole-word (look-say) method that teaches children to recognize words as units rather than by sounding out letters. These experts think that the phonetic method, which teaches children the names of letters and their sounds first, provides a better foundation for reading. They claim that the child who learns to read by the phonetic method will be able to learn new words easily and to recognize words in print that are unfamiliar as well as to spell words in written form after hearing them pronounced. Other reading authorities believe that combining the whole-word and the phonetic approaches is the most effective way to teach reading. Using this method children memorize many words as units, but they also learn to apply phonetic rules to new words. Whatever method they support, experts who think that instructional practices may cause dyslexia agree that strengthening the beginning reading programs in all schools would significantly decrease the number and the severity of reading problems among school children.

Nature of the English Language. Many common English words do not follow phonetic principles, and learning to read and to spell these words can be difficult, especially for the dyslexic. Words such as cough, was, where, and laugh are typical of those words that must be memorized since they cannot be sounded out. While such words undoubtedly contribute to reading problems, they constitute only a small percent of words in English and so cannot be considered a primary cause of dyslexia.

Intelligence Tests. The commonly accepted definition of dyslexia as a reading disability affecting children of normal intelligence is based on the assumption that we can measure intelligence with a fair degree of accuracy. Intelligence test results, usually referred to as IQ scores, must be interpreted carefully. IQ scores may be affected by factors other than intelligence. Those IQ tests which require the child to read or write extensively pose special problems for the dyslexic. Scores from such tests may reflect poor language skills rather than actual intelligence. Even those IQ tests that are individually administered and demand little or no reading and writing may fail to give a fair measure of intelligence; dyslexics often develop negative attitudes toward all testing situations. In addition, conditions such as noise, fatigue, or events immediately preceding the testing session may adversely affect test results. With such a range of possible influences on IQ scores, we must regard these scores as at best, an estimate of the range of the child's scholastic aptitude, and at worst, a meaningless number that can unjustly label the student.

Psychological Causes

Some researchers attribute dyslexia to psychological or emotional disturbances resulting from inconsistent discipline, absence of a parent, frequent change of schools, poor relationships with teachers or other causes. Obviously a child who is unhappy, angry, or disappointed with his or her relations with parents or other children may have trouble learning. Sometimes such a child is labeled lazy or stupid by parents and friends—even by teachers and doctors. Emotional problems may result from rather than cause reading problems. Although emotional stress may not produce dyslexia, stress can aggravate any learning problem. Any effective method of treatment must deal with the emotional scars of dyslexia.

Biological Causes

A number of investigators believe that dyslexia results from alterations in the function of specific parts of the brain. They claim that certain brain areas in dyslexic children develop more slowly than is the case for normal children, and that dyslexia results from a simple lag in brain maturation. Others consider the high rate of left-handedness in dyslexics as an indication of differences in brain function. This theory has been widely debated, but recent evidence indicates that it may have some validity. Another theory is that dyslexia is caused by disorders in the structure of the brain. Few researchers accepted this theory until very recently when brains of dyslexics began to be subjected to post-mortem examination. These examinations have revealed characteristic disorders of brain development. It now seems likely that structure disorders may account for a significant number of cases of severe dyslexia.

Genetics probably play a role as well. Some studies have found that 50 percent or more of affected children come from families with histories of dyslexia or related disorders. The fact that more boys than girls are affected means that nongenetic biological factors as well as environmental/sociological factors could contribute to the problem.

Treatment

Educators and psychologists generally agree that the remedial focus should be on the specific learning problems of dyslexic children. Therefore, the usual treatment approach is to modify teaching methods and the educational environment. Just as no two children with dyslexia are exactly alike, the teaching methods used are likewise varied.

Children suspected of being dyslexic should be tested by trained educational specialists or psychologists. By using a variety of tests, the examiners are able to identify the types of mistakes the child commonly makes. The examiner is then able to diagnose the problem and if the child is dyslexic, make specific recommendations for treatment such as tutoring, summer school, speech therapy, or placement in special classes. The examiner may also recommend specific remedial approaches. Since no method is equally effective for all children, remediation should be individually designed for each child. The child's educational strengths and weaknesses, estimated scholastic aptitude (IQ), behavior patterns, and learning style, along with the suspected causes of the dyslexia, should all be considered when developing a treatment plan. The plan should spell out those skills the child is expected to master in a specific time period, and it should describe the methods and materials that will be used to help the child achieve those goals.

Treatment programs for dyslexic children fall into three general categories: developmental, corrective, and remedial. Some programs combine elements from more than one category.

The developmental approach is sometimes described as a "more of the same" approach: Teachers use the methods that have been previously used believing that these methods are sound, but that the child needs extra time and attention. Small-group or tutorial sessions in which the teacher can work on reading with each child allow for individual attention. Some researchers and educators believe, however, that this method is not effective for many children.

The corrective reading approach also uses small groups in tutorial sessions, but it emphasizes the child's assets and interests. Those who use this method hope to encourage children to rely on their own special abilities to overcome their difficulties.

The third approach, called remedial, was developed primarily to deal with shortcomings of the first two methods. Proponents of this method try to resolve the specific educational and psychological problems that interfere with learning. The instructor recognizes a child's assets but directs teaching mainly at the child's deficiencies. Remedial teachers consider it essential to determine the skills that are the most difficult and then to apply individualized techniques in a structured, sequential way to remedy deficits in those skills. Material is organized logically and reflects the nature of the English language. Many educators advocate a multisensory approach, involving all of the child's senses to reinforce learning: Listening to the way a letter or word sounds; seeing the way a letter or word looks; and feeling the movement of hand or mouth muscles in producing a spoken or written letter, word or sound.

Prognosis

For dyslexic children, the prognosis is mixed. The disability affects such a range of children and presents such a diversity of symptoms and such degrees of severity that predictions are hard to make.

Parents of dyslexic children may be told such things as "the child will read when he is ready" or "she'll soon outgrow it." Comments like these fail to recognize the seriousness of the problem. Recent research shows that dyslexia does not go away, that it is not outgrown and that extra doses of traditional teaching have little impact.

Fortunately, educators are becoming more aware of the complexities of dyslexia, placing greater emphasis on choosing the most appropriate teaching method for each child. Teachers are more willing to provide remedial teaching over longer periods of time, whereas prior practice often has been to cut off services if observable changes fail to occur in a limited time. Some dyslexics improve quickly, others make steady but very slow progress, and still others are highly resistant to instruction. Many have persistent spelling problems. Some acquire a basic reading skill but cannot read fluently.

A child's ability to conquer dyslexia depends on many things. An appropriate remedial program is critical. However, environmental and social conditions can undermine any treatment program. The child's relationships with family, peers, and teachers have a major effect on the outcome of instruction. In a supportive atmosphere, a child's chance of success is enhanced. Attitudes such as "expectancy," the degree to which a teacher expects a child to learn, are important. Children who sense that they are not expected to succeed seldom do. Since slight progress in reading ability can make an enormous difference in academic success and vocational pursuits, children need to know that they are expected to progress.

The earlier dyslexia is diagnosed and treatment started, the greater the chance that the child will acquire adequate language skills. Untreated problems are compounded by the time a child reaches the upper grades, making successful treatment more difficult. Older students may be less motivated because of repeated failure, adding another obstacle to the course of treatment. The time at which remediation is given also affects a dyslexic's chances. Often, remedial programs are offered only in the early grades even though they may be needed through high school and college. Remedial programs should be available as long as the student makes gains and is motivated to learn. Adults can make significant progress, too, although there are fewer programs for older students.

A dyslexic child's personality and motivation may influence the severity of the condition. Because success in reading is so vital to a child, dyslexia can affect his or her emotional adjustment. Repeated failure takes its toll. The child with dyslexia may react to repeated failure with anger, guilt, depression, resignation, and even total loss of hope and ambition; he or she may require counseling to overcome these emotional consequences of dyslexia. With help a dyslexic child can make gains but the assistance must be timely and thorough, dealing with everything that affects progress. For the child whose dyslexia is identified early, with supportive family and friends, with a strong self-image, and with a proper remedial program of sufficient length, the prognosis is good.

Books on Dyslexia

Books of Interest to Teachers

Ansara, A. (1982). The Orton-Gillingham approach to remediation in developmental dyslexia. In R.N. Malatesha & P.G. Aaron (Eds.), *Reading Disorders: Varieties and Treatments*. New York: Academic Press.

Chall, J. (1967). *Learning to Read: The Great Debate*. New York: McGraw-Hill.

Chall, J. (1983). *Learning to Read: The Great Debate*. (Updated edition.) New York: McGraw-Hill.

Childs, S.B., (Ed.) (1968). *Education and Specific Language Disability: The Papers of Anna Gillingham, M.A.* Baltimore: The Orton Dyslexia Society.

Clark, D. B. (1988). *Dyslexia: Theory and Practice of Remedial Instruction*. Baltimore: York Press.

Critchley, M. (1968). *The Dyslexic Child*. Springfield, IL: Charles C. Thomas.

Critchley, M., & Critchley, E. (1978). *Dyslexia Defined*. Chichester, Sussex, Great Britain: R.J. Acford, Limited.

Crosby, R.M.N., & Liston, R.A. (1976). *The Waysiders: A New Approach to Reading and the Dyslexic Child*. New York: John Day.

Gerber, A. (1993). *Language-related Learning Disabilities: Their Nature and Treatment*. Baltimore: Brookes.

Gillingham, A., & Stillman, B. (1956). *Remedial Training for Children with Specific Disability in Reading, Spelling and Penmanship* (5th ed.). Cambridge, MA: Educators Publishing Service.

Goldberg, H.K., & Schiffman, G. (1972). *Dyslexia: Problems of Reading Disabilities*. New York: Grune & Stratton.

Goldberg, H.K., Schiffman, G.B., & Bender, M. (1983). *Dyslexia: Interdisciplinary Approaches to Reading Disabilities*. New York: Grune & Stratton.

Hutson, A.M. (1987). *Common Sense About Dyslexia*. Latham, MD: Madison Books.

Lyman, D.E. (1986). *Making the Words Stand Still*. Boston: Houghton-Mifflin.

Malatesha, R.N., & Aaron, P.G. (1982). *Reading Disorders: Varieties and Treatments*. New York: Academic Press.

Books of Interest to Parents and Teachers

Brutten, M., Richardson, S.O., & Mangel, C. (1979). *Something's Wrong with My Child*. New York: Harcourt Brace Jovanovich.

Clarke, L. (1973). *Can't Read, Can't Write, Can't Talk Too Good,* Either. New York: Walker.

Cordoni, B. (1990). *Living with a Learning Disability* (Rev. Ed.). Carbondale, IL: Southern Illinois University Press.

Duane, D.D., & Rawson, M.B. (Eds.). (1977). *Developmental Dyslexia*. New York: Insight Publishing.

Duane, D.D., & Rome, P.D. (Eds.) (1977). *The Dyslexic Child*. Cambridge, MA: Educators Publishing Service.

Garnett, K., & LaPorta, S. (1984). *Dispelling the Myths: College Students and Learning Disabilities*. New York: Hunter College.

Hampshire, S. (1982). *Susan's Story*. New York: St. Martin's Press.

Healy, J. (1990). *Endangered Minds: Why Our Children Don't Think*. New York: Simon and Schuster.

Levine, M. (1990). *Keeping a Head in School*. Cambridge, MA: Educators Publishing Service.

MacCracken, M. (1986). *Turnabout Children*. Boston: Little, Brown & Co.

McGuinness, D. (1985). *When Children Don't Learn*. New York: Basic Books.

Miles, T.R., & Gilroy, E. (1986). Dyslexia at College. New York: Methuen.

Miles, T.R., & Miles, E. (1983). *Help for Dyslexic Children*. London: Methuen.

Osman, B.B. (1982). *No One to Play With: The Social Side of Learning Disabilities*. New York: Random House.

Rawson, M.B. (1988). *The Many Faces of Dyslexia*. Baltimore: The Orton Dyslexia Society.

Silver, L.B. (1984). *The Misunderstood Child*. New York: McGraw-Hill.

Simpson, E. (1979). *Reversals: A Personal Account of Victory Over Dyslexia*. New York: Houghton-Mifflin.

Smith, S. (1978). *No Easy Answers: The Learning Disabled Child*. Washington, DC: USDHEW, National Institute of Mental Health.

Stevens, S.H. (1991). *Classroom Success for the Learning Disabled*. Winston-Salem, NC: Blair.

Stevens, S.H. (1991). *The Learning Disabled Child: Ways that Parents Can Help*. Winston-Salem, NC: Blair.

Stuart, M. (1988). *Personal Insights into the World of Dyslexia*. Cambridge, MA: Educators Publishing Service.

Vail, P.L. (1987). *Smart Kids with School Problems*. New York: E. P. Dutton.

Vail, P.L. (1990). *About Dyslexia: Unraveling the Myth*. Rosemont, NJ: Modern Learning Press.

Vail, P.L. (1991). *Common Ground: Whole Language and Phonics Working Together*. Rosemont, NJ: Modern Learning Press.

Books of Interest to Researchers and Teachers

Aaron, P.G., & Joshi, R.M. (1992). *Reading Problems: Consultation and Remediation*. New York: Guilford Press.

Ansara, A., Geschwind, N., Galaburda, A., Albert, M., & Gartrell, N. (1981). *Sex Differences in Dyslexia*. Baltimore: The Orton Dyslexia Society.

Benton, A.L., & Pearl, D. (Eds.) (1978). *Dyslexia: An Appraisal of Current Knowledge*. New York: Oxford University Press.

Boder, E. (1973). Developmental dyslexia: a diagnostic approach based on three atypical reading-spelling patterns. *Developmental Medicine and Child Neurology*, 15, 663–687.

Downing, J., & Leong, C.K. (1982). *Psychology of Reading*. New York: Macmillan. (See chapter 15, "Specific Reading Disability").

Ellis, A.W. (1984). *Reading, Writing and Dyslexia: A Cognitive Analysis*. London: Lawrence Erlbaum Associates.

Gray, D.. & Kavanaugh, J. (Eds.). (1989). *Biobehavioral Measures of Dyslexia*. Baltimore: York Press.

Hynd, G., & Cohen, M. (1983). *Dyslexia: Neuropsychological Theory, Research, and Clinical Differentiation*. New York: Grune & Stratton.

Kline, C.L. (1982). Dyslexia in adolescents, In R.N. Malatesha & P.G. Aaron (Eds.). *Reading Disorders: Varieties and Treatments*. New York: Academic Press.

Liberman, I.Y., & Mann, V.A. (1981). Should reading instruction and remediation vary with the sex of the child? In A. Ansara et al (Eds.), *Sex Differences in Dyslexia*. Towson, MD: The Orton Dyslexia Society.

Lyon, G.R., Gray, D.B., Kavanaugh, J.F., & Krasnegor, N.A. (1993). *Better Understanding Learning Disabilities: New Views From Research and Their Implications for Education and Public Policies*. Baltimore: Brookes.

Money, J. (1966). *The Disabled Reader*. Baltimore: Johns Hopkins Press.

Myklebust, H. (1978). *Progress in Learning Disabilities* (Volume IV). New York: Grune & Stratton.

Orton Dyslexia Society (1987). *Intimacy with Language*. (Proceedings of The Orton Dyslexia Society Symposium on Dyslexia and Evolving Educational Patterns.)

Orton, S.T. (1937). *Reading, Writing and Speech Problems in Children*. New York: W. W. Norton.

Pavlidis, G. T. (Ed.). (1990). *Perspectives on Dyslexia* (Vol. 1-2). New York: Wiley and Sons.

Pavlidis, G.T., & Miles, T.R. (1981). *Dyslexia Research and its Applications to Education*. New York: John Wiley and Sons.

Sawyer, D.J., & Fox, B.J. (1991). *Phonological Awareness in Reading: The Evolution of Current Perspectives*. New York: Springer-Verlag.

Seymour, P. (1986). *Cognitive Analysis of Dyslexia*. New York: Routledge & Kegan Paul.

Stanovich, K.E. (Ed). (1988). *Children's Reading and the Development of Phonological Awareness*. Detroit: Wayne State University Press.

Thompson, L.J. (1966). *Reading Disability: Developmental Dyslexia*. Springfield, IL: Charles C. Thomas.

Valett, R.E. (1980). *Dyslexia: A Neuropsychological Approach to Educating Children with Severe Reading Disabilities*. Belmont, CA: Fearon-Pitman.

Vellutino, F.R. (1979). *Dyslexia: Theory and Research*. Cambridge, MA: MIT Press.

West, T.G. (1991). *In the Mind's Eye: Visual Thinkers, Gifted People with Learning Difficulties, Computer Images, and the Ironies of Creativity*. Buffalo: Prometheus Books.

Young, P., & Tyre, C. (1983). *Dyslexia or Illiteracy: Realizing the Right to Read*. Bury St. Edmunds, Suffolk, GB: St. Edmundsbury Press.

Note

Parents and teachers are encouraged to read *PERSPECTIVES*, the quarterly newsletter of The Orton Dyslexia Society. Parents, teachers and researchers will also want to read the journal, *Annals of Dyslexia* (formerly "Bulletin of The Orton Society"), published annually and containing timely articles on current research and practice in the field of dyslexia. For further information contact:

The Orton Dyslexia Society
Chester Building, Suite 382
8600 LaSalle Road
Baltimore, MD 21286-2044
Telephone: (410) 296-0232

—Bibliography compiled by
Marcia Henry, Ph.D., July 1993

Chapter 11

Academic Interventions for Children with Dyslexia Who Have Phonological Core Deficits

Overview

Approximately 3% to 6% of all school-aged children are believed to have developmental reading disabilities, or dyslexia. In fact, almost 50% of children receiving special education have learning disabilities, and dyslexia is the most prevalent form. Consequently, dyslexia has been given considerable attention by researchers and extensive literature exists on instruction and remediation methods.

Dyslexia is a neurocognitive deficit that is specifically related to the reading and spelling processes. Typically, children classified as dyslexic are reported to be bright and capable in other intellectual domains. Current research indicates that the vast majority of children with dyslexia have phonological core deficits. The severity of the phonological deficits varies across individuals, and children with these deficits have been shown to make significantly less progress in basic word reading skills compared to children with equivalent IQs. For example some experts report that between ages 9 and 19, children with dyslexia who have phonological deficits improve slightly more than one grade level in reading, while other children with learning disabilities (LD) in the same classroom improve about six grade levels. Without direct instruction in phonemic awareness and sound-symbol correspondences, these children generally fail to attain adequate reading levels.

ERIC Digest, #E539, EDO–EC–95–2, August 1995.

Definition

Phonological core deficits entail difficulty making use of phonological information when processing written and oral language. The major components of phonological deficits involve phonemic awareness, sound-symbol relations, and storage and retrieval of phonological information in memory. Problems with phonemic awareness are most prevalent and can coexist with difficulties in storage and retrieval among children with dyslexia who have phonological deficits.

Phonemic awareness refers to one's understanding of and access to the sound structure of language. For example, children with dyslexia have difficulty segmenting words into individual syllables or phonemes and have trouble blending speech sounds into words.

Storage of phonological information during reading involves creating a sound-based representation of written words in working memory. Deficits in the storage of phonological information result in faulty representations in memory that lead to inaccurate applications of sound rules during reading tasks.

Retrieval of phonological information from long-term memory refers to how the child remembers pronunciations of letters, word segments, or entire words. Children with dyslexia may have difficulty in this area, which leads to slow and inaccurate recall of phonological codes from memory.

Classification and Identification

Historically, classification criteria for developmental dyslexia have been vague and, consequently, open to interpretation. For example, according to the *Diagnostic and Statistical Manual of Mental Disorders*, revised 3rd edition (DSM-III-R), developmental reading disorder (dyslexia) may be diagnosed if reading achievement is "markedly below" expected level; interferes with academic achievement or daily living skills, and is not due to a defect in vision, hearing, or a neurological disorder. Because of such imprecise guidelines, educators and clinicians use a wide variety of criteria when defining dyslexia. School psychologists classify children based on federal and state learning disability placement criteria. The federal guidelines for LD placement are as follows:

1. Disorder in one or more of the basic psychological processes (memory, auditory perception, visual perception oral language, and thinking).

2. Difficulty in learning (speaking, listening, writing, reading, and mathematics).

3. Problem is not primarily due to other causes (visual or hearing impairment, motor disabilities, mental retardation, emotional disturbance, or economic environment or cultural disadvantage).

4. Severe discrepancy between apparent potential and actual achievement.

While the federal guidelines are more specific than the DSM-III-R criteria, they are still rather nonspecific. Consequently, eligibility criteria for LD services for reading disabilities vary from state to state. Fortunately, there is some general agreement among educators, clinicians, and researchers in terms of identifying phonological deficits in children with dyslexia. Phonological processing impairment is generally identified by significantly impaired performance (generally, a standard score less than 85) on phonological processing tasks. Table 11.1 includes some assessment measures that may be used to identify these phonological core deficits.

Suggested Interventions

- Teach metacognitive strategies. Teach children similarities and differences between speech sounds and visual patterns across words.

- Provide direct instruction in language analysis and the alphabetic code. Give explicit instruction in segmenting and blending speech sounds. Teach children to process progressively larger chunks of words.

- Use techniques that make phonemes more concrete. For example, phonemes and syllables can be represented with blocks where children can be taught how to add, omit, substitute, and rearrange phonemes in words.

- Make the usefulness of metacognitive skills explicit in reading. Have children practice them. Try modeling skills in various reading contexts. Review previous reading lessons and relate to current lessons.

- Discuss the specific purposes and goals of each reading lesson. Teach children how metacognitive skills should be applied.

- Provide regular practice with reading materials that are contextually meaningful. Include many words that children can decode. Using books that contain many words children cannot decode may lead to frustration and guessing, which is counterproductive.

- Teach for automaticity. As basic decoding skills are mastered, regularly expose children to decodable words so that these words become automatically accessible. As a core sight vocabulary is acquired, expose children to more irregular words to increase reading accuracy. Reading-while-listening and repeated reading are useful techniques for developing fluency.

Table 11.1. Measures that May be Used to Identify Phonological Core Deficits

Features	Assessment Techniques
General reading ability	Metropolitan Achievement Tests-Reading Gray Oral Reading Tests, 3rd Ed. WRAT-R-Reading WRMT-Word Identification
Storage and Retrieval	SB-4-Memory for Sentences Verbal Selective Reminding Test Rapid Automatized Naming Test Boston Naming Test
Phonological awareness	WRMT-Word Attack Test of Awareness of Language Segments (TALS) Test of Auditory Analysis Skills (TAAS) Lindamood Auditory Conceptualization Test Decoding Skills Test

- Teach for comprehension. Try introducing conceptually important vocabulary prior to initial reading and have children retell
  the story and answer questions regarding implicit and explicit
  content. Teach children the main components of most stories
  (i.e., character, setting, etc.) and how to identify and use these
  components to help them remember the story.

- Teach reading and spelling in conjunction. Teach children the
  relationship between spelling and reading and how to correctly
  spell the words they read. Provide positive explicit and corrective feedback. Reinforce attempts as well as successes. Direct
  instruction and teacher-child interactions should be emphasized.

Resources for Teachers

Adams, M.J. (1990). *Beginning reading instruction in the United States*. ERIC Digest. Reston, VA: ERIC Clearinghouse on Disabilities and Gifted Education. ED321250

Bradey, S., & Shankweller, D. (Eds.) (1991). *Phonological processes in literacy*. Mahwah, NJ: Lawrence Erlbaum Associates.

Lyon, G.R., Gray, D.B., Kavanagh, J.F., & Krasnegor, N.A. (Eds.) (1995). *Better understanding learning disabilities: New views from research and their implications for education and public policies*. Baltimore: Paul H. Brookes Publishing Company.

Stahl, S.A. (1990). *Beginning to read: Thinking and learning about print: A summary*. Cambridge, MA: University of Illinois Center for the Study of Reading. ED315740

Wong, B.Y.L. (1991). *Learning about learning disabilities*. San Diego: Academic Press.

—by Julie A. Frost and Michael J. Emery

Chapter 12

Mullisensory Approaches to Working with Dyslexic Students

Introduction

Orton, Gillingham, and Stillman showed a way through the torturous barricades [faced by dyslexics who are learning to read] and, because they were not static thinkers, probably would have relished the other openings which have emerged from the original passage. Their disciples taught disciples and, as the years have gone along, their theme remains constant but the practice takes on many forms. Each of those will, in turn, produce other forms. All the while, real people have been helped through the barricades. [This chapter presents] a sampling of the forms.

Texas Scottish Rite Hospital for Children

In 1993, it is estimated that approximately 27 million Americans are functionally illiterate. This is a staggering statistic. It has called many citizens, and especially educators, to develop programs throughout the country that work toward overcoming this costly national problem. However, at Texas Scottish Rite Hospital for Children (TSRHC) in Dallas, Texas, the staff has worked diligently since 1965 to help children diagnosed as dyslexic to remediate their language learning differences.

Taken from "Through the Barricades: Multisensory Approaches," in *Perspectives*, published by the Orton Dyslexia Society, Suite 382, Chester Building, 8600 LaSalle Road, Baltimore MD 21286-2044; reprinted with permission.

At that time Lucius Waites, M.D., was asked to join the TSRHC staff. He and an interdisciplinary team initiated a "remedial language training" program to teach children in small groups. An intense study of several hundred children for the next ten years led to the development of a complete curriculum for teaching written language skills and the structure of written language.

Meanwhile, Aylett R. Cox and her staff at the hospital adapted, modified, structured, and sequenced the original material of Anna Gillingham. The result was *Alphabetic Phonics*. In 1985, the Texas legislature passed the "dyslexia laws," which mandated screening for dyslexia and the training of teachers to help students identified as being "at risk" for dyslexia.

Today, the dyslexia program at the hospital has grown to include the *Dyslexia Training Program*, a series of video tapes and accompanying written materials, designed to teach the structure of written English to elementary school-aged children in public schools who would not otherwise receive appropriate remediation. A veteran therapist teaches and directs the lesson while a facilitating team teacher in the classroom assists and monitors the students' activities throughout the lesson.

In 1992, *The Literacy Program* videotaped series was developed to provide classroom remediation for the dyslexic student at the secondary school level and adults with literacy difficulties. This program moves at a much faster pace and includes extension activities designed for the special needs of this specific target audience of older students.

Teacher Training returned to TSRHC in 1987. An intensive two year training program prepares teachers to step out of "the teaching mode" and into the more flexible role of the person who redesigns and implements the daily lessons to meet the specific requirements of the students while teaching the structure of English, using multisensory techniques and strategies that encourage the daily success of the students.

The *Dyslexia Training Program and Alphabetic Phonics* curricula are multisensory and based on the Orton-Gillingham approach for teaching phonics and the structure of the written English language. They are phonetic programs which teach alphabet and dictionary skills, reading accuracy, cursive handwriting, spelling skills. expression, listening and reading comprehension by engaging the visual, auditory, and kinesthetic modalities simultaneously.

This basic English language training program can be taught to individuals or small groups in daily one-hour sessions. Each lesson is structured to include ten different activities taught in the same daily sequence, deliberately alternating modalities. The methodology and philosophy of teaching engage strategies designed to meet the specific needs of the dyslexic learner. A lesson includes the following activities:

- Language Development: Aspects of the development of our language. Students are taught that they can learn to read, write and spell 80 percent of standard English if they learn the scientific, alphabetic, phonetic code on which our language is based.

- Alphabet: Alphabet study including identification, sequencing, accent and rhythm, alphabetizing, dictionary, and reference book skills, leads to efficient usage of the alphabetic symbol system of our language.

- Review of Graphemes: Reinforcement activity to identify and instantly name each grapheme, then translate the letter or letter cluster into the appropriate speech sounds.

- Review of Phonemes: Reinforcement activity to instantly translate each phoneme into the letter or letters which most often represent that sound in the initial, medial, or final position in a base word or derivative.

- Multisensory Introduction of New Learning: Letters and letter clusters are introduced for reading, writing, and spelling through eight multisensory linkages. Concepts, including rules and formulas, are also introduced during this portion of the daily lesson.

- Reading Practice: Practice in applying decoding skills, syllable division formulas, and reading fluency in a reading experience activity.

- Handwriting Practice: Cursive handwriting is employed throughout the curriculum, with emphasis on the multisensory writing technique of naming each letter before it is written. Near and far point copying skills are also taught and practiced during this portion of the lesson.

- Spelling Practice: Daily practice in spelling involves the student's application of the sound-symbol relationship. Phonemic segmentation, application of spelling generalizations, practice in spelling derivatives, and dictation are the building blocks of this important and difficult portion of the lesson.

- Daily Review: A brief review of the day's new discoveries, as well as previous concepts which were not practiced during other portions of the lesson, encourages students by allowing them to rehearse the concepts they have learned.

- Expression, Listening, and Reading Comprehension: Practice in organization of thoughts, strategies for understanding and expressing ideas, and listening to high interest selections read by the instructor encourages application of the language skills that were taught and practiced during the earlier activities in the day's lesson. At the most advanced levels the same strategies are applied to composition and reading comprehension.

The staff at Texas Scottish Rite Hospital for Children endeavors to provide essential services for the dyslexic child who deserves the opportunity to reach his potential in life.

The Herman Method Institute

The Herman Method Institute is a private educational organization dedicated to serving learning-disabled-dyslexic (LDD) students. The Institute's primary emphasis is to:

- conduct seminars and practicums for educators in the learning disability field;

- provide school districts with a cost efficient multisensory reading curriculum geared to the public school setting (namely, "The Herman Method for Reversing Reading Failure" described below);

- instruct, and then supervise, trained Herman Method Consultants who present workshops for educators of LDD students;

- develop instructional techniques and materials to supplement and update "The Herman Method for Reversing Reading Failure";

- complete a three-year longitudinal study in conjunction with researchers from Baylor University to: (a) determine if differential effects occur in the reading growth of LDD students when teachers are trained in and use special instructional methods, and (b) ascertain what constitutes an effective educational prescription for LDD students.

The Herman Method for Reversing Reading Failure is a remedial reading, writing and spelling curriculum designed for dyslexic students, ages eight through adult. It evolved from the Orton-Gillingham approach and maintains the integrity of the original model: use of kinesthetic and tactile input while teaching a phonetic, structured, sequential reading curriculum. The Herman Method is unique, and differs from other Orton Gillingham approaches by incorporating the following instructional techniques and strategies:

- deliberate, simultaneous input to both cerebral hemispheres: bimanual/bipedal writing, mirror feedback, multisensory left-to-right tracking, rhythmic activities;

- specific instructional techniques to help students compensate for auditory as well as visual misperceptions;

- metronomic pacing to encourage fluency in reading and writing;

- a variety of review opportunities to maintain student interest and, at the same time, offer the intensive practice that is essential for retention: phrase, sentence and story reading; software games and activities; instructional filmstrips, word-wheels, sight-word ladders, workbook exercises; and consistent reinforcement with sequences of multisensory/bihemispheric input.

Teacher education is the primary focus of the Herman Method Institute. We have found that school administrators, teachers and boards of education are not insensitive to the needs of dyslexic students. Most school districts have been unable to implement an effective multisensory approach because public schools are burdened with limited budgets that do not allow for extensive and costly teacher-training workshops. The Herman Method Institute offers a three-day teacher education program.

Student success is closely linked to teacher success. No dyslexic student needs to fail. When teachers learn to teach dyslexics, dyslexics will learn to read!

Lindamood-Bell Learning Process

The Lindamood-Bell Learning Process offers diagnosis and treatment of learning disabilities in all ages of individuals. Headquartered in San Luis Obispo, California, they also have centers in Sacramento, San Diego, Kansas City, and Chicago. Lindamood-Bell Directors Patricia Lindamood, Nanci Bell, and Phyllis Lindamood have authored programs to develop three sensory cognitive processes which underlie basic language processing:

- **Language Comprehension and Thinking:** A cause of language comprehension problems is difficulty creating an imaged gestalt—a whole. This weakness causes students to get only "parts" of what they read or hear, and have difficulty following directions and thinking critically. The Visualizing and Verbalizing program presents specific steps for stimulating imagery from single words, to sentences, paragraphs, and pages of content, extending into study skills, writing, and higher order thinking skills.

- **Work Attack, Word Recognition, and Spelling:** A cause of decoding and spelling problems is difficulty in phonological awareness—the ability to judge sounds within words. This weakness causes students to omit, substitute, and reverse sounds and letters when they read and spell. The Lindamood program develops awareness of the motor-kinesthetic features of speech sounds, and these features are labeled to heighten their distinctiveness and enable clear communication about their sequence within single- and multi-syllable words, enabling individuals to grasp and apply the logic of our alphabet system.

- **Visual-Motor Function:** A cause of difficulty with drawing, printing, and handwriting, and following directions is weak visual-motor processing. This weakness causes individuals to miss the gestalt or distort important parts when drawing or copying, and have difficulty organizing their work on the page, using maps and finding their way in unfamiliar territory. The Drawing with Language Program develops the use of language to guide visual-motor problem solving. Students learn to label distance, direction, and types of lines that compose drawings and symbols, and to apply this specific language to guide themselves through a visual motor task.

In addition to offering diagnosis and clinical treatment in these areas, Lindamood-Bell is involved in "workplace literacy," and provides training and consulting for educators. They incorporate the concept of *intensive treatment*—a familiar concept in the medical world which has been implemented in the learning world—and have been extremely effective. In providing services, the primary concern *is the consistency with which treatment produces superior results*. All aspects of clinical interaction are oriented to enhance clients' self-worth, and to develop their trust in their ability to think, reason, and learn.

Orton-Gillingham Academy

There has long been a need to establish standards of training and practice among Orton-Gillingham educators. An advisory board has been convened, hosted by Dyslexia Institute of Minnesota under the leadership of Paula Rome, to develop recommendations for the structure and standards of such a body, tentatively titled the Orton-Gillingham Academy.

The Organizing Committee of the Orton-Gillingham Academy has elected Arlene Sonday as Chair and Sharon Rome as Secretary. Four committees have been designated to gather information and develop recommendations: Philosophy Committee, chaired by Roger Saunders; Administrative Committee, chaired by Amy Bailin; Credentials Committee, chaired by Phyllis Meisel; Curriculum Committee, chaired by Helaine Schupack.

The Orton-Gillingham Academy Organizing Committee has been working in committees and in large group sessions to draft documents which define the Orton-Gillingham Academy philosophy statement, mission statement, by-laws, fee structure, levels of membership, curriculum requirements at each membership level, and procedures for application, review and acceptance of members in the Orton-Gillingham Academy. A review of prepared documents is now in progress. When this process in completed, the Orton-Gillingham Academy will apply for incorporation according to the laws governing educational organizations.

The mission of the Orton-Gillingham Academy is to:

- Promote professional, instructional, and ethical standards of the highest quality for Orton-Gillingham practitioners and instructors through programs which certify practitioners and instructors and accredit programs;

- Insure professional growth of Orton-Gillingham practitioners and instructors by sponsoring continuing education programs which are relevant to teaching practice and which reflect the most current research;

- Expand current knowledge about teaching practice by encouraging research relevant to Orton-Gillingham instructional techniques and teaching strategies;

- Broaden public awareness of the importance and success of the Orton-Gillingham approach in education;

- Broaden public awareness of the nature of dyslexia and the potential of persons affected by it.

Project Read/Language Circle

- Project Read/Language Circle is a mainstream language arts program that provides an alternative to whole word, inductive instruction.

- It is for the child/adolescent who needs a systematic, direct, multisensory learning experience.

- It was designed to be delivered in the regular classroom by the classroom teacher. However, the program is also used by special education and chapter one teachers as well as reading specialists.

- Project Read is taught wherever the child/adolescent with language learning problems receives instruction whether in the regular classroom or in a special setting.

- The classroom teacher is trained by a Project Read Teacher going into the classroom and demonstrating the curriculum and technology with the identified group of learners as the classroom teacher observes. After a period of time the classroom teacher resumes teaching the group. The demonstration teacher returns periodically to work with the group as the classroom teacher observes. Thus the primary training strategy is through model teaching.

- The demonstration teacher is trained through formal training sessions in each "strand" of the program by the authors of the program or their designated consultants.

- Project Read is administered according to the sponsoring department of the district. In many districts it is a collaborative effort between regular and special education (or other special need programs).

- The recommended staff are a Project Read Coordinator and demonstration teachers. Often this is accomplished by redefining the roles and responsibilities of persons already on staff. However, individual teachers certainly can and are implementing this program even if their district/school has not formally adopted it.

- Project Read is funded through various sources depending on the sponsoring department or agency.

- Project Read is cost effective. The cost per Project Read student is 10% of the cost of funding a special education student in a "pull out" program. The majority of students are taught in the regular classroom by the classroom teacher thus reducing the number of students referred for special services.

- Project Read was designed to be an early intervention program for grades one through six; however it can be used with adolescents and adults as well. All "strands" are integrated at all grade levels but specific "strands" are emphasized at certain grade levels.

- Many students need Project Read. Numbers vary from district to district as some populations are more "at risk" than others. The average is about 15-20% of primary age students, 10-12% of intermediate and 5% of secondary students (if the program has been implemented from grade one).

- Project Read has been in existence since 1970 when it was implemented in the Bloomington Public Schools located in a large suburb of Minneapolis, Minnesota. Since its initial implementation, it has been implemented in many districts throughout the nation and Canada.

The Slingerland Approach

The Slingerland Institute is a non-profit, tax-exempt organization, founded in 1977 to carry on the work of Beth H. Slingerland in providing classroom teachers with the techniques, knowledge and understanding necessary for identifying and teaching children with Specific Language Disability (Dyslexia).

The Slingerland Approach is a simultaneous, multisensory approach that begins with a single unit of sight, sound, or thought and proceeds to the more complex. From the very beginning, the emphasis in the Slingerland Approach has been to teach through the intellect. Building understanding of the concepts rather than rote learning helps the intelligent child transfer the knowledge gained to other areas of learning. The child's self-esteem is enhanced as he learns how to learn. The success by the student provides motivation for further learning; his attitude, behavior and personality responds exceptionally well to the positive learning environment created by the use of the Slingerland Approach.

The Slingerland Approach was originally designed as a preventive approach to help the child before failure takes its toll. Its structure, sequence, and thoroughness, however, make it a very successful remedial program for people of all ages. Illiterate adults are now learning to read and write when taught with the Slingerland Approach.

Beth H. Slingerland began her teacher education program in 1960 with graduate-level college credit being offered. Today, The Slingerland Institute sponsors teacher education courses during the summer. Each four-week session presents a totally integrated language approach made up of oral language development, organization, phonics, encoding, decoding, spelling, written expression and reading comprehension. Each eight hour day includes a classroom demonstration with children taught by Slingerland staff teachers. Each participant practices the techniques under staff guidance with an individual child each day. Lectures on phonics, techniques, and background knowledge as well as guidance in making daily plans to meet individual needs are provided by Slingerland directors.

Mrs. Slingerland devised a daily plan for integrating the three modalities of language learning in a structured, sequential manner. It begins with *Learning to Write*, which leads into the *Auditory Approach*. The goal is for the student to be able to do propositional and creative writing. The *Visual Approach* leads to independent reading of the student's choice. This format provides the structure for the linkage of the modalities to take place. It also builds from the single unit to the more complex.

212

Mrs. Slingerland originally chose to use manuscript writing in the first and second grades because the public schools used it in the primary grades. As she continued to work with young children, she saw the value of having them initially learn letter forms that were very similar to the letters they saw in their text books. However, she retained the Orton-Gillingham's use of cursive writing for the older children.

Mrs. Slingerland observed that in both encoding and decoding, the stumbling block most often is the vowel sound. She decided to have the child attend to the vowel sound first, then proceed with blending or unlocking the word. This worked well for most children, so it became part of her approach. Children with severe deficits, however, found it too confusing. So Mrs. Slingerland taught both procedures, relying upon skilled teachers to use the pattern most effective for a particular child.

To prepare the child to read successfully from a book, Mrs. Slingerland devised four preliminary steps in which vocabulary, phrase concept, and eye span are developed with phrases extracted from the reading selection and placed on the board for the reading group to see. These four steps closely parallel the phenomenal way in which language is learned.

Reading from a book begins immediately in first grade with the Slingerland Approach. Motivation to learn to read is perhaps at its highest level at this time. The natural, phenomenal language and the intellect of the child pleads for more "story" than is possible when only limited phonetic elements are used in a reading selection. With the Slingerland Approach, strictly phonetic material is used for instruction only with the severely disabled child.

The purpose of the Slingerland Screening Procedures, also one of Beth Slingerland's contributions, is to screen from among a group of children those who are beginning to show difficulties in the area of language and those with already present specific language disabilities. The screenings can be given by classroom teachers to as many as fifteen students at one time. Each test takes from one to two hours, excluding rest periods to administer. A Slingerland college level screening, authored by Carol Murray, has recently been published.

Beth H. Slingerland remained grateful to Anna Gillingham and Bessie Stillman for their part in her work. Today, the Slingerland Institute continues to recognize the solid foundation from which the Slingerland Approach evolved.

The Spalding Education Foundation: An Overview

The illiteracy rate in the United States continues to climb, signaling the importance of improving the regular education program for all children. The Spalding Method is a unique program designed for the regular classroom that incorporates the use of the Orton phonograms to teach the sounds of the language; multisensory instruction; and intensive, systematic phonics instruction. Dr. Robert Aukerman, in *Approaches to Beginning Reading*, describes the Spalding Method as a total language arts method because it integrates the four essential elements of listening and reading comprehension, speaking. and writing. It was designed to challenge students who have facility with language as well as those who have great difficulty learning. Therefore, it is one answer to the need for an effective regular education program.

The Spalding Education Foundation, a non-profit organization, is committed to the worldwide promotion of the Spalding Method, the certification of qualified instructors and tutors, the ongoing training of teachers, and distribution of materials. It was incorporated in 1986 with Mrs. Romalda Spalding as the chairman and Mr. Warren North as president of the Board of Directors. Mrs. Spalding has been directly involved in both the establishment of the goals and policies of the Foundation.

The Spalding Foundation facilitates courses in 17 states and three countries as well as certifying over 124 instructors. In addition, the Louisiana effort has resulted in a three-year pilot project bringing the method to parishes throughout the state. In Arizona the method has been used very successfully. One of the top five districts has adopted Spalding in kindergarten through eighth grade and their scores are now in the top three in the state.

The Foundation offers beginning, intermediate, and advanced courses in *The Writing Road to Reading*. These courses can be taken for college credit and include teaching comprehension. The Foundation also offers Writing Across the Curriculum in which teachers learn techniques used in narrative, descriptive, and expository writing. In addition, certified Spalding Teacher instructors participate in annual seminars sponsored by the Foundation. Materials needed for instructing teachers and students in *The Writing Road to Reading* are a notebook used for spelling and vocabulary development, a spelling scale to chart progress, comprehension lessons, and quality literature.

Wilson Language Training

The purpose of Wilson Language Training is to assist in the effort to spread the effective and necessary multisensory, structured language methodology, especially in adult education and public school settings.

Wilson Language Training was formed due to the great need for multisensory language teaching. WLT is dedicated to spreading the success of the Wilson Reading System beyond its origin at the Wilson Learning Center in Hopedale, Massachusetts. Wilson Language Training:

- Publishes the Wilson Reading System;
- Provides Wilson Overview Workshops to schools, organizations and literacy providers;
- Conducts Level I Wilson Certified Training in public schools.

The Wilson Reading System is a remedial reading and writing program for individuals with a language-based learning disability. This program is based on Orton-Gillingham philosophy and principles and current phonological coding research. The Wilson Reading System was developed by Barbara A. Wilson at the Wilson Learning Center in Hopedale, MA, resulting from her work at the Massachusetts General Hospital Language Disorders Unit. This program directly teaches the structure of words in the English language so that students master the phonological coding system for reading and spelling. The material is presented in 12 steps in a systematic, sequential and cumulative manner. The teaching techniques utilize visual-auditory-kinesthetic tactile (multisensory) methods. The Wilson Reading System materials include phonetically-controlled readers that are geared for older students. These readers are appropriate for use with any Orton-Gillingham-based program.

Wilson Overview Workshop presentations provide a description of the program for teachers and tutors. Topics presented are: What is Dyslexia?, The Ten Critical Points of the Wilson Program, Description and Sequence of Materials, The Description and Demonstration of the Wilson Lesson Plan, and Student Initiation.

Wilson Level I Training is conducted in public schools. Teachers work with language-learning disabled students under the supervision of a trainer for one academic year (September-June). On-site monthly seminars assist teachers with the implementation of the Wilson program. Pre-post student testing is a requirement. These results have demonstrated significant gains in reading and spelling with students who have been unsuccessful with other teaching methods that did not follow multisensory, structured language principles.

Resource Information

Alphabetic Phonics
(Texas Scottish Rite Hospital for Children, Dyslexia Therapy)
2222 Welborn Street
Dallas, TX 75219-3993
(214) 559-7425
Contact: Connie Burkhalter

The Herman Method Institute
4700 Tyrone Avenue
Sherman Oaks, CA 91423
(818) 784-9566
Contact: Renee Herman

Lindamood-Bell Learning Processes
416 Higuera Street
San Luis Obispo, CA 93401
(805) 541-3836
Contact: Pat Lindamood or Nanci Bell

Orton-Gillingham Academy
1322 7th Street SW
Rochester, MN 55902
(507) 288-5271
Contact: Sharon O'C. Rome

Project Read/Language Circle
P.O. Box 20631
Bloomington, MN 55420
(612) 884-4880
Contact: Victona Greene or Mary Lee Enfield

The Spalding Education Foundation
15410 N. 67th Avenue, Suite 8
Glendale, AZ 85306
(602) 486-5881

Slingerland Institute
One Bellevue Center
411 108th Avenue NE, Suite 230
Bellevue, WA 98004
(206) 453-1190
Contact: Clara McCulloch

Wilson Language Training
162 West Main Street
Millbury, MA 01527
(508) 865-5699
Contact: Barbara A. Wilson

Chapter 13

The Alphabetic Principle

Overview

Proper application of the alphabetic principle rests on an awareness of the internal phonological (and morphophonological) structure
of words that the alphabet represents. Unfortunately for the would-be
reader-writer, such awareness is not an automatic consequence of
speaking a language, because the biological specialization for speech
manages the production and perception of these structures below the
level of consciousness. Not surprisingly, then, awareness of phonological structures is normally lacking in preliterate children and adults;
the degree to which it does exist is the best single predictor of success in learning to read; lack of awareness usually yields to appropriate instruction; and such instruction makes for better readers. That
some children have particular difficulty in developing phonological
awareness (and in learning to read) is apparently to be attributed to
a general deficiency in the phonological component of their natural
capacity for language. Thus, these children are also relatively poor
in short-term memory for verbal information, in perceiving speech in
noise, in producing complex speech patterns, and in finding the words
that name objects. All children will benefit from instruction that is
intelligently designed to show them what the alphabet is about.

From *Phonology and Reading Disability: Solving the Reading Puzzle,*
Isabelle Y. Liberman, Donald Shankweiler, and Alvin M. Liberman, eds. Ann
Arbor: MI, University of Michigan Press, © 1989 by the University of Michi-
gan; reprinted with permission.

For some fifteen years, we have been exploring the sources of the problems beginners encounter in learning to read. Since children are quite fluent in their native language when first encountering the language in print, we began by asking what seemed to us the obvious question: what is required of the child in reading a language but not in speaking or listening to it? The first answer that came to mind, of course, was the discrimination of the visual shapes of the letters. But investigators who had done comprehensive studies of many different aspects of the reading process (see Doehring 1968), or who had compiled exhaustive reviews of the visual factors involved in reading (Benton and Pearl 1978; Stanovich 1982; Vellutino 1979; Vernon 1957), were all in agreement that beginners who were making little progress in learning to read generally showed no significant difficulty in the visual identification of letters.

Beyond letter identification, reading requires mastery of a system that maps letter shapes to units of speech. However, as we noted years ago (Liberman 1973), there is no evidence that children of normal intelligence, given proper instruction, have difficulty in associating individual letters of the alphabet with their appropriate speech equivalents. Perhaps, then, they are defeated by the often complex and irregular relations in English between spelling and language. Surely, the complexities of English spelling do create some problems. But even when the items to be read include only those words that map the sound in a simple, consistent way, many children still fail (Savin 1972).

Learning to identify the letters, learning to associate them with consonant and vowel sounds, learning to cope with the irregularities of English spelling—none of these is the primary obstacle in learning to read. What is it then that makes reading so hard while speech is relatively so easy? In the seventies, we (Liberman 1971; Shankweiler and Liberman 1972) and other investigators (Elkonin 1973; Gleitman and Rozin 1977; Klima 1972; Mattingly 1972) proposed another possible source of difficulty in reading that is not present in speech. Although both reading and speech require some degree of mastery of language, reading requires, in addition, a mastery of the alphabetic principle. This entails an awareness of the internal phonological structure of the words of the language, an awareness that must be more explicit than is ever demanded in the ordinary course of listening and responding to speech. If this is so, it should follow that beginning learners with a weakness in phonological awareness would be at risk.

We here first set forth the considerations that led us to that view, followed by the evidence that supports it. Then we say why we should consider that deficits in awareness of the phonological structure may be only one symptom of a more general underlying deficiency in the phonological component of the beginning reader's capacity for language. Finally we consider the implications for instruction.

Phonology and the Alphabetic Principle

We begin, then, with the assumption that reading by an alphabetic writing system requires mastery of the alphabetic principle. Surprisingly, this assumption, which seems to us a truism, is not accepted by everyone in the field, as we will see. But even among those who think the principle important, many take it—we would say mistake it—to mean simply an understanding by the would-be reader that the discrete letters of the alphabet represent the discrete sounds of speech. Our view (Liberman 1983) is different. As we see it, the letters of the alphabet do not represent sounds as such, but rather the more remote phonological (and morphophonological) segments those sounds convey. This is not to quibble. For surely it must be somewhat confusing to children to be told that the word bag is spelled with three letters, when their ears tell them plainly that it has but one sound. The confusion is only worse confounded if the teacher insists, against the evidence of what the child hears, that bag can be divided into three sounds, and that these can then be "blended" so as to re-form the word. For there is, in fact, no way, with or without the marvels of modern technology, to divide bag into pieces of sound that correspond in any reasonable way to the sounds of the three letters, nor is there any way to synthesize the word by somehow putting the letter sounds together. Though bag does truly consist of three segments—it differs from sag in the first, from big in the second, and from bat in the third—these segments are to be found only in the underlying phonology, not in the surface appearances of the sound (Liberman et al. 1967).

To emphasize that letters stand for sounds also risks making it that much harder for a reader to understand perfectly reasonable aspects of English spelling—for example, cats and dogs, instead of cats and dogz; or bat and batter, instead of bat and badder; or an apple, instead of uh napple; and so on. As for those aspects of English spelling that are most egregiously unreasonable—for example, through, rough, and the like—we confess that even a proper understanding of the alphabetic principle is not likely to be of much help, but then neither will anything else, short of learning about how the language has changed since the orthography was developed. (Such spellings need not be a hindrance if they are introduced only after the more systematic aspects of the orthography have been understood.)

The identification of letters with sounds promotes yet another misunderstanding, this one about the nature of words and how they are perceived. For it accords all too well with the commonplace notion that it is only spoken words that are made of phonological units. Words that come to us via print are incorrectly thought to be different, in that they supposedly can (and perhaps should) be perceived independently of phonology. On this basis, some advise that the reader be taught from the very beginning to skip the phonology (read this as skipping the sound) and go "direct to meaning" (Goodman 1976; Smith 1971). Others grant that going through the phonology—which is taken to mean "sounding it out"—may be useful for the beginning reader, or for the mature reader who encounters a strange word, but they otherwise hold that the putatively "direct" (nonphonological) route is the way to go (Coltheart 1978; Waters, Seidenberg and Bruck 1984).

We believe that these assumptions seriously misconstrue the nature of words and the processes by which they are produced and perceived, in print as in speech. Consider, in this connection, a critical difference between language and all other natural forms of communication. In all the nonlinguistic systems—whether the medium is acoustic, optical, electrical, or chemical—meanings are conveyed by signals that differ holistically, one from another. That is to say that there are no words. The inevitable consequence is that the number of meanings that can be communicated is limited to the number of holistically different signals the animal can produce and perceive, a number that is always quite small. Even if that number can somehow be increased, there is no way of doing it so as to guarantee that the new signals will be immediately recognized as belonging naturally to a system that has a specifically communicative function.

Language is different in a most important way. Meanings are not conveyed directly by signals that differ holistically, but rather by words that are distinct from each other in their internal structure. This structure is formed of a small number of meaningless phonological segments we know as consonants and vowels, and governed according to a highly systematic combinatorial scheme called phonology. The consequence is that words can (and do) number in the tens of thousands. Moreover, there is a perfectly natural basis for accommodating new words, since the phonological system, which all speakers of the language have in common, automatically recognizes a new, but legal, structure as a word that stands ready to have meaning attached to it. It is only because children have this phonological system that they are able to acquire new words and their meanings with such astonishing ease and rapidity (Studdert-Kennedy 1987).

What follows, then, is that phonology governs all words, whether dead, living, or waiting to be born. So, whatever else a word is, and regardless of whether it is spoken or printed, it is always a phonological structure. If listeners or readers correctly perceive a word, they correctly perceive the structure that distinguishes it. They may very well be unsure of its meaning—indeed, may even have got the meaning wrong—but if they have the phonological structure, they have a perfectly adequate basis for ultimately getting its meaning properly sorted out. As for going directly to meaning—that is, independently of phonology—surely that is done when a person sees a picture, for example, or hears the roar of a lion, but not when one perceives a word as it is spoken or read.

From our point of view, then, there is no reason to ask, as some do, whether readers must, or should get to meaning via the phonology. To make sense of this question, one must make three false assumptions. The first is that the meanings can be communicated in language independently of words (that is, phonological structures), but in fact they cannot. The second is that the phonological units that form all words are equivalent to the sounds of speech, but in fact they are not. And the third is that an alphabetic transcription specifies, on a segment by segment basis, how the speech organs are to be articulated and coarticulated so as to produce the sounds of speech, but in fact it does not. What the reader must do is to match the alphabetic transcription to the abstract phonological structure of the word it represents. In the case of a familiar word, this structure and its associated meaning(s) are available in the reader's lexicon; in the case of an unfamiliar word, given a command of the alphabetic principle, the structure is easily formed and thus made ready for whatever meanings may subsequently be attached to it. Once the reader has the phonological form of the word, the appropriate phonetic structure and its associated articulatory movements are automatically available for use in working memory, or for reading aloud if the occasion should call for that.

Phonological Processing in Reading-Writing and in Listening-Speaking

Why is it normally so much harder and less natural to deal with phonological structures in reading and writing than it is in listening and speaking? A serious attempt to answer this question would take us quite deeply into the phonological system and its biology, for the answer requires explaining, among other things, why speech could have evolved in the history of our species but writing systems could not, and why speech can develop in the child without explicit instruction but reading and writing typically cannot (Liberman, in press). Here, we can offer only a truncated account.

Like all members of the animal kingdom, human beings have highly specialized ways of communicating with their fellows. In the human case, and only there, this specialization includes, as a critical component, the phonological system that, as we have seen, makes large vocabularies possible. As this system evolved in the race, and as it develops anew in each child, it employs abstract motor structures—let us call them gestures—that ultimately control the movements of the speech organs (Browman and Goldstein 1985; Liberman and Mattingly 1985; Liberman and Mattingly 1989). These gestures are adapted for one purpose and for one purpose only: the production of strings of consonants and vowels at rates many times more rapid than could otherwise be achieved. These rates, which run about eight to ten per second on average, are managed by precisely overlapping and merging the articulatory movements that produce the phonologically significant aspects of the speech sounds. This coarticulation, as it is called, is a most complex process, but it does not appear so in the normal exercise of speech functions, because it is done automatically and naturally by this aspect of the specialization for language. A consequence is that a neurologically normal child, put in a speech environment, can hardly be prevented from learning to form phonological structures and to exploit coarticulation for that purpose. (Lacking this specialization, nonhuman primates do not, and cannot, learn to produce these structures: this is to say that they cannot produce words.) A more important consequence for our purposes is that to speak a word one need not know how it is spelled. The speaker need only think of the word; the phonological component of his grammar "spells" it for him. Indeed, the automaticity of this specialization makes it that much harder to be aware of how the word is spelled, or even to know that such a thing as spelling exists.

Perception of the speech signal is correspondingly complex and automatic. Given coarticulation, there is no direct correspondence between the phonological structure intended by the speaker and the surface properties of the sound. Most relevant to our concerns is the fact that, as we have so often pointed out, the number of segments in the sound is not equal to the number of segments in the phonological structure it conveys (Liberman et al. 1967). Thus, the three consonants and vowels of a word like bag are so thoroughly coarticulated as to produce a single segment of sound. But this is no problem for listeners, for they have only to rely on their phonological specialization to automatically process the speech signal and recover the coarticulated gestures that caused it (Liberman and Mattingly 1989). It is a problem for would-be readers, however, because, given the complex relation between phonological structure and sound, and the automaticity with which this relation is dealt in speech, they find it just that much harder to be aware that the word does have an internal structure and thus to appreciate why an alphabetic transcription makes sense.

Small wonder then that an alphabetic writing system is such a comparatively recent development in the history of our species. In contrast to the naturally evolved phonological structures it represents, it is an artifact. The development of this artifact had to wait on the discovery—and it was a discovery—that words have an internal structure. Once that discovery was available, someone could and did invent the notion that, by representing the units of that structure with arbitrarily chosen optical shapes, people could read and write all the words of the language—those they were already familiar with and those they had yet to encounter. But they could exploit this wonderful invention only if they understood the discovery on which it was based.

Awareness of Phonological Structure and Reading

Development of Phonological Awareness in Children

Considerations such as these led us at the very outset of our research on reading to suppose that preliterate children would not naturally have made the discovery that underlay the invention of the alphabet, from which it would follow that they would not be prepared to understand and apply the alphabetic principle. So we began to examine developmental trends in phonological awareness by testing the ability of young children to segment words into their constituent elements. We investigated the children's segmentation of spoken words both by syllable and phoneme (Liberman et al. 1974). (The latter class of units of the phonological representation comprise the consonants and vowels. Heretofore we have referred to these only by the general term phonological segments. From now on we will call then phonemes to distinguish them from syllables.) We found that normal preschool

225

children performed rather poorly, but that the phonemes presented the greater difficulty by far.

It was clear from these results that awareness of phoneme segments, the basic units of the alphabetic orthography, is initially harder to achieve than awareness of syllable segments, and develops later, if at all. More relevant to our present purposes, it was also apparent that a large number of children, about 30 percent of our sample, had not attained an understanding of the internal phonemic structure of words, even at the end of a full year in school. Surely, they are the ones we need to worry about, because they are the ones who are deficient in the linguistic awareness that may provide entry into the alphabetic system.

Lack of Phonological Awareness and Reading Failure in Children

Is lack of phonological awareness in fact related to failure in reading and writing? That the answer is yes is strongly supported by studies in a number of languages. In English, the relation has been found, for example, in studies by Blachman (1984), Bradley and Bryant (1983), Fox and Routh (1980), Goldstein (1976), Helfgott (1976), Treiman and Baron (1981) and Vellutino and Scanlon (1987). Their findings have been supported by studies in Swedish by Lundberg and associates (Lundberg, Olofsson and Wall 1980) and Magnusson and Naucler (1987), in Spanish by de Manrique and Gramigna (1984), in French by a group of Belgian researchers (Alegria, Pignot, and Morais 1982), and recently in Italian by Cossu and associates (Cossu et al. 1988).

The study carried out by Lundberg and his associates in Sweden (Lundberg, Olofsson, and Wall 1980) is worthy of special mention on two counts. It provides one of the most intensive examinations of the linguistic abilities of kindergartners. It is noteworthy as well because it also addresses the question of whether the children's deficiency is, in fact, linguistic or whether it might be attributable to a deficiency in general analytic ability. Their battery of eleven tests given to 200 kindergartners included both linguistic and nonlinguistic tasks. In the linguistic set were: (1) word synthesis tasks that varied in two dimensions of two levels each—with or without memory load and using either phoneme or syllable units, and (2) word analysis tasks analogous to those for synthesis and, in addition, three others demanding analysis of phoneme position in words, reversal of phoneme segments in words, and rhyming. Since the linguistic tasks required the child to shift attention from meaning to abstract form, thus possibly reflecting a general cognitive function not exclusively limited to linguistic material, nonlinguistic control tasks that simulated those cognitive demands were also included. The most powerful predictors of later reading and writing skills in the entire battery turned out to be those requiring phonological awareness, specifically the analytic ability to manipulate phonemes in words. In contrast, the poor readers showed no particular deficiency in the nonlinguistic tasks.

These findings that tasks of linguistic, rather than nonlinguistic analysis, and specifically phonemic analysis, were predictive of reading failure have since received support from other studies here and abroad. For example, in a study of six to nine year olds with severe reading disability (Morais, Cluytens, and Alegria 1984) it was found that these children were poorer on segmenting words into their constituent parts but performed just as well as normal readers in a matched task that required them to deal analytically with musical tone sequences instead of words. The question of a possible general analytic deficit was also addressed in two complementary experiments, one with good and poor readers in the third grade and the other with good and poor readers in adult education classes (Pratt 1985). All the subjects were given three linguistic awareness tests and one nonspeech control task identical in format to one of the linguistic measures. Significant differences were found between the good and poor readers at both age levels on all three linguistic measures, but not on the nonspeech control task. Thus the poor readers, whether young or old, had no more difficulty in segmental analysis than the good readers when the task was nonlinguistic; their problem was limited to the segmental analysis of speech.

Not only reading, but early spelling proficiency has also been found to be closely related to analytic phonological skills. In a study of kindergartners (Liberman et al. 1985), the children's ability to produce invented spellings, given only some knowledge of letter names was related to their performance on a series of language-based tasks. It was found that the children's proficiency in spelling was more closely tied to phonological awareness than to any of the other aspects of language development tested. Of the eight tasks in the study, only the three that unquestionably tapped phonological analysis skills made a difference statistically. They combined to account for 93 percent of the variance in proficiency in invented spelling. A phoneme analysis test patterned after Lundberg, Olofsson. and Wall (1980) made the largest contribution—67 percent of the variance. A test of the ability to write letters to phoneme dictation accounted for 20 percent more, and a phoneme deletion task ("Say milk without the m") added another

6 percent. (A fourth task, picture naming, added 1 percent, but did not reach significance in the correlation. As we will note later, however, naming can be a subtle indicator of more general phonological difficulties.)

Among the four language-based tests that did not contribute to the invented spelling performance were three that are frequently included in clinical evaluations: receptive vocabulary, articulation as measured by the repetition of simple words, and letter naming or writing. The fourth was a syllable deletion test ("Say bookcase without the book"). Being able to segment words by syllable was, as we would expect, not enough to equip the child to produce alphabetically written words.

The Remedial Effect of Training in Awareness

Given the abundant evidence that phonological awareness is predictive of success in reading, it is of interest to know that such awareness can be trained even in preschool and kindergarten (Bradley and Bryant 1983; Content et al. 1982; Lundberg. Frost and Petersen 1988; Olofsson and Lundberg 1983). It is of special interest to find, moreover, that the training can have a salutary effect on future reading skill. Impressive evidence for the efficacy of the training comes from a pair of experiments by Bradley and Bryant (1983). The first experiment confirmed the high correlations found by others between preschoolers' phonological awareness and later reading skill. This was done by a comparison of children's performance on rhyming tasks and their achievement in reading and spelling several years later. The second experiment was directed to an examination of the effect of various kinds of early training on the later academic achievements of children considered to be at risk for failure. To this end. the children who had been found in the first experiment to have a low level of phonological awareness were divided into four groups. One group was trained to sort pictured words on cards by phonological categories. A second received the same training except that letters corresponding to the phonemic categories were added. A third group was trained to sort by semantic categories. A control group was given equal time and unrelated card play. The two phonologically trained groups were found to be superior to the others in subsequent tests of reading and spelling. Moreover, in follow-up studies, they continued to maintain their advantage.

Further evidence for the positive effect of early training in phonological awareness is found in the longitudinal study by Lundberg and associates (Lundberg, Frost, and Petersen 1988). An experimental group of kindergartners who had participated in a variety of analytic word games was found at year-end to be superior in phoneme awareness to a matched control group. When compared in academic achievement in the first grade, the experimental group was slightly below the controls in math and IQ but significantly superior in both reading and spelling. Moreover their advantage was maintained when the children were retested in the second grade.

Lack of Phonological Awareness and Adult Literacy

What about phonological awareness in adult nonreaders? Is it still a problem for them? The question as to whether phonological awareness improves spontaneously with age or requires some form of instruction is a crucial one, with obvious implications not only for preschool instruction but also for the design of literacy teaching programs geared to adolescents and adults. This question was explored in an unusual investigation by a Belgian research group who examined the phonological awareness of illiterate adults in a rural area of Portugal (Morais et al. 1979). They found that the illiterate adults could neither delete nor add phonemes at the beginning of nonsense words, whereas others from the same community who had received reading instruction in an adult literacy class succeeded in performing those tasks. The authors concluded that awareness of phoneme segmentation does not develop spontaneously even by adulthood but arises as a concomitant of reading instruction and experience.

In view of these findings, we believed it would prove of value to test the phonological awareness of adults who had reading instruction but were nonetheless poor readers. To this end, our reading research group (Liberman et al. 1985) tested the members of a community literacy class, all of whom were having serious decoding problems despite years of schooling. What we found was that these adults performed with difficulty on a very simple task in which the subjects were required only to identify the initial, medial, or final sound in monosyllabic words. Though this is an exercise that one might expect a first grader to be able to perform, our adults managed to produce correct responses on only 58 percent of the items. Moreover, they clearly found it to be singularly frustrating and unpleasant. This inability of adults with literacy problems to perform well on tasks demanding explicit understanding of phonological structure has also been found by other investigators—Byrne and Ledez (1983) in Australia, Marcel (1980) in England, and Read and Ruyter (1985) in a prison population in the United States.

A Broader Phonological Deficiency and Reading

Why do some people have difficulty in achieving the understanding of phonological structure that application of the alphabetic principle requires? One possibility, as we noted before, is that they may suffer from a general deficiency in the ability to divide objects of all kinds into their constituent elements. But as we pointed out, the results of several studies suggest that the difficulty is specifically linguistic. Another possibility—one that we and others have pursued—is that the poor reader's difficulty with analyzing words into their constituent units is one among several symptoms of a general deficiency in the phonological component of the child's natural capacity for language. If the underlying biology tends to set up phonological structures weakly, then it should follow that these structures would be that much harder for the child to bring to a level of explicit awareness. But there would be other consequences for the processing of language, and these we consider below.

Problems in Short-Term Memory and Sentence Comprehension

Because short-term memory depends on the ability to gain access to phonological structure and to use it to hold linguistic information (Conrad 1964; Liberman, Mattingly, and Turvey 1972), we might expect people who have underlying phonological deficiencies to show various limitations on verbal tasks that tap short-term memory. This expectation is amply borne out.

The research literature contains many reports that young children who are poor readers are deficient in short-term memory. Typically they retain fewer items from a set of fixed size than age-matched good readers (see Mann, Liberman, and Shankweiler 1980; Shankweiler et al. 1985; Shankweiler, Smith, and Mann 1984; Wagner and Torgesen 1987). However, memory difficulties for poor readers appear to arise only under specific conditions; chiefly, they occur when the items to be retained are words and nameable objects. When the test materials do not lend themselves to verbal (i.e., phonological) encoding, as in memory for nonsense shapes or unfamiliar faces, memory testing does not find poor readers at a disadvantage (Katz, Shankweiler and Liberman 1981; Liberman et al. 1982). The problem seems, therefore, to be a material-specific one, not an all embracing memory impairment.

It is noteworthy, in addition, that memory differences between good and poor readers may also depend on other demands of the task—tasks that require rote recall of a list of unstructured items may be less differentiating than tasks that require both storage and further processing of the incoming material as in sentence processing (Daneman and Carpenter 1980; Perfetti and Goldman 1976). Since language structures are hierarchically organized and sequentially transmitted, comprehension of language, either by ear or by eye, depends on a short-term memory system that transiently stores and continuously processes the incoming segments of the linguistic message. In keeping with current usage (see Baddeley and Hitch 1974; also Shankweiler and Crain 1986), we call this form of memory *working memory*. A phonological deficiency would understandably impair the functions of working memory and could be expected, in turn, to have repercussions on comprehension, whether of spoken discourse or printed text. For example, in sentence processing, the parsing of phonological segments into lexical units and the groupings of these units into higher-level phrasal structures requires phased control of the flow of linguistic information through the language apparatus.

We could therefore expect that children with reading disability would sometimes comprehend sentences poorly because of their difficulties in setting up and retaining phonological structures. The difficulty should be especially acute in reading, where the problem of decoding from print would create an additional processing load in an unskilled reader who decodes poorly. The important insight that the lower-level and higher-level reading problems of the poor reader are causally connected through constriction of working memory was contributed by Perfetti and Lesgold (1979). In their terms, poor decoding skills coupled with the limitations of working memory create in the poor reader a "bottleneck" in information flow with severe repercussions for comprehension.

But, as Crain and Shankweiler discuss, comprehension difficulties of poor readers are not limited to reading. From our working memory perspective, difficulties should also arise in spoken language processing, especially if the sentence material contains remote dependencies or structural ambiguities that necessitate reanalysis, or if the comprehension task presents additional complexities that further dilute memory resources. Several reports in the literature indicate that disabled readers do have problems in comprehending such sentences in spoken form as well as in reading (Byrne 1981; Mann, Shankweiler, and Smith 1984; Stein, Cairns, and Zurif 1984). More recent findings

231

indicate that the poor readers fail not because they lag behind their good reading peers in comprehension of grammar as such, but because working memory is overloaded due to deficient phonological processing.

By changing the task in various ways to reduce the demands on memory while testing the same grammatical structures, it has been shown that poor readers can succeed as well as good readers in comprehending complex grammatical structures (Crain et al., forthcoming; Smith et al., forthcoming). Thus, a memory impairment stemming from a weakness in phonological processing can masquerade as a grammatical or semantic deficit.

Other Language-Related Problems

Thus far we have discussed difficulties involving the phonological components of language that directly affect reading. Reading is affected both by the difficulties of accessing and mentally manipulating phonemic segments and by the limitations on use of the working memory that we have just discussed (though in the case of working memory the consequences are not confined to reading). We now turn to other deficits displayed by poor readers that are phonological in nature, but do not affect reading directly. These are worth mentioning, both for their diagnostic value, and because they add to the weight of the evidence that all the elements of the syndrome of many poor readers may stem ultimately from a deficiency in phonological processing.

One such deficit is suggested by some preliminary research into the speech perception of poor readers that was carried out by Brady and associates at Haskins Laboratories (Brady, Shankweiler, and Mann 1983). In their experiments, good and poor readers were tested on two auditory perception tasks, one involving words and the other nonspeech environmental sounds. The identification tasks were presented under two conditions—with favorable and unfavorable noise ratios. The findings were that the poor readers did show a deficit, but it was specific to the speech stimuli and occurred only in the noise-masked condition. They did not differ from the good readers in the perception of nonspeech environmental sounds, whether the sounds were noise-masked or not. Note that the poor readers apparently needed a higher quality of signal than the good readers for error-free performance in speech, but not for nonspeech environmental sounds. These results suggest that the minor deficit displayed by the poor readers may derive from phonological structures that are set up more weakly than in good readers, or are more difficult to activate.

Additional evidence for a broader phonological deficit in poor readers is provided by a study of speech production, specifically, the errors of junior high school students (Catts 1986). The critical finding was that the reading-disabled students made significantly more errors than matched normals on three different tasks in which their speech production was stressed. The author concluded, as we would, that their difficulties in speech production may be an extension of deficits in the phonological realm.

More evidence for a broad phonological deficit in poor readers was provided by a study of the performance of second graders on a naming test (Katz 1986). This study confirmed what others had shown—that poor readers named more words incorrectly. But it went further to show that their difficulties are often phonological and not semantic, as might be assumed. Three kinds of evidence were presented in this regard. First, when quizzed about the characteristics of the object they had named incorrectly (e.g., "tornado" for volcano), the poor readers were often able to describe it accurately. They clearly knew what the object was. That is they described a volcano, not a tornado. Second, given the name of the item, they could select it from a group of pictured objects. That is, they could identify it correctly. And third, their naming errors were often related to the phonological and not the semantic aspect of the word. For example, though the name given to the picture of a volcano was incorrect, it shared syllable count, stress pattern, and vowels with the target word.

Distorted production of the word for an item that had been correctly identified could stem either from deficient specification of the phonological structure in the lexicon, or from deficient retrieval and processing of the stored phonological information. In either case, the source of the difficulty relates to the phonological structure of the words and not to their meanings.

Phonology and the Successful Deaf Reader

The congenitally deaf constitute a population with a phonological impairment arising from an entirely different source. Surprisingly, this group represents some of the most compelling evidence for the importance of phonological abilities for reading. It is well known that profound deafness from birth or early life usually results in attainment of a low level of reading skill. The hearing impaired of all ages tend to read far below grade expectations. But, nonetheless, differences in reading achievement are related to differences in phonological abilities even in deaf populations. Moreover, a few congenitally, profoundly deaf individuals can read well, even up to the college level.

How are these successful deaf readers different from the majority? Vicki Hanson and her associates at Haskins Laboratories asked that question in a series of experiments (Hanson 1982; Hanson and Fowler 1987; Hanson, Liberman, and Shankweiler 1984). Briefly, they found that the successful deaf readers were not limited to reading English words as if they were logographs; that is, they were not, as one might assume, dependent on a limited store of words learned in paired associate fashion as visual designs. The results showed that unlike their poor reading peers among the deaf, these subjects, despite so little exposure to sound, were able to access phonological knowledge both in reading and in retaining verbal material in short-term memory.

In reading, the good readers among the deaf displayed their phonological sensitivity by responding differentially to rhyming and nonrhyming pairs of words (save/wave vs. have/cave) and by being able to name the real word equivalents of nonwords (flame for f-l-a-i-m; tall for t-a-u-l). In a short-term memory experiment, the successful deaf readers were more affected by phonetically confusing words than by those that were orthographically confusing or whose signs were formationally confusing. These results certainly suggest that successful deaf readers are using phonological processing, a conclusion also reached by Conrad with a less severely impaired population of deaf readers (Conrad 1979).

The question of how the congenitally, profoundly deaf might develop phonological sensitivity without being able to hear the sounds of speech is explored by Hanson. She identifies several sources of information that may be helpful. The orthography itself tells them something about the systematic phonological forms of words. In addition, oral training when available supplies information about the gestures used to produce speech. Lip-reading also provides considerable useable information, and the deaf individual's own attempts at speech may reflect more phonological sensitivity than is apparent to the hearing listener.

Implications for Instruction

In view of all the evidence that has accumulated in the past fifteen years to support the critical importance of phonological sensitivity for the attainment of literacy in an alphabetic system, one would surely expect teacher training to reflect these findings. Unfortunately, all too often it does not. Many teachers are being trained to teach reading without themselves ever having learned how an alphabetic orthography represents the language, why it is important for beginners to understand how the internal phonological structure of words relates to the orthography, or why it is hard for children to achieve this understanding.

In fact, teachers are all too often being provided with an instructional procedure that directs them specifically not to trouble the learner with details of how the alphabet works. Instead, they are told to view reading as a "guessing game" (Goodman 1976) in which the general import of the message, and not the actual words of the text, is to be emphasized. Beginners are encouraged to memorize the appearance of words as visual patterns by whatever means they can muster and to use their store of memorized words and their "whole language" capability as a basis for guessing the rest of the message from picture cues and context. Thus, they are not to be corrected when reading "kids" for children in a story about a playground, "Crest" for toothpaste in a story about dental hygiene, and "cats" for dogs in a story about pets.

Fortunately, many children—the lucky 75 percent or so who learn to read whatever the method—manage to pick up the alphabetic principle without much explicit instruction, if any. That is, given experience with printed material, they begin to discover for themselves the commonalities between similarly spoken and written words. When tested in kindergarten, these children turn out to be the ones with strengths in the phonological domain. For the large group of children with phonological deficiencies who do not understand that the spoken word has segments, and who have not discovered on their own that there is a correspondence between those segments and the segments of the printed word, the current vogue for the so-called (and from our point of view, misnamed) psycholinguistic guessing game and its offshoots, the "whole language" and "language experience" approaches, are likely to be disastrous. Many children taught this way are likely to join the ranks of the millions of functional illiterates in our country who stumble along, guessing at the printed message from their inadequate store of memorized words, unable to decipher a new word they have never seen before.

For those beginners who do not discover the alphabetic principle unaided, an introductory method that provides them with direct instruction in what they need to know is critical (Liberman 1985; Liberman and Shankweiler 1979). Direct instruction could begin with language analysis activities that are incorporated into the daily reading lesson. These activities can take many different forms, limited in number and variety only by the creativity of the teacher. The Auditory Discrimination in Depth Program of Lindamood and Lindamood (1975) is an ingenious method for helping the student to apprehend the internal phonological structure of words. It does this by calling the student's attention to the perceived distinctiveness of the articulatory gestures for the various phonemic constituents of spoken words and then demonstrating their sequences in syllables with variously colored blocks. The method was originally developed for individual reading remediation, but is currently being adapted for classroom use.

Adaptations of three exercises that we advocated some years ago (Liberman et al. 1980) have recently been shown by one of our colleagues (Blachman 1987) to be effective in improving reading skills even in an inner city school with a high incidence of reading failure. In the first procedure, one originally devised by the Soviet educator Elkonin (1973), Blachman presents the child with a simple line drawing representing the word to be analyzed. A rectangle under the drawing is divided into squares equal in number to the phonemes in the picture word. The children are taught to say the word slowly, placing a counter in the appropriate squares of the diagram as the word is being slowly articulated. The words selected must begin with a fricative, liquid, or nasal rather than a stop consonant in order to permit their component phonemes to be accessed readily. Later, as the child progresses, the counters are color-coded-one color for vowels, another for consonants. Letter symbols can be added as well. In another activity, this one adapted from Engelmann (1969), the children are taught how to read as a single unit the combination of a consonant followed by a vowel. For example, the teacher writes a consonant on the blackboard (preferably, a fricative, nasal, or liquid)—the letter s, for example—and produces it, holding it over time until she writes the vowel and pronounces that. The length of time between the pronunciations of the initial consonant and the vowel (as well as a line drawn between them on the board) is then reduced step by step until the two phonemes are pronounced as a single unit—"sa". By adding stop consonants in the final position and pronouncing the resultant words, the children can begin to accumulate a pool of real words (sag, sat, sad, etc.). Thereafter, new vowels and new consonants can be introduced in the same way, and built into new words that are incorporated into stories to be read and written.

A similar effect can be produced by a third procedure, adapted from Slingerland (1971), in which a small pocket chart is used by the child at each desk to manipulate individual letters to form new words and learn new phonemes. The words thus constructed, along with a few nonphonetic "sight" words, can be used in stories and poems to be read and written by the child. Note that the child is now reading and writing words the structure of which is no longer a mystery and the understanding of which can be used productively to form related words (bag, bat, bad, big, bit, bid, etc.).

All these language analysis activities and others like them can be played as games in which the introduction of each new element not only informs but delights. Beginning readers with adequate phonological ability will require only a relatively brief exposure to such activities. They will soon develop skills that will enable them to decode the new words of the text and to go from them to the meaning of the passage. For such readers, language analysis can be quickly followed, or even accompanied, by practice with interesting reading materials from other sources. These children will benefit from the added skill that comes from increased reading practice and the further enhancement of vocabulary and knowledge that comes with expanded reading and life experience. But unless they receive extra assistance, the many beginners with weakness in phonological skills, who may include as many as 20 to 25 percent of the children, will remain locked into a sight-word stage of reading, able to cope only with those few words they have already memorized. They will not learn to decode new words—the essence of true reading skill—unless the method initially includes more intensive, direct, and systematic training in phonological structure and demonstrates how it relates to the way words are written. Research support for this view has been available for at least twenty years (see Chall 1967 or Pflaum et al. 1980). It is surely time to put the research into practice.

Note

Parts of this chapter were adapted from "Phonology and the problems of learning to read and write," *Remedial and Special Education*, 6 (1985):8–17. This research was supported in part by grant HD–01994 to Haskins Laboratories and by grant NIH–21888 to Yale University and Haskins Laboratories from the National Institute of Child Health and Human Development.

—by Isabelle Y. Liberman,
Donald Shankweiler,
Alvin M. Liberman

References

Alegria, J.; Pignot. E.; and Morais, J. 1982. Phonetic analysis of speech and memory codes in beginning readers. *Memory and Cognition* 10:451–56.

Baddeley, A.D., and Hitch, G. 1974. Working memory. In *The Psychology of Learning and Motivation*, vol. 8, ed. G.H. Bower. New York: Academic Press.

Benton, A.L., and Pearl, D. 1978. *Dyslexia: An Appraisal of Current Knowledge*. New York: Oxford University Press.

Blachman, B. 1984. The relationships of rapid naming ability and language analysis skills to kindergarten and first grade reading achievement. *Journal of Educational Psychology* 76:610–22.

Blachman, B. 1987. An alternative classroom reading program for learning disabled and other low-achieving children. In *Intimacy with Language: A Forgotten Basic in Teacher Education*, ed. W. Ellis. Baltimore: Orton Dyslexia Society.

Bradley, L., and Bryant, P.E. 1983. Categorizing sounds and learning to read—a causal connection. *Nature* 301:419–21.

Brady, S.A.; Shankweiler, D.; and Mann, V.A. 1983. Speech perception and memory coding in relation to reading ability. *Journal of Experimental Child Psychology* 35:345–67.

Browman, C.P., and Goldstein, L. M. 1985. Dynamic modeling of phonetic structure. In *Phonetic Linguistics*, ed. V. Fromkin. New York: Academic Press.

Byrne, B. 1981. Deficient syntactic control in poor readers: Is a weak phonetic memory code responsible? *Applied Psycholinguistics* 2:201–12.

Byrne, B., and Ledez, J. 1983. Phonological awareness in reading disabled adults. *Australian Journal of Psychology* 35:185–97.

Catts, H.W. 1986. Speech production/phonological deficits in reading disordered children. *Journal of Learning Disabilities* 19 (8):504–8.

Chall, J. 1967. *Learning to Read: The Great Debate*. New York: McGraw Hill.

Coltheart, M. 1978. Lexical access in simple reading tasks. In *Strategies in Information Processing*, ed. G. Underwood. London: Academic Press.

Conrad, R. 1964. Acoustic confusions in immediate memory. *British Journal of Psychology* 55:75–84.

Conrad, R. 1979. *The Deaf Child*. London: Harper and Row.

Content, A.; Morais, J.; Alegria, J.; and Bertelson, P. 1982. Accelerating the development of phonetic segmentation skills in kindergartners. *Cahiers de psychologie cognitive* 2:259–69.

Cossu, G.; Shankweiler, D.; Liberman, I.Y.; Tola, G.; and Katz, L. 1988. Awareness of phonological segments and reading ability in Italian children. *Applied Psycholinguistics* 9:1–16.

Crain, S.; Shankweiler, D.; Macaruso, P.; and Bar-Shalom, E. Forthcoming. Working memory and sentence comprehension: Investigations of children with reading disorder. In *Neuropsychological Impairments of Short-Term Memory*, ed. G. Vallar and T. Shallice. Cambridge: Cambridge University Press.

Daneman, M., and Carpenter, P.A. 1980. Individual differences in working memory and reading. *Journal of Verbal Learning and Verbal Behavior* 19:450–66.

Doehring, D.G. 1968. *Patterns of Impairment in Specific Reading Disability*. Bloomington: Indiana University Press.

Elkonin, D.B. 1973. U.S.S.R. In *Comparative Reading*, ed. J. Downing. New York: Macmillan.

Englemann, S. 1969. *Preventing Failure in the Primary Grades*. Chicago: Science Research Associates.

Fox, B., and Routh, D.K. 1980. Phonetic analysis and severe reading disability in children. *Journal of Psycholinguistic Research* 9:115–19.

Gleitman, L.R., and Rozin, P. 1977. The structure and acquisition of reading. Relations between orthographies and structure of language. In *Toward a Psychology of Reading*, ed. A.S. Reber and D.L. Scarborough. Hillsdale, N.J.: Erlbaum.

Goldstein, D.M. 1976. Cognitive-linguistic functioning and learning to read in preschoolers. *Journal of Educational Psychology* 68:680–88.

Goodman, K.S. 1976. Reading: A psycholinguistic guessing game. In *Theoretical Models and Processes of Reading*, ed. H. Singer and R.B. Ruddell. Newark, Del.: International Reading Association.

Hanson, V.L. 1982. Short-term recall by deaf signers of American Sign Language: Implications of encoding strategy for order recall. *Journal of Experimental Psychology: Learning, Memory, and Cognition* 8:572–83.

Hanson, V.L., and Fowler, C.A. 1987. Phonological coding in word reading: Evidence from hearing and deaf readers. *Memory and Cognition* 15(3):199–207.

Hanson, V.L.; Liberman, I.Y.; and Shankweiler, D. 1984. Linguistic coding by deaf children in relation to beginning reading success. *Journal of Experimental Child Psychology* 37:398–93.

Helfgott, J. 1976. Phoneme segmentation and blending skills of kindergarten children: Implications for beginning reading acquisition. *Contemporary Education Psychology* 1:157–69.

Katz, R.B. 1986. Phonological deficiencies in children with reading disability: Evidence from an object-naming task. *Cognition* 22:225–57.

Katz, R.B.; Shankweiler, D.; and Liberman, I.Y. 1981. Memory for item order and phonetic recoding in the beginning reader. *Journal of Experimental Child Psychology* 32:474–84.

Klima, E.S. 1972. How alphabets might reflect language. In *Language by Ear and by Eye: The Relationships between Speech and Reading*, ed. J.F. Kavanagh and I.G. Mattingly. Cambridge, Mass: MIT Press.

Liberman, A.M. in press. Reading is hard just because listening is easy. In *Wenner-Gren International Symposium Series: Brain and Reading*, ed. C. Von Euler. Hampshire, England: Macmillan.

Liberman, A.M.; Cooper, F.S.; Shankweiler, D.P.; and Studdert-Kennedy, M. 1967. Perception of the speech code. *Psychological Review* 74:431–61.

Liberman, A.M., and Mattingly, I.G. 1985. The motor theory of speech perception revised. *Cognition* 21:1–36.

Liberman, A.M., and Mattingly, I.G. 1989. A specialization for speech perception. *Science* 243:489–94.

Liberman, I.Y. 1971. Basic research in speech and lateralization of language: Some implications for reading disability. *Bulletin of the Orton Society* 21:71–87.

Liberman, I.Y. 1973. Segmentation of the spoken word and reading acquisition. *Bulletin of the Orton Society* 23:65–77.

Liberman, I.Y. 1983. A language-oriented view of reading and its disabilities. In *Progress in Learning Disabilities*, Vol. 5, ed. H. Myklebust. New York: Grune and Stratton.

Liberman, I.Y. 1985. Should so-called modality preferences determine the nature of instruction for children with learning disabilities? In *Dyslexia: A neuroscientific approach to clinical evaluation*, ed. F.H. Duffy and N. Geschwind. Boston: Little, Brown.

Liberman. I.Y.; Mann, V.; Shankweiler, D.; and Werfelman, M. 1982. Children's memory for recurring linguistic and nonlinguistic material in relation to reading ability. *Cortex* 18:367–75.

Liberman. I.Y.; Rubin, H.; Duques, S.; and Carlisle, J. 1985. Linguistic abilities and spelling proficiency in kindergartners and adult poor spellers. In *Biobehavioral Measures of Dyslexia*. ed. J. Kavanagh and D. Gray. Parkton, Md.: York Press.

Liberman, I.Y.; and Shankweiler, D. 1979. Speech, the alphabet and teaching to read. In *Theory and Practice of Early Reading*, ed. L.B. Resnik and P.A. Weaver. Hillsdale, N.J.: Erlbaum.

Liberman, I.Y.; and Shankweiler, D. 1985. Phonology and the problems of learning to read and write. *Remedial and Special Education* 6:8–17.

Liberman, I.Y.; Shankweiler, D.; Blachman, B.; Camp, L.; and Werfelman, M. 1980. Steps toward literacy. In *Auditory Processing and Language: Clinical and Research Perspectives*, ed. P. Levinson and C. Sloan. New York: Grune and Stratton.

Liberman, I.Y.; Shankweiler, D.; Fischer, F.W.; and Carter, B. 1974. Explicit syllable and phoneme segmentation in the young child. *Journal of Experimental Child Psychology* 18:201–12.

Lindamood, C.H.. and Lindamood, P.C. 1975. *The A.D.D. Program, Auditory Discrimination in Depth*. Hingham, Mass.: Teaching Resources.

Lundberg, I.; Frost, J.; and Petersen, O-P. 1988. Effects of an extensive program for stimulating phonological awareness in preschool children. *Reading Research Quarterly* 23(3):263–84.

Lundberg, I.; Olofsson, A.; and Wall, S. 1980. Reading and spelling skills in the first school years, predicted from phonemic awareness skills in kindergarten. *Scandinavian Journal of Psychology* 21:159–73.

Magnusson, E., and Naucler. K. 1987. Language disordered and normally speaking children's development of spoken and written language: Preliminary results from a longitudinal study. *Reports from Uppsala University, Linguistics Department* 16:35–63.

Mann, V.; Liberman, I.Y.; and Shankweiler, D. 1980. Children's memory for sentences and word strings in relation to reading ability. *Memory and Cognition* 8:329–35.

Mann, V.; Shankweiler. D.; and Smith. S. 1984. The association between comprehension of spoken sentences and early reading ability: The role of phonetic representation. *Journal of Child Language* 11:607–43.

de Manrique, A.M.B., and Gramigna. S. 1984. La segmentacion fonologica y silabica en ninos de preescolar y primer grado. *Lectura y Vida* 5:4–13.

Marcel, A. 1980. Phonological awareness and phonological representation: Investigation of a specific spelling problem. In *Cognitive processes in spelling*, ed. U. Frith. London: Academic Press.

Mattingly, I.G. 1972. Reading, the linguistic process, and linguistic awareness. *In Language by Ear and by Eye: The Relationships between Speech and Reading*, ed. J.F. Kavanagh and I.G. Mattingly. Cambridge. Mass.: MIT Press.

Morais, J.; Cary, L.; Alegria, J.; and Bertelson, P. 1979. Does awareness of speech arise spontaneously? *Cognition* 7:323–31.

Morais, J.; Cluytens, M.; and Alegria, J. 1984. Segmentation abilities of dyslexics and normal readers. *Perceptual and Motor Skills* 58:221–22.

Olofsson, A., and Lundberg, I. 1983. Can phonemic awareness be trained in kindergarten? *Scandinavian Journal of Psychology* 24:35–44.

Perfetti, C.A., and Goldman, S.R. 1976. Discourse memory and reading comprehension skill. *Journal of Verbal Learning and Verbal Behavior* 14:33–42.

Perfetti, C.A., and Lesgold, A.M. 1979. Coding and comprehension in skilled reading and implications for reading instruction. In *Theory and Practice of Early Reading*, vol. 1, ed. L.B. Resnick and P.A. Weaver. Hillsdale, N.J.: Erlbaum.

Pflaum, S.W.; Walberg, H.J.; Karegianes, M.L.; and Rasher, S.P. 1980. Reading instruction: A quantitative analysis. *Educational Research* 9:12–18.

Pratt, A. 1985. The relationship of linguistic awareness to reading skill in children and adults. Ph.D. diss., University of Rhode Island.

Read, C. 1986. *Children's Creative Spelling*. London: Routledge and Kegan Paul.

Read, C. and Ruyter, L. 1985. Reading and spelling skills in adults of low literacy. *Reading and Special Education* 6:43–52.

Savin, H. 1972. What the child knows about speech when he starts to learn to read. *In Language by Ear and by Eye: The Relationships between Speech and Reading,* ed. J.F. Kavanagh and I.G. Mattingly. Cambridge, Mass.: MIT Press.

Shankweiler, D., and Crain, S. 1986. Language mechanisms and reading disorders: a modular approach. *Cognition* 24:139–68.

Shankweiler, D., and Liberman, I.Y. 1972. Misreading: A search for causes. In *Language by Ear and by Eye: The Relationships between Speech and Reading*, ed. J.F. Kavanagh and I.G. Mattingly. Cambridge, Mass.: MIT Press.

Shankweiler, D.; Liberman, I.Y.; Mark, L.S.; Fowler, C.A.; and Fischer, F.W. 1979. The speech code and learning to read. *Journal of Experimental Psychology: Human Learning and Memory* 5: 531–45.

Shankweiler, D.; Smith, S.T.; and Mann, V. 1984. Repetition and comprehension of spoken sentences by reading disabled children. *Brain and Language* 12:241–57.

Slingerland, B.H. 1971. *A Multisensory Approach to Language Arts for Specific Language Disability Children: A Guide for Primary Teachers*. Cambridge, Mass.: Educators Publishing Service.

Smith, F. 1971. *Understanding Reading: A Psycholinguistic Analysis of Reading and Learning to Read*. New York: Holt, Rinehart and Winston.

Smith, S.T.; Macaruso, P.; Shankweiler, D.; and Crain, S. Forthcoming. Syntactic comprehension in young poor readers. *Applied Psycholinguistics*.

Stanovich, K.E. 1982. Individual differences in the cognitive processes of reading: I. Word decoding. *Journal of Learning Disabilities* 15:449–572.

Stein, C.L.; Cairns, H.S.; and Zurif, E.B. 1984. Sentence comprehension limitations related to syntactic deficits in reading disabled children. *Applied Psycholinguistics* 5:305–22.

Studdert-Kennedy, M. 1987. The phoneme as a perceptuo-motor structure. In *Language Perception and Production*, ed. A. Allport, D. MacKay, W. Prinz, and E. Sheerer. London: Academic Press.

Treiman, R.A., and Baron, J. 1981. Segmental analysis ability: Development and relation to reading ability. In *Reading Research: Advances in Theory and Practice*, vol. 3, ed. G.E. MacKinnon and T.G. Walker. New York: Academic Press.

Vellutino, F.R. 1979. *Dyslexia: Theory and Research*. Cambridge, Mass.: MIT Press.

Vellutino, F.R., and Scanlon, D. 1987. Phonological coding, phonological awareness, and reading ability. Evidence from longitudinal and experimental study. *Merrill-Palmer Quarterly* 33(3):321–63.

Vernon, M.D. 1957. *Backwardness in Reading, a Study of Its Nature and Origin*. Cambridge: Cambridge University Press.

Wagner, R.K., and Torgesen, J.K. 1987. The nature of phonological processing in the acquisition of reading skills. *Psychological Bulletin* 101:192–212.

Waters, G.S.; Seidenberg, M.S.; and Bruck, M. 1984. Children's and adults' use of spelling-sound information in three reading tasks. *Memory and Cognition* 12:293–305.

Chapter 14

Dysgraphia: Learning Disabilities in Writing

Definition and Identification

Definitions of dysgraphia, found in the learning disability literature, are used to describe any persistent problem associated with the act of writing. Since writing is a complex cognitive process that requires the integration of many skills, labeling a student dysgraphic identifies that a problem exists but does not by itself suggest the learner's specific needs. The next logical step is an in-depth analysis of the student's writing strengths and deficits which leads to a "needs list." Priorities are established from this "needs list" and appropriate strategies are developed. Successful strategies are "over learned"; continuous assessment redefines the priorities so that progress becomes an integral aspect of the dysgraphic's monitored program.

Writing Problems Often Manifest Themselves in Three Developmental Stages

- **The first is usually noted in the young child who has difficulty in the very act of writing.** Teachers and parents identify children who are much more awkward than their peers in

An undated document written by Dorothy A. Stracher, Ph.D. and distributed by the National Center for Learning Disabilities, 381 Park Avenue South, New York, NY 10016; reprinted with permission.

holding writing instruments, and who have extreme difficulty in forming legible, uniform letters.

- **The second stage is observed in the young writer whose spelling is considerably less developed than that of his peers.** We see learning disabled adults who write either totally phonetically or whose word representations have very little relationship to the real model.

- **The third stage is signaled by those learning disabled writers who have problems in organizing writing clearly and tersely, and/or who may have problems in using the syntactic structures of language accurately.** Language problems manifested in dysgraphic writing will be the main focus of this chapter.

The three stages listed above are arbitrary divisions that have been used for clarity and to indicate the developmental matter noted in dysgraphia. People can have one, two or all three of these problems simultaneously.

An individual student may have one or more of the writing problems already noted but not be dysgraphic. To be identified as learning disabled means that a neurological processing problem exists. While some people, in testing, exhibit "hard signs," that is, neurological testing that can identify brain anomalies, most identification of learning disabilities is done via "soft signs." These include family history, school and anecdotal records, psychological and educational testing. Thereafter, the testers meet together to discuss the individual case and to determine if the term "learning disabled" is appropriate. Frequently, we will interview students whose set of educational symptoms strongly suggest a learning disability; however, we still recommend a total testing battery that usually validates our hypothesis.)

Assessment

To begin to plan necessary strategies to help the dysgraphic student requires assessment of that student's strengths and deficits in writing. We give the student a general expository topic, ask him to develop a well-organized essay and then analyze the results. At the end of each semester, the student is asked to write an expository essay; each essay is reanalyzed to note growth and further writing needs that require alternate strategy development.

Strategies

Although writing, as noted previously, is a complex cognitive process, there are some universals, identified in the literature, that are shared by all proficient writers. One of these is that every good writer is a good reader of fine literature. Some dysgraphic students also have great difficulty in reading. This prevents them from using the printed word as the medium through which to absorb that literature which defines our culture and extends our knowledge base. Not only is the student deprived of great stories, but also of the richness of vocabulary, language and higher level reasoning.

Fortunately, we live in a technological era that offers our reading disabled youngsters other options. Books on tapes and videos are useful alternatives. Parents and teachers are encouraged to read aloud to these students. Tapes of books can be used while the learners "read" the books.

Writing Strategies/Word Processing

Listed below are some of the writing strategies developed by our graduate tutors in their work with individual dysgraphic college students. While the strategies provide needed structure for our students, our success is also predicated upon the use of collaborative learning. Tutor and student discuss the writing strengths and needs of the learner. They jointly develop goals and work together toward its accomplishment. They will discuss individual words, sentences, paragraphs and organization but the final choice is always the writer's. The tutors respect the students autonomy as writers and thinkers.

The word processor is unique in the support it offers the writing disabled students. All writers, with this aid, can comfortably use the keyboard in lieu of writing utensils and can automatically present neatly written material. A word processor with a spell check program means that dyslexic students can much more accurately use the orthography of our language.

Further, the word processor can be used to plan and organize initial ideas and to store the information for another day. Even editing, once the bane of dysgraphic students, can be accomplished easily as students move words, sentences and paragraphs at will.

The pre-writing strategies center around the dysgraphic student reasoning through the theme to be presented in an essay. Some of the strategies are:

- Have the student brainstorm all the information to be included on a topic. Some of the students are most comfortable if they state the ideas and the listing is written by their tutor.

- Then ask the student to identify relationships between and among the listed items. These become the major categories of the paper.

- Encourage the student to verbalize the major theme that binds all the categories together. This theme sentence is written at the top of the page or first card.

How to Outline

Teach the dysgraphic student three ways to outline.

1. One is the vertical listing of each major topic and supporting details.

2. The second is semantic mapping which presents the information in a graphic form.

3. The third is a variation of the second. That is the use of cards that list the main idea of each paragraph inside an oval circle and has the supporting details on lines radiating from the circle.

Use a Card System

One of the advantages of the card system is that the student can visually and physically alter the placement of paragraphs prior to beginning the rough draft. The advantages of the first two systems are that the student can immediately place the information on the word processor and then alter, expand or expunge easily and quickly. The successful strategy is the one that "feels most comfortable" to the dysgraphic student.

The rough draft is the student's first writing of the essay. This is immediately placed on the word processor; the key is to include all the information that the student previously developed in outline form. A successful strategy that has worked for many of our dysgraphic students is to concentrate on the ideas and to disregard the spelling, language, sentence structure and paragraph development.

Editing Strategy

The next stage is the editing phase. Some of the strategies used at this point are:

1. **The rough draft is read through to determine that the main idea is developed throughout each paragraph.** Every paragraph is analyzed to determine that it has a main idea, supporting details and a summary or topic sentence. Transitional words, such as "first," "then," "next," "in addition," "in summary," "finally," etc. are considered if appropriate.

2. **Each individual sentence is then examined to determine that it clearly states the student's thought.** Strunk and White's (*Elements of Style*) advice to "omit needless words" is considered at this stage. As the dysgraphic students increase their control over their writing, their tutors encourage the joining together of simple sentences comfortably; they are beginning to express their higher level reasoning in their writing. Complex sentences indicate that the writer perceives a subordinate idea controlled by an independent clause.

3. **Next, the essay is reviewed for possible word changes.** The dysgraphic student is familiar with both the dictionary and the thesaurus. The tutor suggests that any word that is overused or is not specific be replaced by a synonym. The nuance of each word is discussed by tutor and tutee.

4. **Finally, the essay is reread for a final editing and proofreading.** Some of our dysgraphic students can better attend to their writing when they hear it read aloud. The tutor will read it slowly so that the student can identify any changes to be made. Again, the student determines the changes; the tutor helps the dysgraphic writer at that particular stage. The writing is now completed.

Summary

Dysgraphic students are identified as learning disabled students who have writing problems. To help the students develop successful strategies to compensate for their deficits, a comprehensive needs assessment is completed. Then, pre-writing strategies are developed for helping dysgraphic students organize their writing. Word processors are suggested as useful tools for dysgraphic writers. After a rough draft, strategies are offered for proofreading and editing that include concept, paragraph, sentence and word reviews.

Writing is a thinking process. With the development of appropriate strategies, dysgraphic students can become competent writers.

—by Dorothy A. Stracher, Ph.D.

Chapter 15

Dyspraxia: Learning Disabilities in Movement

Dyspraxia is a dysfunction or difficulty with praxis or motor planning. Praxis is the ability to conceive, plan, sequence, and execute a non-habitual or unfamiliar motor task. Dyspraxia can affect skill development in any motor area, including gross motor (sports skills), fine motor (cutting, handwriting), self care (buttons, zipping, tying shoes), oral motor and even academic and social skills. A child who is dyspraxic may demonstrate any or all of the following:

- appears clumsy, uncoordinated
- does things in an inefficient way
- poor organization of body or materials in space
- slow development of motor skills of any type
- slow, laborious handwriting, poor legibility, or poor quality
- poor self-esteem or low self-concept, particularly in regards to motor skills
- may be "accident prone"—bumping into things, falling frequently

If the family of a 9 year old child or younger suspects that their child has problems with motor planning, an evaluation using the Sensory Integration and Praxis Tests administered by a therapist certified in the administration of these tests is recommended, to provide

An undated document written by Sally Smith and distributed by the National Center for Learning Disabilities, 381 Park Avenue South, New York, NY 10016; reprinted with permission.

a specific diagnosis and precise recommendation for formal therapy, if needed. (An older child can also be evaluated and treated by a certified therapist, who is experienced in dealing with these issues in the pre-adolescent and adolescent children.) Lists of available certified therapists can be obtained from:

Sensory Integration International
1402 Cravens Avenue
Torrance, CA 90501-2701
(310) 533-8338

A non-certified therapist can provide treatment, as long as she has training in sensory integration theory and treatment. Sensory integration certified therapists are usually registered occupational or physical therapists.

It is important to note that a child with motor planning difficulties may have difficulty learning new and unfamiliar tasks. He can develop skill in any motor area with enough motivation, time, patience, and hard work. Parents need to help children master necessary tasks by giving the child extra time to learn, breaking down a new task into each of its parts and teaching each part separately, providing extra external structure and organization for the child, not requiring speed and perfection, providing ways to compensate for tasks which are particularly hard (such as allowing a child with poor handwriting to dictate homework to the parent who writes it), and much patience.

Recommended reading for parents include:

• *A Parent's Guide to Understanding Sensory Integration* revised in 1991 and published by Sensory Integration International.

• Ayres, A. Jean; *Sensory Integration and the Child*, 1979, Western Psychological Services, Los Angeles, CA.

Both of these can be obtained from Sensory Integration International.

Occupational Therapy Evaluation

Occupation therapy evaluation can encompass a wide variety of assessment goals and instruments. A comprehensive occupation therapy assessment for an elementary school-aged child which includes evaluating sensory integrative processing would evaluate non-motor visual-perceptual skills, visual-motor integration, fine and gross motor skills and coordination, kinesthetic body awareness, tactile discrimination, sensory defensiveness, praxis (motor planning), balance, bilateral coordination, crossing the body midline, postural control, muscle tone, reflex integration, ocular-motor functions, and other neuromuscular responses related to learning and behavior.

Assessment would include instruments such as the Sensory Integration and Praxis Tests, the Bruininks-Useretsky Test of Motor Proficiency, clinical observations, and tests of visual perceptual and visual-motor integration. It is time-consuming, expensive, and requires special expertise and certification on the part of the evaluator. Occupational therapists employed in public schools assessing a child for school-based occupational therapy needs may not use all of these assessment tools. A child in the public schools can only be referred for an occupational therapy assessment if certified as needing special education and will receive services if it is determined that his needs for O.T. will enable him to benefit from that special education.

A school-based occupational therapist may consider or informally assess sensory integration needs depending upon the expertise, experience, and knowledge of that therapist and the time and policy constraints placed on that therapist by the local education agency. Parents can seek a private, sensory integration certified occupational therapist to administer each assessment (and appropriate therapy) and may receive medical insurance reimbursement or handle the expenses themselves.

If an occupational therapy evaluation is recommended for a pre-school or school-aged child, then the parents need to look at the experience, training, and theoretical orientation of the evaluating therapist, ask which areas of function/dysfunction will be assessed, and determine for themselves if these match the areas of difficulty which their child is experiencing. Sensory integration assessment and treatment is not appropriate for all conditions or difficulties and should not be administered unless indicated. It is important to know that balance, bilateral coordination, and problems in postural control can impact upon the development of fine motor and visual perception skills.

Sensory integration is the organization of sensory input for use. The "use" may be a perception of the body or the world, or an adaptive response, or a learning process, or the development of some neural function. Through sensory integration, the many parts of the nervous system work together so that a person can interact with the environment effectively and experience appropriate satisfaction.

Sensory integration dysfunction is an irregularity or disorder in brain function that makes it difficult to integrate sensory input effectively. Sensory integrative dysfunction may be present in motor, learning, social/emotional, speech/language or attention disorders.

To learn more, the reader is referred to: *A Parent's Guide to Understanding Sensory Integration,* published by Sensory Integration International, 1402 Cravens Avenue, Torrance, CA, 90501-2701, (310) 533-8338.

— by Sally Smith

Chapter 16

Dyscalculia: Learning Disabilities in Mathematics

What Constitutes a Learning Disability in Mathematics?

There is no single mathematics disability. In fact, mathematics disabilities are as varied and complex as those associated with reading. Furthermore, there are some arithmetic disabilities which can exist independent of a reading disability and others which do not. One type of learning disability affecting mathematics can stem from an individual's difficulty processing language, another might be related to visual spatial confusion, while yet another could include trouble retaining math facts and keeping procedures in the proper order. While extremely rare, there are some learners who cannot successfully compare the lengths of two sticks and others who have almost no ability to estimate. Finally, some people experience emotional blocks so overwhelming as to preclude their ability to think responsibly and clearly when attempting math, and these students are disabled, as well.

How Is Mathematics Learning Related to Mathematics Learning Disabilities?

Ginsburg (1977) and Baroody (1987) have identified the initial, intuitive stages of mathematics learning as the "informal" stage. A

An undated document written by Dr. C. Christina Wright, Ph.D. for the National Center for Learning Disabilities, 318 Park Avenue South, New York, NY 10016; reprinted with permission.

young child learns the language of magnitude (more, less; bigger, smaller) and equivalence (same) at home, long before schooling begins. In much the same way a child learns to chant the alphabet before knowing how to use it, children learn the counting sequence. This sequence is a kind of song, they discover, and it must go in a particular order.

Informal mathematics includes the ability to match one item with another item, as in setting the table. Later, sometime during the first years of formal school, the child comes to realize that five objects, no matter what size, no matter how spread out, no matter what the configuration, are still counted as five. This gradual realization, called "conservation" of number is an exciting transition and cognitive metamorphosis. It heralds the child's growing ability to use numerals symbolically with real meaning.

A learning disability at this age may revolve around using language, manipulating objects, or judging size at a glance. Those who are visually impaired require experiences touching and judging more/less, bigger/smaller. There is a very small group of children who seem unable to visually compare length and amount.

When children enter school, they will gradually learn the formal aspects of number, i.e., adding with exchanging and trading. In the best circumstances, children begin with informal mathematics, usually with manipulatives, and gradually build to the more abstract, less inherently meaningful formal procedures.

Many children do not make this connection and characterize math as a collection of unconnected facts which must be memorized. They don't look for patterns or meaning and can feel puzzled by classmates who seem to learn with so much less effort. In other cases, adults move in prematurely with children who are eager and excited to memorize, teaching them procedures which they can imitate but not understand. While this informal/formal gap is not, strictly speaking, a learning disability, it probably is a factor in a majority of math learning difficulties.

The pace at which children move from informal to formal arithmetic is far more gradual than most educators or parents realize. Even as adult learners we need a considerable chunk of time with the concrete, "real" aspect of a new piece of learning before we move on to making generalizations and other abstractions.

There are some children who have a language impairment, who do not easily process and understand the words and sentences they hear. Sometimes these children also have difficulty grasping the connection and the organizing hierarchy of "little" ideas and "big" ones.

These children are also likely to view math as an ocean full of meaningless facts and procedures to be memorized.

Visual processing difficulties play a different sort of role in reading than they do in mathematics. In math there are fewer symbols to recognize, produce, and decode, and children can "read" math successfully even when they cannot yet read words. Children with visual/spatial perceptual difficulties may exhibit two kinds of problems. In the less severe instance, some will understand math quite clearly but be unable to express this using paper and pencil. More severe is the case where children cannot translate what they see into ideas which make sense to them.

How Do You Assess a Mathematics Disability?

One need not be a mathematics expert to evaluate a child's ability and style of doing math. A one-to-one mathematics interview is the best format for noting details. In the interview one focuses as intently on how the child does mathematics as on what or how correctly they do it. It is essential to keep in mind that you are searching for what does work at the same time as you are probing to find out what doesn't work.

A mathematics interview should include the use of manipulatives, i.e. coins, base ten blocks, geoboards, cuisenaire rods, and tangrams. A calculator is an important tool and can be used to uncover the difference between comprehension and computation difficulties.

The interviewer needs to remember to look at the full range of mathematical areas. In addition to computation, one should explore the child's ability to make predictions based on understanding patterns, to sort collections of blocks or objects in a logical way, to organize space with flexibility, and to measure.

To aid in making a diagnosis which will result in useful recommendations, look carefully at strengths and weaknesses. Note whether the child talks to herself, whether she draws a picture to help her understand a situation, or whether he asks you to repeat. See if the child has a mathematics "proofreading" capacity by asking him to estimate before he computes. This is an important strength.

How Do You Help A Child Who Is Having Difficulty?

The fundamental principle in helping a child with a disability in mathematics is to work with the child to define his or her strengths. As these strengths are acknowledged, one uses them to re-configure what is difficult.

When learners have lost (or never had) the connection between mathematics and meaning, it is helpful to encourage them to estimate their answers before they begin computing. When children work together in small groups to solve problems, they often ask more questions, get more answers, and do more quality thinking than when they work quietly, alone.

When children have difficulty organizing their written work on a page, they often do better with graph paper. A less expensive solution is to turn lined paper sideways so that the lines serve as vertical columns. This is especially helpful for long division.

The task of learning the facts can be transformed into one requiring verbal reasoning. Instead of being asked to memorize 7 + 8, one boy was asked, "How do you remember that 7 + 8 = 15?" His strategies, in this case, that 7 + 7 = 14, so 7 + 8 = 15, were practiced and reinforced and he became able to retain his facts. A general principle is that through drill and practice children will get faster at whatever they're already doing. This technique of focusing on strategies is one which fosters a healthy sense of self reliance and diminishes the need for meaningless memorization.

When children do not have a strong language base, it is even more important for the language of explanations to be absolutely accurate (concrete) and parsimonious. In other words, elaborations confuse rather than help this type of child. Give the instructions or explanation once and give the child time and the materials to think about what has been said so that he or she can formulate a meaningful question, if necessary. Asking these children to process quickly is unrealistic and not helpful.

By contrast, the group of children who use language as a tool to keep themselves on track and to organize their thinking are often extremely quick to respond. Language is their preferred medium, after all. These children often respond well to the use of metaphor in explanations. These children are often impatient and do not understand that good thinking is not instantaneous. They need reassurance and a relaxed structure so that they go beyond the superficial quickness and do some real thinking.

Finally, those who are afraid to even attempt math are often unaware of their very real strengths. This group believes that math = computation, when in fact computation is but a small slice of mathematics. The increasing acceptance of calculators refocuses teachers and students on the real issue at hand: problem solving. Math anxious students often will take risks if their fears are acknowledged and support is provided. Students will gradually feel more powerful as they experience themselves as successful thinkers.

Summary

Mathematics learning disabilities do not often occur with clarity and simplicity. Rather, they can be combinations of difficulties which may include language processing problems, visual spatial confusion, memory and sequence difficulties, and/or unusually high anxiety. With the awareness that math understanding is actively constructed by each learner, we can intervene in this process to advocate for or provide experience with manipulatives, time for exploration, discussion where the "right" answer is irrelevant, careful and accurate language, access to helpful technologies, and understanding and support.

References

Baroody, A. (1987). *Children's Mathematical Thinking*. New York: Teachers College Press.

Ginsburg, H. (1977). *Children's Arithmetic: The Learning Process*. New York: Van Nostrand.

—by C. Christina Wright, Ph.D.

Part Four

Sensory and Communication Disorders

Chapter 17

Background Information on Developmental Speech and Language Disorders

Eliza, age 2-1/2, toddles around her nursery school classroom, the straps of her purple overalls slipping off her shoulders. She watches and smiles, and generally she follows directions, but Eliza is silent. The only words she utters are *dog* to describe a wooden plaything and—when it's time to go home—*bus*.

Ben is older, nearly 5, and as sweet-faced as little Eliza. But his only "words"—used sparingly in two-word phrases—are all but unintelligible to a stranger. Ben wants to join in the activities of his class, but he cannot understand his teacher's instructions about putting a beanbag on his head, on his shoe, on his shoulder. He simply holds on to the beanbag and smiles, waiting to imitate the other children's responses.

Eliza and Ben are in a special program for preschoolers with speech and language disorders. Eliza is language disordered and has a brain dysfunction: she is delayed primarily in her ability to translate thoughts into language, even though she understands almost everything that a child her age is expected to. Ben is disordered in both speech and language. His problems involve the neurological motor skills that produce speech, as well as the brain function of understanding language. The treatment he requires is more complex. And if Ben has normal intelligence—which can be determined by specialized testing—then this intelligence is masked by his halting, stumbling phrases.

NIH Publication No. 88-2757. March 1988. An update on the information in this chapter appears in the next chapter.

What causes speech and language disorders in children like these? How can the problems be treated? Will children who are slow to speak and understand what is said to them also be slow to read, to write, to think logically? Evidence suggests that the answer to the latter question may be yes for some children, but scientists continue to search for causes and effective treatments that will give parents and professionals a basis for hope. Encouraged by the National Institute of Neurological and Communicative Disorders and Stroke (NINCDS), the primary source of Federal support for research on the brain and disorders of speech and language, investigators around the country are developing new techniques for studying normal and disordered speech and language acquisition as well as treatments for speech and language impairments.

Eliza and Ben have a chance of being helped because their problems have been discovered and are being treated early in life. But many questions will remain unanswered for years. The children will be watched closely when they enter school—Ben probably in a special classroom, Eliza perhaps mainstreamed into a regular school—to see whether their speech and language delays show up later in other guises, particularly as reading disabilities. And as they reach adulthood, another question looms: Will they pass their speech and language difficulties on to their own children?

The Scope of the Problem

A child with a language disorder has difficulty understanding language or putting words together to make sense, indicating a problem with brain function. A child with a speech disorder has trouble producing the sounds of language, often resulting from a combination of brain-coordination and neurological motor dysfunction. Either child will lag significantly behind the level of speech and language development expected of a playmate of the same age, environment, and intellectual ability.

Language impairment may show itself in several ways:

- Children may have trouble giving names to objects and using those names to formulate ideas about how the world is organized. For example, they cannot learn that a toy they play with is called <u>car</u>, or that a toy car of another color, or a real car, can also be called <u>car</u>.

- They may have trouble learning the rules of grammar. Such children might not learn, for example, how to use prepositions and other small words like <u>in</u> or <u>the</u>.

- They may not use language appropriately for the context; for example, they might respond to a teacher's question by reciting an irrelevant jingle heard on television.

Speech problems seem to be more prevalent than language problems. Both disorders appear to decline as children get older. Speech disorders affect an estimated 10 to 15 percent of preschoolers, and about 6 percent of children in grades 1 through 12. Language disorders affect about 2 to 3 percent of the preschool population and about 1 percent of the school-age population. In all, nearly 6 million children under the age of 18 are speech or language disordered. Two-thirds of them are boys.

It is difficult to be more precise about just how prevalent the problem is, because the definition itself is so unwieldy. How delayed must a child be to qualify as "disordered"? How does one recognize the delay in the first place?

When Is There a Problem?

Experts use phrases such as *developmental language disorder, delayed speech, impaired language, motor disorder,* and *idiopathic* (no known cause) speech and language disorders to describe a variety of speech and language difficulties in children. In this pamphlet, delayed speech or delayed language means a problem that appears in the course of the child's development and for which there is no apparent cause. Eliminated from this discussion are speech or language problems that can be traced to deafness, mental retardation, cerebral palsy, or autism.

Speech-language pathologists generally define children as disordered if they lag significantly behind their age peers in reaching certain speech and language milestones. The significance of this lag is determined by a thorough professional examination. British studies show that the range of normal for early language acquisition is enormous. Normal children speak their first word at anywhere from 6 to 18 months, and combine words into phrases for the first time at anywhere from 10 to 24 months. It takes a skilled practitioner to distinguish between a slow child who will eventually catch up and a child with a true delay.

Speech and language professionals have devised a general outline of what speech sounds should have been acquired by a certain age. A child who is not quite on schedule, of course, is not necessarily delayed or disordered; it may just be that the child's individual timetable is different from most children's.

Language problems are most obvious among 2- to 3-year-olds, whose language skills are usually developing very rapidly. Many of these problems subsequently resolve themselves; others require the aid of therapy.

Among older children, speech and language disorders might emerge in a different guise. A 5- or 6-year-old might have caught up in language and social skills sufficiently to communicate with others, but not sufficiently for good reading or thinking. Such a child could be considered reading- or learning-disabled.

The Physical Tools of Speech

Speech has four components: articulation, phonation, resonance, and rhythm:

- *Articulation* is the ability to make specific sounds: the g in gum, the b in bear, the s in snake. Articulation is the component most often affected in children with speech disorders of unknown cause.

- *Phonation* is the utterance of vocal sounds—the voice—produced in the larynx or "voice box."

- *Resonance* is the modification of the voice after it leaves the larynx. The voice is modified by the cavities inside the mouth, nose, and pharynx (the throat).

- *Rhythm*, or what scientists call *prosody* involves the rate and timing of speech.

For speech to begin, the brain and the vocal and auditory systems must be in good working order. The human vocal system components are perfectly adapted for speech. Our teeth, for example, are usually evenly spaced and equal in size (unless there are dental problems), and our top and bottom teeth can get close enough to pronounce such sounds as s, f, sh, and th. Our lips have more developed muscles than the lips of other primates, and our relatively small mouths can open and shut rapidly to form sounds such as p and b. The size of our mouth opening can be varied to pronounce a range of vowel sounds.

The location of the larynx is perhaps the most important feature of the human vocal system. In the adult human, the larynx, where the vocal cords are located and voice sounds originate, is located farther down in the throat than is the larynx of any other primate. This extra room allows humans to modulate speech and to pronounce such sounds as the consonants in gut and cut.

Defects in the structure of the lips, palate, or teeth can interfere with a child's ability to make speech sounds correctly. A hole in the palate—the "cleft palate" seen in some newborns—is the most common such problem. A cleft palate can usually be corrected surgically, but even after surgery affected children may have too much nasal resonance and difficulty producing certain speech sounds. Other children with growths in the larynx or vocal cords may have voices with a harsh, husky sound.

The auditory system comprises the three parts of the ear—the outer ear, the middle ear, and the inner ear—and the connections between the inner ear and the auditory center of the brain. The middle ear is prone to infection during childhood because of the angle of the Eustachian tube, which connects the middle ear to the throat. When a child has a cold, the short Eustachian tube cannot drain excess mucus properly, and the fluid that builds up becomes a breeding ground for bacteria. The resulting condition is called otitis media.

If the auditory system is not in good order and a hearing loss exists as a result of continual ear infections and fluid buildup, the child may mishear adult speech and produce it incorrectly. To avoid this problem, an otolaryngologist, a physician who specializes in ear, nose, and throat disorders, should be consulted at the first sign of a hearing loss. The otolaryngologist may refer the child for testing to an audiologist, an expert on the hearing process.

The Role of the Brain

If scientists were asked to identify the most important feature of the brain that enables humans to speak, they would point to the brain's functional division into left and right hemispheres. This characteristic appears to be related in most people to the brain's asymmetry. Even at birth one can see evidence of this asymmetry: the left hemisphere tends to be larger than the right in most newborns.

Although most complex functions involve both sides of the brain to some extent, certain functions can be traced to one hemisphere or the other. In approximately 90 percent of us, the right hemisphere controls how we see spatial relationships (such as the recognition of faces) and recognize patterns (such as a musical melody). In that same 90 percent of us, the left hemisphere controls how we process sequences of information involving language.

Neuroscientists once thought that a person's handedness showed which side of the brain was dominant for language: right-handed people were thought to derive language skills from the left hemisphere, left-handed people were thought to draw these skills from the right hemisphere. But we now know that the tendency is for most individuals, no matter which hand they prefer, to rely on the left hemisphere for language abilities. In certain situations, however, the right hemisphere can take over language function. In young children, for example, the loss of left-hemisphere language function after certain kinds of brain surgery can be well compensated for by the right hemisphere. But in adolescents and young adults the right hemisphere is less able to take over language or speech production.

The maturing nervous system. The development of the brain's asymmetry is part of the overall maturation of the nervous system which occurs before birth. Scientists believe that sometime in the middle of gestation, nerve cells, or neurons, migrate from germinal zones—areas where cells reproduce—to the regions of the brain in which they will reside. This brain cell migration usually begins at about the 16th week and ends by the 24th week.

If the migration of cells to the brain is incomplete or interrupted by something in the fetus' environment (perhaps an antibody developed by the body in response to a foreign substance), the fetus could die before or shortly after birth. If migration occurs, but with errors, the result could be language delay.

After mid-gestation, and probably through the first decade of life, the neurons of a child's brain begin to mature. As neurons develop, they grow axons: long connecting arms linking one brain cell to another. As neuronal development continues, these axons are covered by a myelin sheath, a fatty casing that protects the axons and helps them transmit messages more efficiently. This myelinization of message pathways in the brain occurs at a rapid rate until about age 2 and continues at a slower pace until puberty. The process is crucial to the child's growing capacity for understanding and expressing language.

The brain's language centers. Two areas in the brain are known to be involved in speech and language. Broca's area, named after the French surgeon Pierre-Paul Broca, is in the left frontal lobe, close to the part of the brain that controls movements of the tongue, larynx, and other structures involved in speech. Broca's area is responsible for translating thoughts into speech.

Wernicke's area, named after the German neurologist Karl Wernicke, is located behind Broca's area, just around the temples. It contributes to the understanding of the spoken and written word, and in most individuals is larger in the left hemisphere than in the right. Wernicke's area is quite close to the auditory cortex, the brain region that controls the input and analysis of sound.

The difference in function of the two language regions is apparent when either area is damaged. Aphasia is the loss of language after a brain injury. An adult aphasic with damage to Broca's area has reduced speech that sounds like a message in a telegram: asked about the weather, he might respond "rainy" or, if pressed, "rainy day. " An adult with damage to Wernicke's area may articulate well and form grammatically correct sentences, but provides very little coherent information in his speech. Such a patient might answer a question about the weather by saying, "I think it's not good. I don't like it when it's like that. " Many aphasic patients may have other language problems as well.

Translating sounds into meaning. Some children may have language difficulty because of a problem with the brain's ability to analyze speech. Research scientists have studied dozens of language-delayed children and found that they are unable to process rapid speechlike signals produced by a computer. But they can be trained to differentiate among sounds if the time between sounds is prolonged.

Scientists now know that soon after birth, babies are able to detect differences between speech sounds. Investigators have found that infants as young as 1 month can detect the minute differences between closely related speech sounds such as pat and bat.

Most children develop a phonological system, an internal sense of how different categories of speech sounds are used, by about age 3. This system differs according to the child's native language. An English-speaking child, for instance, does not have within his phonological system the same s sound as a Spanish-speaking child, a sound that is somewhere between the English s and th, or the gutteral kh sound of a German-speaking child.

Children must first perceive the unique characteristics of a sound in order to be able to repeat it. But many sounds in the English language differ only minutely—and sometimes the differences are a matter of timing. The difference between the initial sounds for the words bin and pin, for example, is a function of something called voice onset time. To utter the b sound, the vocal cords begin to vibrate almost as soon as the speaker releases air by opening the lips. For the p sound, there is a delay of about 20 extra milliseconds between the time the lips first open and the time the vocal cords start vibrating.

Even though these differences are very small, most persons can discriminate between b and p, or d and t, or g and k—consonants distinguishable by short differences in voice onset time. Speech-language pathologists believe that when children consistently fail to make these distinctions, they may have incorrectly established the sounds in their phonological systems.

Think of what happens to an adult trying to learn a foreign language. The adult can generally imitate the sounds of that language after hearing a word about 50 to 100 times, but still does not know the phonology—the range of possible sounds of the language and the rules for their order. Similarly, a child can imitate the sounds his speech pathologist urges him to make, but to him they're like a foreign tongue. A little boy who speaks like Elmer Fudd, the cartoon character who calls Bugs Bunny a "scwewy wabbit," may be capable of making an r sound the way he's told to, but to him the r sound isn't supposed to sound like an r. He thinks it should sound like a w.

Other Influencing Factors

The normal development of speech and language depends largely on the health of the brain and the vocal and auditory systems. But children who are abnormally slow in speech or language acquisition may show no signs of physical problems that could explain the delay. In such cases, certain other factors may be slowing things down.

Ear Infections. Controversy exists about the relationship between chronic otitis media and the rapidity with which a child learns to speak. Most studies investigating the question have found no clear association between otitis media and language disorder, unless a hearing loss is present. The prudent course is to treat ear infections promptly and to be alert to signs of poor hearing—inattentiveness, failure to respond, requests to have words repeated or to have the television volume raised—in a child with frequent otitis media. Treatment may include antibiotic therapy and the insertion of a tube into the middle ear to drain the fluid. Recent NINCDS-supported studies found that decongestant and antihistamine compounds are ineffective for otitis media but that the antibiotic amoxicillin is effective.

Poor models in the home. The role of the environment in language acquisition has never been fully explained. For example, a normal child whose parent suffers from a language problem may reach full language competence despite an environment in which language models are scant. Psycholinguists, who study the psychological and biological roots of language, believe most children have an innate drive to learn the language of the community no matter what the environment.

But children whose brain structures are abnormal, even in quite subtle ways, may be born with a tendency toward language problems, and if their environments are language-deficient they just don't have the inner resources to compensate. In addition, a vicious cycle of silence is all too easy to establish in the home of a language-impaired child. Parents react to the cues their babies give them. If a baby does not respond with sounds and words, the parent is unlikely to know that the baby is indeed ready for conversation. According to one scientist, the communication difficulties of language-impaired children have a direct impact on the parent's efforts to talk to them.

A Collection of Disorders

Speech and language disorders wear many faces. Common speech disorders include:

- *Phonological impairment*, also called misarticulation. Here the child says the sounds wrong, or omits or duplicates certain sounds within a word. The problem may reflect poor neurological motor skills, a learning error, or difficulty in identifying certain speech sounds. Examples of common errors are <u>wabbit</u> for <u>rabbit</u>, <u>thnake</u> for <u>snake</u>, <u>dood </u>for <u>good</u>, and <u>poo</u> for <u>spoon</u>.

  Another phonological impairment is unstressed syllable deletion, in which a child simply skips over a syllable in a long word, as in <u>nana</u> for <u>banana</u> or <u>te-phone</u> for <u>telephone</u>. Many of these misproductions are a part of normal development and are expected in the speech of very young children, but when they persist past the expected age they are considered abnormal and usually indicate brain dysfunction.

- *Verbal dyspraxia*. This term is used by some scientists and clinicians to describe the inability to produce the sequential, rapid, and precise movements required for speech. Nothing is wrong with the child's vocal apparatus, but the child's brain cannot give correct instructions for the motor movements involved in speech. This disorder is characterized by many sound omissions. Some verbally dyspraxic children, for instance, speak only in vowels, making their speech nearly unintelligible. One little boy trying to say "My name is Billy" can only manage "eye a eh ee-ee. " These children also have very slow, halting speech with many false starts before the right sounds are produced. Their speech errors may be similar to those of children with phonological impairment.

- *Dysarthria.* Here muscle control problems affect the speech-making apparatus. Dysarthria most commonly occurs in combination with other nervous system disorders such as cerebral palsy. A dysarthric child cannot control the muscles involved in speaking and eating, so the mouth may be open all the time or the tongue may protrude.

A child with a language problem has difficulty comprehending or using language, and several different types of errors may result. Three of the more common are:

- *Form errors.* These are present when the child cannot understand or use the rules of grammar. A child with this problem might say "We go pool" instead of "We went to the pool."

  Language-disordered children seem to have particular difficulty with complex sentence constructions such as questions and negative forms.

  Examples of Form Errors:

Correct sentences	Disordered sentences:
They won't play with me	They no play with me.
I can't sing	I no can sing.
He doesn't have money	He no have money.
When will he come?	When he will come?
What is that?	What that?

- *Content errors.* This language disorder is involved when the semantics, or what the child understands or talks about, is limited or inaccurate. The child may have a limited vocabulary or may fail to understand that the same word—match, for example— can have multiple meanings.

- *Use errors.* This term concerns what linguists call pragmatics, the ability of the child to follow the rules of communication: when to talk, how to request information, how to take turns. A child with a use error might be unable to ask an adult for help, even though he knows that help is needed and the adult can provide it. Autistic children who have difficulty communicating with people may have use errors.

Categorizing Patients

If children with a speech or language problem are to benefit from different treatment approaches now available, they must be accurately subgrouped according to type of impairment. In categorizing speech- and language-impaired children, experts tend to ask two questions. First, is the disorder expressive, receptive, or a mixture of both? Second, is the child simply delayed in speech or language development, or is the child not only delayed but abnormal in speech and language when these skills begin to develop?

Expressive or receptive? Some language-impaired children have primarily expressive (speaking) disorders; others have mainly receptive (understanding) disorders. Most have a combination of both.

Clinicians often encounter children who may be unable to communicate effectively, but nonetheless show signs of understanding others quite well. Consider Becky, a 6-year-old girl seen at a speech clinic. Her conversation with a clinician goes like this:

> *Clinician:* What is your favorite game?
> *Becky:* Doctor.
> *Clinician:* How many can play that game?
> *Becky:* Two four.
> *Clinician:* Two or four?
> *Becky:* Or three.
> *Clinician:* How do you play doctor?
> *Becky:* One has to be doctor.
> *Clinician:* Anything else?
> *Becky:* One operation man.
> *Clinician:* Anything else?
> *Becky:* No.
> *Clinician:* What do you want to be?
> *Becky:* A nurse.
> *Clinician:* Oh, you need a nurse?
> *Becky:* No, you don't.

Becky has an expressive language disorder. Her responses are limited to incomplete sentences that may be inappropriate to the question, and they reveal Becky's inability to use verbs, conjunctions, or any of the subtleties of language. Like some children with expressive language problems, Becky has a good vocabulary, but she has difficulty connecting words. Even though she is 6, she talks like a 2-year-old.

Children with expressive language problems may or may not have articulation problems. But even if their speech is perfectly articulated, communication is impaired because language remains ungrammatical, reduced, babyish.

Paul, who is 7 years old, is Becky's opposite, a child with a receptive language disorder who has difficulty understanding language. Receptive language problems rarely occur alone; usually they are accompanied by at least some degree of expressive language disorder. The condition often is misdiagnosed as attention problems, behavioral problems, or hearing problems. Standardized language tests may reveal, though, that a child with a receptive language disorder is trying to cooperate but simply cannot understand the instructions.

Paul, for instance, cannot point to a picture that best reveals his understanding of single vocabulary words or of grammatical associations between words. When asked to point to a picture of "the ball under the table," Paul might just as readily point to a picture of a ball on the table. When asked to point to the picture of "the boy running after the girl," he might instead choose the one of a girl running after a boy.

Delay or disorder? Scientists have not agreed on whether language-impaired children acquire language normally—but more slowly—than other children or whether they develop language in an abnormal way when they begin to talk and understand. If any consensus has been reached in the past decade, it is that both sides may be right. There may be two quite separate conditions, one in which speech or language is delayed, and another in which speech or language is not only delayed but also incorrect.

In the 1970s, several groups of scientists tackled the problem. Generally, children had been categorized according to certain measures of language development such as the average length of spontaneous sentences. One study found that language-impaired children used simpler grammatical sentences and fewer questions than other children. Another study found that language-impaired children understood the meanings and relationships of words in much the same way that other children did. Language-impaired children seemed to develop their ability to express themselves in the same progression as normal children, but only after they had reached a higher-than-normal level of language comprehension.

The general consensus from research of recent years is: many language-impaired children seem to be merely delayed, but a sizable number also develop language in an abnormal way. The distinction is important, because it can help clinicians recognize that some children should be treated aggressively and others left alone.

A Visit to the Doctor

A child whose parents suspect a speech or language disorder will probably enter the health care system through the pediatrician's office. Before referral to a speech-language pathologist for assessment, the physician will try to determine if there are underlying conditions that might be the indirect cause of the speech or language delay.

A child is likely to be tested to rule out the following conditions:

- *Hearing problems.* Language acquisition is a continual process of hearing, imitating or spontaneously trying a word or phrase, hearing one's own productions, and refining them. Scientists have observed that infants who have impaired hearing from birth tend to be delayed in their instinctive babbling and produce fewer different sounds.

  A physician faced with a child over 2 years old who does not speak often will refer that child for complete audiological testing. Such tests involve the use of tones delivered through headphones: as soon as the tone is heard, the child responds by raising a finger or performing some other behavior or gesture. Occasionally, children with hearing problems may unintentionally hide their conditions from their parents because they become so adept at using environmental cues—facial expressions, vibrations, and what little hearing they have—to get by. These cues fall short of helping the children learn the complex sounds of language.

- *Mental retardation.* The developmental language disorders described in this chapter occur in children of normal or above-normal intelligence. However, language problems are also common among the mentally retarded. Experts estimate that nearly half of all mildly retarded children, 90 percent of severely retarded children, and 100 percent of profoundly retarded children have language disorders of some sort.

277

A pediatrician may suspect mental retardation if the delay in achieving speech and language milestones is accompanied by a delay in other mental and physical milestones. Gross neurological motor development—sitting, standing, crawling, and walking—and fine motor development—reaching, grasping, building towers of blocks—are often interpreted as clues to whether a child's mental capacities are normal. If mental retardation is a source of concern, tests are available to see just where a child ranks with his or her age peers in mental and physical areas of development. These tests involve such tasks as having the child imitate an examiner's arrangement of blocks or copy geometric shapes.

- *Autism.* One of the hallmarks of the disorder called autism is the inability of the child to communicate. Autism begins before age 2-1/2 years; it includes particular speech and language problems: total lack of language, a pervasive lack of responsiveness to people, and peculiar speech patterns. The latter include immediate or delayed echoing of another's comments, speaking in metaphors, or reversing pronouns. In addition to having communication problems, autistic children may be resistant to change, may be overly attached to objects, and may have bizarre and unexpected responses to their environments. A child neurologist will ask about the child's behavior to rule out autism.

- *Cerebral palsy.* The muscle control problems characteristic of cerebral palsy can sometimes interfere with speaking. When this happens, children may understand language better than they can speak. They may have trouble expressing themselves because of difficulty moving their lips or tongue.

- *Acquired aphasia.* Children are considered aphasic when the brain injury that causes loss of language occurs after speech and language have begun to develop. Aphasia can occur after severe head trauma or a brain infection. Some acquired aphasia is an unfortunate consequence of surgery, as in those rare cases when children undergoing a heart operation suffer a stroke after blood flow to the brain is blocked.

Children who suffer damage to the left half of the brain exhibit many of the symptoms that adult aphasics do. Their problems are predominantly expressive but also may be receptive. They may have speech articulation problems or make errors in syntax. They may also speak in reduced, incomplete sentences, just as adults do when there is damage to Broca's area.

But a child with acquired aphasia is different from an adult aphasic in one important way: the child is better able to recover. Because the brain continues to reorganize itself until adolescence, neurons seem to be capable of compensating for an injury that happens early in life.

- *Other conditions.* A handful of genetic conditions also are characterized by language or speech problems. These include *Cri Du Chat Syndrome*, which leads to mental retardation and a tendency to make catlike mewing sounds, and *Tourette Syndrome*, a neurological disorder characterized by involuntary sounds such as barking, clicking, and yelping.

A Team of Experts

Once a child has been identified as having a speech or language disorder, most successful diagnosis and treatment involves a team of experts. The audiologist, an expert in the process of hearing, evaluates and assists those with hearing disorders. The audiologist may work in consultation with an otolaryngologist, a physician who specializes in ear, nose, and throat disorders. These two health professionals determine which hearing conditions can be treated—and perhaps corrected—medically or surgically, and which require rehabilitative techniques such as hearing aids or lip reading.

The speech-language pathologist, also called a speech therapist, studies the normal and abnormal processes of speech and language and measures and diagnoses speech and language problems. The pathologist can also enhance early learning of language, teach the correct production of speech and language, and help a child learn to understand words and sentences.

The neurologist is a physician with expertise in the workings of the brain and nervous system. The neurologist may use modern brain imaging techniques to "see" through the skull and detect brain abnormalities in a child with speech or language delay. A range of pencil-and-paper and physical tests have also been devised to help diagnose any underlying brain disorder that might account for the language problem.

The psychologist studies the science of human development and personality, and can administer tests to evaluate the child's cognitive capabilities. Such tests can help determine how the child's language age compares to his or her mental and chronological ages.

The New Therapy

In the 1970s, language-delayed children were taught to repeat sentences in a robotlike fashion. As one NINCDS scientist puts it, "These children could say, 'We went swimming today' perfectly, but they couldn't change it to say the same thing with different words. "Today the emphasis in therapy is less on imitation than on grasping the context of language. Children play with toys and are taught to translate their activities into words—a mode of learning that is more meaningful for them and that gives them the tools to construct their own sentences.

For the child whose speech is impaired or delayed, treatment may focus on one sound group at a time, starting with the sounds that babies naturally learn first. Young clients are encouraged to use the sounds in a variety of contexts, to watch the clinician make the sound—even putting their hands on the clinician's throat or mouth while the sound is spoken—and to watch themselves make the sound, putting their hands on their own mouths and watching themselves in a mirror.

The most important and continuous help comes from parents. Guided by speech and language pathologists, parents can do a great deal to improve the language environment in their home.

Parents can learn better ways to respond to their children's utterances so that language skills improve. When a child says, "more milk," a parent may respond several ways. The least helpful are silently to refill the milk glass, or to say, "here milky in cuppy," or some other form of nongrammatical babytalk. But adults are tempted to give such answers with youngsters who never seem to benefit from more sophisticated replies such as, "Do you want more milk?" A better response would be the simple statement, "More milk for Sam."

If the parent peppers responses with what linguists call *expansions*—new words, new sentence constructions, new rules of grammar—the child can eventually learn new bits of language. Expansions introduce new information or help the parent develop the child's words into a grammatically correct sentence.

Ways Adults Can Help a Child Learn Language

- Expand the statement, preserving the child's intent.
  a. Expand the statement using the same noun.
     Child: kitty jump.
     Adult: The kitty is on the chair.
  b. Replace the noun with a pronoun.
     Child: kitty jump.
     Adult: She is jumping.
  c. Expand the statement adding new information.
     Child: kitty jump.
     Adult: The dog is jumping, too.

- Respond by indicating the truth value of the child's utterance, rather than its linguistic accuracy (or inaccuracy).
     Child: kitty jump.
     Adult: Yes, the kitty is jumping

The Long-Term Outlook

How do speech- and language-impaired children fare in adolescence and adulthood? Most followup studies indicate that speech disorders tend to be outgrown by adolescence, but that difficulties involving language use, production, or understanding can persist into adulthood.

One study from the University of Iowa examined 36 adults, 18 of whom had been diagnosed as speech-disordered and 18 as language-disordered when they were children. Nine of the language-disordered children still had communication and learning difficulties in adulthood, compared to only one in the speech-disordered group.

A Cleveland-based study of 63 preschoolers with speech and language disorders found that 5 years after initial diagnosis, 40 percent of the children still had speech and language problems, and 40 percent had other learning problems such as below-normal achievement in reading and in math. NINCDS-supported scientists at the University of California at San Diego are now conducting a study of 100 language-impaired 4-year-olds to see how they fare up to 5 years after identification of their language problems. Preliminary results suggest that children with only expressive language losses have a lower risk of long-term problems than do children with both expressive and receptive impairments.

The Promise of Research

Scientists are pursuing research leads that promise improved therapy for children with speech and language disorders. Studies of these disorders are supported by NINCDS, other Federal agencies including the National Institute of Mental Health and the National Institute of Child Health and Human Development, and private and medical institutions.

The brain's organization. Studies of cell structure in the brains of dyslexic individuals—otherwise normal people who have extraordinary difficulty learning to read—show that speech and language disorders may be caused by abnormal development of the brain's language centers sometime before or soon after birth.

"From the middle of gestation until about the first or second year, the actual floor plan of the brain is being laid down," says one of the NINCDS grantees who conducted these studies at Boston's Beth Israel Hospital.

Using a technique called cytoarchitectonics, in which the actual structure and arrangement of cells is revealed, the investigators examined the brains of seven adults who had been diagnosed as dyslexic. They found a series of abnormalities in the cerebral cortex. These included *ectopias*, neurons found in the language centers of the brain that seem to have arisen elsewhere and migrated to the wrong area; *dysplasias*, or misshapen neurons; and so-called brain warts, neurons that are nodular in appearance. The brains also failed to show the normal degree of asymmetry.

Other methods are being used to study how the brain may be abnormal in children with speech or language disorders. Some scientists are using brain imaging techniques to try to locate the site of auditory processing in the brains of children with expressive and receptive language impairments. These investigators hope to pinpoint regions where speech sounds are processed and to see how those regions differ between language-impaired and normal children.

The genetic connection. Speech and language problems seem to run in families. This could be accounted for by environmental influences: a home in which language is misused is a home where children develop poor language skills. But most scientists think there may be a large genetic component. Investigators are now studying families with speech and language problems to find out how these disorders are inherited.

Speeding things up. Some language disorders may originate in the abnormally slow rate at which the child's brain is able to process information. To test this theory, scientists are experimenting with ways to train language-impaired children to process speech and language more rapidly. NINCDS grantees at the University of California at San Diego are using computers to teach children to hear the most subtle sound shifts—such as those that differentiate ba from da—by exaggerating those differences. The computer produces and gradually speeds up speech sounds until the children can hear the ba/da distinction at the rate at which it occurs in ordinary conversation.

Some language-delayed children avoid words that are hard to pronounce. In an NINCDS-supported study of word avoidance, scientists at Purdue University are asking both normal and language-delayed children to say the hard-to-pronounce nonsense names assigned to unusual objects and toys. By characterizing the patterns of word avoidance in the two groups, the scientists hope to devise improved treatment methods for the language-delayed children.

As scientists learn more about how the normal brain controls language and initiates speech, they will also discover just what goes wrong in brains when problems arise. After the underlying mechanisms are detected, investigators hope to develop new treatment techniques to help the millions of children whose thoughts and feelings are poorly expressed.

Where to Get Help

A number of private organizations have been set up to help people with speech and language disorders. These organizations distribute educational materials and, in some cases, provide lists of treatment experts. For more information, call or write to the following organizations:

American Speech-Language-Hearing Association
10801 Rockville Pike
Rockville, MD 20852
(301) 897-5700

The Council for Exceptional Children
Division of Children with Communication Disorders
1920 Association Drive
Reston, VA 22091
(703) 620-3660

National Association for Hearing and Speech Action
Suite 1000
6110 Executive Boulevard
Rockville, MD 20852
(301) 897-8682

National Easter Seal Society, Inc.
2023 West Ogden Avenue
Chicago, IL 60612
(312) 243-8400

The Orton Dyslexia Society, Inc.
724 York Road
Towson, MD 21204
(301) 296-0232

Tourette Syndrome Association
42-40 Bell Boulevard
Bayside, NY 11361
(718) 224-2999
(800) 237-0717 (toll free)

NINCDS Information

For more information about the research programs of the NINCDS, contact:

Office of Scientific and Health Reports
National Institute on Deafness and Other Communication Disorders
National Institutes of Health
Bethesda, MD 20892
(301) 496-7243
(301) 402-0252

Chapter 18

Update on Developmental Speech and Language Disorders

The National Institute on Deafness and Other Communication Disorders (NIDCD) has primary responsibility at the National Institutes of Health (NIH) for supporting research on developmental speech and language disorders. The NIDCD, which became one of the institutes of the NIH in October 1988, supports research and research training on normal and disordered processes of hearing, balance, smell, taste, voice, speech, and language. This publication provides an update of current research and recent advances in understanding developmental speech and language disorders.

Language Impairments

Overview. It is estimated that between six and eight million people in the United States have some form of language impairment. A person with a language impairment or disorder has difficulty communicating with others because the ability to understand or produce language is impaired. Understanding spoken words and sentences may be difficult, and the disorder may lead to problems with speaking, reading and writing. Scientists study development of language to understand the nature of the disorders affecting language development and to design teaching or therapeutic strategies to improve

---

The text in this chapter is taken from a document published in December 1991, as an update of the original National Institute on Deafness and other Communication Disorders (NIDCD) booklet on Developmental Speech and Language Disorders (No. 88-2757) which is reprinted in the previous chapter.

285

the communication process for persons with developmental language disorders.

There are different causes of language disorders in children. Some language disorders are a result of hearing loss, autism, mental retardation, emotional disorders, or neural impairment. However, for a larger number of children, the cause of the disorder is unknown. Scientists use the term specific language impairment (SLI) to describe language disorders of unknown cause. SLI is the type of disorder discussed in this update.

Early studies of SLI children found that only a small percentage of these children showed evidence of a neural impairment. However, studies since then have shown that children with SLI may have temporal processing difficulties, in that some perform especially poorly when asked to identify specific sounds when hearing a series of rapid sound changes. Children with SLI also may have problems in coordinating incoming sensations (e.g., sight, sound, touch) with motor activity.

Early studies of children with SLI centered on the features of syntax (sentence structure), morphology (word formation and pronunciation), phonology (the sounds of words), and semantic relations or the meaning of words in a sentence in relation to their location in the sentence. Scientists found that children with SLI had problems in all of these areas. The studies revealed that these children not only develop language more slowly than other children with normal language, but also differently than younger children who are developing language normally. Certain features (e.g., word formation) caused more serious difficulty. Long-term studies of children with language-related learning problems showed that these language problems may continue into adulthood. Young children with language-related learning problems are clearly at risk for later problems in reading.

Recent Advances. Diagnostic techniques, such as magnetic resonance imaging (MRI), are being used to determine if neurogenic disorders might be found in language-impaired children. MRI produces detailed images of the body's inner structures without the use of x-rays.

Genetic studies of SLI children have also been undertaken. The findings from these studies suggest that SLI children are more likely than are normal children to have other family members with language problems. An NIDCD-supported scientist is conducting a genetic study at the University of Iowa to determine factors that contribute to this familial aspect of specific language impairment.

Scientists at the Salk Institute, La Jolla, California, are examining the neurobehavioral development (the brain's impact on behavioral development) in normal children and in language-impaired and reading-disabled (LI/RD) children. They are comparing brain functions during tasks involving sensing, thinking, and language reception and production in normal children and LI/RD children at different ages and different stages of language and thought development. This research will provide an understanding of the best type and timing of intervention for language-impaired individuals.

New studies include comparisons of treatment for children with SLI. Current research includes studies on the lexical (vocabulary) and pragmatic (communicative-conversational) abilities of SLI children. Scientists at the Pennsylvania State University are exploring ways to combine imitation training, in which the child imitates the clinician's or teacher's speech, and conversation-based treatment which involves the child in conversation. At an NIDCD-sponsored research study at the University of Washington investigators are looking at the language acquisition process in preschool SLI children to determine whether there are optimum times to begin treatment.

Some of the research priorities of the NIDCD include the integration of speech perception (children's recognition, organization, and interpretation of speech) and speech motor abilities and the relationship of these processes to language acquisition. NIDCD-supported researchers at Purdue University, for example, are examining differences in the processes of speech perception and speech production in normal and SLI children. They are using tests of speech production to determine whether a primary speech motor deficit or a speech motor learning impairment is the cause of language problems in children. These tests will help the scientists determine what extent speech production abilities (i.e., speech motor skills) may be related to how children interpret and produce sentences. Another study by scientists at Indiana University is examining the relationships between speech perception and the more abstract linguistic (language) and cognitive (thinking) processes involved in the understanding of spoken language.

Children with SLI often exhibit difficulties with the way words are used, such as use of past tense and function words, which include articles (i.e., a, an, the) and auxiliary verbs (i.e., be, have, do). A research project is underway at Purdue University to explore the possible bases of these grammatical word limitations and to examine how such limitations may hinder other aspects of these children's language development.

Speech Disorders

Overview. Speech development is a gradual process that requires years of practice. Children spend several years "playing with speech sounds" and imitating the sounds they hear. Most children have mastered all of the speech sounds by six years of age; however, they will continue to refine their speech production for several more years.

By first grade, it is estimated that five percent of children have noticeable speech disorders, the majority of which have no known cause. Although most of these children eventually learn normal speech, about 20 percent will remain speech impaired for the rest of their lives. According to the American Speech-Language-Hearing Association, the major class of speech disorders are articulation disorders of unknown cause. An articulation disorder is an incorrect production of specific speech sounds (e.g., producing a lisp by substituting the /s/ sound for the /th/ sound). These children comprise 40 percent of those seen by school speech clinicians.

Another category of speech disorder is fluency disorders or stuttering. This disorder is characterized by a disruption in the flow of speech. It includes repetitions of speech sounds, hesitations before and during speaking, and/or prolongations of speech sounds. It can be accompanied by evidence of a struggle to speak. The speaker will frequently avoid certain words or phrases and avoid certain difficult speech situations (for example, the telephone). Although stuttering is a type of speech disorder, it is not a developmental speech disorder and is not the focus of this text.

Recent Advances. NIDCD continues to support research to identify the causes of articulation disorders and to identify factors that may be used in treatment. A research project at Indiana University, for example, is examining whether children perceive distinctions in their own sound productions that are not perceived by other listeners. The researchers will determine if treatment of perceptual knowledge (the listener's interpretation of speech sounds) is as important to learning sounds as treatment of productive knowledge (the process of sound production). It is important to know if some articulation disorders result from a problem in a child's understanding of language messages or a defect in the child's motor system, i.e., the ability to make the movements to produce the sounds. The results of this project will help to identify processes that are essential to learning a sound system. A large research program is being conducted by investigators at the University of Wisconsin to describe, predict, manage, and prevent developmental articulation disorders. Scientists are determining how to predict normal speech following indirect (caregiver-based) and direct (clinician-based) management of speech problems. These findings will have a direct impact on service delivery for preschool children identified as having speech disorders of unknown origin.

As scientists continue to learn more about the underlying causes of speech and language disorders, they will be able to design and develop more appropriate treatment strategies for children with developmental speech and language disorders.

About the NIDCD

The NIDCD conducts and supports research and research training on normal and disordered mechanisms of hearing, balance, smell, taste, voice, speech and language. The NIDCD achieves its mission through a diverse program of research grants for scientists to conduct research at medical centers and universities around the country and through a wide range of research performed in its own laboratories.

The institute also conducts and supports research and research training related to disease prevention and health promotion; addresses special biomedical and behavioral problems associated with people who have communication impairments or disorders; and supports efforts to create devices that substitute for lost and impaired sensory communication function. The NIDCD is committed to understanding how certain diseases or disorders may affect women, men and members of the underrepresented minority populations differently.

The NIDCD has established a national clearinghouse of information and resources. Additional information on developmental speech and language disorders may be obtained from the NIDCD Clearinghouse. Write to:

NIDCD Clearinghouse
P.O. Box 37777
Washington, DC 20013-7777

For additional information:

American Speech-Language-Hearing Association
10801 Rockville Pike
Rockville, MD 20852
Voice/TDD (301) 897-5700
Consumer Helpline (800) 638-8255

Central Institute for the Deaf (CID)
818 South Euclid Avenue
St. Louis, MO 63110-1594
(314) 652-3200 voice/TDD

The Council for Exceptional Children
Division of Children with Communication Disorders
1920 Association Drive
Reston, VA 22091
(703) 620-3660

National Rehabilitation Information Center (NARIC)
8455 Colesville Road, Suite 935
Silver Spring, MD 20910
(301) 588-9284 voice/TDD
(800) 34-NARIC

Orton Dyslexia Society
724 York Road
Baltimore, MD 21204
(301) 296-0232
(800) ABCD-123

Chapter 19

Prevalence of Communication Disorders among Children in Special Education Classes

The number of children with disabilities, ages 6-21, served in public schools under IDEA (Individuals with Disabilities Education Act of 1990) Part B and Chapter 1 of ESEA (SOP)[14] in the 1992-93 school year was 4,633,674. Of these 4.6 million children:

- 1,000,154 (21.6%) received services for speech or language disorders, 60,896 (1.3%) received services for hearing disorders.

- In the 1991-92 school year, 85.5% of students with speech or language disorders and 27% of students with hearing disorders were mainstreamed into regular classrooms.[1]

Hearing

- In 1993, 17 in every 1,000 children under 18 years of age had some degree of hearing loss.[2]

- Of deaf and hard-of-hearing students, 47.4% were born with hearing loss (heredity, at 13%, was the leading known cause), 23.2% acquired a loss after birth (meningitis, at 8.1%, was the leading known cause), and the onset was unknown or unreported for 29.4%.[3]

- Approximately 1 child in every 1,000 is born deaf.[4]

Communication Facts, 1995 Edition, American Speech-Language-Hearing Association; reprinted with permission.

- The average age of identification of hearing loss is almost 3 years of age[4] despite the availability of several methods for assessing infants' hearing within the first 3 months. ABR and OAE can be used as early as the first 24 hours. ASHA's Joint Committee on Infant Hearing recommends identification before 3 months, ideally soon after birth.[5] Because of late identification, for many infants and children with hearing loss much of the critical period for language and speech development—the first two years of life—is lost.[4]

- Nearly 1 child in 1,000 has early onset sensorineural hearing loss to the extent that it impedes normal language acquisition; even with special education, one half of these children attain only a fourth-grade level of education by the time they graduate from high school.[6]

- Severe congenital sensorineural hearing loss affects about 1 child in 1,000.[6]

- An estimated 90% of all children experience at least one bout of otitis media by age 6, making it the most common treatable illness for which children see a physician. Otitis media accounts for over 10 million physician visits each year at an estimated annual cost of over 1 billion dollars.[7]

Table 19.1. Students, age 6-12, served under IDEA Part B and Chapter 1 of ESEA (SOP), 1992-93, by disability (Source: U.S. Department of Education, 1994).

Disability	Percent
Learning Disability	51.2%
Speech-Language Disorder	21.6%
Mental Retardation	11.5%
Emotional Disturbances	8.7%
Other*	3.4%
Multiple Disabilities	2.2%
Hearing Disorder	1.3%

*Other: Orthopedic impairments, other health impairments, visual impairments, autism, deaf-blindness, traumatic brain injury

Speech

- Of the individuals who were reported to have a chronic speech disorder, 43% were under age 18.[2]

- An estimated 6 million children under the age of 18 have a speech or language disorder. Boys make up two thirds of this population.[8]

- About 10-15% of preschoolers and about 6% of children in grades 1-12 have a speech disorder.[8]

- It is estimated that 2 million Americans,[12] and more than 15 million people around the world, stutter. Most begin to stutter at an early age.[9] One child in 30 goes through a period of stuttering that can last 6 months or longer. Boys are 4 times more likely to stutter than girls. Approximately 80% of children who stutter are able to speak normally by the time they reach adulthood.[10]

- Cerebral palsy develops in an estimated 9,000 babies each year, and is found in about 1% of all children. About 750,000 Americans of all ages have the condition.[11] This group of neurological disorders may affect the motor control centers involved in speech production and result in a speech disorder.

Language

- Language disorders affect between 2-3% of preschoolers and about 1% of the school-age population.[8]

- Nearly two thirds of children identified before age 2 as late or slow talkers continue to show delays in expressive language at age 3. For the more than half of these children who continue to have language problems at age 4, the risk of developing learning disabilities is very high. Such findings indicate the importance of early intervention, which may help prevent later learning disabilities.[12]

- The prevalence of mild cognitive deficits and learning disabilities is estimated between 10-15% of all children.[11]

- Impaired language development is most prevalent in individuals with mental retardation.[13] Nearly 50% of children with mild retardation, 90% of children with severe retardation, and 100% of children with profound retardation have a language disorder.[8]

- An estimated 5% of preschool children have specific language impairment. The causes and mechanisms of the disorder are unknown.[13]

- Some language disorders are acquired through brain injury. The estimated annual incidence of head trauma in children is as high as 200 in 100,000, the annual incidence of stroke in children is nearly 3 in 100,000.[13]

- Autism occurs in roughly 5 births in 10,000, and primarily in boys.[6] Severe communication problems often occur in autism.

References

1. U.S. Department of Education. (1994). To *assure the free appropriate public education of all Americans: Sixteenth annual report to Congress on the implementation of The Individuals with Disabilities Education Act* (ED/OSERS Publication No. 065–00000700–2). Washington, DC: U.S. Government Printing Office.

2. Benson, V. & Marano, M.A. (1994, December). *Current estimates from the National Health Interview Survey. 1993.* Vital and Health Statistics Series 10(190). Hyattsville, MD: National Center for Health Statistics.

3. Holt, J.A. & Hotto, S.A. (1994). *Demographic aspects of hearing impairment: Questions and answers, third edition.* Washington, DC: Center for Assessment and Demographic Studies, Gallaudet University.

4. National Institutes of Health. (1993). *Early identification of hearing impairment in infants and young children* (Program and abstracts from the NIH Consensus Development Conference). Bethesda, MD: Author.

5. Joint Committee on Infant Hearing. (1994). 1994 position statement. *Asha*, 36, pp. 38–41.

6. National Advisory Neurological and Communicative Disorders and Stroke Council. (1989) Decade *of the brain: Answers through scientific research* (NIH Publication No. 88–2957). Bethesda, MD: Author.

7. National Deafness and Other Communication Disorders Advisory Board. (1992). *Research in human communication* (NIH Publication No. 93–3562). Bethesda, MD: National Institute on Deafness and Other Communication Disorders.

8. Office of Scientific and Health Reports (1988). *Developmental speech and language disorders: Hope through research* (NIH Publication No. Pamphlet 882757). Bethesda, MD: National Institute of Neurological and Communicative Disorders and Stroke.

9. Program Planning and Health Reports Branch. (1991). *Update on stuttering* (Insert to *Stuttering* NIH Publication No. Pamphlet 81–2250). Bethesda. MD: National Institute on Deafness and Other Communication Disorders.

10. Office of Scientific and Health Reports. (1981). *Stuttering* (NIH Publication No. Pamphlet 81–2250). Bethesda, MD: National Institute of Neurological and Communicative Disorders and Stroke.

11. National Advisory Neurological Disorders and Stroke Council. (1990). *Implementation plan: Decade of the brain*. Bethesda, MD: National Institute of Neurological Disorders and Stroke.

12. National Deafness and Other Communication Disorders Advisory Board. (1991). *Research in human communication* (NIH Publication No. 92–3317). Bethesda, MD: National Institute on Deafness and Other Communication Disorders.

13. National Institute on Deafness and Other Communication Disorders. (1991). *National strategic research plan for balance and the vestibular system and language and language impairments* (NIH Publication No. 91–3217). Bethesda, MD: Author.

14. Individuals with Disabilities Education Act (IDEA), formerly the Education of the Handicapped Act; Elementary and Secondary Education Act, State Operated Programs (ESEA [SOP]).

Chapter 20

Questions and Answers about Central Auditory Processing Deficits

What is the difference between a hearing loss and a central auditory processing deficit? The term hearing generally refers to the operation of the parts of the ear starting at the outer ear and ending at the auditory nerve, which carries auditory information to the brain. It is at the brain level that we make use of the auditory signal. The use we make of this auditory signal is what is called central auditory processing (CAP). Children with central auditory processing deficits (CAPD), typically have normal hearing sensitivity, but experience difficulty analyzing or making sense of what they hear.

Are the terms "central auditory processing" and "auditory processing" interchangeable? Yes, the terms are currently being used interchangeably. And although not as common or popular, the terms auditory perception, central deafness, word deafness, auditory comprehension deficit, and auditory perceptual processing dysfunction have also been used.

What behavioral characteristics might indicate that a child may have a CAPD? Children with CAPD may demonstrate difficulties in speech, language, and/or learning, especially in the areas of spelling and reading. They may also appear hearing impaired, be inattentive, easily distractable, and have difficulty following oral directions.

"Central Auditory Processing: What Is It?" *Parent Journal*, Spring 1995. Parent's Educational Resource Center, 1660 S. Amphlett Blvd, Suite 200, San Mateo, CA 94402.

How is a CAPD diagnosed? What tests should be performed? Who should perform the testing? Often the speech and language therapist is the first to assess a child who has difficulty listening and following directions, but a CAP problem cannot be completely assessed without the help of an audiologist. Both the speech and language therapist and the audiologist use standardized testing, question-naires, and behavioral inventories to evaluate CAPDs.

The speech and language therapist concentrates on evaluating the linguistic characteristics of this disorder, and the audiologist concentrates on the broader aspects of hearing. For example, the speech and language therapist would look at speech production, how well the child follows increasingly more difficult directions, discriminates speech sounds, or understands language. The audiologist would first make sure the child has normal hearing acuity, and normal middle ear function. Middle ear condition is known to affect central auditory performance and so must be assessed before more sophisticated tests can be done. The ability to understand speech in the presence of background noise, competing speech, and less than optimal listening conditions can then be tested.

What is the role of CAP in learning? CAP is crucial to learning. At all grade levels most information communicated in the classroom is auditory, and much casual learning is auditory as well. By the time a child is ready for fourth grade, most auditory discrimination, speech and language development, and memory and processing skills are mature and intact, except in children with CAPD. Taking notes becomes difficult if listening requires all of a child's attention. Remembering assignments given verbally becomes difficult if a child has an auditory memory problem.

If a person has a CAPD how might that affect speech and language? A CAPD could affect speech in subtle ways. Some children who have difficulty hearing the difference between speech sounds, or confuse syllable sequences, will manifest this difficulty in their pronunciation. Some examples are "bizgetti" for "spaghetti," and "ephelants" for "elephants." These difficulties can persist beyond the age when they are considered cute, and tend instead to become an embarrassment to the speaker. In addition, vocabulary development and receptive language can be affected.

How are reading and writing affected by a CAPD? It is not known why certain children with CAPD have reading and writing difficulties. We have only found correlates (that is that if certain CAP problems are identified, then we can expect certain reading and writing problems to be present), but the "why" is not clear. Depending on the CAP difficulty, reading, comprehension, spelling, and vocabulary will be affected.

Can anything be done to improve or cure a CAPD? Remediation techniques are definitely helpful, particularly since the central auditory processing system is not complete until somewhere between ages 11 and 14, allowing the child to be more responsive to change. Once the child is assessed, environmental modifications for home and school can be suggested, and specific remediation techniques can be employed by teachers and therapists.

Chapter 21

Auditory Processing Disorder and Interventions

Introduction

Auditory processing is the processes of recognizing and interpreting information taken in through the sense of sound. The terms, "auditory processing" and "auditory perception," are often used interchangeably. Although there are many types of perception, the two most common areas of difficulty involved with a learning disability are visual and auditory perception. Since so much information in the classroom and at home is presented visually and/or verbally, the child with an auditory or visual perceptual disorder can be at a disadvantage in certain situations. The information presented here and in the next chapter describes these two types of disorders, their educational implications, some basic interventions, and what to do if there is a suspected problem.

For the sake of consistency, the term used in this chapter is auditory processing disorder. Other terms which refer to the same disorder include auditory perceptual disorder, auditory processing deficits, central auditory processing disorders, and other similar combinations of these terms.

What Is Auditory Processing Disorder?

An auditory processing disorder interferes with an individual's ability to analyze or make sense of information taken in through the

An undated document produced by the National Center for Learning Disabilities, 381 Park Avenue South, Suite 1420, New York, NY 10016; reprinted with permission.

ears. This is different from problems involving hearing per se, such as deafness or being hard of hearing. Difficulties with auditory processing do not affect what is heard by the ear, but do affect how this information is interpreted, or processed by the brain.

An auditory processing deficit can interfere directly with speech and language, but can affect all areas of learning, especially reading and spelling. When instruction in school relies primarily on spoken language, the individual with an auditory processing disorder may have serious difficulty understanding the lesson or the directions.

Common Areas of Difficulty and Some Educational Implications

Phonological awareness. Phonological awareness is the understanding that language is made up of individual sounds (phonemes) which are put together to form the words we write and speak. This is a fundamental precursor to reading. Children who have difficulty with phonological awareness will often be unable to recognize or isolate the individual sounds in a word, recognize similarities between words (as in rhyming words), or be able to identify the number of sounds in a word. These deficits can affect all areas of language including reading, writing, and understanding of spoken language.

Though phonological awareness develops naturally in most children, the necessary knowledge and skills can be taught through direct instruction for those who have difficulty in this area.

Auditory discrimination. Auditory discrimination is the ability to recognize differences in phonemes (sounds). This includes the ability to identify words and sounds that are similar and those which are different.

Auditory memory. Auditory memory is the ability to store and recall information which was given verbally An individual with difficulties in this area may not be able to follow instructions given verbally or may have trouble recalling information from a story read aloud.

Auditory sequencing. Auditory sequencing is the ability to remember or reconstruct the order of items in a list or the order of sounds in a word or syllable. One example is saying or writing "ephelant" for "elephant."

Auditory blending. Auditory blending is the process of putting together phonemes to form words. For example, the individual phonemes "c," "a," and "t" are blended to from the word, "cat."

Interventions

First, a few words about interventions in general. Interventions need to be aimed at the specific needs of the child. No two children share the same set of strengths or areas of weaknesses. An effective intervention is one that utilizes a child's strengths in order to build on the specific areas in need of development. As such, interventions need to be viewed as a dynamic and ever changing process. Although this may sound overwhelming initially, it is important to remember that the process of finding successful interventions becomes easier with time and as the child's learning approach, style, and abilities become more clear. The following examples provide some ideas regarding a specific disability. It is only a beginning, which is meant to encourage further thinking and development of specific interventions and intervention strategies.

The following represent a number of common interventions and accommodations used with children in their regular classroom:

Do not rely solely on an area of weakness. If instructions are given orally, try to supplement this with written or other visual cues. While it is important to address the area of need directly and try to build up areas of weakness, it is also necessary that the student be able to function successfully in the classroom. A simple accommodation like backing up verbal directions with visual or written cues is one way to facilitate this.

Keep the area of difficulty in mind. Simplifying verbal directions, slowing the rate of speech, and minimalizing distractions can make a big difference to a person with auditory processing difficulties.

Plan specific activities for the areas of difficulty. There are many activities that can help build auditory processing skills, whether it be in the area of phonological awareness, auditory discrimination, or any of the other areas in this realm. Rhyming games, for example, can help build phonological awareness as well as discriminating between similar and different sounds. Sorting games can help build auditory memory, as the number of variables and steps involved in the sorting can be easily controlled to adjust the level of difficulty.

What to Do If You Suspect a Problem?

The following suggestions are presented in a sequence which should help ensure that your concerns do not go ignored. Of equal importance, this sequence should help avoid setting off any premature alarms, which may not be in the child's best interests.

1. **Write down the reasons you suspect a problem might be present or developing, carefully documenting examples in which the concerning behavior is taking place.** This will help in two ways. First, it will help confirm or alleviate your concerns. If there is cause for concern, it will help you get a more focussed idea of where the difficulty lies. This list will also be helpful if further action or meetings with other professionals are necessary.

2. **Contact the school.** Speak to the child's teacher and other professionals who interact with your child to see if they see similar behaviors or have similar concerns. If the child is already working with specialists or receiving special education services, a consultation with these people can be helpful in identifying the problem and working out solutions.

3. **If concerns remain, an evaluation by a specialist familiar with these issues could help isolate the problem.** Evaluations can be done through the public schools or through private practitioners. Please refer to NCLD's legal rights packet for a full explanation of your rights, the process, and the school's responsibilities to you. In addition, the evaluation should help identify strengths and weaknesses in general and the therapist should be able to recommend accommodations and strategies to best facilitate your child's learning.

4. **If it is felt that special services or accommodations are warranted, arrange a meeting with the school professionals involved in your child's education to make plans for meeting the specific needs of your child.** In some cases, children meet the requirements to be legally entitled to special services. In other cases, children do not meet the criteria for legal entitlement. In either case, it is the school which will have to arrange and implement these decisions. Legally bound or not,

some people and school systems are more responsive to people's needs than others. For this reason, it is important to try to establish and maintain a useful rapport with the people to whom you entrust your child' s education. Often there are local resources available to help meet and support the variety of needs which accompany any person and his/her family when a disability is discovered. These organizations often prove tremendously valuable in providing additional resources and strategies which can make the difference between your child receiving the help s/he needs or not.

References

Bloom, Jill. (1990). *Help Me to Help My Children: A Sourcebook for Parents of Learning Disabled Children.* Waltham, MA: Little, Brown, and Company.

Parent Journal. (Spring 1995). "Central Auditory Processing Disorder." San Mateo, CA: Parents' Education Resource Center.

Hayden, A.H., Smith, R.K., von Hippel, C.S., & Baer, S.A. (1986). *Mainstreaming Preschoolers: Children with Learning Disabilities.* US Department of Health and Human Services.

Lerner, Janet. (1989) *Learning Disabilities: Theories. Diagnosis and Teaching Strategies.* 6th edition. Boston, MA: Houghton Mifflin.

Levine, M. (1990). *Keeping Ahead in School.* Cambridge, MA: Educators Publishing Services, Inc.

Understanding Learning Disabilities: A Parent Guide and Workbook. (1991). National Center for Learning Disabilities and The Learning Disabilities Council. Richmond, VA.

Chapter 22

Visual Processing Disorder and Interventions

Introduction

Visual processing is the processes of recognizing and interpreting information taken in through the sense of sight. The terms, "visual processing" and "visual perception," are often used interchangeably. Although there are many types of perception, the two most common areas of difficulty involved with a learning disability are visual and auditory perception. Since so much information in the classroom and at home is presented visually and/or verbally, the child with an auditory or visual perceptual disorder can be at a disadvantage in certain situations. The information here and in the preceding chapter describes these two types of disorders, their educational implications, some basic interventions and what to do if there is a suspected problem.

For the sake of consistency, the term used in this chapter is visual processing disorder. Other terms which refer to the same disorder include visual perceptual disorders, visual processing deficits, and other similar combinations of these terms.

What Is Visual Processing Disorder?

A visual processing, or perceptual, disorder refers to a hindered ability to make sense of information taken in through the eyes. This

An undated document produced by the National Center for Learning Disabilities, 381 Park Avenue South, Suite 1420, New York, NY 10016; reprinted with permission.

is different from problems involving sight or sharpness of vision. Difficulties with visual processing affect how visual information is interpreted, or processed by the brain.

Common Areas of Difficulty and Some Educational Implications

Spatial relations. This refers to the position of objects in space. It also refers to the ability to accurately perceive objects in space with reference to other objects.

Reading and math are two subjects where accurate perception and understanding of spatial relationships are very important. Both of these subjects rely heavily on the use of symbols (letters, numbers, punctuation, math signs). Examples of how difficulty may interfere with learning are in being able to perceive words and numbers as separate units, directionality problems in reading and math, confusion of similarly shaped letters, such as b/d/p/q. The importance of being able to perceive objects in relation to other objects is often seen in math problems. To be successful, the person must be able to associate that certain digits go together to make a single number (i.e., 14), that others are single digit numbers, that the operational signs (+,-,x,=) are distinct from the numbers, but demonstrate a relationship between them. The only cues to such math problems are the spacing and order between the symbols. These activities pre-suppose an ability and understanding of spatial relationships.

Visual discrimination. This is the ability to differentiate objects based on their individual characteristics. Visual discrimination is vital in the recognition of common objects and symbols. Attributes which children use to identify different objects include: color, form, shape, pattern, size, and position. Visual discrimination also refers to the ability to recognize an object as distinct from its surrounding environment. In terms of reading and mathematics, visual discrimination difficulties can interfere with the ability to accurately identify symbols, gain information from pictures, charts, or graphs, or be able to use visually presented material in a productive way. One example is being able to distinguish between an /n/ and an /m/, where the only distinguishing feature is the number of humps in the letter. The ability to recognize distinct shapes from their background, such as objects in a picture, or letters on a chalkboard, is largely a function of visual discrimination.

Visual closure. Visual closure is often considered to be a function of visual discrimination. This is the ability to identify or recognize a symbol or object when the entire object is not visible.

Difficulties in visual closure can be seen in such school activities as when the young child is asked to identify, or complete a drawing of, a human face. This difficulty can be so extreme that even a single missing facial feature (a nose, eye, mouth) could render the face unrecognizable by the child.

Object recognition (Visual Agnosia). Many children are unable to visually recognize objects which are familiar to them, or even objects which they can recognize through their other senses, such as touch or smell. One school of thought about this difficulty is that it is based upon an inability to integrate or synthesize visual stimuli into a recognizable whole. Another school of thought attributes this difficulty to a visual memory problem, whereby the person can not retrieve the mental representation of the object being viewed or make the connection between the mental representation and the object itself.

Educationally, this can interfere with the child's ability to consistently recognize letters, numbers, symbols, words, or pictures. This can obviously frustrate the learning process as what is learned on one day may not be there, or not be available to the child, the next. In cases of partial agnosia, what is learned on day one, "forgotten" on day two, may be remembered again without difficulty, on day three.

Whole/part relationships. Some children have a difficulty perceiving or integrating the relationship between an object or symbol in its entirety and the component parts which make it up. Some children may only perceive the pieces, while others are only able to see the whole. The common analogy is not being able to see the forest for the trees and conversely, being able to recognize a forest but not the individual trees which make it up.

In school, children are required to continuously transition from the whole to the parts and back again. A "whole perceiver," for example, might be very adept at recognizing complicated words, but would have difficulty naming the letters within it. On the other hand, "part perceivers" might be able to name the letters, or some of the letters within a word, but have great difficulty integrating them to make up a whole, intact word. In creating artwork or looking at pictures, the "part perceivers" often pay great attention to details, but lack the ability to see the relationship between the details. "Whole perceivers," on the other hand, might only be able to describe a piece of artwork in very general terms, or lack the ability to assimilate the pieces to make any sense of it at all. As with all abilities and disabilities, there is a wide range in the functioning of different children.

Interaction with Other Areas of Development

A common area of difficulty is visual-motor integration. This is the ability to use visual cues (sight) to guide the child's movements. This refers to both gross motor and fine motor tasks. Often children with difficulty in this area have a tough time orienting themselves in space, especially in relation to other people and objects. These are the children who are often called "clumsy" because they bump into things, place things on the edges of tables or counters where they fall off, "miss" their seats when they sit down, etc. This can interfere with virtually all areas of the child's life: social, academic, athletic, pragmatic. Difficulty with fine motor integration effects a child's writing, organization on paper, and ability to transition between a worksheet or keyboard and other necessary information which is in a book, on a number line, graph, chart, or computer screen.

Interventions

First, a few words about interventions in general. Interventions need to be aimed at the specific needs of the child. No two children share the same set of strengths or areas of weaknesses. An effective intervention is one that utilizes a child's strengths in order to build on the specific areas in need of development. As such, interventions need to be viewed as a dynamic and ever changing process. Although this may sound overwhelming initially, it is important to remember that the process of finding successful interventions becomes easier with time and as the child's learning approach, style, and abilities become more easily seen. The following examples provide some ideas regarding a specific disability. It is only a beginning which is meant to encourage further thinking and development of specific interventions and intervention strategies.

The following represent a number of common interventions and accommodations used with children in their regular classroom:

Reading

Enlarged print for books, papers, worksheets or other materials which the child is expected to use can often make tasks much more manageable. Some books and other materials are commercially available; other materials will need to be enlarged using a photocopier or computer, when possible.

There are a number of ways to help a child keep focussed and not become overwhelmed when using printed information. For many children, a "window" made from cutting a rectangle in an index card helps keep the relevant numbers, words, sentences, etc. in clear focus while blocking out much of the peripheral material which can become distracting. As the child's tracking improves, the prompt can be reduced. For example, after a period of time, one might replace the "window" with a ruler or other straight-edge, thus increasing the task demands while still providing additional structure. This can then be reduced to, perhaps, having the child point to the word s/he is reading with only a finger.

Writing

Adding more structure to the paper a child is using can often help him/her use the paper more effectively. This can be done in a number of ways. For example, lines can be made darker and more distinct. Paper with raised lines to provide kinesthetic feedback is available. Worksheets can be simplified in their structure and the amount of material which is contained per worksheet can be controlled. Using paper which is divided into large and distinct sections can often help with math problems.

Teaching Style

Being aware and monitoring progress of the child's skills and abilities will help dictate what accommodations in classroom structure and/or materials are appropriate and feasible. In addition, the teacher can help by ensuring the child is never relying solely on an area of weakness, unless that is the specific purpose of the activity. For example, if the teacher is referring to writing on a chalkboard or chart paper, s/he can read aloud what is being read or written, providing an additional means for obtaining the information.

Part Five

Other Neurological Disorders that Impede Learning

Chapter 23

Attention-Deficit/Hyperactivity Disorder (AD/HD)

Every year the National Information Center for Children and Youth with Disabilities (NICHCY) receives thousands of requests for information about the education and special needs of children and youth with Attention Deficit Disorder (ADD). Over the past several years, ADD has received a tremendous amount of attention from parents, professionals, and policy makers across the country—so much so, in fact, that nearly everyone has now heard about ADD.

While helpful to those challenged by this disability, such widespread recognition creates the possibility of improper diagnostic practice and inappropriate treatment. Now, more than ever, parents who suspect their child might have ADD and parents of children diagnosed with the disorder need to evaluate information, products, and practitioners carefully.

This chapter is intended to serve as a guide to help parents and educators know what ADD is, what to look for, and what to do. While acknowledging that adults, too, can have ADD, this paper focuses on the disorder as it relates to children and youth.

Is ADD Something New?

References to ADD-type symptoms have been found in the medical literature for almost 100 years. In fact, this syndrome is one of the most widely researched of all childhood disorders. Scientific experts have long

National Information Center for Children and Youth with Disabilities (NICHCY), *NICHCY Briefing Paper*, Revised Edition, October 1994.

315

understood ADD as a disability that can and does cause serious lifelong problems, particularly when nothing is done to manage the difficulties associated with the disorder.

Throughout all these years of research, the children with ADD have not changed. The characteristics of ADD evident 40 years ago are still the same seen today. It is our understanding of ADD that has evolved. The knowledge we have gained through research has, in fact, led to a change in the disorder's name and in the way it is viewed.

What Is Attention Deficit Disorder?

ADD is officially called Attention-Deficit/Hyperactivity Disorder, or AD/HD (American Psychiatric Association, 1994), although most lay people, and even some professionals, still call it ADD (the name given in 1980). The disorder's name has changed as a result of scientific advances and the findings of careful field trials; researchers now have strong evidence to support the position that AD/HD (as we will refer to the disorder throughout the remainder of this chapter) is not one specific disorder with different variations. In keeping with this evidence, AD/HD is now divided into three subtypes, according to the main features associated with the disorder: inattentiveness, impulsivity, and hyperactivity. The three subtypes are:

- AD/HD Predominantly Combined Type,
- AD/HD Predominantly Inattentive Type, and
- AD/HD Predominantly Hyperactive-Impulsive Type.

These subtypes take into account that some children with AD/ HD have little or no trouble sitting still or inhibiting behavior, but may be predominantly inattentive and, as a result, have great difficulty getting or staying focused on a task or activity. Others with AD/HD may be able to pay attention to a task but lose focus because they may be predominantly hyperactive-impulsive and, thus, have trouble controlling impulse and activity. The most prevalent subtype is the Combined Type. These children will have significant symptoms of all three characteristics.

What Causes AD/HD?

AD/HD is a neurobiologically based developmental disability estimated to affect between 3-5% of the school age population (Professional Group for Attention and Related Disorders, 1991). No one knows exactly what causes AD/HD. Scientific evidence suggests that the disorder is genetically transmitted in many cases and results from a chemical imbalance or deficiency in certain neurotransmitters, which are chemicals that help the brain regulate behavior. In addition, a landmark study conducted by the National Institute of Mental Health showed that the rate at which the brain uses glucose, its main energy source, is lower in subjects with AD/HD than in subjects without AD/HD (Zametkin et al., 1990).

Even though the exact cause of AD/HD remains unknown, we do know that AD/HD is a neurologically-based medical problem. Parents and teachers do not cause AD/HD. Still, there are many things that both can do to help a child manage his or her AD/HD-related difficulties. Before we look at what needs to be done, however, let us look at what AD/HD is and how it is diagnosed.

What Are the Signs of AD/HD?

Professionals who diagnose AD/ HD use the diagnostic criteria set forth by the American Psychiatric Association (1994) in the Diagnostic and Statistical Manual of Mental Disorders; the fourth edition of this manual, known as the DSM-IV, was released in May 1994. The criteria in the DSM-IV (discussed below) and the other essential diagnostic features listed below are the signs of AD/HD.

As can be seen, the primary features associated with the disability are inattention, hyperactivity, and impulsivity. The discussion below describes each of these features and lists their symptoms, as given in the DSM-IV.

Inattention

A child with AD/HD is usually described as having a short attention span and as being distractible. In actuality, distractibility and inattentiveness are not synonymous. Distractibility refers to the short attention span and the ease with which some children can be pulled off-task. Attention, on the other hand, is a process that has different parts. We focus (pick something on which to pay attention), we select (pick something that needs attention at that moment) and we sustain (pay attention for as long as is needed). We also resist (avoid things that remove our attention from where it needs to be), and we shift (move our attention to something else when needed).

When we refer to someone as distractible, we are saying that a part of that person's attention process is disrupted. Children with AD/HD can have difficulty with one or all parts of the attention process. Some children may have difficulty concentrating on tasks (particularly on tasks that are routine or boring). Others may have trouble knowing where to start a task. Still others may get lost in the directions along the way. A careful observer can watch and see where the attention process breaks down for a particular child.

Symptoms of inattention, as listed in the DSM-IV, are:

- often fails to give close attention to details or makes careless mistakes in schoolwork, work, or other activities;
- often has difficulty sustaining attention in tasks or play activities;
- often does not seem to listen when spoken to directly;
- often does not follow through on instructions and fails to finish schoolwork, chores, or duties in the workplace (not due to oppositional behavior or failure to understand instructions);
- often has difficulty organizing tasks and activities;
- often avoids, dislikes, or is reluctant to engage in tasks that require sustained mental effort (such as schoolwork or homework);
- often loses things necessary for tasks or activities (e.g., toys, school assignments, pencils, books, or tools);
- is often easily distracted by extraneous stimuli;
- is often forgetful in daily activities (American Psychiatric Association, 1994, pp. 83–84).

Hyperactivity

Excessive activity is the most visible sign of AD/HD. The hyperactive toddler/preschooler is generally described as "always on the go" or "motor driven." With age, activity levels may diminish. By adolescence and adulthood, the overactivity may appear as restless, fidgety behavior (American Psychiatric Association, 1994).

Symptoms of hyperactivity, as listed in the DSM-IV, are:

- often fidgets with hands or feet or squirms in seat;
- often leaves seat in classroom or in other situations in which remaining seated is expected;
- often runs about or climbs excessively in situations in which it is inappropriate (in adolescents or adults, may be limited to subjective feelings of restlessness);
- often has difficulty playing or engaging in leisure activities quietly;
- is often "on the go" or often acts as if "driven by a motor;"
- often talks excessively (APA, 1994, p. 84).

Impulsivity

When people think of impulsivity, they most often think about cognitive impulsivity, which is acting without thinking. The impulsivity of children with AD/HD is slightly different. These children act *before* thinking, because they have difficulty waiting or delaying gratification. The impulsivity leads these children to speak out of turn, interrupt others, and engage in what looks like risk-taking behavior. The child may run across the street without looking or climb to the top of very tall trees. Although such behavior is risky, the child is not really a risk-taker but, rather, a child who has great difficulty controlling impulse. Often, the child is surprised to discover that he or she has gotten into a dangerous situation and has no idea how to get out of it.

Symptoms of impulsivity, as listed in the DSM-IV (p. 84), are:

- often blurts out answers before questions have been completed;
- often has difficulty awaiting turn;
- often interrupts or intrudes on others (e.g., butts into conversations or games).

It is important to note that, in the DSM-IV, hyperactivity and impulsivity are no longer considered as separate features. According to Barkley (1990), hyperactivity impulsivity is a pattern stemming from an overall difficulty in inhibiting behavior.

In addition to problems with inattention or hyperactivity-impulsivity, the disorder is often seen with associated features. Depending on the child's age and developmental stage, parents and teachers may see low frustration tolerance, temper outburst, bossiness, difficulty in following rules, disorganization, social rejection, poor self-esteem, academic underachievement, and inadequate self-application (American Psychiatric Association, 1994).

Defining Attention Deficit/Hyperactivity Disorder

Instead of a single list of 14 possible symptoms as listed in the prior edition of the DSM (the DSM-III-R), the DSM-IV categorically sorts the symptoms into three subtypes of the disorder:

- Combined Type—multiple symptoms of inattention, impulsivity, and hyperactivity;
- Predominantly Inattentive—multiple symptoms of inattention with few, if any, of hyperactivity-impulsivity;

- Predominantly Hyperactive-Impulsive Type—multiple symptoms of hyperactivity-impulsivity with few, if any, of inattention.

Other essential diagnostic features of AD/HD include:

- Symptoms of inattention, hyperactivity, or impulsivity must persist for at least six months and be maladaptive and inconsistent with developmental levels;
- Some of the symptoms causing impairment must be present before age 7 years;
- Some impairment from the symptoms is present in two or more settings (e.g., at school/work, and at home);
- Evidence of clinically significant impairment is present in social, academic, or occupational functioning;
- Symptoms do not occur exclusively during the course of Pervasive Developmental Disorder, Schizophrenia, or other Psychotic Disorder and are not better accounted for by another mental disorder (e.g., Mood Disorder, Anxiety Disorder, Dissociative Disorder, or Personality Disorder).

The above information was drawn from the American Psychiatric Association (1994), Diagnostic and Statistical Manual of Mental Disorders (4th ed.), pp. 83–85.

Don't All Children Show These Signs Occasionally?

From time to time, all children will be inattentive, impulsive, and overly active. In the case of AD/HD, these behaviors are the rule, not the exception. When a child exhibits the behaviors listed above as symptomatic of AD/HD, even if he or she does so consistently, do not draw the conclusion that the child has the disorder. Until a proper evaluation is completed, you can only assume that the child *might* have AD/HD.

Conversely, people have been known to read symptom lists and, finding one or two exceptions, rule out the possibility of the disorder's presence. AD/HD is a disability that, without proper identification and management, can have long-term complications. Parents and teachers are cautioned against making the diagnosis by themselves.

How Do I Know For Sure If My Child Has AD/HD?

Unfortunately, no simple test such as a blood test or urinanalysis exists to determine if a child has this disorder. Diagnosing AD/HD is complicated and much like putting together a puzzle. An accurate diagnosis requires an assessment conducted by a well-trained professional (usually a developmental pediatrician, child psychologist, child psychiatrist, or pediatric neurologist) who knows a lot about AD/HD and all other disorders that can have symptoms similar to those found in AD/HD. Until the practitioner has collected and evaluated all the necessary information, he or she must follow the same rule of thumb as the parent or teacher who sees the behavior and suspects that the child has the disorder: Assume the child *might* have AD/HD.

The AD/HD diagnosis is made on the basis of observable behavioral symptoms in multiple settings. This means that the person doing the evaluation must use *multiple sources* to collect the information needed. A proper AD/HD diagnostic evaluation includes the following elements:

1. A thorough medical and family history
2. A physical examination
3. Interviews with the parents, the child, and the child's teacher(s)
4. Behavior rating scales completed by parents and teacher(s)
5. Observation of the child
6. A variety of psychological tests to measure I.Q. and social and emotional adjustment, as well as to indicate the presence of specific learning disabilities.

It is important to realize that, almost characteristically, children with AD/HD often behave well in new situations, particularly in those that are one-on-one. Therefore, a well-trained diagnostician knows not to make a determination based solely on how the child behaves during their time together.

Sophisticated medical tests such as EEGs (to measure the brain's electrical activity) or MRIs (an X-ray of the brain's anatomy) are NOT part of the routine assessment. Such tests are usually given only when the diagnostician suspects another problem, and those cases are infrequent. Similarly, positron emission tomography (PET Scan) has recently been used for research purposes but is not part of the diagnostic evaluation.

After completing an evaluation, the diagnostician makes one of three determinations:

1. the child has AD/HD;
2. the child does not have AD/ HD but his or her difficulties are the result of another disorder or other factors; or

3. the child has AD/HD and another disorder (called a co-existing condition).

To make the first determination—that the child has AD/HD—the professional considers his or her findings in relation to the criteria set forth in the *Diagnostic and Statistical Manual of Mental Disorders* (4th edition), the DSM-IV, of the American Psychiatric Association (1994). A very important criterion for diagnosis is that the child's symptoms be present prior to age 7. They must also be inappropriate for the child's age and cause clinically significant impairment in social and academic functioning.

To make the second determination—that the child's difficulties are the result of another disorder or other factors—the professional considers the exclusionary criteria found in the DSM-IV and his or her knowledge of disorders with similar symptomatology. According to the DSM-IV, "Attention-Deficit/Hyperactivity Disorder is not diagnosed if the symptoms are better accounted for by another mental disorder (e.g., Mood Disorder, Anxiety Disorder, Dissociative Disorder, or Personality Disorder, Personality Change Due to a General Medical Condition, or a Substance-Related Disorder.) In all these disorders, the symptoms of inattention typically have an onset after age 7 years, and the childhood history of school adjustment generally is not characterized by disruptive behavior or teacher complaints concerning inattentive, hyperactive, or impulsive behavior" (American Psychiatric Association, 1994, p. 83).

Furthermore, psychosocial stressors, such as parental divorce, child abuse, death of a loved one, environmental disruption (such as change in residence or school), or disasters can result in temporary symptoms of inattention, impulsivity, and overactivity. Under these circumstances, symptoms generally arise suddenly and, therefore, would have no long-term history. Of course, a child can have AD/HD and also experience psychosocial stress, so such events do not automatically rule out the existence of AD/HD.

To make the third determination—that the child has AD/HD and a co-existing condition—the assessor must first be aware that AD/HD can and often does co-exist with other difficulties, particularly learning disabilities, oppositional defiant disorder, and conduct disorder. All factors must be considered to ensure the child's difficulties are evaluated and managed comprehensively.

Clearly, diagnosis is not as simple as reading a symptom list and saying, "This child has AD/HD!" This chapter explores the issue of diagnosis in some depth, because no one wants children to be misdiagnosed.

As parents, the more we know, the more we can help our children to succeed. We probably do not need to know how to use the DSM-IV. We probably *do* need to know that the person evaluating our child is using the specified criteria for AD/HD and all the components of a comprehensive assessment.

How Do I Have My Child Evaluated for AD/HD?

When a child is experiencing difficulties which suggest that he or she may have AD/HD, parents can take one of two basic paths to evaluation. They can seek the services of an outside professional or clinic, or they can request that their local school district conduct an evaluation.

In pursuing a private evaluation or in selecting a professional to perform an assessment for AD/HD, parents should consider the clinician's training and experience with the disorder, as well as his or her availability to coordinate the various treatment approaches. Most AD/HD parent support groups have knowledge of clinicians trained to evaluate and treat children with AD/HD. Parents may also consult their child's pediatrician, community mental health center, university mental health clinics, or hospital child evaluation units.

It is important for parents to realize, however, that the schools have an affirmative obligation to evaluate a child (aged 3-21) if school personnel suspect that he or she might have AD/HD or any other disability that is adversely affecting educational performance. This evaluation is provided free of charge to families and must, by law, involve more than one standardized test or procedure.

Thus, if you suspect that your child has an attention or hyperactivity problem, or know for certain that your child has AD/HD, and his or her educational performance appears to be adversely affected, you should first request that the school system evaluate your child. When making this request, it is a good idea to be as specific as possible about the kinds of educational difficulties your child is experiencing.

If your child is an infant or toddler, you may want to investigate what early intervention services are available in your state through the Part H program of the Individuals with Disabilities Education Act (IDEA). You can find out about the availability of these services in your state by contacting the State Department of Education or local education agency (both of which are listed on NICHCY's *State Resource Sheet*), by asking your pediatrician, or by contacting the nursery or child care department in your local hospital. While your state may not specifically list AD/HD as a disability to be addressed through the Part H program, most states have a category such as "atypical children" or "other" under which an AD/HD assessment might be made.

Preschoolers (children aged 3-5) may be eligible for services under Part B of the IDEA. If your child is a preschooler, you may wish to contact the State Department of Education or local school district, ask your pediatrician, or talk with local day care providers about how to access special education services in order to have your child assessed.

Also, under the 1993 Head Start regulations, AD/HD is considered a chronic or acute health impairment entitling the child to special education services when the child's inattention, hyperactivity, and impulsivity are developmentally inappropriate, chronic, and displayed in multiple settings, and when the AD/HD severely affects performance in normal developmental tasks (for example, in planning and completing activities or following simple directions).

If your child is school-aged, and you suspect that AD/HD may be adversely affecting his or her educational performance, you can ask your local school district to conduct an evaluation. With the exception of the physical examination, the assessment can be conducted by the child study team, provided a member of the team is knowledgeable about assessing Attention-Deficit/ Hyperactivity Disorder. If not, the district may need to utilize an outside professional consultant trained in the assessment of AD/ HD. This person must know what to look for during child observation, be competent to conduct structured interviews with the parent, teacher(s), and child, and know how to administer and interpret behavior rating scales.

Identifying where to go and whom to contact in order to request an evaluation is just the first step in the process. Unfortunately, many parents experience difficulty in the next step—getting the school system to agree to evaluate their child. If the school district does not believe that the child's educational performance is being adversely affected, it may refuse to evaluate the child. In this case, parents may wish to pursue a private evaluation. It is also important to persist with the school, enlisting the assistance of an advocate, if necessary. Parents can generally find this type of assistance by contacting the Parent Training and Information (PTI) center for their state, the Protection and Advocacy (P&A) agency, or the local parent group. A school district's refusal to evaluate a child suspected of having AD/HD involves issues that must be addressed on an individual basis; these organizations will typically be able to provide information on parent's legal rights, offer direct assistance, in many cases, and give specific suggestions on how to proceed.

For children who are evaluated by the school system, eligibility for special education and related services will be based upon evaluation results and the specific policies of the state. Many parents have found this to be a problematic area as well, and so eligibility for special education services is discussed in greater detail towards the end of this chapter. For the moment, however, let us look at what we know about managing AD/HD and the specific difficulties associated with the disorder.

How Is AD/HD Treated?

No cure or "quick fix" exists to treat AD/HD. The symptoms, however, can be managed through a combination of efforts. Management approaches need to be designed to assist the child behaviorally, educationally, psychologically, and, in many instances, pharmacologically.

Called multi-modal management, this approach consists of four basic parts: education about and understanding of AD/HD, behavior management, appropriate educational interventions, and, frequently, medication. In some instances, individual or family counseling is also advised.

Understanding AD/HD

AD/HD has been called an environmentally dependent disability. The significant people in the life of those who have AD/HD need to understand that difficulties rise and fall in relation to the environments demands and expectations. Problems often arise in environments where children are expected to be seen and not heard, to pay careful attention, and to use great self-control. Often, when children with AD/HD fall short meeting these expectations, we try to change the children, rather than changing aspects of the environment, including our actions and reactions.

Parents and teachers need be aware of the symptoms of AD/HD and how those symptoms impact child's ability to function at home, in school, and in social situations. When the adults in the child's life understand the nature of the disorder, they will be able to structure situations to enable the child to behave appropriately and achieve success. Remember, the child who has difficulty with attention, impulse control, and in regulating physical activity needs help and encouragement to manage these problems.

From a thorough understanding of AD/HD comes a change in the way the child's behavior is viewed. This change sets the stage for the effective use of the other components of the AD/HD management system.

Behavior Management

The main goal of all behavior management strategies is to increase the child's appropriate behavior and decrease inappropriate behavior. The best way to influence any behavior is to pay attention to it. The best way to increase a desirable behavior is to *catch the child being good*.

Behavior is defined as a specific act or actions. When thinking about managing behavior, many people focus on the act or actions. In actuality, behavior management is much broader. It takes into account that, before a specific act or action occurs, there is something that sets the stage for the act to happen (called an antecedent), and something that follows which either encourages or discourages a repetition of the act (called a consequence). Behavior management involves changing the antecedents and consequences so that the child's behavior changes.

Whether at home or in school, children with AD/HD respond best in a structured, predictable environment. Here, rules and expectations are clear and consistent, and consequences are set forth ahead of time and delivered immediately. Demands are limited. Rewards are plenty. Praise is frequent. Negative feedback is minimal.

By establishing structure and routines, preparing the child for changes in the routine, building opportunities for the child to be successful, setting consequences ahead of time, and anticipating where difficulties may arise, parents and teachers can change the antecedents and cultivate an environment that encourages the child t behave appropriately. When adults in the child's life do what they say they are going to do, and do so on a consistent basis so that the child knows their word has meaning, the they are providing the consequence to encourage the child to continue behaving appropriately, plus discouraging any undesired behavior.

Behavior management is a skill. It requires practice—and it require patience. Changing behavior takes time.

Behaviorally trained professionals often encourage the use of behavior modification charts. Charts are designed to provide the child with a clear picture of what behaviors are expected. The child then has the choice of whether to meet those expectations. Parents or teachers provide feedback to the child about his or her choices by delivering consequences. Charts provide high motivation and enable the child to develop an internal sense of self-control—specifically, that he or she can behave appropriately.

There are two basic types of chart programs:

- Token Economy—Here, the child earns tokens (chips, stickers, stars) for appropriate behavior. Tokens can be exchanged for various rewards.

- Response Cost—In this chart program, the child is given tokens for free. Tokens are withdrawn for inappropriate behavior (e.g., out of seat, off-task, etc.).

The most effective programs use both types of chart systems and work on a give-and-take basis. In this combination system, the child is given a token for behaving appropriately and loses a token when misbehaving.

When creating and implementing a behavior modification chart, you may wish to follow these suggestions:

- Make a list of problematic behaviors or ones that need improving.

- Select the behaviors to be modified. Parents (or teachers), with input from the child, review the list of problematic behaviors and select three, four, or five to work on at a given time. The behaviors charted should be ones that occur daily, such as going to bed on time, doing homework, or getting ready for school on time.

- Design a reward system (Token Economy, Response Cost, or a combination). Parents (or teachers) need to pay attention to the child's behavior throughout the course of the day and provide frequent rewards when the child behaves appropriately. At the end of the day, tokens can be exchanged for rewards, such as extended bed time, playing a game with Mom or Dad, or a favorite snack. Remember, a reward is only effective when it has value to the child. Rewards might have to be changed frequently.

About Punishment. Children with AD/HD respond best to motivation and positive reinforcement. It is best to avoid punishment. When punishment is necessary, use it sparingly and with sensitivity. It is important for parents and teachers to respond to this child's inappropriate behavior without anger and in a matter-of-fact way. These children need to be taught to replace inappropriate behavior with appropriate behavior.

About Time-out. When the child is misbehaving or out of control, time-out is an effective way to manage the problem. Time-out means the child is sent to a predetermined location for a short period of time. A place out of the mainstream of activity is best; for example, one particular chair may be specified as the "time-out chair." The time-out location should not be a traumatic place, such as a closet or dark basement. The purpose of time-out is to provide the child with a cooling-off period wherein he or she can regain control.

An important aspect to time-out is that the child no longer has the privilege of choosing where he or she would like to be or how time is spent. In general, the child stays in time-out and must be quiet for five minutes. Preschool-aged children are usually given two or three minutes in time-out. For toddlers, 30 seconds to a minute is appropriate.

Medication

Medication has proven effective for many children with AD/HD. Most experts agree, however, that medication should never be the only treatment used. The parents' decision to place a child on medication is a personal one and should be made after a thorough evaluation of the child has taken place and after careful consideration by both the parents and the physician.

Stimulants are the medication most widely prescribed for AD/HD. These drugs—for example, Ritalin (the most widely used), Dexedrine, Cylert—are believed to stimulate the action of the brain's neurotransmitters, which enables the brain to better regulate attention, impulse, and motor behavior. In general, the short-acting stimulant medications (e.g., Ritalin, Dexedrine) have few and mild side effects. For children who cannot take stimulant drugs, anti-depressant medications or Clonidine are used.

The prescribing physician should explain the benefits and drawbacks of medication to the parents and, when appropriate, to the child. Doses are generally administered gradually, so that the child receives the lowest dose needed to achieve the best therapeutic benefit. Parents should dispense the medication as prescribed and monitor closely how their child responds to the medication, including side effects. Such monitoring generally includes feedback from the child's teacher(s), which is usually based on the use of behavior rating scales. Parents should communicate with the physician as often as is necessary to determine when medication has reached the proper level for the child, and to discuss any problems or questions.

A note of caution: Many parents and teachers have heard that megavitamins, chiropractic scalp massage, visual/ocular motor training, biofeedback, allergy treatments, and diets are useful treatments for AD/HD. However, these treatments have not been recommended by AD/HD experts for the simple reason that they have not stood up under careful scientific scrutiny. As their child's primary caregivers and advocates, parents need to become informed consumers and exercise caution when considering such treatments.

Educational Intervention

Many children with AD/HD experience the greatest difficulty in school, where demands for attention and impulse and motor control are virtual requirements for success. Although AD/HD does not interfere with the ability to learn, it does wreak havoc on performance. Thus, in the school arena, AD/HD is an educational performance problem. When little or nothing is done to help these children improve their performance, over time they will evidence academic achievement problems. This underachievement is not the result of an inability to learn. It is caused by the cumulative effects of missing important blocks of information and skill development that build from lesson to lesson and from one school year to the next.

Generally, AD/HD will affect the student in one or more of the following performance areas:

- starting tasks,
- staying on task,
- completing tasks,
- making transitions,
- interacting with others,
- following through on directions,
- producing work at consistently normal levels, and
- organizing multi-step tasks.

Those teaching or designing programs for these students need to pinpoint where each student's difficulties occur. Otherwise, valuable intervention resources may be spent in areas where they are not critical. For example, one child with AD/HD may have difficulty starting a task because the directions are not clear, while another student may fully understand the directions but have difficulty making transitions and, as a result, get stuck in the space where one task ends and another begins. With the first child, intervention needs to focus upon making directions clear and in helping the child to understand those directions. The second child would need help in making transitions from one activity to another.

The sooner educational interventions begin, the better. They should be started when educational performance problems become evident and not delayed because the child is still holding his or her own on achievement tests.

Specific suggestions for educational intervention are presented in a separate heading below.

What about Special Education?

The type of special education services a child receives will depend upon the nature and severity of his or her difficulties. Not all of these children will need special education services. And not all of these children can receive an appropriate education without special education services. Decisions about children's need for special education and their subsequent placement must be made on a case-by-case basis.

A series of steps is typically necessary in order for the child to receive special education services. First, the child must be experiencing educational performance problems. Second, when such problems become evident, the parent or teacher can refer the child to the local school district's child evaluation team and request an evaluation. Third, an evaluation is performed to determine if the child does indeed have a disability according to eligibility criteria set forth in state and federal law and if that disability is adversely affecting the child's educational performance. If so, the child may then be found eligible for special education services.

When a child is found eligible for special education, his or her parents collaborate with school personnel to develop an Individualized Education Program (IEP) designed to address the child's specific problems and unique learning needs. Here, strengths are considered as well. Strategies to improve social and behavioral problems are also addressed in the IEP. After specifying the nature of the child's special needs, the IEP team, including parents, determines what types of services are appropriate for addressing those needs and whether these services will be delivered in the regular education classroom or elsewhere (such as the resource room or through individualized attention).

Researchers estimate that half of the children with AD/HD will be able to perform to their ability levels without special education services, *provided the disorder is recognized, understood, and curriculum adjustments to the regular program of instruction are made.*

The majority of children with AD/HD who require special education services (approximately 35%-40%) will receive them through combined placements which might include the regular education classroom, with or without in-class support, and the resource room. Support personnel are likely to be used as case managers and consultants to regular education teachers.

Some children (approximately 10%) may need to be served in a self-contained classroom with minimal mainstreaming. Such children are likely to have severe AD/HD and will probably have co-existing conditions as well.

Guidelines for Educational Intervention

Here are several general guidelines for improving the social and academic performance of children with AD/HD in both regular and special education settings.

Place the student with teachers who are positive, upbeat, highly organized problem-solvers. Teachers who use praise and rewards liberally and who are willing to "go the extra mile" to help students succeed can be enormously beneficial to the student with AD/HD.

Provide the student with a structured and predictable environment. As part of this environment:

- display rules;
- post daily schedules and assignments;
- call attention to schedule changes;
- set specific times for specific tasks;
- design a quiet work space for use upon request;
- seat the child with positive peer models;
- plan academic subjects for morning hours;
- provide regularly scheduled and frequent breaks;
- use attention-getting devices (e.g., secret signals, color codes).

Modify the curriculum. In many cases, AD/HD students can benefit from the "less is more" maxim. That is to say, if the student can demonstrate proficiency in 10 problems, 20 do not need to be assigned. Curriculum modification can also include:

- mixing high and low interest activities;
- providing computerized learning materials;
- simplifying and increasing visual presentations;
- teaching organization and study skills;

- using learning strategies such as mnemonic devices and links; and
- using visual references for auditory instruction.

Additional Principals of Remediation

These guidelines were designed by Sydney Zentall, Ph.D. (1991).

For Excessive Activity:

- Channel activity into acceptable avenues. For example, rather than attempting to reduce a student's activity, teachers can encourage directed movement in classrooms when it is not disruptive, or allow standing during seatwork, especially at the end of a task.

- Use activity as a reward. For example, to reward a child's appropriate behavior or improvement, a teacher might allow him or her to run an errand, clean the board, organize the teacher's desk, or arrange the chairs in the room.

- Use active responses in instruction. Teaching activities that encourage active responses such as talking, moving, organizing, or working at the board are helpful to many students with AD/HD, as are activities such as writing in a diary or painting.

For Inability to Wait:

- Give the child substitute verbal or motor responses to make while waiting. This might include teaching the child how to continue on easier parts of a task (or a substitute task) while waiting for the teacher's help.

- When possible, allow daydreaming or planning while the child waits. For example, the child might be allowed to doodle or play with clay while waiting, or might be guided to underline or write directions or relevant information.

- When inability to wait becomes impatience or bossiness, encourage leadership. Do not assume that impulsive statements or behavior are aggressive in intent. Suggest alternative ways or behaviors (e.g., line reader, paper passer). It may be important to cue a student when an upcoming task will be difficult and extra control will be needed.

For Failure to Sustain Attention to Routine Tasks and Activities:

- Decrease the length of the task. There are many ways to do this, including breaking one task into smaller parts to be completed at different times or giving fewer spelling words or math problems.

- Make tasks interesting. Teachers can heighten interest in tasks by allowing students to work with partners or in small groups, by using an overhead projector, and by alternating high and low interest activities. Make a game out of checking work, and use games to over-learn rote material.

For Noncompliance and Failure to Complete Tasks:

- Generally increase the choice and specific interest of tasks for the child. Teachers may allow the student with AD/HD a limited choice of tasks, topics, and activities. Teachers may also find it useful to determine which activities the student prefers and to use these as incentives.

- Make sure tasks fit within the student's learning abilities and preferred response style. Students are more likely to complete tasks when they are allowed to respond in various ways (e.g., typewriter, computer, on tape) and when the difficulty of assignments varies (i.e., not all tasks are equally difficult). *It is important to make sure that disorganization is not the reason the student is failing to complete tasks.*

For Difficulty at the Beginning of Tasks:

- Increase the structure of tasks and highlight important parts. This includes encouraging notetaking; giving directions in writing as well as orally; stating the standards of acceptable work as specifically as possible; and pointing out how tasks are structured (e.g., topic sentences, headers, table of contents).

For Completing Assignments on Time:

- Increase the student's use of lists and assignment organizers (notebooks, folders), write assignments on the board, and make sure that the student has copied them.

- Establish routines to place and retrieve commonly used objects such as books, assignments, and clothes. Pocket folders are helpful here; new work can be placed on one side and completed work on the other. Parents can be encouraged to establish places for certain things (books, homework) at home. Students can be encouraged to organize their desk or locker with labels/ places for certain items.

- Teach the student that, upon leaving one place for another, he or she will self-question, "Do I have everything I need?"

What Do I Do If My Child Is Found Ineligible for Services?

The eligibility of AD/HD children for special education services is an area of great concern to schools, parents, and advocates alike. Every year, NICHCY receives hundreds of telephone calls from parents whose children have been found ineligible for services, despite the fact that they have AD/HD. Accordingly, this section looks at what the laws have to say about the legal rights of children with AD/HD to special education.

The primary law under which schools evaluate children for special education, and then provide services to those they find eligible, is called the Individuals with Disabilities Education Act, or IDEA. This law entitles children with disabilities to a free appropriate public education by mandating special education and related services for students who meet eligibility requirements. In order for a student to be eligible, he or she must have a disability according to the criteria established in state or federal law, or be suspected of having such a disability, and that disability must adversely affect his or her educational performance. Thus, a medical diagnosis of AD/ HD alone is not sufficient to render a child eligible for services. Educational performance must be adversely affected.

Presently, the IDEA lists 13 categories of disability under which a child might be found eligible for special education services. Your child must meet the criteria for one of these categories.

In accordance with federal law, each state has to have a state law that entitles students with disabilities to a free appropriate public education. All state special education laws must meet the standards of federal law. Local school districts, then, must follow the state law and its accompanying rules and regulations. Yet many local school districts may not understand their obligation to provide special education to children with AD/HD in cases where the disability adversely affects the student's educational performance.

As a result of the considerable confusion in the field, the U.S. Department of Education has issued two memoranda intended to clarify state and local responsibility under federal law for addressing the needs of children with AD/HD in the schools. The first memorandum, issued in 1991, states that "children with ADD should be classified as eligible for services under the "other health impaired" category in instances where the ADD is a chronic or acute health problem that results in limited alertness, which adversely affects educational performance" (U.S. Department of Education, 1991, p. 3). Children with AD/HD are also eligible for services under any other category, if they meet the criteria established for those disabilities—for example, "specific learning disabilities."

According to the memorandum, students with AD/HD might also be eligible for services under Section 504 of the Rehabilitation Act of 1973. Section 504 is a civil rights statute prohibiting discrimination on the basis of disability by recipients of federal funds. Under Section 504, a person with a disability means any person with an impairment that "substantially limits one or more major life activities." Because "learning" is included in Section 504's definition of "major life activities," many students with AD/HD qualify as a person with a disability. Schools are then required under Section 504 to provide them with a "free appropriate public education," which can include regular or special education and related services, depending upon each student's specific needs.

Therefore, if a school district finds a child ineligible for services under the IDEA, there are a number of actions parents can take to have this decision re-considered. Parents may:

- Ask the school system for information about parent rights and the appropriate procedures for appealing the decision, including mediation and due process. Due process is a right under the IDEA State and local laws will specify the procedures to be followed, as required by the IDEA.

- Ask to have their child evaluated under the criteria of Section 504. Many children who have not met eligibility criteria under IDEA do meet those under Section 504.

- Contact sources of assistance. Each state has a Parent Training and Information Center (PTI) that is an excellent resource of information about state policy, state disability definitions, appeal procedures, and legal requirements of both IDEA and Section 504. Another resource available to parents, particularly those in disagreement with the school system, is the Protection and Advocacy (P&A) Agency within the state, which can provide guidance and assistance. Both of these organizations are listed on the NICHCY *State Resource Sheet*. Trained advocates with private consulting businesses also exist in many areas.

- Become familiar with federal and state laws regarding special education and the rights of children with disabilities. Numerous resources can provide this information, including NICHCY's *Questions and Answers About the Individuals with Disabilities Education Act* (1993).

How Can I Help My Child Improve Self-Esteem?

Most undiagnosed and untreated children with AD/HD suffer from low self-esteem. Many will also show signs of being mildly depressed. These feelings stem from the child's sense of personal failure. For the child with AD/HD, the world is often an unkind place. Negative feedback in the form of punishment or blame tends to be a constant in this child's life. Early diagnosis and treatment help to stem the feelings of poor self-esteem.

To encourage a good sense of self, this child must be helped to recognize personal strengths and to develop them. Using many of the behavior management techniques and intervention strategies described in this chapter will help. The child's self-esteem will improve when he or she feels competent. These are not children who can't, or won't. They can, and do. It's just that "can" and "do" come harder for them.

Where Can I Find a Parent Support Group?

For those parents, teachers, and children challenged by this disorder, AD/HD can be a truly unique experience. While some days the struggles seem insurmountable, it's important for parents to realize that, when AD/HD is properly managed, these children and youth can and do turn their liabilities into assets.

Until such time, help and hope are available. AD/HD parent support groups exist in every state. For information about a group in your area, contact CH.A.D.D. (Children and Adults with Attention Deficit Disorders) at 499 NW 70th Avenue, Suite 109, Plantation, FL 33317, Telephone: (305) 587-3700. If there is no parent support group in your area, the CH.A.D.D. staff can give you guidance in how to start a group. In addition, CH.A.D.D. offers many publications, including *CH.A.D.D.er Box* and *Attention!*

References

American Psychiatric Association. (1994). *Diagnostic and statistical manual of mental disorders* (4th ed.). Washington, DC: Author.

Barkley, R. (1990). *Attention deficit hyperactivity disorder, a handbook for diagnosis and treatment*. New York: Guilford Press.

Fowler, M. (1993). *Maybe you know my kid: A parent's guide to identifying, understanding, and helping your child with ADHD* (2nd ed.). New York: Birch Lane Press.

Professional Group for Attention and Related Disorders (PGARD). (1991). *PGARD response to Department of Education notice of inquiry*. Washington, DC: Author.

U.S. Department of Education. (1991). *Clarification of policy to address the needs of children with attention deficit disorders within general and/or special education*. Washington, DC: Author.

Zametkin, A., Mordahl, T.E., Gross, M., King, A.C., Semple, W.E., Rumsey, J., Hamburger, S., & Cohen, R.M. (1990). Cerebral glucose metabolism in adults with hyperactivity of childhood onset. *New England Journal of Medicine*, 323(2), 1361–1366.

Zentall, S. (1991). Testimony presented to Council of Exceptional Children's Task Force on At-Risk Students, New Orleans, Louisiana.

Materials on AD/HD for Families

Fowler, M. (1993). *Maybe you know my kid: A parent's guide to identifying, understanding, and helping your child with ADHD* (2nd ed.). New York: Birch Lane Press. (Available from Birch Lane Press, 120 Enterprise Avenue, Secaucus, NJ 07094. Telephone: 1-800-447-2665.)

Goldstein, S., & Goldstein, M. (1993). *Hyperactivity—Why won't my child pay attention? A complete guide to ADD for parents, teachers, and community agencies*. New York: Wiley. (Available from Wiley, Eastern Distribution Center, 1 Wiley Drive, Somerset, NJ 08475-1272. Telephone: 1-800-225-5945.)

Hallowell, E.M., & Ratey, J. (1994). *Driven to distraction*. New York: Pantheon Books. (Available from Random House, 400 Hahn Road, Westminster, MD 21157. Telephone: 1-800-733-3000.)

Latham, P.S., & Latham, P.H. (1992). *Attention deficit disorder and the law: A guide for advocates*. Washington, DC: JKL Communications. (Available from JKL Communications, P.O. Box 40157, Washington, DC 20016. Telephone: (202) 223-5097.)

Moss, D. (1989). *Shelly the hyperactive turtle*. Rockville, MD: Woodbine House. (Intended for children aged 4-8. Available from Woodbine House, 6510 Bells Mill Road, Bethesda, MD 20817. Telephone: 1-800-843-7323; 1-301-897-3570.)

Wodrich, D.L. (1994). *Attention deficit hyperactivity disorder: What every parent wants to know*. Baltimore, MD: Paul H. Brookes. (Available from Paul H. Brookes Publishing Company, P.O. Box 10624, Baltimore, MD 21285-0624. Telephone: 1-800-638-3775.)

Materials on AD/HD for Schools and Practitioners

ADHD Report. Newsletter published six times a year for practitioners, educators, and researchers. Provides up-to-date information on clinical practices involving individuals with ADHD. (Available from Guilford Press, 72 Spring Street, New York, NY 10012. Telephone: 1-800-365-7006.)

Barkley, R. (1990). *Attention deficit hyperactivity disorder, a handbook for diagnosis and treatment*. New York: Guilford Press. (Available from Guilford Press, 72 Spring Street, New York, NY 10012. Telephone: 1-800-365-7006.)

DuPaul, G.J., & Stoner, G. (1994). *ADHD in the schools: Assessment and intervention strategies*. New York: Guilford. (Available from Guilford Press, 72 Spring Street, New York, NY 10012. Telephone: 1-800-365-7006.)

Fowler, M. (1992). *CH.A.D.D. educators manual: An indepth look at attention deficit disorders from an educational perspective.* Plantation, FL: CH.A.D.D. (Available from Caset Associates, 3927 Old Lee Highway, Fairfax, VA 22030. Telephone: 1-800-545-5583.)

Goldstein, M., & Goldstein, S. (1990). *Managing attention disorders in children: A guide for practitioners.* New York: Wiley Interscience Press. (Available from Wiley, Eastern Distribution Center, 1 Wiley Drive, Somerset, NJ 08875-1272. Telephone: 1-800-225-5945.)

Parker, H.C. (1992). *The ADD hyperactivity handbook for schools: Effective strategies for identifying and treating ADD students in elementary and secondary schools.* Plantation, FL: Impact. (Available from the A.D.D. Warehouse, 300 NW 70th Avenue, Plantation, FL 33317. Telephone: 1-800-233-9273.)

Selected Materials on Behavior Management

Kendall, P.C., & Braswell, L. (1993). *Cognitive-behavioral therapy for impulsive children* (2nd ed.). New York: Guilford. (Available from Guilford Press, 72 Spring Street, New York, NY 10012. Telephone: 1-800-365-7006.)

Kupper, L. (Ed.). (1994). A bibliography of materials on behavior management in the schools. *NICHCY Bibliography*, 1-8. (Available from NICHCY, P.O. Box 1492, Washington, DC 20013. Telephone: 1-800-695-0285.)

Martin, G. (1991). *Behavior modification: What it is and how to do it* (4th ed.). Englewood Cliffs, NJ: Prentice Hall. (Available from Allyn and Bacon, Order Processing Center, P.O. Box 11071, Des Moines, IA 50336-1071. Telephone: 1-800-947-7700.)

Smith, M.D. (1993). *Behavior modification for exceptional children and youth.* Stoneham, MA: Andover Medical Publishers. (Available from Butterworth-Heinemann, 225 Wildwood Avenue, Unit B, Woburn, MA 01801. Telephone: 1-800-366-2665.)

Selected Materials on Special Education

Anderson, W., Chitwood, S., & Hayden, D. (1990). *Negotiating the special education maze: A guide for parents and teachers* (2nd ed.).

Rockville, MD: Woodbine House. (Available from Woodbine House, 6510 Bells Mill Road, Bethesda, MD 20817. Telephone: 1-800-843-7323; 1-301-897-3570.)

Cutler, B.C. (1993). *You, your child, and "special" education: A guide to making the system work*. Baltimore, MD: Paul H. Brookes. (Available from Paul H. Brookes Publishing Company, P.O. Box 10624, Baltimore, MD 21285-0624. Telephone: 1-800-638-3775.)

Des Jardins, C. (1993). *How to get services by being assertive*. Chicago, IL: Family Resource Center on Disabilities. (Available from Family Resource Center on Disabilities, 20 East Jackson Boulevard, Room 900, Chicago, IL 60604. Telephone: (312) 939-3513.)

Ferguson, S., & Ripley, S. (1991). Special education and related services: Communicating through letter writing. *A Parent's Guide, 11*(1), 1-20. [Available from NICHCY, P.O. Box 1492, Washington, DC 20013. Telephone: 1-800-695-0285 (V/TT).]

Kupper, L. (Ed.). (1993). Questions and answers about the IDEA. *NICHCY News Digest, 3*(2). 1–16.

Organizations

CH.A.D.D. (Children and Adults with Attention Deficit Disorders), 499 NW 70th Avenue, Suite 109, Plantation, FL 33317. Telephone: (305) 587-3700.

Council for Exceptional Children, 1920 Association Drive, Reston, VA 22091. Telephone: (703) 620-3660.

Family Resource Center on Disabilities, 20 East Jackson Boulevard, Room 900, Chicago, IL 60604. Telephone: 1-800-952-4199; 1-312-939-3513.

Learning Disabilities Association, 4156 Library Road, Pittsburgh, PA 15234. Telephone: (412) 341-1515.

National Center on Learning Disabilities, 99 Park Avenue, New York, NY 10016. Telephone: (212) 687-7211.

Office of Civil Rights (OCR): Responsible for overseeing compliance with Section 504 of the Rehabilitation Act of 1973. There are 10 regional offices of OCR. To locate the one serving your area, call 1-800-421-3481.

ADD Policy Clarifications Issued by the U.S. Department of Education

U.S. Department of Education. (1991, September 16). *Clarification of policy to address the needs of children with attention deficit disorders within general and/or special education.* Washington, DC: Author.

U.S. Department of Education. (1993, April 29). *Clarification of school districts responsibilities to evaluate children with attention deficit disorders (ADD).* Washington, DC: Author.

Both of these policy memoranda are available by contacting NICHCY, P.O. Box 1492, Washington, DC 20013. Telephone: 1-800-695-0285 (V/TT); 1-202-884-8200 (V/TT).

—by Mary Fowler

Chapter 24

The Effects of Stimulant Medication on Children with Attention Deficit Disorder

Introduction

This report presents a review and synthesis of a large literature addressing the use of stimulant medication to treat children with Attention Deficit Disorder (ADD). This topic was chosen as one of the critical areas to be addressed by the four ADD Centers established in 1991 by the U.S. Department of Education.

In this report, the term ADD is used as the general label for a condition of childhood once commonly called "hyperactivity" and now generally called "attention deficit disorder" (ADD) or "attention-deficit hyperactivity disorder" (AD/HD). Also, in this report the term stimulant medication will be used to refer to the class of drugs which includes d-amphetamine (Dexedrine), methylphenidate (Ritalin), and pemoline (Cylert).

Historically, the recognition of ADD as a disorder has been linked to the response of children with ADD to stimulant medication. In the

This chapter contains excerpts from *The Effects of Stimulant Medication on Children with Attention Deficit Disorder: A Review of Reviews*, by James M. Swanson, University of California-Irvine ADD Center, 1992. The document was prepared for the Division of Innovation and Development, Office of Special Education programs, Office of Special Education and Rehabilitative Services, U.S. Department of Education. A copy of the entire report may be ordered for a fee from ERIC Document Reproduction Service (operated by DynEDRS, Inc.); call (800) 443-ERIC and ask for document ED 363086. The U.S. Food and Drug Administration's update on Ritalin at the end of the chapter is from *FDA Consumer*, April 1996.

face of diagnostic uncertainty and changing labels, this has created a persistent controversy about the use of stimulant medication. The definition of response to stimulant medication and the basis for controversies about the use of medication were identified as important topics to be addressed in this report.

The University of California-Irvine (UCI) ADD Center decided to perform a "review of reviews," instead of performing just another traditional review, to synthesize the large literature which spans over 55 years of research on the use of stimulants to treat children with ADD. This literature is massive: a list of over 5,000 original articles has been accumulated for this report, and over 300 reviews of this literature have been located. The first study in the literature on the use of stimulant medication to treat children with ADD is commonly attributed to Bradley (1937), but rigorous research on this topic started in the 1960s. By 1970, the use of stimulant medication had become so widespread that it created controversy. Controversies have persisted for the last two decades, but the prevalence of stimulant therapy has remained relatively high: the literature suggests that from 2% to 6% of all elementary school-aged children may be treated with stimulant medication and that from 60% to 90% of school-aged children with an ADD diagnosis are treated with stimulant medication for a prolonged period of time.

ADD: Revised Criteria and Labels

In this report, ADD is used as the general label for a condition of childhood once commonly called "hyperactivity" and now generally called "attention-deficit hyperactivity disorder" (AD/HD). These definitions changed over the 55 years covered by this review. Initially, much of the defining literature on ADD was contributed by pediatricians, and reviews appeared in journals for the profession of pediatrics. The labels were based on a presumed association with brain damage and motor dysfunction and learning disabilities. In the 1950s and 1960s, a succession of labels including "hyperkinetic impulse disorder," "minimal brain damage, and "minimal brain dysfunction" [were used].

In the 1970s, the defining literature began to be contributed by psychologists and psychiatrists, and reviews began to appear in journals for the professions of psychology and psychiatry. In 1980, the American Psychiatric Association (APA) took the lead by incorporating the research finding into revised psychiatric definitions in the *Third Edition of the Diagnostic and Statistical Manual* (*DSM-III*).

Based on the literature, the label "hyperkinetic reaction of childhood" (*DSM-II*, 1968) was replaced by the label Attention Deficit Disorder with or without Hyperactivity (ADD or ADDH), based on the assumption that the core symptoms of the disorder were due to a cognitive rather than motor dysfunction.... [In *DSM-IV*,] the AD/HD label was retained but the criteria changed by returning to multiple symptom lists to define the disorder.

History of Five Decades of Reviews

To illustrate the history of reviews, seven time periods were selected for emphasis: pre-1966, 1966-1970, 1971-1975, 1976-1980, 1981-1985, 1986-1990, post-1990. The pattern of primary topics addressed by reviews in these seven eras was contrasted.

The classification of reviews by era gives a brief description of the stated main purpose or critical issue addressed by each review. From this evaluation, the following main trends have been identified which have emerged over the past half century:

1. The initial period (pre-1966) addressed basic clinical issues about how to define the patient population and what forms of stimulant medications to use.

2. The next era (1966-1970) represents the development of scientific methods in a new discipline (pediatric psychopharmacology).

3. The third era (1970-1975) was an era of public controversy, sparked by newspaper articles and congressional hearings on this topic.

4. The fourth era (1975-1980) was marked by the introduction of methodologies for measuring the differential effects of stimulants on activity, attention, cognition, and social interaction, as well as the difference between dramatic short-term effects and negligible long-term effects.

5. The fifth era (1981-1985) emphasized refined methods for the investigation of time, course, and dose effects of the stimulants.

6. The sixth era (1986-1990) emphasized the combination of psychosocial treatments with stimulants.

7. The current era (post-1990) seems to be emphasizing the effects of stimulants on academic productivity and aggression, as well as the definition of boundary conditions which may limit the long-term effects of stimulants.

Interpretation of Reviews

The organization of the multiple reviews and some of the historical trends have been described above. Based on this organization, ten topics were selected to synthesize the information contained in the multiple reviews. These ten topics are:

- response rate
- effects on diagnostic symptoms
- effects on associated features
- side effects
- long-term effects
- paradoxical response
- effects on high order processes
- prediction of response
- recommendations for clinical use
- recommendation for multimodality treatment

Response Rate

Not all children with ADD respond favorably to stimulant drugs. Across a subset of reviews which addressed this topic, the prevalence of a favorable response was about 70% and was about the same across 55 years despite changes over time in the diagnostic criteria and labels used to define the disorder.

Effects on Diagnostic Symptoms

In the majority of ADD children who responded favorably to stimulants, the response included temporary management of the diagnostic symptoms of ADD (i.e., a decrease in inattention, impulsivity, and hyperactivity) and a time-limited increase in concentration and goal-directed effort. Across relevant reviews, 97% agreed with this description of short-term effects.

Effects of Associated Features

In reviews which addressed common associated features of ADD which occur in some affected children (such as deviant deportment,

346

high levels of aggression, inappropriate social interaction, and poor academic productivity), 94% agreed that a component of response to stimulant medication was a decrease in the manifestation of these disruptive behaviors.

Side Effects

In reviews which addressed side effects (such as minor problems of anorexia and insomnia, serious problems associated with motor and verbal tics, and psychological impairment in the areas of cognition and social interaction), almost all (99%) acknowledged the existence of side effects and the clinical necessity to monitor and manage these effects.

Long Term Effects

In the reviews which addressed the issue of long-term effects of stimulant medication, 88% acknowledged the lack of demonstrated long-term effects on important outcome domains (i.e., social adjustment and academic achievement).

Paradoxical Response

Some early influential reviews asserted that stimulant medication "calmed or subdued" children with ADD, which was represented as a paradoxical response. This probably was because the response to high doses of stimulant drugs in other literature (e.g., the abuse literature) commonly was described as an euphoric or "speeding" response. However, in reviews which addressed this topic, 78% concluded that in children with ADD the behavioral, physiological and psychological responses to clinical doses of stimulant medications (i.e., increased concentration and goal-directed effort) were not qualitatively different from the responses of normal children and adults to equivalent doses. Thus, most reviews of the use of stimulant medication to treat children with ADD did not classify the typical clinical response as a paradoxical response.

Effects on High Order Processes

A subset of reviews addressed the effects of stimulant medication on complex behavior requiring high order skills (e.g., learning, reading, etc.) as well as on simple behavior requiring low order skills (e.g., performing rote tasks, monitoring a repetitive display, etc.). Most

Table 24.1. What Should and Should Not be Expected

What Should Be Expected

1. Temporary Management of Diagnostic Symptoms
   a. overactivity (improved ability to modulate motor behavior)
   b. inattention (increased concentration or effort on tasks)
   c. impulsivity (improved self-regulation)

2. Temporary Improvement of Associated Features
   a. deportment (increased compliance and effort)
   b. aggression (decrease in physical and verbal hostility)
   c. social interactions (decreased negative behaviors)
   d. academic productivity (increased amount and accuracy of work)

What Should Not Be Expected

1. Paradoxical Response
   a. responses of normal children are in same directions
   b. responses of normal adults are in same direction
   c. responses of affected adults and children are similar

2. Prediction of Response
   a. not by neurological signs
   b. not by physiological measures
   c. not by biochemical markers

3. Absence of Side effects
   a. infrequently the appearance or increase in tics
   b. frequently problems with eating and sleeping
   c. possible psychological effects on cognition and attribution

4. Large Effects on Skills or Higher Order Processes
   a. no significant improvement of reading skills
   b. no significant improvement of athletic or game skills
   c. no significant improvement of positive social skills
   d. improvement on learning/achievement < behavior/attention

5. Improvement in Long-term Adjustment
   a. no improvement in academic achievement
   b. no reduction in antisocial behavior or arrest rate

Table 24.1. Notes to Table: What Should and Should Not be Expected

The "review of reviews" revealed that reviews may acknowledge very similar patterns of benefits and limitations of stimulant medications but still draw very different conclusions and make very different recommendations about pharmacological treatment of ADD children. Consider the recent review by Jacobvitz, et al.[1] which criticizes current clinical practice, and the review by Stevenson and Wolraich[2], which supports current clinical practice. As shown in this table, both reviews describe a pattern of expected benefits which is expressed in the literature. Also shown is a summary of the limitations which were acknowledged in both reviews.

Jacobvitz, et al. acknowledged the short-term benefits outlined above but focused on the limitations. As a conclusion, they urged a "greater caution and a more restricted use of stimulant treatment" (p. 685). In contrast, Stevenson and Wolraich acknowledged the limitations outlined above but focused on the temporary suppression of symptoms. As a conclusion, they stated: "Stimulant medications are an effective treatment modality for most children with AD/HD" (p. 1193).

[1] Jacobvitz, D., Sroufe., L.A., Stewart, M., and Leffert, N. (1990). Treatment of attentional and hyperactivity problems in children with sympathomimetic drugs: A comprehensive review. Journal of the American Academy of Child and Adolescent Psychiatry, 29, 677-688.

[2] Stevenson, R.D., and Wolraich, M.L. (1989) Stimulant medication therapy in the treatment of children with attention deficit hyperactivity disorder. Pediatric Clinics of North America, 36, 1183-1197.

(72%) of these reviews acknowledged the lack of a demonstrated beneficial effect on performance of complex tasks or behaviors which required the use of high order processes.

Prediction of Response

Some reviews addressed the methods of evaluating a trial response to stimulant medication, and the prediction of response on the basis of behavioral, cognitive, physiological, biochemical, or neurological measures. Most reviews (86%) acknowledged poor prediction by these measures.

Recommendations about Clinical Use

Across the past half century, most reviews were written by clinicians and most (91%) supported some clinical use of stimulant medication to treat children with ADD. However, in each era of the past half century, some reviews have addressed the same issues which generate controversy and have questioned this established clinical practice.

Recommendations for Multimodality Treatment

Many reviews ended with a recommendation for combinations of psychosocial and pharmacological interventions, but in most (70%) of these reviews, specific references to support this common-sense recommendation were not provided, and when references were specified they provided little empirical data to support this specific recommendation.

Summary of Interpretations

This evaluation produced a qualitative estimate of agreement across reviews. The agreement across reviews may be interpreted as reflecting a *consensus about the effects* of stimulant medication. Specific disagreements which endured over time were interpreted as *controversy about the use* of stimulant medication. The literature covered by the reviews suggested that in most (but not all) cases a clear and immediate short-term benefit was perceived by parents, teachers, and physicians in terms of the management of symptoms and associated features of ADD. The controversies which have persisted over time (and are consistent with acknowledged effects of stimulant mediation) are the lack of diagnostic specificity for short-term effects, the lack of effects on learning or complex cognitive skills, potential side effects and adverse effects, and the lack of evidence of significant long-term effects.

The consensus about the effects of stimulant medication and the enduring controversies about its widespread use suggest a careful approach be taken in the clinical decision to treat a child with ADD.

Current Questions and Investigations

The following critical questions have been addressed by the most recent reviews:

1. What are some boundary conditions which limit the effects of medication on school behavior and performance?

2. Does stimulant medication have an effect on the academic performance of AD/HD children?

3. Does stimulant medication have an effect on the aggression manifested by some AD/HD children?

4. Does the combination of psychosocial and pharmacological interventions improve the long-term outcome of AD/HD children treated with stimulant medication?

In this section of the "review of the reviews," each of these important reviews will be discussed to provide examples of current critical questions being addressed by investigators studying AD/HD and stimulant medication.

Boundary Conditions

The purpose of the Swanson et al. review (Swanson, J.M., Cantwell, D.P., Lerner, M., McBurnett, K., Pfiffner, L., and Kotkin, R. (1992). Treatment of AD/HD: Beyond medication. *Beyond Behavior*, 4, 13-22) was to emphasize the "...limitations that are not usually emphasized but have important implications for educators" (p. 13). The seven issues addressed in this selective review are presented below:

1. Is stimulant medication overused?
2. Does the short length of action critically limit the benefits of typical treatment with stimulants?
3. At what dose (if any) does cognitive toxicity occur?

351

4. How many AD/HD cases are adverse responders to stimulants?
5. Why does treatment with stimulants stop in most cases?
6. Does treatment with medication have any residual effects that continue after the pharmacological effects dissipate?
7. Are double-blind assessments or laboratory assessments useful in the treatment of AD/HD children with stimulants?

The purpose, conclusions, and speculations of the Swanson et al. (1992) paper are presented below:

-   **Purpose:** to emphasize the limitations of the effects of typical treatment with stimulant medication.

-   **Conclusions:** the short-term effects of stimulants should not be considered "... to be a permanent solution to chronic ADD symptoms."

-   **Speculations:** stimulant medication may improve learning in some cases but impair learning in other cases; in practice, prescribed doses of stimulants may be too high for optimal effects on learning, the length of action of most stimulants is too short to produce an effect on academic achievement

Academic Productivity

The purpose of the Carlson and Smith article (Carlson, C.L. and Smith, M. (1993?). Effects of methylphenidate on the academic performance of children with attention deficit hyperactivity disorder. *School Psychology Review*) was to examine "...whether short-term gains can be translated into long-term improvements in academic achievement" (p. 3). To accomplish this, they proposed to "...describe some of the research relevant to this topic, attempt to draw conclusions about many of the important questions related to stimulant effects on learning, and provide suggestions that may assist school personnel in helping to collaborate with physicians in evaluating these effects" (p. 1). Early reviews concluded that treatment of AD/HD children with stimulant medication did not improve long-term academic achievement, but more recent work reviewed by Carlson and Smith provide clear evidence of short-term improvement in performance on academic tasks, in both the laboratory and the classroom settings. Investigations of AD/HD children with comorbid learning problems (e.g., specific reading deficits or general academic deficits) were reviewed, pointing out the lack of a long-term effect of medication combined with specific interventions (e.g., reading remediations or cognitive therapy). However, in AD/HD cases without concurrent academic problems, stimulant medication clearly improves practice to a degree that should improve learning. Serious methodological problems in the literature were reviewed by Carlson and Smith, including lack of random assignment of comparison groups, lack of control of dose or length of treatment with stimulants, psychometric properties (lack of sensitivity, ceiling effects, etc.). In the absence of any definitive answer about the long-term effects of stimulants on AD/HD children, Carlson and Smith recommended ways to avoid the limitations suggested by the methodological weaknesses, including "...performing thorough, individualized medications evaluations" using standardized procedures for administering "real life" academic tasks, the results of which are communicated to the physicians to titrate dose.

Effects of Stimulant Medication on Aggression

The purpose of the Hinshaw review (Hinshaw, S.P. (1991). Stimulant medication and the treatment of aggression in children with attention deficits. *Journal of Clinical Child Psychology*, 20, 301-312) was to "(a) assess the role of the most prevalent treatment for children with attentional deficits—stimulant medication—in the amelioration of aggressive behavior; and (b) discuss relevant methodologic, clinical, and theoretical issues that pertain to the role of medication in treating aggressive acts" (p. 301). He reviewed the literature on subcategories of aggressive acts (e.g., eruptive/impulsive versus antisocial/hostile and covert versus overt), the weak effects of stimulants on aggression in the artificial settings of laboratory testing or playroom observation, and the strong effects of stimulants on aggression in the natural setting of the classroom and playground. He also reviewed the role of aggression in the long-term outcome of AD/HD children, the minimal effects of stimulant medication on important areas of functioning related to aggression (e.g., peer status and academic achievement), the role of environmental factors (e.g., low socioeconomic status and conflictual family environments) in maintaining an aggressive pattern of behavior, and the effects of combined (e.g., psychosocial and pharmacological) treatments on aggression in AD/HD children. Hinshaw challenged the accepted belief in the field that "...whereas the core deficits of AD/HD—which are presumably biologically based—are best treated with pharmacological agents, aggressive behavior requires psychosocial intervention, preferably family-oriented, behavioral treatment" (p. 303). He concluded that the literature suggests "small and usually nonsignificant effects of medication in the laboratory or playroom" but large effects in "...naturalistic observations of aggression in the classroom or outdoor play settings" (p. 307). However, Hinshaw also concluded that any short-term amelioration of aggressive acts with stimulant medication is likely to be countered by "(a) compliance problems, (b) unmedicated periods in peer and neighborhood environments, and (c) the continuous, stressful interchanges that occur in the lives of children" (p. 309).

Combination Interventions

The Request for Applications (RFA) for a "Multi-site, Multimodality Treatment Study of Ad/HD," issued by the National Institute of Mental Health (NIMH) Child and Adolescent Research Branch, provided a comprehensive discussion and review of the dramatic short-term but negligible long-term effects of stimulant medication on AD/HD children. The NIMH-RFA listed 10 topics that should be addressed in future studies of the effects of stimulants on AD/HD children. These topics are:

1. Why have no long-term effects been demonstrated?
2. In the short-term, how many AD/HD children are nonresponders?
3. Do high doses impair learning?
4. Does state-dependent learning occur?
5. Do effects depend on age and IQ?
6. Do effects depend on comorbid conditions?
7. Are the effects of different stimulants the same?
8. Do attributions of success to the pill offset benefits?
9. Why are links to biological factors not well established?
10. Why has length of treatment in most cases been so limited?

These issues are being addressed in the NIMH Multi-site Multimodality Treatment Study. One of the most important issues addressed by this study will be the effect of combined intervention which is recommended by almost all reviews on the effects of stimulant medication on AD/HD children.

An Update from the U.S. Food and Drug Administration about Ritalin's Cancer-Causing Potential

An animal study of Ritalin (methylphenidate hydrochloride), a stimulant widely prescribed for children with attention deficit hyperactivity disorder (AD/HD), has produced a "weak signal" that the drug may have the potential to cause cancer, according to FDA, which has taken steps to alert health professionals to the possible problem.

The agency has asked the drug's sponser, Ciba Pharmaceuticals, to include the study findings in the labeling for Ritalin, and to alert prescribers by sending them a Dear Doctor letter. The company complied in late January (1996). FDA also plans to initiate additional follow-up studies, including both animal tests and epidemiological studies in humans using Ritalin.

The agency continues to regard Ritalin as a safe and effective drug, but says the potential risk needs to be considered and further studied because of the increasing and often long-term use of Ritalin in children. In the last five years, there has been about a two- to threefold increase in the use of the product.

The agency's actions are based on findings of a draft report by the National Toxicology Program on cancer-causing potential of Ritalin in a study in mice and a study in rats.

The study in rats revealed no cancer-causing activity. The findings in mice included increased rates of noncancerous liver tumors and, in males only, the occurrence of cancerous liver tumors.

FDA considers the studies' results a signal of a weak cancer-causing potential because:

- The positive findings were seen in one species of rodent (the mouse) and in only one organ—the liver—which is know to be particularly likely to develop tumors to a wide variety of stimuli.

- The increased rates were seen primarily in nonmalignant tumors.

- There was no increase in mortality associated with the tumors.

The agency also noted that animal studies do not necessarily reflect human findings. The kind of liver tumor found in mice is extremely rare in people, and its occurrence in recent years has not increased despite the increased use of Ritalin.

Chapter 25

Readings and Resources on AD/HD

Publications

Crook, W.G. (1991). *Help for the hyperactive child.* **Professional Books, PO Box 3246, Jackson, TN 38302. 245pp.**

This guide for parents focuses on treating hyperactivity and attention deficit disorders, as well as related behavior and learning problems, through allergy detection, nutritional changes, and avoidance of environmental toxins, rather than drug treatment. Suggestions are given to parents, teachers and other professionals including; dietary changes, good nutritional supplements, food allergies, lifestyle changes, control of candida, psychological support and discipline and helping the child succeed in school.

DuPaul, G.J., & Stoner, G. (1994). *ADHD in the schools: Assessment and intervention strategies.* **Guilford Publications Inc., 72 Spring Street, New York, NY 10012. 269pp.**

This book addresses school-related problems associated with attention deficit hyperactivity disorder (ADHD), such as academic underachievement, noncompliance with classroom rules, and problematic peer relationships. Eleven appendices provide examples of ADHD

ERIC Mini-Bib, Clearinghouse on Disabilities and Gifted Education, Office of Educational Research and Improvement, U.S. Department of Education, September 1995.

identification criteria, a teacher handout on ADHD medications, an ADHD self-report rating scale, suggested readings, and samples for professional communications.

Fouse, B., & Brians, S. (1993). *A primer on attention deficit disorder.* **(Fastback 354). Phi Delta Kappa, PO Box 789, Bloomington, IN 47402-0789. 45pp. (ED370319 microfiche only)**

This pamphlet explains briefly what is known about attention deficit disorder (ADD) to help parents and educators have a more positive influence on the ADD child's life. It begins with definitions of terminology, characteristics of preschool, school-age, and adult individuals with ADD, and causes of ADD. It discusses special problems associated with ADD, including academic problems, behavior problems, interpersonal difficulties, and self-esteem difficulties. Strategies effective in managing ADD are outlined, including medical management, behavioral strategies, cognitive-behavioral therapy, modifications in assignments and tests, and instruction in learning strategies.

Friedman, R.J., & Doyal, G.T. (1992). *Management of children and adolescents with attention deficit-hyperactivity disorder.* **(3rd ed.) Pro-ed, 8700 Shoal Creek Blvd., Austin, TX 78758-6897. 198pp.**

This book combines medical and psychological research findings with clinical experience gained from work with children with attention deficit hyperactivity disorder (ADHD) and their families. The book begins with definitions and statistical information and then goes on to review medical, psychological, and educational management programs.

Gordon, S.B., & Asher, M.J. (1994). *Meeting the ADD challenge: A practical guide for teachers.* **Research Press, 2612 N. Mattis Avenue, Champaign, IL 61821. 188pp.**

This book is designed to help classroom teachers meet the challenge of serving students with attention deficit disorder (ADD) by presenting practical information about the needs and treatment of these children and adolescents. A five-stage model for behavioral assessment is described, involving problem identification measurement and functional analysis, matching intervention to students, assessment of intervention strategies, and evaluation of the intervention plan. Specific assessment methods for use within this model are then discussed, and basic issues to be addressed prior to the design of an intervention strategy are analyzed.

Hartman, T. (1994). *Focus your energy: Hunting for success in business with attention deficit disorder*. Pocket Books, Simon & Schuster Consumer Group, 1230 Avenue of the Americas, New York, NY 10020. 138pp.

This book examines common characteristics of individuals with attention deficit disorder (ADD) who have succeeded in business, and draws on these findings to provide suggestions for adults with ADD. Guidelines for finding appropriate jobs in existing businesses are provided, as are tips on starting one's own business. Specific suggestions focus on how to harness and manage ADD in the workplace, including goal-setting, running meetings, and interpersonal relationships.

Johnson, D.D. (1992). *I can't sit still: Educating and affirming inattentive and hyperactive children*. Suggestions for parents, teachers and other care providers of children to age 10. ETR Associates, PO Box 1830, Santa Cruz, CA 95061-1830. (800) 321-4407. 178pp.

Causes, symptoms and challenges related to attention deficit hyperactivity disorder are discussed, with a strong emphasis on cultivating students' self-esteem. Diagnosis of attention problems is described, as are treatments such as behavior management, drug therapy, and cognitive-behavioral therapy. Self-esteem is approached as a combination of feeling valued, feeling in control, feeling capable and avoiding embarrassment. Methods for parents, teachers and students to moderate and control their frustration and anger are described.

Johnston, R.B. (1991). *Attention deficits, learning disabilities, and Ritalin: A practical guide*. (2nd ed.) Singular Publishing Group Inc., 4284 41st Street, San Diego, CA 92105-1197; (800) 521-8545. 178pp.

This book reviews practical aspects of identifying learning and attention disabilities; examines the problems and pitfalls in diagnosis and treatment; explores the expectations, limitations, and precautions necessary in using Ritalin® (brand name for methylphenidate); attempts to demystify what physicians do, addresses the dynamics of an effective team approach, and argues the need to demedicalize learning and attention disabilities.

Lerner, J.W. (1995). *Attention deficit disorders: Assessment and teaching.* **Brooks/Cole Publishing Co., 511 Forest Lodge Road, Pacific Grove, CA 93950. 259pp.**

This book on attention deficit disorders (ADD) is designed to prepare current and prospective teachers and other school personnel to teach and work with students with ADD in the schools. The book reviews assessment methods, the diagnostic process and testing instruments; describes methods that regular teachers can use in the classroom; describes interventions used by special educators; and discusses the challenges faced by the parent of a child with ADD, methods of counseling, and home management for parents. Issues involved in using medications and the kinds of medications administered to children with ADD are reviewed.

Moss, R.A., & Dunlap, H.H. (1990). *Why Johnny can't concentrate.* **Bantam Books, 666 Fifth Avenue, New York, NY 10103. 225pp.**

This book explains the components of attention deficit disorder (ADD) in children, acknowledges the diversity of children with these dysfunctions and the limitations of the labels used to categorize them, and offers suggestions regarding the practical management of these children. The book offers a general picture of the characteristics of ADD and the process of diagnosis, and provides chapters that look at ADD in four age-groups: preschoolers, early elementary school, late elementary and junior high, and adulthood. The book also provides specific information to equip parents to help their children and to find qualified professionals when needed.

Nadeau, K. (Ed.) (1995). *A comprehensive guide to attention deficit disorder in adults: Research, diagnosis, and treatment.* **Brunner/Mazel Publishers, 19 Union Square West, New York, NY 10003. 408pp.**

This book is written for professionals who diagnose and treat adults with attention deficit disorder (ADD), it provides information from psychologists and physicians on the most current research and treatment issues regarding our understanding of ADD as a neurobiological disorder. Authors examine ADD with and without hyperactivity and describe a wide range of assessment tools that can be useful in developing a full diagnostic picture of different conditions that must be addressed in treating adults with the disorder.

Nadeau, K.G., & Dixon, E.B. (1991). *Learning to slow down and pay attention.* **Chesapeake Psychological Services, P.C., 5041 A & B, Backlick Road, Annandale, VA 22003. 52pp.**

This booklet designed for children with problems of attention impulsivity, and concentration, is to be read along with their parents. Sections include a check list for students to assess their problems at school, at home, and with friends; ways that other people can help the student, such as a talking with a counselor; and things the student can do to help himself or herself. Tips on doing homework, getting ready for school, paying attention in class, and solving problems are included. The book is written in easy-to-understand language and illustrated with cartoons.

Nadeau, K.G. (1994). *Survival guide for college students with ADD or LD.* **Brunner/Mazel Publishers, 19 Union Square West, New York, NY 10003. 56pp.**

This book is written for college students with attention deficit disorders, hyperactivity, or learning disabilities who are applying to or are already enrolled in college. Chapters include questions to consider in choosing a college, on-campus accommodations, coping strategies, specific tips for organizing important information and managing time, choosing a major, career guidance, tutoring, learning self-advocacy, and resources and services available elsewhere in the community.

Neuville, M.B. (1995). *Sometimes I get all scribbly.* **(Rev. ed.) Pro-ed, 8700 Shoal Creek Blvd., Austin, TX 78757-6897. 159pp.**

This first-person account of life with a child with attention deficit hyperactivity disorder (ADHD) addresses the author's struggles to help and understand her son. The story is a mother's testament to the day-to-day, moment-to-moment existence of life with a child who is hyperactive. It validates the struggles and triumphs of their lives.

Paltin, D.M. (1993). *The parents' hyperactivity handbook: Helping the fidgety child.* **Plenum Publishing Corporation, 233 Spring Street, New York, NY 10013. (800) 221-9369. 291pp.**

This book is written to provide information and suggestions on aspects of attention deficit hyperactivity disorder (ADHD) which parents of children with ADHD find most challenging. The first part of the book deals with behavior problems rooted in inattention, impulsivity, and hyperactivity. Aspects of children's affective development are discussed, including relationships among children and the interaction among self-concept, self-esteem, and self-mastery. The second part of the book then addresses specific issues such as medication, discussing ADHD with affected children, and working with schools and teachers.

Quinn, P.O. (Ed.). (1994). *ADD and the college student: A guide for high school and college students with attention deficit disorder.* **Magination Press, Brunner/Mazel Publishers, 19 Union Square West, New York, NY 10003. (800) 825-3089. 113pp.**

This handbook was designed to help high school and college students who have attention deficit disorder (ADD) make a successful transition to college life. Chapters examine various aspects of ADD and its effects on college preparation and selection.

Quinn, P.O., & Stern, J.M. *Putting on the brakes: Young people's guide to understanding attention deficit disorder (ADHD).* **(1991). 64pp.;** *The "Putting on the Brakes" activity book for young people with ADHD.* **(1993). 88pps. Brunner/Mazel Publishers, 19 Union Square West, New York, NY 10003.**

This guide and accompanying activity book were designed to teach children between 8 and 13 the facts about attention deficit hyperactivity disorder (ADHD) and how to gain a sense of control. Tips are provided for organizing their lives through time management, improved study habits, and developing test taking skills. The activity book uses pictures, puzzles, and other techniques to assist in the learning of a wide range of skills.

Rief, S.F. (1993). *How to reach and teach ADD/ADHD children: practical techniques, strategies, and interventions for helping children with attention problems and hyperactivity.* **Council for Exceptional Children, 1920 Association Drive, Reston, VA 22091-1589. (800) 232-7323. 256pp.**

This book provides information, techniques, and strategies to help students with attention deficit disorder (ADD) or attention deficit hyperactivity disorder (ADHD) succeed. This book is organized into 30 sections that provide practical guidance on such topics as: preventing behavioral problems in the classroom through effective management techniques; multisensory strategies for teaching academic skills; learning styles; cooperative learning techniques; protocol and steps for referring students and communicating effectively with parents, physicians, and agencies; and how administrators can help teachers and students to succeed.

Weaver, C. (Ed.) (1994). *Success at last!: Helping students with AD(H)D achieve their potential.* **Heinemann, 361 Hanover Street, Portsmouth, NH 03801-3912. (800) 541-2086. 290pp.**

This book presents a collection of papers on attention deficit hyperactivity disorder (ADHD) from parents, classroom teachers, teacher educators, researchers, curriculum specialists, administrators, and other stakeholders. Sections cover understanding and educating students with attention deficit (hyperactivity) disorders, student support services, different instructional paradigms, and seeing how ADHD students flourish when teachers change. Appendices include a U.S. Department of Education Memorandum on ADHD.

Weiss, L. (1992). *Attention deficit disorder in adults.* **Taylor Publishing Company, 1550 W. Mockingbird Lane, Dallas, TX 75235. 217pp.**

This book explores the manifestations of attention deficit disorder (ADD) in adults and what can be done to cope with its effects. Adults who live with ADD share their stories, as do their spouses and family members. Treatment options such as medication, group therapy, and creative visualization are described. Coping strategies for individuals hoping to control their temper, bolster self-esteem, and manage attention problems within an independent adult lifestyle are presented.

Wodrich, D.L. (1994). *Attention deficit hyperactivity disorder (ADHD).* **Paul H. Brookes Publishing Co., PO Box 10624, Baltimore, MD 22185-0624; (800) 638-3775. 291pp.**

This book aims to provide current information on attention deficit hyperactivity disorder (ADHD) in a clear, concise fashion to help parents deal with the various manifestations of this problem and the impact it has on their family life, as well as on the child's interpersonal life at home and at school. Information is presented on the various types of educational programs that might be useful for children with ADHD, and sources of financial help are discussed.

Materials from Federally Funded Research Projects

In 1991 the U.S. Dept. of Education, Office of Special Education Programs (OSEP), funded four centers to synthesize the existing research on assessment and intervention practices to meet the needs of children with ADD. Titles are:

- *Assessment and Characteristics of Children with Attention Deficit Disorder* (ED363084), Arkansas Children's Hospital;

- *A Synthesis of the Research Literature on the Assessment and Identification of Attention Deficit Disorder* (ED363087), University of Miami;

- *Research Synthesis on Education Interventions for Students with Attention Deficit Disorder* (ED363085), Research Triangle Institute, NC; and

- *The Effects of Stimulant Medication on Children with Attention Deficit Disorder* (ED363086), University of California-Irvine.

A fifth project was funded to investigate and report on promising classroom practices for children with attention deficits: *Promising Practices in Identifying and Educating Children with Attention Deficit Disorder* (ED363088) Federal Resource Center for Special Education, University of Kentucky.

A practitioner-oriented piece based on the above ADD research and other research on academic interventions for difficult-to-teach students was produced by Research Triangle Institute, NC: *Promising Classroom Interventions for Students with Attention Deficit Disorder* (ED363086).

The Chesapeake Institute, Washington DC published several documents based on the federally funded research syntheses: *Attention Deficit Disorder: Adding up the facts* (ED370334), *Attention Deficit Disorder: Beyond the Myth* (ED370335), *Attention Deficit Disorder What Teachers Should Know* (ED370336), *Attention Deficit Disorder: What Parents Should Know* (ED370337), *Where Do I Turn? A Resource Directory of Materials About Attention Deficit Disorder* (ED370333), *Teaching Strategies: Education of Children with Attention Deficit Disorder* (ED370332), *Executive Summaries of Research Syntheses and Promising Practices on the Education of Children with ADD* (ED363083).

The first in a series of policy briefs on ADHD has been produced by the Appalachia Educational Laboratory, Charleston, WV: *ADHD-New Legal Responsibilities for Schools* (ED378750).

Documents with an ED number can also be ordered for a fee through EDRS (ERIC Document Reproduction Service): (800) 443-ERIC (3742).

Videos

A.D.D. Warehouse, 300 NW 70th Avenue, Suite 102 Plantation, FL 33317. (800) 233-9273.

- *1-2-3 MAGIC: Training Your Preschooler & Preteen to Do What You Want Them to Do!*
- *ADHD/ADD Video Resource for Schools with Attention without Tension*
- *Educating Inattentive Children: A Guide for the Classroom*
- *How to Use Time-out Effectively*
- *Understanding A.D.D.*
- *Understanding Attention Disorders: Preschool through Adulthood*
- *The Video SOS! Help for Parents*
- *Why Won't My Child Pay Attention?*

CACLD (Connecticut Association for Children with Learning Disabilities), 18 Marshall Street S., Norwalk, CT 06854. (203) 838-5010.

- *Understanding Attention Deficit Disorder*

CEC (Council for Exceptional Children),1920 Association Drive, Reston, VA 22091-1589. (800) 232-7323.

- *Facing the Challenges of ADD: A Kit for Parents & Teachers* (2 videos)
- *A.D.D. from A to Z* (4 videos)

Filmakers Library, 124 E. 40th Street, New York, NY 10016. (212) 808-4980.

- *Out of Control*

LDA (Learning Disabilities Association), 4156 Library Road, Pittsburgh, PA 15234. (412) 341-1515.

- *Living with A.D.D.*

Guilford Publications, 72 Spring Street, New York, NY 10012. (800) 365-7006.

- *ADHD What Can We Do?*
- *ADHD What Do We Know?*

JKL Communications, PO Box 40157, Washington, DC 20016. (202) 223-5097.

- *The ABC's of ADD*
- *Succeeding in the Workplace*

National Professional Resources, Inc., Dept. B-2, 25 S. Regent Street, Port Chester, NY 10573. (914) 937-8879.

- *It's Just Attention Disorder—A Video Guide for Kids*
- *Inclusion of Children & Youth with Attention Deficit Disorder*

StarBase One Limited, Box 1447, Nevada City, CA 95959.

- *Peer Support ADHD ADD Teens Speak Out!*

University of Kentucky, Medical Television, 207 HSLC, 760 Rose Street, Lexington, KY 40536-0232.

- *Attention Deficit Hyperactivity Disorder: Diagnosis and Management; A Training Program for Teachers*

University of Minnesota, Dept. of Professional Development and Conference Services, 214 Nolte Center, 315 Pillsbury Drive, SE, Minneapolis, MN 55455-0139.

- *Creative Approaches to Attention Deficit Hyperactivity Disorder: Active Partnerships*

Journals

Attention, CHADD (Children with Attention Deficit Disorder), 499 Northwest 70th Avenue, Suite 101, Plantation, FL 33317; (305) 587-3700.

Journal of Learning Disabilities, Pro-ed, 5341 Industrial Oaks Blvd., Austin, TX 78735-8809; (512) 451-3246.

Learning Disabilities Quarterly, Council for Learning Disabilities, PO Box 40303, Overland Park. KS 66204; (913) 492-8755.

Journals (Special Issues)

Exceptional Children. Issues in the Education of Children with Attention Deficit Disorder, Vol.60 No.2, Oct/Nov 1993 Council for Exceptional Children, 1920 Association Dr., Reston, VA 22091 1589; (800) 232-7323.

Intervention in School and Clinic. Attention-Deficit/Hyperactivity Disorder: Academic Strategies, Comprehensive Assessment, Students with ADHD in the Inclusive Classroom, Vol.30 No. 4 Mar 1995, Pro-ed, 5341 Industrial Oaks Blvd., Austin, TX 787358809; (512) 451-3246.

Topics in Language Disorders. ADD and Its Relationship to Spoken and Written Language, Vol.14 No.4, Aug 1994, Aspen Publishers, Inc.,200 Orchard Ridge Dr., Gaithersburg, MD 20878; (800) 638-8437.

Newslettes

ADDendum (for and by ADD adults)
c/o CPS 5041A Backlick Road
Annandale, VA 22003

ADD-ONS
PO Box 675
Frankfort, IL 60423

ADDult News
Newsletter of ADDult Support Network
2620 Ivy Place
Toledo, OH 43613

Brakes
Magination Press
Brunner/Mazel Publishers
19 Union Square West
New York, NY 10003
(800) 825-3089

CH.A.D.D.ER and *CH.A.D.D.E.R. Box* Newsletters of CHADD (Children with Attention Deficit Disorder)
499 NW 70th Avenue, Suite 308
Plantation, FL 33317

Challenge
Newsletter of ADDA (Attention Deficit Disorder Association)
PO Box 2001
West Newbury, MA 01985

Resources

Attention Deficit Disorder Association (ADDA)
PO Box 972
Mentor, OH 44061
(800) 487-2282

Attention Deficit Information Network (AD-IN)
475 Hillside Avenue
Needham, MA 02194
(617) 455-9895

Children with Attention Deficit Disorder (CHADD)
499 NW 70th Avenue, Suite 308
Plantation, FL 33317
(305) 587-3700 (call for number of your local CHADD group)

National Information Center for Children and Youth with Disabilities (NICHCY)
PO Box 1492
Washington, DC 20013
(800) 695-0285

Internet Resources

Gopher sites:

gopher sjuvm.stjohns.edu
St. John's University
Electronic Rehabilitation Resource Center
Norman Coombs, Jay Leavitt

gopher hawking.u.washington.edu
University of Washington
Dean Martineau (demar@u.washington.edu)

FTP Sites:

ftp://com 13.netcom.com/pub/lds/add/add.faq

ftp://mos.com:/mcsnet.users/falcon/add

ftp.netcom:/pub/lds/add

Worldwide Web Homepages

These homepages have disability-related information:

http://www.seas.upenn.edu/~mengwong/add/20q.html

http://www.seas.upenn.edu/~mengwong/add/gifts.html

http://www.usfca.edu/usf/wesfford/wesfford.html

http://www.eskimo.com/~jlubin

http://www.eskimo.com/~dempt

http:/lwww.digimark. net/a+/ada.htlm (Americans w/Disabilities)

http://disability.com (disability resources, products, and services) Site features disability tips of the month, One Step Ahead newsletter, Disability Mall. Site is sponsored by Evan Kemp Associates, a company managed by people with disabilities. For more info, contact: webmaster@eka.com

If you subscribe to America Online (AOL), there are several weekly ADD conferences in the Issues in Mental Health Forum (use the keyword IMH).

If you subscribe to CompuServe, there is an ADD Forum (GO ADD), a DISABILITIES FORUM (GO DISABILITIES), and an EDUCATION Forum (GO EDFORUM) that address special needs.

If you subscribe to Delphi, there are two forums: ADDvantage Mental Health and ADD Parents Playhouse.

—by Janet Drill and Barbara Sorenson

Chapter 26

Understanding Autism

The Image and Reality of Autism

Autistic individuals suffer from a biological defect. Although they cannot be cured, much can be done to make life more hospitable for them.

The image often invoked to describe autism is that of a beautiful child imprisoned in a glass shell. For decades, many parents have clung to this view, hoping that one day a means might be found to break the invisible barrier. Cures have been proclaimed, but not one of them has been backed by evidence. The shell remains intact. Perhaps the time has come for the whole image to be shattered. Then at last we might be able to catch a glimpse of what the minds of autistic individuals are truly like.

Psychological and physiological research has shown that autistic people are not living in rich inner worlds but instead are victims of a biological defect that makes their minds very different from those of normal individuals. Happily, however, autistic people are not beyond the reach of emotional contact.

Thus, we can make the world more hospitable for autistic individuals just as we can, say, for the blind. To do so, we need to understand what autism is like—a most challenging task. We can imagine being blind, but autism seems unfathomable. For centuries, we have known that blindness is often a peripheral defect at the sensory-motor level of the nervous system, but only recently has autism been appreciated as a central defect at the highest level of cognitive processing. Autism, like blindness, persists throughout life, and it responds to special efforts in compensatory education. It can give rise to triumphant feats of coping but can also lead to disastrous secondary consequences—anxiety, panic and depression. Much can be done to prevent problems. Understanding the nature of the handicap must be the first step in any such effort.

Identifying Autism

Autism existed long before it was described and named by Leo Kanner of the Johns Hopkins Children's Psychiatric Clinic. Kanner published his landmark paper in 1943 after he had observed 11 children who seemed to him to form a recognizable group. All had in common four traits: a preference for aloneness, an insistence on sameness, a liking for elaborate routines, and some abilities that seemed remarkable compared with the deficits.

Concurrently, though quite independently, Hans Asperger of the University Pediatric Clinic in Vienna prepared his doctoral thesis on the same type of child. He also used the term "autism" to refer to the core features of the disorder. Both men borrowed the label from adult psychiatry, where it had been used to refer to the progressive loss of contact with the outside world experienced by schizophrenics. Autistic children seemed to suffer such a lack of contact with the world around them from a very early age.

Kanner's first case, Donald, has long served as a prototype for diagnosis. It had been evident early in life that the boy was different from other children. At two years of age, he could hum and sing tunes accurately from memory. Soon he learned to count to 100 and to recite both the alphabet and the 25 questions and answers of the Presbyterian catechism. Yet he had a mania for making toys and other objects spin. Instead of playing like other toddlers, he arranged beads and other things in groups of different colors or threw them on the floor, delighting in the sounds they made. Words for him had a literal, inflexible meaning.

Donald was first seen by Kanner at age five. Kanner observed that the boy paid no attention to people around him. When someone interfered with his solitary activities, he was never angry with the interfering person but impatiently removed the hand that was in his way. His mother was the only person with whom he had any significant contact, and that seemed attributable mainly to the great effort she made to share activities with him. By the time Donald was about eight years old, his conversation consisted largely of repetitive questions. His relation to people remained limited to his immediate wants and needs, and his attempts at contact stopped as soon as he was told or given what he asked for.

Some of the other children Kanner described were mute, and he found that even those who spoke did not really communicate but used language in a very odd way. For example, Paul, who was five, would parrot speech verbatim. He would say "You want candy" when he meant "I want candy." He was in the habit of repeating, almost every day, "Don't throw the dog off the balcony," an utterance his mother traced to an earlier incident with a toy dog.

Twenty years after he had first seen them, Kanner reassessed the members of his original group of children. Some of them seemed to have adapted socially much better than others, although their failure to communicate and to form relationships remained, as did their pedantry and single-mindedness. Two prerequisites for better adjustment, though no guarantees of it, were the presence of speech before age five and relatively high intellectual ability.

The brightest autistic individuals had, in their teens, become uneasily aware of their peculiarities and had made conscious efforts to conform. Nevertheless, even the best adapted were rarely able to be self-reliant or to form friendships. The one circumstance that seemed to be helpful in all the cases was an extremely structured environment.

As soon as the work of the pioneers became known, every major clinic began to identify autistic children. It was found that such children, in addition to their social impairments, have substantial intellectual handicaps. Although many of them perform relatively well on certain tests, such as copying mosaic patterns with blocks, even the most able tend to do badly on test questions that can be answered only by the application of common sense.

Autistic Behavior

The traits most characteristic of autistic people are aloneness, an insistence on sameness and a liking for elaborate routines. At the same time some autistic individuals can perform complicated tasks provided that the activity does not require them to judge what some other person might be thinking. These traits lead to characteristic forms of behavior, a number of which are listed here:

- Displays indifference
- Indicates needs by using an adult's hand

373

- Parrots words
- Laughs and giggles inappropriately
- Does not make eye contact
- Joins in only if an adult insists and assists
- Does not play with other children
- Does not pretend in playing
- Prefers sameness
- Is one-sided in interactions
- Talks incessantly about one topic
- Behaves in bizarre ways
- Handles or spins objects
- Yet some do certain things well if the task does not involve social understanding.

The Brain in Autism

Autism is rare. According to the strict criteria applied by Kanner, it appears in four of every 10,000 births. With the somewhat wider criteria used in current diagnostic practice, the incidence is much higher: one or two in 1,000 births, about the same as Down's syndrome. Two to four times as many boys as girls are affected.

For many years, autism was thought to be a purely psychological disorder without an organic basis. At first, no obvious neurological problems were found. The autistic children did not necessarily have low intellectual ability, and they often looked physically normal. For these reasons, psychogenic theories were proposed and taken seriously for many years. They focused on the idea that a child could become autistic because of some existentially threatening experience. A lack of maternal bonding or a disastrous experience of rejection, so the theory went, might drive an infant to withdraw into an inner world of fantasy that the outside world never penetrates.

These theories are unsupported by any empirical evidence. They are unlikely to be supported because there are many instances of extreme rejection and deprivation in childhood, none of which have resulted in autism. Unfortunately, therapies vaguely based on such notions are still putting pressure on parents to accept a burden of guilt for the supposedly avoidable and reversible breakdown of interpersonal interactions. In contrast, well-structured behavior modification programs have often helped families in the management of autistic children, especially children with severe behavior problems. Such programs do not claim to reinstate normal development.

The insupportability of the psychogenic explanation of autism led a number of workers to search for a biological cause. Their efforts implicate a defective structure in the brain, but that structure has not yet been identified The defect is believed to affect the thinking of autistic people, making them unable to evaluate their own thoughts or to perceive clearly what might be going on in someone else's mind.

Autism appears to be closely associated with other clinical and medical conditions. They include maternal rubella and chromosomal abnormality, as well as early injury to the brain and infantile seizures. Most impressive, perhaps, are studies showing that autism can have a genetic basis. Both identical twins are much more likely to be autistic than are both fraternal twins. Moreover, the likelihood that autism will occur twice in the same family is 50 to 100 times greater than would be expected by chance alone.

Structural abnormalities in the brains of autistic individuals have turned up in anatomic studies and brain-imaging procedures. Both epidemiological and neuropsychological studies have demonstrated that autism is strongly correlated with mental retardation, which is itself clearly linked to physiological abnormality. This fact fits well with the idea that autism results from a distinct brain abnormality that is often part of more extensive damage. If the abnormality is pervasive, the mental retardation will be more severe, and the likelihood of damage to the critical brain system will increase. Conversely, it is possible for the critical system alone to be damaged. In such cases, autism is not accompanied by mental retardation.

Neuropsychological testing has also contributed evidence for the existence of a fairly circumscribed brain abnormality. Autistic individuals who are otherwise able show specific and extensive deficits on certain tests that involve planning, initiative and spontaneous generation of new ideas. The same deficits appear in patients who have frontal lobe lesions. Therefore, it seems plausible that whatever the defective brain structure is, the frontal lobes are implicated.

Identifying the Damaged Cognitive Component

Population studies carried out by Lorna Wing and her colleagues at the Medical Research Council's Social Psychiatry Unit in London reveal that the different symptoms of autism do not occur together simply by coincidence. Three core features in particular—impairments in communication, imagination, and socialization—form a distinct triad. The impairment in communication includes such diverse phenomena as muteness and delay in learning to talk, as well as problems in comprehending or using nonverbal body language. Other autistic individuals speak fluently but are over literal in their understanding of language. The impairment in imagination appears in young autistic children as repetitive play with objects and in some autistic adults as an obsessive interest in facts. The impairment in socialization includes ineptness and inappropriate behavior in a wide range of reciprocal social interactions, such as the ability to make and keep friends. Nevertheless, many autistic individuals prefer to have company and are eager to please.

The question is why these impairments, and only these, occur together. The challenge to psychological theorists was clear: to search for a single cognitive component that would explain the deficits yet still allow for the abilities that autistic people display in certain aspects of interpersonal interactions. My colleagues at the Medical Research Council's Cognitive Development Unit in London and I think we have identified just such a component. It is a cognitive mechanism of a highly complex and abstract nature that could be described in computational terms. As a shorthand, one can refer to this component by one of its main functions, namely the ability to think about thoughts or to imagine another individual's state of mind. We propose that this component is damaged in autism. Furthermore, we suggest that this mental component is innate and has a unique brain substrate. If it were possible to pinpoint that substrate—whether it is an anatomic structure, a physiological system or a chemical pathway—one might be able to identify the biological origin of autism.

The power of this component in normal development becomes obvious very early. From the end of the first year onward, infants begin to participate in what has been called shared attention. For example, a normal child will point to something for no reason other than to share his interest in it with someone else. Autistic children do not show shared attention. Indeed, the absence of this behavior may well be one of the earliest signs of autism. When an autistic child points at an object, it is only because he wants it.

In the second year of life, a particularly dramatic manifestation of the critical component can be seen in normal children: the emergence of pretense, or the ability to engage in fantasy and pretend play. Autistic children cannot understand pretense and do not pretend when they are playing. The difference can be seen in such a typical nursery game as "feeding" a teddy bear or a doll with an empty spoon. The normal child goes through the appropriate motions of feeding and accompanies the action with appropriate slurping noises. The autistic child merely twiddles or flicks the spoon repetitively. It is precisely the absence of early and simple communicative behaviors, such as shared attention and make-believe play, that often creates the first nagging doubts in the minds of the parents about the development of their child. They rightly feel that they cannot engage the child in the emotional to-and-fro of ordinary life.

A Theoretical Model

My colleague Alan M. Leslie devised a theoretical model of the cognitive mechanisms underlying the key abilities of shared attention and pretense. He postulates an innate mechanism whose function is to form and use what we might call second-order representations. The world around us consists not only of visible bodies and events, captured by first-order representations, but also of invisible minds and mental events, which require second-order representation. Both tapes of representation have to be kept in mind and kept separate from each other.

Second-order representations serve to make sense of otherwise contradictory or incongruous information. Suppose a normal child, Beth, sees her mother holding a banana in such a way as to be pretending that it is a telephone. Beth has in mind facts about bananas and facts about telephones—first-order representations. Nevertheless, Beth is not the least bit confused and will not start eating telephones or talking to bananas. Confusion is avoided because Beth computes from the concept of pretending (a second-order representation) that her mother is engaging simultaneously in an imaginary activity and a real one.

As Leslie describes the mental process, pretending should be understood as computing a three-term relation between an actual situation, an imaginary situation and an agent who does the pretending. The imaginary situation is then not treated as the real situation. Believing can be understood in the same way as pretending. This insight enabled us to predict that autistic children, despite an adequate mental age (above four years or so), would not be able to understand that someone can have a mistaken belief about the world.

Explaining the Deficit in Autism

Together with our colleague Simon Baron-Cohen, we tested this prediction by adapting an experiment originally devised by two Austrian developmental psychologists, Heinz Wimmer and Josef Perner. The test has become known as the Sally-Anne task. Sally and Anne are playing together. Sally has a marble that she puts in a basket before leaving the room. While she is out, Anne moves the marble to a box. When Sally returns, wanting to retrieve the marble, she of course looks in the basket. If this scenario is presented as, say, a puppet show to normal children who are four years of age or more, they understand that Sally will look in the basket even though they know the marble is not there. In other words, they can represent Sally's erroneous belief as well as the true state of things. Yet in our test, 16 of 20 autistic children with a mean mental age of nine failed the task—answering that Sally would look in the box—in spite of being able to answer correctly a variety of other questions relating to the facts of the episode. They could not conceptualize the possibility that Sally believed something that was not true.

Many comparable experiments have been carried out in other laboratories, which have largely confirmed our prediction: autistic children are specifically impaired in their understanding of mental states. They appear to lack the innate component underlying this ability. This component, when it works normally, has the most far reaching consequences for higher-order conscious processes. It underpins the special feature of the human mind, the ability to reflect on itself. Thus, the triad of impairments in autism—in communication, imagination and socialization—is explained by the failure of a single cognitive mechanism. In everyday life, even very able autistic individuals find it hard to keep in mind simultaneously a reality and the fact that someone else may hold a misconception of that reality.

The automatic ability of normal people to judge mental states enables us to be, in a sense, mind readers. With sufficient experience we can form and use a theory of mind that allows us to speculate about psychological motives for our behavior and to manipulate other people's opinions, beliefs and attitudes. Autistic individuals lack the automatic ability to represent beliefs, and therefore they also lack a theory of mind. They cannot understand how behavior is caused by mental states or how beliefs and attitudes can be manipulated. Hence, they find it difficult to understand deception. The psychological undercurrents of real life as well as of literature—in short, all that gives spice to social relations—for them remain a closed book. "People talk to each other with their eyes," said one observant autistic youth. "What is it that they are saying?"

Lacking a mechanism for a theory of mind, autistic children develop quite differently from normal ones. Most children acquire more and more sophisticated social and communicative skills as they develop other cognitive abilities. For example, children learn to be aware that there are faked and genuine expressions of feeling. Similarly they become adept at that essential aspect of human communication, reading between the lines. They learn how to produce and understand humor and irony. In sum, our ability to engage in imaginative ideas, to interpret feelings and to understand intentions beyond the literal content of speech are all accomplishments that depend ultimately on an innate cognitive mechanism. Autistic children find it difficult or impossible to achieve any of these things. We believe this is because the mechanism is faulty.

Summary

This cognitive explanation of autism is specific. As a result, it enables us to distinguish the types of situations in which the autistic person will and will not have problems. It does not preclude the existence of special assets and abilities that are independent of the innate mechanism my colleagues and I see as defective. Thus it is that autistic individuals can achieve social skills that do not involve an exchange between two minds. They can learn many useful social routines, even to the extent of sometimes camouflaging their problems. The cognitive deficit we hypothesize is also specific enough not to preclude high achievement by autistic people in such diverse activities as musical performance, artistic drawing, mathematics and memorization of facts.

It remains to be seen how best to explain the coexistence of excellent and abysmal performance by autistic people on abilities that are normally expected to go together. It is still uncertain whether there may be additional damage in emotions that prevents some autistic children from being interested in social stimuli. We have as yet little idea what to make of the single-minded, often obsessive, pursuit of certain activities. With the autistic person, it is as if a powerful integrating force—the effort to seek meaning—were missing.

The old image of the child in the glass shell is misleading in more ways than one. It is incorrect to think that inside the glass shell is a normal individual waiting to emerge, nor is it true that autism is a disorder of childhood only. The motion picture *Rain Man* came at the right time to suggest a new image to a receptive public. Here we see Raymond, a middle-aged man who is unworldly, egocentric in the extreme and all too amenable to manipulation by others. He is incapable of understanding his brother's double-dealing pursuits, transparently obvious though they are to the cinema audience. Through various experiences it becomes possible for the brother to learn from Raymond and to forge an emotional bond with him. This is not a farfetched story. We can learn a great deal about ourselves through the phenomenon of autism.

Yet the illness should not be romanticized. We must see autism as a devastating handicap without a cure. The autistic child has a mind that is unlikely to develop self-consciousness. But we can now begin to identify the particular types of social behavior and emotional responsiveness of which autistic individuals are capable. Autistic people can learn to express their needs and to anticipate the behavior of others when it is regulated by external, observable factors rather than by mental states. They can form emotional attachments to others. They often strive to please and earnestly wish to be instructed in the rules of person-to-person contact. There is no doubt that within the stark limitations a degree of satisfying sociability can be achieved.

Autistic aloneness does not have to mean loneliness. The chilling aloofness experienced by many parents is not a permanent feature of their growing autistic child. In fact, it often gives way to a preference for company. Just as it is possible to engineer the environment toward a blind person's needs or toward people with other special needs, so the environment can be adapted to an autistic person's needs.

On the other hand, one must be realistic about the degree of adaptation that can be made by the limited person. We can hope for some measure of compensation and a modest ability to cope with adversity. We cannot expect autistic individuals to grow out of the unreflecting mind they did not choose to be born with. Autistic people in turn can look for us to be more sympathetic to their plight as we better understand how their minds are different from our own.

Further Reading

Autism: Explaining The Enigma. Uta Frith. Blackwell Publishers, 1989.

The Cognitive Basis Of A Biological Disorder: Autism. Uta Frith, John Morton and Alan M. Leslie in *Trends in Neurosciences*, Vol. 14, No. 10, pages 433–438; October 1991.

Autism and Asperger Syndrome. Edited by Uta Frith. Cambridge University Press, 1992.

Understanding Other Minds: Perspectives From Autism. Edited by Simon Baron-Cohen, Helen Tager-Flusberg and Donald J. Cohen. Oxford University Press, 1993.

— by Uta Frith

Uta Firth is a senior scientist in the Cognitive Development Unit of the Medical Research Council in London. Born in Germany, she took a degree in psychology in 1964 at the University of the Saarland in Saarbrücken, where she also studied the history of art. Four years later she obtained her Ph.D. in psychology at the University of London. Besides autism, her interests include reading development and dyslexia. She has edited a book in the field of reading development, *Cognitive Processes in Spelling*, and is the author of *Autism: Explaining the Enigma*.

Chapter 27

Autism and Pervasive Developmental Disorder (PDD)

Definition

Autism and Pervasive Developmental Disorder-NOS (not otherwise specified) are developmental disabilities that share many of the same characteristics. Usually evident by age three, autism and PDD-NOS are neurological disorders that affect a child's ability to communicate, understand language, play, and relate to others.

In the diagnostic manual used to classify disabilities, the *DSM-IV* (American Psychiatric Association, 1994), "autistic disorder" is listed as a category under the heading of "Pervasive Developmental Disorders." A diagnosis of autistic disorder is made when an individual displays 6 or more of 12 symptoms listed across three major areas: social interaction, communication, and behavior. When children display similar behaviors but do not meet the criteria for autistic disorder, they may receive a diagnosis of Pervasive Developmental Disorder-NOS (PDD not otherwise specified). Although the diagnosis is referred to as PDD-NOS, throughout the remainder of this fact sheet, we will refer to the diagnosis as PDD, as it is more commonly known.

Autistic disorder is one of the disabilities specifically defined in the Individuals with Disabilities Education Act (IDEA), the federal legislation under which children and youth with disabilities receive special education and related services. IDEA, which uses the term "autism," defines the disorder as "a developmental disability significantly

National Information Center for Children and Youth with Disabilities (NICHCY), Document FS1, July 1995.

affecting verbal and nonverbal communication and social interaction, usually evident before age 3, that adversely affects a child's educational performance. Other characteristics often associated with autism are engagement in repetitive activities and stereotyped movements, resistance to environmental change or change in daily routines, and unusual responses to sensory experiences." (In keeping with the IDEA and the way in which this disorder is generally referred to in the field, we will use the term autism throughout the remainder of this chapter.)

Due to the similarity of behaviors associated with autism and PDD, use of the term pervasive developmental disorder has caused some confusion among parents and professionals. However, the treatment and educational needs are similar for both diagnoses.

Incidence

Autism and PDD occur in approximately 5 to 15 per 10,000 births. These disorders are four times more common in boys than in girls.

The causes of autism and PDD are unknown. Currently, researchers are investigating areas such as neurological damage and biochemical imbalance in the brain. These disorders are not caused by psychological factors.

Characteristics

Some or all of the following characteristics may be observed in mild to severe forms:

- Communication problems (e.g., using and understanding language);
- Difficulty relating to people, objects, and events;
- Unusual play with toys and other objects;
- Difficulty with changes in routine or familiar surroundings; and
- Repetitive body movements or behavior patterns.

Children with autism or PDD vary widely in abilities, intelligence, and behaviors. Some children do not speak; others have language that often includes repeated phrases or conversations. Persons with more advanced language skills tend to use a small range of topics and have difficulty with abstract concepts. Repetitive play skills, a limited range of interests, and impaired social skills are generally evident as well. Unusual responses to sensory information—for example, loud noises, lights, certain textures of food or fabrics—are also common.

Educational Implications

Early diagnosis and appropriate educational programs are very important to children with autism or PDD. PL 101–476, the Individuals with Disabilities Education Act (IDEA), formerly PL 94–142, includes autism as a disability category. From the age of three, children with autism and PDD are eligible for an educational program appropriate to their individual needs. Educational programs for students with autism or PDD focus on improving communication, social, academic, behavioral, and daily living skills. Behavior and communication problems that interfere with learning sometimes require the assistance of a knowledgeable professional in the autism field who develops and helps to implement a plan which can be carried out at home and school.

The classroom environment should be structured so that the program is consistent and predictable. Students with autism or PDD learn better and are less confused when information is presented visually as well as verbally. Interaction with nondisabled peers is also important, for these students provide models of appropriate language, social, and behavior skills. To overcome frequent problems in generalizing skills learned at school, it is very important to develop programs with parents, so that learning activities, experiences, and approaches can be carried over into the home and community.

With educational programs designed to meet a student's individual needs and specialized adult support services in employment and living arrangements, children and adults with autism or PDD can live and work in the community.

Resources

Harris, S. (1994). *Siblings of children with autism: A guide for families*. Bethesda, MD: Woodbine House. (Telephone: (800) 843-7323; (301) 897-3570.)

Hart, C.A. (1993). *A parent's guide to autism: Answers to the most common questions*. New York: Pocket Books, Simon & Schuster Co. (Telephone: (800) 223-2336.)

Journal of Autism and Developmental Disorders. (Available from Plenum Publishing Corporation, 233 Spring Street New York, NY 10013. Telephone: (800) 221-9369.)

New Jersey Center for Outreach and Services for the Autism Community (COSAC). (1994, December). *National directory of programs serving individuals with autism and related pervasive developmental disorders.* Ewing, NJ: Author. (Available from COSAC, 1450 Parkside Avenue, Suite 22, Ewing, NJ 08638. Telephone: (609) 883-8100.)

Powers, M.D. (Ed.). (1989). *Children with autism: A parent's guide.* Rockville, MD: Woodbine House. (Telephone: (800) 843-7323; (301) 897-3570.)

Schopler, E., & Mesibov, G.B. (Eds.). Several books are available in the "Current Issues in Autism" book series: *Autism in adolescents and adults* (1983); *Effects of autism on the family (1984); Communication problems in autism* (1985); *Social behavior in autism* (1986); *High-functioning individuals with autism* (1990); *Preschool issues in autism* (1993); and *Learning and cognition in autism* (1995). (All are available from Plenum Publishing at the address above. Telephone: (800) 221-9369.)

Organizations

Autism Hotline
Autism Services Center
P.O. Box 507
Huntington, WV 25710-0507
Telephone: (304) 525-8014

Autism National Committee
7 Teresa Circle
Arlington, MA 02174

Autism Society of America
7910 Woodmont Avenue, Suite 650
Bethesda, MD 20814
Telephone: (301) 657-0881
For information and referral, call (800) 328-8476

Institute for the Study of Developmental Disabilities
Indiana Resource Center for Autism
Indiana University
853 East 10th Street
Bloomington, IN 47408-2601
(812) 855-6508

Chapter 28

Antidepressant Holds Promise for Treating Autism

Scientists have discovered that an antidepressant medication can help to reduce some of the abnormal behaviors associated with autism, a severe developmental disorder that affects 4 out of every 10,000 children. In the June 15 issue of the *Archives of General Psychiatry*, researchers at the National Institute of Mental Health reported that clomipramine can relieve many of the obsessive-compulsive symptoms of autistic disorder.

In addition, the authors—Charles T. Gordon, Rosanne C. State, Jean E. Nelson, Susan D. Hamburger, and Judith L. Rapoport, all with the Child Psychiatry Branch at NIMH—discovered that clomipramine improved some of the core symptoms of autism. These include stereotyped motor behaviors such as jumping, twirling and hand flapping, as well as abnormal social interaction.

"We are far from finding a cure for this devastating disorder, but these results offer considerable hope for people with autism and their families," said NIMH director Dr. Frederick K. Goodwin. "At the conclusion of the study, in fact, nearly 80 percent of the parents of study participants elected for their children to remain on clomipramine treatment."

Autism is a significant public health problem with great cost to the individual, family and community. Only 5 to 10 percent of autistic children become independent as adults; 25 percent improve but still

Excerpted from *The NIH Record*, August 3, 1993, Vol. XLV No 16, U.S. Department of Health and Human Services, National Institutes of Health.

require supervision; and the remainder continue to be severely impaired and in need of high-level institutionalized care. The disorder often coexists with mental retardation.

Autism is distinguished by impaired social interaction, lack of development of language and communication skills, and the inability to engage in imaginative activity. Autistic children, for example, typically are unable to form relationships with other people; they may not speak at all or may use language inappropriate to the situation; and they often cannot play creatively with other children. Certain obsessive-compulsive behaviors—such as positioning objects in a particular way, or performing tasks a certain number of times—are a common symptom of autistic disorder.

According to Gordon, clomipramine is known to be effective for treating obsessive-compulsive disorder—a mental illness causing recurrent, distressing thoughts that lead people to perform senseless behaviors like repetitive handwashing, checking locks, and counting objects. The research team hypothesized that clomipramine could, therefore, help reduce the obsessive-compulsive behaviors in autism.

"What was unexpected—and exciting—was the patients' improvement in making eye contact and initiating social interaction," he said. "It was a very consistent effect—we observed improvement in all of the patients taking clomipramine. The difference was slight in some patients, more marked in others—but it was noticeable."

In the study, 12 autistic children completed a 10-week double-blind crossover comparison of clomipramine and desipramine, and 12 different autistic children completed a similar comparison of clomipramine and placebo. While clomipramine was superior to desipramine in reducing both obsessive-compulsive and core autistic symptoms, the drugs were equally effective in reducing hyperactivity—another common feature of autistic disorder. Additionally, clomipramine helped to reduce self-injurious behaviors—biting, hitting and pinching themselves—in all of the four children in the study who exhibited such behaviors.

Of the 24 children studied, Gordon said, about one-sixth showed major improvement in social and behavioral functioning. About half of the group demonstrated moderate improvement. About one-sixth showed small improvement, and the remaining one-sixth had none.

Until now, medication studies in autism have yielded relatively disappointing results. The most studied and consistently useful medication has been the neuroleptic drug haloperidol, but it has problematic side effects—most notably tardive dyskinesia, a disorder causing involuntary movements of the facial muscles, limbs and trunk.

"Clomipramine is the most effective medication, certainly, that we've seen in quite some time," said Rapoport. "And even long-term use poses no significant risk of side effects, which is not the case with neuroleptic medications."

According to Rapoport, the precise physical cause of autism remains unknown; however, it has been hypothesized that autism is caused by excessive levels of serotonin, a neurotransmitter, or by underdevelopment of parts of the brain.

Clomipramine belongs to the class of drugs known as serotonin reuptake inhibitors. While its exact neurochemical mechanism is unknown, the drug is presumed to influence obsessive and compulsive behaviors through its effects on serotonergic neuronal transmissions.

"This is the first double-blind, controlled trial of a serotonin reuptake inhibitor for autistic disorder," Rapoport said. "We believe that the results shown for clomipramine could be applicable for other drugs of this type."

In addition, she said, future studies comparing haloperidol and clomipramine treatments for autistic disorder could prove to be useful.

— by Caree Vander Linden

Part Six

Legal and Social Information for Parents of Learning Disabled Children

Chapter 29

Legal Rights of Children and Youth Who Have Learning Disabilities (LD)

Introduction

Perhaps the most commonly asked questions by callers and correspondents to NCLD's office (National Center for Learning Disabilities) can be summed up in the sentence:

> My child has learning disabilities and I want
> to know how the school can help my child.

Considerable efforts were made in the early 1970s to win the enactment of Federal legislation which would ensure the right of children with disabilities to a free, appropriate education in the least restrictive environment. It was acknowledged that different children would require different prescriptions of treatment in their school settings. Nobody was to be excluded from the possibility of a good education.

That we receive so many anxious requests from parents about the laws and implementing regulations suggests that:

- the school system may not be being as responsive to the child's needs and parental concern as it might be, and
- the provisions of the various laws are not always well known.

Legal Rights of Children and Youth Who Have Learning Disabilities, by William Ellis, written for the National Center for Learning Disabilities, 381 Park Avenue South, Suite 1420, New York, NY 10016; reprinted with permission.

As a parent of a child with learning disabilities I recognized early on that I would have to be my child's chief advocate. I also understood that in order to be an effective advocate I would need to be very well informed. This text is designed to help you to know what your rights are so that, as you work with the school system, you have a clear sense not only of the provisions of the law but the kinds of questions that you have a right to ask.

This, of course, is only a starting place, and the National Center for Learning Disabilities and the other advocacy groups listed at the end of this chapter are very pleased to assist you. Please do not feel that you are alone.

—Introduction by Anne Ford, Chairman
National Center for Learning Disabilities

Why Should Parents Understand the Rights of Children and Youth Who Have Learning Disabilities?

Over several years, legislative protection for the rights of disabled individuals, including the learning disabled, was granted. Implementation of the regulations mandated by that legislation was given to the States. There are variations among the States in their implementation of the laws. This becomes particularly important to understand if you relocate from one State to another.

Public Law 94-142 (The Education for all Handicapped Children Act of 1975) as amended by Public Law 101-476 (The Individuals with Disabilities Education Act of 1990—IDEA) and Public Law 102-119 (The Individuals with Disabilities Act of 1991—IDEA) granted the right of parents, on behalf of their children, to be informed and involved. **The law provides the right to specific legal safeguards for your child**.

A parent is the most effective advocate for their child and a knowledge of the legal rights enables the parent to obtain the appropriate services for the child. In order to gain access to these services parents should initially contact the Principal's office or the child's counselor.

The greater your understanding of the law, the better the chances you have for the mandates of the law to be implemented on behalf of your child.

What Are My Rights as a Parent of a Child with Learning Disabilities?

Identification of the Disability

When you suspect that your child has a learning disability, you have the right to:

- Request that a comprehensive assessment be conducted by the school system at no cost to you.

- Receive notice and give (or refuse to give) consent before evaluation may take place.

- Examine all of your child's records.

- Have your child tested in all areas related to the suspected disability.

- See the results of the evaluation(s) and have them explained. You may request an independent evaluation at public expense (if you disagree with the school division's evaluation).

- Have the school division consider all independent evaluations in determining your child's educational needs.

- Have the school division consider all reports from professionals independent of the school system.

- A complete reevaluation every three years or, more frequently, upon request.

Special Education Service Eligibility Determination

To determine if your child is eligible for special services, you have the right to:

- Have eligibility for special education services be determined by a team of people including: the building principal or his/her designee, the supervisor of special education or his/her designee, the child's current teacher and at least one person who participated in your child's evaluation. You may ask to attend and to bring someone for moral and/or technical support.

- Receive free special education (and related services if necessary) regardless of family's insurance coverage.

IEP Development

If your child is deemed eligible for Special Education services, you have the right to:

- Have an Individualized Educational Program (IEP) in effect within thirty days of the date when it was determined your child was eligible for LD services.

- Participate in all meetings regarding the development, revision, and review of the IEP. You also have the right to have the meeting(s) scheduled at a time which is mutually convenient for you and school personnel.

- Have an advocate or someone of your choice accompany you to the IEP meeting(s).

- Have an interpreter present at the meeting(s) if you are hearing impaired or if your native language is other than English.

- Receive a copy of your child's IEP.

- Consent to the proposed placement before services are delivered.

- Have your child placed in a program which is appropriate, as close as possible to your home, and delivered in the least restrictive environment appropriate to your child's needs.

- Request a re-evaluation after your child is placed in a program if you feel his or her condition or needs have changed.

- Follow and be informed of your child's progress in the program in which he or she is placed.

Impartial Due Process Hearing

If you are unhappy at the way the IEP is working, you have the right to:

- Request an impartial due process hearing, within six months of a disagreement, when the school division proposes to initiate or refuses to initiate or change the identification, evaluation, or the provision of a free and appropriate public education for your child.

- Present evidence, confront, cross-examine, and compel witnesses to attend the hearing.

- Prohibit introduction of any documentary evidence or witnesses at the hearing which have not been disclosed to the other party at least five working days before the hearing.

- Request and obtain a written or electronic verbatim record of the hearing, when either party appeals the local hearing decision.

- Obtain findings of fact and decisions rendered by the hearing officer.

- Be informed by the school division of any low-cost legal and/or other relevant services available in the area when: (a) you request such information, or (b) a hearing is initiated by you or the school.

- Have your child present at an impartial due process hearing.

- Appeal the decision of the hearing officer to a reviewing officer.

- Appeal the decision of the reviewing officer to either a U.S. District Court or the State court in your jurisdiction.

- Recover from the school system reasonable attorney's fees if the hearing officer or judge rules in your favor. Included are expenses incurred in providing competent representation, such as witness fees, medical and diagnostic expenses, and costs for transcripts, depositions, travel, etc. These fees cannot be recovered if the school system prevails in the case, or if the school division offers to settle the case ten days before the hearing and the settlement is substantially similar to the outcome. An award of fees is in the discretion of the court.

School Records

You have the right to:

- Receive, upon request, a list of the types of records kept on your child, their location, and how you may obtain access to them.

- Inspect, review, and copy any of your child's records without unnecessary delay.

- Have someone at school explain or interpret information or material in your child's records.

- Receive copies of the records if this is the only way to insure access to them.

- Have a representative of your choosing inspect and review the records.

- Ask the school to change or delete any statement or information contained in your child's records which you believe is incorrect or misleading. The school must respond, and either change this statement or refuse. If the school refuses, school officials must inform you of their refusal and advise you of your rights to a hearing on the matter.

- A hearing on the change you requested in the records, conducted by a school official who does not have a direct interest in its outcome. **If the hearing is decided in your favor**, school officials must change the information and inform you in writing that this has been done. **If the hearing is decided in the school division's favor,** you have the right to add a statement to the record. This statement must remain with the record for as long as the records are kept. If your child's records are shown to anyone, this statement must also be included.

Additional Parent Rights

You have the right to:

- Provide written consent before the school division may proceed in: (a) Pre-placement evaluations; (b) Your child's initial placement in a program providing special education and related services.

- Not be bound by what the school division can offer in services that are needed, but the right to focus in all transactions on what your child needs.

- A fully paid private school special education placement if your school division refers you to such a setting because it is deemed appropriate while the one the school can offer is deemed not appropriate.

- Contact the Complaints Officer at your state's Department of Education if you feel the school division has not or is not complying with special education law and regulation.

- File a formal complaint with the federal Office of Civil Rights serving his/her state if you feel you or your child have been the subject of discrimination based on a physical or mental handicap (see following section).

Filing a Discrimination Complaint

When anyone feels that discrimination on the basis of physical or mental handicap exists in any education-related program operated by an institution receiving federal funding from the U.S. Department of Education, that person may file a formal complaint with the federal Office of Civil Rights serving his or her state.

The complaint should be filed in writing no later than 180 days after the discrimination occurred. The letter should explain who was discriminated against, how the person was harmed, who to contact for further information, and the name, address, and telephone number of the person filing the complaint. Include as much background information as possible. If necessary, ask regional office personnel for help in writing the complaint.

Below is a list of Office of Civil Rights regional offices and states served by each office:

Region I: Connecticut, Maine, Massachusetts, New Hampshire, Rhode Island, Vermont

J.W. McCormack Post Office and Courthouse
Room 222
Boston, MA 02109-4557
(617) 223-9662

Region II: New Jersey, New York, Puerto Rico, the Virgin Islands

26 Federal Plaza, Room 33-130
New York, NY 10278-0082
(212) 264-5180

Region III: Delaware, the District of Columbia, Maryland, Pennsylvania, Virginia, West Virginia

Gateway Building
3535 Market Street, Room 6300
Philadelphia, PA 19104-3326
(215) 596-6772

Region IV: Alabama, Florida, Georgia, North Carolina, South Carolina, Tennessee

Post Office Box 2048
Atlanta, GA 30301-2048
(404) 331-2954

Region V: Illinois, Indiana, Minnesota, Michigan, Ohio, Wisconsin

401 South State Street, Room 700C
Chicago, IL 60605-1202
(312) 886-3456

Region VI: Arkansas, Louisiana, Mississippi, Oklahoma, Texas

1200 Main Tower Building, Suite 2260
Dallas, TX 75202-9998
(214) 767-3959

Region VII: Iowa, Kansas, Kentucky, Missouri, Nebraska

10220 North Executive Hill Blvd., 8th Floor
Kansas City, MO 64153-1367
(816) 891-8026

Region VIII: Arizona, Colorado, Montana, North Dakota, Utah, South Dakota, Wyoming, New Mexico

1244 Spear Blvd.
Denver, CO 80204-3582
(303) 844-5695

Region IX: California

Old Federal Building
50 United Nations Plaza, Room 239
San Francisco, CA 94102-4102
(415) 556-7000

Region X: Alaska, Hawaii, Idaho, Nevada, Oregon, Washington (State of)

915 Second Avenue, Room 3310
Seattle, WA 98174-1099
(206) 553-6811

What Is an IEP?

An IEP (Individualized Education Program) is a written statement of special education and related services for a child. All children who receive special education services under PL 94-142 and IDEA must have an IEP.

An IEP should include:

- A statement of your child's present educational performance level; including academic achievement, social adaptation, prevocational and vocational skills, sensory and motor skills, self-help skills and speech and language skills.

- A statement of annual goals and reasonable short-term instructional objectives designed to achieve those goals.

- The extent and duration of both regular and special education and related services.

- The dates for initiation and anticipated duration of services.

- A statement of specific special education and related services to be provided and who will provide them.

- A statement of the extent to which the child can participate in regular education programs.

- Objective criteria, evaluation procedures, and schedules for determining at least **annually** whether instructional objectives are being achieved.

- *For students 14 years of age and older* a **statement of transition services** which will help the student move successfully from school to the "real world," with a listing of those agencies, besides the school, which will provide services. The school is responsible for obtaining services from other agencies where necessary and for reconvening the IEP team to seek alternatives if another agency fails to provide the services specified.

Who Develops the IEP?

Participants are:

- A representative of the school or public agency other than the child's teacher. This could be a special education teacher, learning disabilities specialist, or the school principal.

- The child's teacher. If the child has more than one teacher, the state may specify which teacher will participate in the meeting.

- One or both of the child's parents (or guardian).

- The child, where appropriate.

- Other individuals at the discretion of the parents or the state agency.

What Steps Should Be Taken to Have the Child Evaluated?

- A formal evaluation can be initiated at the request of the school or the parent. The parent must agree in writing.

- Before requesting an evaluation, parents are advised to
  - —Clarify their concern.
  - —Gather information and anecdotes about the student's school performance from meetings with school personnel.
  - —Note strengths and weaknesses both in and out of school.
  - —Identify accommodations at school and at home that might alleviate some of the difficulties.
  - —Make accommodations and watch for the effects.
  - —Keep records.

- Evaluations can be arranged through the school system, private clinics or centers, university or hospital centers. Parents should check to see if the school system will honor the test results provided by a private facility.

What Is Involved in the Evaluation?

The evaluation:

- Must be given in an individual's dominant language.
- Must be administered by a qualified individual(s).
- Must use valid tests and testing procedures.
- Must use a variety of tests (no determination of disability or placement is to be based on the results of a single test.)

A comprehensive evaluation includes:

- Background Information
    - —family history
    - —developmental history (e.g., crawling, walking, talking)
    - —medical history social history school history (areas of interest, performance, progress, homework skills)
    - —school attendance

- Assessment of Intellectual Potential
    - —Tests such as the Wechsler Intelligence Scale for Children Revised (WISC-R) or the Stanford Binet Intelligence Scale. *(Note that there are versions of IQ tests designed for very young children and for adults.)*

- Assessment of Performance of Academic Skills
    - —achievement tests
    - —diagnostic tests pinpointing strengths and weaknesses
    - —observations of classroom behavior and learning strategies
    - —analysis of class work discussions with the teacher and other involved individuals
    - —informal diagnosis of learning style

What Types of Placement Are Available to Students in Need of Special Education Services?

PL 94-142 requires that the child's education be appropriate and in the least restrictive environment. Options from least to most restrictive are:

- Regular Class without Accommodations
- Regular Classes In-class Accommodations
- Regular Class plus Supplementary Instructional Services
- Part-time Special Education Class
- Full-time Special Education Class
- Special Day School
- Homebound Instruction in Hospital, Residential, or Total Care Settings

Related services may include:

- counseling/psychotherapy
- occupational therapy
- speech and language therapy

Are There Other Laws under Which My Child Can Receive Free Services?

If a child does not meet the eligibility requirements for services under Part B of The Individuals with Disabilities Education Act (IDEA), but is clearly learning disabled s/he may be eligible for services under Section 504 of the Rehabilitation Act of 1973.

Section 504 of the Rehabilitation Act of 1973 is a civil rights act which protects the civil and constitutional rights of persons with disabilities. It prohibits organizations which receive federal funds from discriminating against otherwise qualified individuals solely on the basis of disability.

The law states that a public school must address the needs of children who are considered "handicapped" as adequately as those of non-handicapped persons. Examples of accommodations include:

- providing a structured learning environment;
- repeating and simplifying instructions about in-class and home-work assignments;
- supplementing verbal instructions with visual instructions;
- using behavioral management techniques;
- adjusting class schedules;
- modifying test delivery;
- using tape recorders, computer aided instruction, and other audio visual equipment;
- selecting modified textbooks and workbooks;
- and tailoring homework assignments.

Under the regulations, "Handicapped" is defined as a person who has physical or mental impairment which substantially limits a "major life activity." "Major life activity" includes learning.

What Are Some of the Areas of Discrimination Affecting Individuals with Learning Disabilities Which Section 504 Prohibits?

Individuals with learning disabilities:

* Must not be denied the opportunity to participate in or benefit from a service which is afforded to non-disabled students.

* Must be provided aids, benefits, or services which are equivalent to those provided to others and which offer an equal opportunity.

* Should not be required to accept different or separate benefits or services unless such action is necessary to be effective for the individual.

* Must not be limited in the enjoyment of any right, privilege, advantage, or opportunity enjoyed by others.

How Can I Gain Access to Services under the Provisions of Section 504?

The school principal and the district office of special education can direct you to the appropriate procedures. Additionally, your regional Office of Civil Rights (OCR) should be able to interpret the provisions of Section 504 as they apply to education.

Are ADD and AD/HD Covered for Services under PL 94-142 and IDEA?

Local Education Authorities (LEA) and State Education Authorities (SEA) are to provide services to AD/HD youngsters even though the term is not specifically listed in the Federal Law. These individuals can be served under current categories such as "specific learning disabilities," "other health impaired," and "seriously emotionally disturbed," if they meet the necessary criteria. This was affirmed in a memorandum dated September 16, 1991 from Assistant Secretary of Education, Robert R. Davila, to Chief State School Officers.

Resources

National Center for Learning Disabilities
381 Park Avenue South, Suite 1420
New York, NY 10016
(212) 545-7510

Federation for Children with Special Needs
Martha Ziegler
Technical Assistance for Parents Programs (TAPP)
95 Berkley Street, Suite 104
Boston, MA 02116
(617) 482-2915

Parent Training and Information Centers (PTI's)

The PTI's are Federally funded advocacy centers which provide training and information to parents to enable them to participate more effectively with professionals in meeting the educational needs of children with disabilities. There is at least one PTI in each state. Organizations such as NCLD, LDA and NICHCY can provide specific listings for your state.

National Information Center for Children and Youth with Disabilities (NICHCY)
1233 20th Street NW, Suite 504
Washington, DC 20036
(800) 695-0285

Learning Disabilities Association of America (LDA)
4156 Library Road
Pittsburgh, PA 15243
(412) 341-1515

Brochures

Legal Rights of Children and Youth with Handicapping Conditions—
Part Four of the manual to the NCLD five part video series, *We Can Learn*, NCLD, 381 Park Avenue South, Suite 1420, NY, NY 10016.
(212) 545-7510.

Understanding Learning Disabilities: A Parent Guide and Workbook. Learning Disabilities Council, Inc., P.O. Box 8451, Richmond, VA 23226. (804) 748-5012.

A Guide to Section 504: How it Applies to Students with Learning Disabilities and ADHD, Learning Disabilities Association of America, 4156 Library Road, Pittsburgh, PA 15234.

Advocacy Manual: A Parents' How-to Guide for Special Education Services, Learning Disabilities Association of America, 4156 Library Road, Pittsburgh, PA 15234.

The Civil Rights of Students With Hidden Disability Under Section 504 of the Rehabilitation Act of 1973. U.S. Department of Education, Office for Civil Rights, Washington D.C. 20202-1328. (Pamphlet)

—by William Ellis

Chapter 30

How Section 504 of the Rehabilitation Act Applies to Students with LD and AD/HD

What Is Section 504

Section 504 is the section of the Rehabilitation Act of 1973 which applies to persons with disabilities. Basically it is a civil rights act which protects the civil and constitutional rights of persons with disabilities. Section 504 prohibits organizations which receive federal funds from discriminating against otherwise qualified individuals solely on the basis of handicap. Section 504 is enforced by the U.S. Department of Education, Office for Civil Rights (OCR).

How Does Section 504 Define "Handicap"?

A person is considered "handicapped" if he/she:

1. has a physical or mental impairment which substantially limits one or more major activities,
2. has a record of such an impairment, or
3. is regarded as having such an impairment.

(In addition to school-age children who are eligible for special education services, this includes, for example, persons with communicable diseases, temporary handicapping conditions, attention deficit disorder

"A Guide to Section 504," an undated brochure produced by Learning Disabilities Association of America (LDA), 4156 Library Road, Pittsburgh, PA 15234; reprinted with permission.

(ADD), behavior disorders, chronic asthma and severe allergies, physical handicaps, and diabetes.)

What Is a "Major Life Activity"?

Major life activities include such things as walking, seeing, hearing, speaking, breathing, learning, working, caring for oneself, and performing manual tasks.

What Types of Discrimination Does Section 504 Prohibit

1. Denial of the opportunity to participate in or benefit from a service which is afforded nonhandicapped students.
   - refusing to allow a student with an IEP the opportunity to be on the honor roll, denying credit to a student whose absenteeism is related to the disability, refusing to dispense Ritalin to a student with ADD (a school cannot require parents to waive liability as a condition of giving medicine; however, it is wise to get your physician's prescription to back up medical accommodations).

2. Provision of opportunity to participate in or to benefit from a service which is not equal to that afforded others.
   - determining sports eligibility on a student's grades without regard to the student's handicapping condition.

3. Provision of aids, benefits or services which are not as effective as those provided to others. Equally effective means equivalent, not identical, and must afford an equal opportunity, not equal results.
   - placing a student with a hearing impairment on the front row instead of providing an interpreter.

4. Provision of different or separate benefits or services unless such action is necessary to be effective.
   - separate classes, schools or facilities.

5. Aiding or perpetuating discrimination by providing assistance to an organization which discriminates.
   - sponsoring a student organization which excludes persons with disabilities.

6. Denial of the opportunity to participate on a planning or advisory board because of an individual's handicapping condition.

7. Otherwise limiting the enjoyment of any right, privilege, advantage or opportunity enjoyed by others.

8. Selecting a site or location which effectively excludes persons with disabilities or subjects them to discrimination.
    -   locating students with disabilities in inferior facilities due to a lack of classroom space.

What Does "Reasonable Accommodation" Mean?

A recipient of federal funds shall make reasonable accommodation to the known physical or mental limitations of an otherwise qualified person unless the recipient can demonstrate that the accommodation would impose an undue hardship on the operation of its program. Courts have required accommodations which achieve "meaningful equal opportunity." Accommodations need to take into account both the functional limitations of the individual and the alternative methods of performing tasks or activities which would permit people of varying abilities to participate without jeopardizing outcomes. Some examples of reasonable accommodations are modified homework requirements, provision of readers, provision of taped textbooks, changes in the way tests are given, provision of a teacher's aide, or seating in the front row of the classroom.

1. Accommodations must be individualized.
2. The individual needs of the persons with a disability should be met to the same extent as the needs of persons without handicapping conditions.
3. Modifications can be made to regular programs or the provision of different programs may be necessary.
4. Accommodations should place the student with a disability at an equal starting level with the nonhandicapped student.

How Does Section 504 Define "Appropriate Education"?

A free appropriate education is one provided by the public elementary or secondary school which includes regular or special education and related aids and services that (i) are designed to meet the individual

411

educational needs of persons with disabilities as adequately as the needs of nonhandicapped persons are met, and (ii) are based upon adherence to evaluation, placement and procedural safeguard requirements.

Does Section 504 Require Evaluations?

Section 504 Regulation, 34 CFR Section 104.35 (a) requires that a district evaluate "any person who, because of handicap, needs or is believed to need special education *or* related services" (emphasis added). An evaluation is also required prior to any significant change in placement. Pre-screening methods which affect a student's eligibility for special education may be considered "evaluations" and are subject to proper notice requirements. EHLR DEC.353.237 (1989).

Section 504 does not require that a district must carry out a full evaluation of a student simply because a parent requests it. However, refusal by the district to do so constitutes an official action with respect to the student's evaluation and placement, and the district must provide the parent with procedural safeguards.

Does Section 504 Require an IEP?

Section 504 requires a written plan describing placement and services. Placement decisions must be based upon information drawn from a variety of sources and all information must be documented and considered. Although a formal IEP is not required, the placement decision must be made by a group of persons knowledgeable about the child, about the meaning of the evaluation data and about placement options.

What Procedural Safeguards Do Parents Have

To be in compliance with Section 504, school districts must:

1. Provide written assurance of nondiscrimination.
2. Designate an employee to coordinate compliance.
3. Provide grievance procedures to resolve complaints.
4. Provide notice of nondiscrimination in admission or access to its programs or activities. Notice must be included in a student/parent handbook.
5. Annually identify and locate all qualified children with disabilities who are not receiving a public education.

6. Annually notify persons with disabilities and their parents or guardians of the district's responsibilities under Section 504.
7. Provide parents or guardians with procedural safeguards:
   (a) notice of their rights
   (b) an opportunity to review relevant records
   (c) an impartial hearing—parents or guardians must be notified of their right to request a hearing regarding the identification, evaluation, or educational placement of persons with handicapping conditions.

How Do I File an OCR Complaint?

Find someone in your regional OCR office who understands the applications of Section 504 on education, and use that person as your contact. Explain the situation, specify the issue, and cite the area of discrimination. OCR should then send a representative to investigate the complaint.

What If I Don't Agree with OCR's Ruling?

Under the Freedom of Information Act ask for a copy of the investigation plan used by the OCR representative, a copy of the investigation report, and a copy of the school's documents. If you don't think that the investigation was a careful and thorough examination of the issue of complaint or the conclusions are wrong, write a letter of appeal saying you don't agree with the Letter of Finding and stating your reasons.

How Is Section 504 Different from P.L. 94-142

1. P.L. 94-142 lists categories of qualifying conditions. Section 504 is much broader.
2. Free Appropriate Education (FAPE) under Section 504 means an education comparable to the education provided to nonhandicapped students.
3. Under Section 504 a student is eligible if he meets the definition of "qualified handicapped person." The student is not required to be in need of special education in order to be protected.
4. Section 504 does not provide additional funds.
5. Section 504 includes detailed regulations regarding building and program accessibility.

6. Section 504 requires notice of procedural safeguards, however it does not have to be *written* notice.
7. Section 504 requires notice, but not consent, prior to an initial evaluation.
8. Under Section 504 school districts must designate an employee to be responsible for assuring compliance and must provide a grievance procedure.

Which Law Takes Precedence?

Schools must comply with both P.L. 94-142 (Individuals with Disabilities Education Act, IDEA) and Section 504 of the Rehabilitation Act of 1973. Compliance with IDEA does not necessarily mean that a district is in compliance with Section 504. One does not take precedence over the other!

Chapter 31

Definitions Under the Individuals with Disabilities Education Act (IDEA)

The IDEA lists 13 separate categories of disabilities under which children may be eligible for special education and related services. This chapter presents the IDEA's definitions verbatim, as found in §300.7(b)(1)–(13).

Autism

"Autism" means a developmental disability significantly affecting verbal and nonverbal communication and social interaction, generally evident before age 3, that adversely affects a child's educational performance. Other characteristics often associated with autism are engagement in repetitive activities and stereotyped movements, resistance to environmental change or change in daily routines, and unusual responses to sensory experiences. The term does not apply if a child's educational performance is adversely affected primarily because the child has a serious emotional disturbance, as defined in paragraph (b)(9) of this section.

Note: If a child manifests characteristics of the disability category "autism" after age 3, that child still could be diagnosed as having "autism" if the criteria in paragraph (b)(1) of this section are satisfied.

National Information Center for Children and Youth with Disabilities (NICHCY) *News Digest*, Vol. 3, No. 2, September 1993.

Deaf-blindness

"Deaf-blindness" means concomitant hearing and visual impairments, the combination of which causes such severe communication and other developmental and educational problems that they cannot be accommodated in special education programs solely for children with deafness or children with blindness.

Deafness

"Deafness" means a hearing impairment that is so severe that the child is impaired in processing linguistic information through hearing, with or without amplification, that adversely affects a child's educational performance.

Hearing Impairment

"Hearing impairment" means an impairment in hearing, whether permanent or fluctuating, that adversely affects a child's educational performance but that is not included under the definition of deafness in this section.

Mental Retardation

"Mental retardation" means significantly subaverage general intellectual functioning existing concurrently with deficits in adaptive behavior and manifested during the developmental period that adversely affects a child's educational performance.

Multiple Disabilities

"Multiple disabilities" means concomitant impairments (such as mental retardation-blindness, mental retardation-orthopedic impairment, etc.), the combination of which causes such severe educational problems that they cannot be accommodated in special education programs solely for one of the impairments. The term does not include deaf-blindness.

Orthopedic Impairment

"Orthopedic impairment" means a severe orthopedic impairment that adversely affects a child's educational performance. The term includes impairments caused by congenital anomaly (e.g., clubfoot, absence of some member, etc.), impairments caused by disease (e.g., poliomyelitis, bone tuberculosis, etc.), and impairments from other causes (e.g., cerebral palsy, amputations, and fractures or burns that cause contractures).

Other Health Impairment

"Other health impairment" means having limited strength, vitality or alertness, due to chronic or acute health problems such as a heart condition, tuberculosis, rheumatic fever, nephritis, asthma, sickle cell anemia, hemophilia, epilepsy, lead poisoning, leukemia, or diabetes that adversely affects a child's educational performance.

Serious Emotional Disturbance

"Serious emotional disturbance" is defined as follows:

- (i) The term means a condition exhibiting one or more of the following characteristics over a long period of time and to a marked degree that adversely affects a child's educational performance
    - —An inability to learn that cannot be explained by intellectual, sensory, or health factors;
    - —An inability to build or maintain satisfactory interpersonal relationships with peers and teachers;
    - —Inappropriate types of behavior or feelings under normal circumstances;
    - —A general pervasive mood of unhappiness or depression; or
    - —A tendency to develop physical symptoms or fears associated with personal or school problems.

- (ii) The term includes schizophrenia. The term does not apply to children who are socially maladjusted, unless it is determined that they have a serious emotional disturbance.

Specific Learning Disability

"Specific learning disability" means a disorder in one or more of the basic psychological processes involved in understanding or in using language, spoken or written, that may manifest itself in an imperfect ability to listen, think, speak, read, write, spell, or to do mathematical calculations. The term includes such conditions as perceptual disabilities, brain injury, minimal brain dysfunction, dyslexia, and developmental aphasia. The term does not apply to children who have learning problems that are primarily the result of visual, hearing, or motor disabilities, of mental retardation, or emotional disturbance, or of environmental, cultural, or economic disadvantage.

Speech or Language Impairment

"Speech or language impairment" means a communication disorder such as stuttering, impaired articulation, a language impairment, or a voice impairment that adversely affects a child's educational performance.

Traumatic Brain Injury

"Traumatic brain injury" means an acquired injury to the brain caused by an external physical force, resulting in total or partial functional disability or psychosocial impairment, or both, that adversely affects a child's educational performance. The term applies to open or closed head injuries resulting in impairments in one or more areas, such as cognition; language; memory; attention; reasoning; abstract thinking; judgment; problem-solving; sensory, perceptual, and motor abilities; psychosocial behavior; physical functions; information processing; and speech. The term does not apply to brain injuries that are congenital or degenerative, or brain injuries induced by birth trauma.

Visual Impairment, Including Blindness

"Visual impairment including blindness" means an impairment in vision that, even with correction, adversely affects a child's educational performance. The term includes both partial sight and blindness.

Chapter 32

Stress Management for the Learning Disabled

Why Does the Education "Spotlight" Need to Be Trained on Stress Management in the Schools?

School-related stress is the most prevalent, untreated cause of academic failure in our schools. It is believed to afflict an alarming 6 to 10 million children a year (Barker 1987). In a classroom of 25 students, between one and three students are at high risk for developing stress-related problems which would probably interfere with learning (Hill & Sarason 1966).

Achievement stress, the widespread "invisible disability" is rarely detected but generally gets worse as children progress through school (Hill & Wigfield, 1984). Untreated, achievement stress may result in academic failure, behavioral/emotional problems, drug abuse, health problems, and even suicide.

Even though it has been demonstrated that reducing stress significantly improves the performance of learning disabled children in reading, arithmetic, spelling (Frey, 1980), and handwriting (Hughes, Jackson, DuBois, & Erwin, 1979), stress management programs in the schools are almost nonexistent (Rubenzer, 1984, 1987). Stress management has also been effective in improving attention skills (Omizo & Michael, 1982) of children with attention problems.

Since the stressed children of today will be the Type A adults of the 21st century, treating stress in the schools now may well relax

ERIC Digest #E452, 1988.

our dangerously stressed society in the future. Currently, stress-related mental disorders are 200 to 400% more prevalent than any other emotional problem requiring clinical treatment (American Psychiatric Association, 1980). Valium, a medication used to relieve stress, is currently the most widely prescribed medication in the United States, thus indicating the epidemic proportions of stress in our society today (Cawood, 1981).

What Is Stress?

Stress is the physiological/emotional reaction to psychological events. Any event triggering the formerly life-saving, ancient "fight or flight" response is a stressor. The constraints of modem society dearly prohibit fleeing from or physically resisting most stressful events (e.g., running out of a classroom when a surprise test is given, arguing with the teacher not to give a test). Unrelieved, the cumulative, physical strain generated by psychological stress can harm the body. Stress is often experienced as a consistent, exaggerated, and overwhelming sense of urgency, often coupled with frustration.

Achievement stress, triggered by school tasks, is a learned, inappropriate distress habit which impairs school performance. The many faces of achievement stress include: test anxiety (Sarson, et al., 1960), math anxiety (Tobias, 1980), "stage fright" (e.g., public speaking, fear of board work in front of the class), writer's block, etc.

What Are Possible Causes of Achievement Stress for the Learning Disabled (LD)?

School Factors: Achievement stress may be the result as well as the cause of poor academic performance. The precise role of stress in academic performance is blurred because of the complexity of anxiety's origin, measurement, and manipulation. The negative relationship between stress and impaired performance is well established however.

Special Education Factors: In addition to the great achievement demands (Elkind, 1981) experienced by all students, learning disabled children may be at particular risk for achievement stress due to frustration stemming from:

1. Insensitivity of significant others who treat these children as if they will not perform, when in fact they cannot perform at their ability level.

2. Self-concept confusion resulting from the vast gap between being able to keep up with the class in some modes (e.g., oral discussion, group work, artistic and creative expression, athletics, etc.) and discrepantly poor academic performance in other modes (reading, writing, board work, standardized achievement tests, etc.).

3. Dependency on the special education teacher for academic survival and the separation anxiety of having this school "life raft" pulled out from under them if they are exited from the program.

4. Label(s) attached (formal and otherwise) to these children by both teachers and students and the isolation and rejection associated with being in any special education class.

5. Hesitancy to ask clarifying questions because of the fear of drawing further criticism.

These frustrations magnify the achievement stress for LD students and place them at particular risk for stress-related underachievement.

How Does Stress "Dim Ability"?

The emotional discomfort of worry, feelings of being overwhelmed, and the unpleasant physical sensations of anxiety (cold, sweaty hands; butterflies in the stomach; fidgeting and squirming; etc.) distract attention from subtle cognitive tasks. Stress can serve as a signal for a panic reaction, or an anxiety attack (e.g., blanking out during a test). Stress can also trigger a "flight" response leading to careless "rushing errors" (missing important details, inadvertently marking wrong responses on tests, poor handwriting, etc.) resulting from the strong urge to "escape" from the unpleasant test situation. A child may learn to avoid stress-producing tasks, resulting in poorer performance, thus amplifying the child's fear of failure of the task in the future. The aim of stress management is to break the link between irrelevant stress reactions (diffused attention, fear, etc.) and academic tasks.

What Are Some Achievement Stress Warning Signals?

1. Sudden dramatic increase or decrease in effort in school.
2. Major change in attitude/temperament (irritability, lack of enthusiasm, carelessness).

3. Withdrawal or outbursts.
4. Overactive/distractible behaviors (fidgeting, making unnecessary trips to the pencil sharpener or bathroom, nervous tics, jumping from task to task, difficulty concentrating, accident proneness, and sighing).
5. Complaints of fatigue and vague illnesses.
6. Problems sleeping.
7. Headaches/stomachaches.
8. Drug use/abuse.
9. Increase in allergic/asthmatic attacks.
10. Avoidance of school or testing situation by direct refusal or convenient illnesses (unnecessary trips to the nurse).
11. Loss of appetite or excessive eating, nail biting, refusing to do chores.
12. Antisocial/disruptive behaviors (Rubenzer, 1987).

A referral to a school psychologist/counselor may be warranted it the quantity and/or intensity of the above warning signals displayed by the child raise concern. Conversely, decreases in these symptoms would indicate improved stress coping skills.

The ABC's of Stress Management

Effective stress management requires a "whole child" approach which addresses the child's Attitude, Behavior (skills), and Circumstances.

Stress-Reducing Attitudes. Foster a relaxed classroom environment. Provide humor as an outlet. Encourage one-thing-at-a-time thinking. Emphasize the importance of affirmative positive thinking on performance. Have the child repeat such phrases as "I can do it," "I am calm and I can remember the right answers," "I have studied hard so I will do well." Encourage the child to discuss his or her problems with counseling personnel and others.

Stress-Reducing Behaviors. After about 10 relaxation training sessions (usually three 10- to 15-minute sessions per week) using such programs as QR, Centering Books, Biofeedback monitor, Stress Dots or Calmpute, have the student practice relaxation while seated at a desk (with eyes open). Make certain the student "unlocks" arms and legs, breathes deeply and slowly, and relaxes muscles. If the chin starts frowning or fidgeting during the task, remind him or her to relax. Sitting at a desk will become a cue for relaxation if the child is rewarded (saying thank you, etc.) for relaxing whenever seated. It may be helpful for a child to engage in some noncompetitive aerobic exercise for a few minutes prior to being seated to help burn off energy.

Stress-Reducing Circumstances. Provide work which is usually within the child's "comfort zone" in terms of success. Only after relaxation and test taking skills have been mastered, give the child mildly challenging work to inoculate him or her against "panic attacks."

Relaxation Centers. To assure that stress management will not be shelved simply to be discussed yearly, a relaxation center can be set up, to which students could be assigned regularly (two to three times per week). A chart indicating the time each student spends at the center may be useful. Designate a small area, relatively free from sound and noise distractions. A study carrel with a comfortable chair should be provided. Decorate the immediate area with calm colors and soothing pictures or wallpaper designs. A cassette recorder/ player with earphones will be needed. A collection of relaxation audio cassettes should be housed along with biofeedback equipment if at all possible.

The special education classroom may be the only place where these children will be equipped with stress management skills which will become increasingly more important as the pressures to achieve academically increase.

Resources

American Psychiatric Association (1980). *Diagnostic and statistical manual of mental disorders* (3rd ed.). Washington, DC: Author.

Barker, B. (1987). Helping students cope with stress. *Learning*, 15(5), 45–49.

Biofeedback Monitor, Tandy Corporation, Radio Shack, Fort Worth, TX 76102.

Calmpute—A biofeedback/stress reduction program. 2180 Belgrave Avenue, Montreal, Quebec, Canada, H4A 2L8. (514) 489-8251.
Cawood, F. (1981). *The side effects of prescription drugs*. Peachtree City, GA: Frank W. Cawood Associates.

Elkind, D. (1981). *The hurried child: Growing up too fast too soon.* Reading, MA: Addison Wesley.

Frey, N. (1980, May). Improving the performance of poor readers through autogenic relaxation training. *The Reading Teacher*, 928–932.

Hendricks, C.G., & Wills, R. (1975). *The centering book. Awareness activities for children, parents, and teachers.* Englewood Cliffs, NJ: Prentice-Hall.

Hill, K.T., & Sarason, S.B. (1966). The relation of test anxiety and defensiveness to test and school performance over the elementary school years. *Monographs of the Society for Research in Child Development*, 31, (2, serial 104).

Hill, K.T., & Wigfield, A. (1984). Test anxiety: A major educational problem and what can be done about it. *The Elementary School Journal*, 85(1).

Hughes, H., Jackson, K., DuBois, K.E., & Erwin, R. (1979). Treatment of handwriting problems utilizing EMG biofeedback training. *Perceptual and Motor Skills*, 48(2), 603–606.

Omizo, N.M., & Michael, W.B. (1982). Biofeedback-induced relaxation training and impulsivity, attention to task, and focus of control among hyperactive boys. *Journal of Learning Disabilities*, 15(7), 414–416.

Rubenzer, R.L. (1984). The effect of biofeedback-induced relaxation on test/math anxiety and related performance for children in a special school for the gifted. Doctoral dissertation, Columbia University. Dissertation Abstracts International.

Rubenzer, R.L. (1987). Helping your children deal with stress. In D. Dinkmeyer, G.D. McKay, D. Dinkmeyer, Jr., J. Dinkmeyer, & J.L. McKay, *The Effective Parent* (p. 84). Circle Pines, MN: American Guidance Service.

Sarason, S.B., Davidson, K.S., Lighthall, F.F., Waite, R.R., & Ruebush, B.K. (1960). *Anxiety in elementary school children.* New York: Wiley.

Stress Dots. Communication Unlimited, 11032 Pinyon Drive, Northglenn, CO 80234, (303) 424–4957.

Tobias, S. (1980) *Overcoming math anxiety.* New York: Houghton Mifflin.

Chapter 33

Building Self-Esteem

Each child is a whole child. Academic performance is not the only issue to be concerned about. Even more important (but closely related), is healthy self-esteem. All too often, children with learning disabilities suffer from low self-esteem. Even as educational remedies are applied, progress will be stilted without healthy self-esteem. More to the point—a child's happiness and belief in herself is by far the most important goal we all should have. Here are a few tips on building your child's self-esteem.

1. Set reasonable expectations and help your child set realistic goals.

2. Give your child frequent, specific and positive praise. Rather than say "You're a good kid," say "It was great that you did so well on your test."

3. Appreciate your child. "I really appreciate that you set the table without being asked," or "Thank you, you are a big help to me."

4. Let your child know she is a capable person and acknowledge the difficulty of a task. Research has shown that over 70 percent of what teachers and parents say to children is critical. "That was a difficult report to research and write. The illustrations are fantastic—you really are a good artist."

"NCLD Tips: Building Self-Esteem," from *Their World*, National Center for Learning Disabilities, 381 Park Avenue South, Suite 1420, New York, NY 10016; reprinted with permission.

5. Focus on your child's strengths and affinities. The more your child participates in something she is good at, the more success she will experience. Nothing builds self-esteem like success.

6. Do allow your child to experience some frustration—tolerance of frustration is a necessary skill for children to develop.

7. Encourage your child's contributions to the family by letting her know you think she is an important part of the family. "You know it is grandmother's birthday next month—what do you think would be a good present for her from our family?"

8. Teach your child how to accept a compliment. "Thank you" works a whole lot better than "Yeah, I got good grades, but the teacher is really an easy grader." It makes it easier for a person to give a compliment when it is accepted rather than negated.

9. Help your child to be independent. Don't do anything for your child that she can do for herself. Maybe it is easier for you to do it, or it is not perfect, but your child will learn how to do things, and she will get better at it with practice.

10. Teach your child to advocate effectively for herself. In communicating needs and desires, she should be specific, clear and positive.

11. Help your child recognize, label and express her own, and others', feelings.

12. Help your child develop appropriate social skills. Learning how to recognize various facial expressions, body language, and vocal cues, will help her integrate with others and build friendships.

13. Allow for mistakes. Talk about mistakes, even your own. Equate mistakes with effort and learning. Help her understand that everyone makes mistakes. Do not dwell on them.

14. Show your child you love her. Listen to your child. Empathize with her bad experiences; rejoice with her good experiences. Tell your child often that you love her.

Chapter 34

Throwing the Book at Them: Remedial Assistance for LD Juvenile Offenders

The teenage defendant—call him Bobby—stood before New York City Family Court Judge Jeffery Gallet in the Bronx. The charge: a felony in connection with a subway mugging. The verdict: guilty. Bobby was awaiting his sentence. Up rose Bobby's special education counselor to plead on his behalf.

Bobby is learning-disabled, his counselor said. He has trouble learning in the usual ways, and he's taken his frustrations out on society. He's been good, until now. Don't lock him up. Leave him in school so that he can get the help he needs.

Judge Gallet listened. He decided in favor of school. The reasons behind his decision lay in some startling facts about learning disabilities and juvenile delinquency.

First is that a learning-disabled ("LD") youngster is much more likely to get into trouble with the law than a youth without a learning disability. About a third of juvenile crimes, a 1977 federal study found, are committed by LD youth. It's not clear why, but social and emotional problems associated with LD seem to play a part.

The good news may be even more remarkable: studies show that, with only 50 to 60 hours of remedial assistance, the vast majority of LD juvenile delinquents never return to crime. Does that mean LD youth should be excused from responsibility for delinquency? Judge Gallet and others believe they should receive help, as well as justice.

GF Magazine, the Gannett Foundation, 1101 Wilson Blvd., Roselyn, VA 22209; reprinted with permission.

"The point is not that learning-disabled youths should get off for stealing cars. But if, after they're convicted, we want to keep them out of the justice system, we have to teach them the basic skills—reading, writing, math," Gallet said. "If you don't do well in school, if you can't get a job, your choices are welfare or crime. Crime pays more and has a higher status.

"Once you're convicted, I own you. I tell youthful offenders that," the judge said. "I can lock them up. I have that power. If I don't use it to get them learning basic skills, then they'll just recycle right back into the system as adults. Shame on me if I let them pass through my court and do nothing."

Gallet, 47, is in a good position to know about learning disabilities. He's LD himself. It wasn't until Gallet was 35 that he took diagnostic tests, at the urging of a friend, to discover he had a learning disability. When he was younger, he found schoolwork incredibly hard. He has always had, and always will have, trouble distinguishing right from left, trouble with spelling and simple math, and difficulty making his eyes follow lines of text. Getting through public school in New York City, he said, was a nightmare. He wasn't stupid. He didn't know it, but his conditions had names: dyslexia, dyscalculia, and dysgraphia.

"I was not the kind of student that teachers like to have," he said, sitting in his judge's chambers in Manhattan. "I was disruptive. I was unhappy. The more unhappy I got, the more unmanageable I became."

But with help from his parents, a college advisor, and his roommates, Gallet graduated from high school, Wilkes College in Pennsylvania, and, in 1967, Brooklyn Law School. He has written five books on law and many journal and magazine articles.

"You can't cure a learning disability," he said, "but you can compensate for it, and you can improve the compensation. I can't tell my right from my left. I wear my watch on my left hand, and when I'm driving, I tighten the band so that I'm aware of it. I know to turn toward the wrist wearing the watchband when I have to turn left. I've compensated—I function the same way you do.

"Sometimes I get angry when people ask me, 'How can you be a judge if you can't read or write?' I can read and write—I just have to adjust to certain difficulties. I don't have problems all the time with everything. For dense prose, I might use a piece of paper to help me follow the lines when I'm reading. For long pieces of writing, I might use a dictating machine and a spelling checker on a word processor."

The problem for so many LD youngsters, as well as adults, though, is that they can't compensate well unless they know what's wrong.

428

They become frustrated in school. Like Gallet, some "act out" in class; their disruptions may lead to counseling in which learning disabilities might be detected. Others withdraw in silence. Both kinds of children, as the studies show, are at risk of descending into delinquency.

In the 1977 study by the National Institute of Juvenile-Justice and Delinquency Prevention, 36.5 percent of a sample of delinquent boys in the juvenile-justice system were found to have previously undiagnosed learning disabilities. Among non-delinquent boys, the figure was only about 19 percent. Other studies put the LD percentage higher but most specialists agree that at least a third of the 100,000 youths in juvenile detention in the United States have undetected learning disabilities.

Fortunately, the law is becoming increasingly aware of the "LD-JD link," as it has come to be called. That's important because, although schools are getting better at identifying LD children, many still get through school undiagnosed. Many more already got through years ago.

The juvenile-justice system got a needed boost toward recognition of the LD-JD connection in 1985, when the Foundation for Children with Learning Disabilities (now the National Center for Learning Disabilities) made its largest grant ever—$100,000. The grant was divided among three organizations: the American Bar Association, the National Council of Juvenile and Family Court Judges, and the Research Development Training Institute, which develops resources for probation officers.

Those groups, representing the professionals who work most closely with LD children, used the NCLD grant to design a three-year national training plan to help lawyers, judges, and probation officers detect learning disabilities. Presentations are made each year at the NCLD's national meetings. Manuals on the LD-JD link have been produced and are in use by thousands of juvenile-justice professionals.

In addition, the Gannett Foundation recently gave NCLD $10,000 toward the $60,000 still needed to produce a series of five videotapes and related materials on all aspects of learning disability and how to provide help. In all, the Gannett Foundation has made five grants totaling $21,250 to NCLD.

The tapes, available in 1990, are narrated by Chuck Scarborough, news anchor at WNBC-TV, New York. They'll be distributed nationally to local bar associations, teacher associations, parent groups, and others, said Julie Gilligan, NCLD director of communications and public affairs.

"We continue to look for ways to help people realize that LD kids are not stupid, not bad—that they just have to be taught in a different way," Gilligan said.

Meanwhile, a number of model programs are helping to serve LD youth in the court system. One, in Newport News, Va., was launched by a $32,000 NCLD grant in 1987 and christened "Sentenced to Literacy." About 100 LD youthful offenders have received mandatory literacy tutoring as a condition of probation in the project, which is a coordinated effort involving local courts, law enforcement, schools, and volunteers. Trained volunteer tutors spend two to four hours a week working one-on-one with the youths. A reporter for the Newport News *Times-Herald* described a judge active in the program as "getting ready to throw the book at juvenile offenders—the textbook."

Project director Walter Dean, administrator of the 7th District Court Service Unit (probation department) in Newport News, said the project will soon try to branch out to include "life skills"—counseling in communication skills, job preparation, and other areas.

A second model, in Brooklyn, N.Y., was designed by Judge Gallet and funded by NCLD and Chase Manhattan Bank. Working with probation officers and judges, the program identified LD youths—81 since its start in 1987, and 19 of those previously undiagnosed.

The courts have sent more than half of those LD youths to detention facilities outside Brooklyn, but, under the Learning Disabilities and the Family Court System project, along with them have gone reports detailing the nature of their LDs and giving educators in those institutions a basis for developing appropriate remedial programs.

For the other 25 youths or so, the project has located educational services in Brooklyn, getting them placed in remedial programs either in public schools or in outside agencies.

But these youths aren't home free simply because their disabilities have been recognized and they are being treated in a program.

Rhianon Allen, who directs the Brooklyn project, noted problems with "non-compliers"—youths who resist taking part in the special education program—and even some cases of depression.

"Putting some of them in services in a sense destroys their myths about themselves," said Allen, an assistant professor of psychology at Long Island University. "They have to face up to the fact that they're not 'all right' in certain ways. But I think that can change later. None of them has had completely smooth sailing, but some are clearly over the hump. Sometimes the first couple of months can be very rocky for them."

However, she added, "None of them has been re-arrested once they entered the remedial services."

Also part of the Brooklyn project is training for probation officers in recognizing LD. A "how-to" guide for finding services for LD youths in Brooklyn is being written. Allen said it could be adapted into a statewide or national procedures manual for locating such services.

Carrie Rozelle, a Gannett Foundation trustee and the founder of NCLD, said that although NCLD's work in cooperation with juvenile-justice has had an, effect, "it's been slow going" and more needs to be done.

"There really is something at the bottom of this (LD-JD problem) that can be remedied so that a real difference can be made in the lives of these kids," she said.

Important next steps, Rozelle said, include working with law schools and teachers' colleges to increase awareness of the LD-JD link.

"Every teacher in America should receive special-education training. That training could very well sensitize teachers to recognize youngsters in their classrooms who might be learning-disabled because they are struggling with their schoolwork," she said.

"The teacher could immediately have the child tested, and if LD is proven, then an IEP (Individual Education Plan) could be set up right away to help the child avoid all of the serious difficulties that a learning-disabled child deals with.

"Why do we have to put everyone in a slot simply according to the grades they make? We all learn differently anyway, and it's time that everyone became aware of that."

Bobby, the LD teen felon, stopped in to see Judge Gallet a few months ago. It had been a year since he had stood before the bench. His year's probation was up. Having completed his remedial work, he was headed for 11th grade.

"He had his report card with him," Gallet said. "A good report card. He had a grin from ear to ear."

— by Brian Buchanan

Chapter 35

Some Reflections on Vulnerable Youth: Learning Disabilities and Substance Abuse

During the past twenty-five years, we have witnessed the development of "learning disabilities" as a concept to describe and understand significant aspects of various academic learning styles and difficulties as well as the behavioral adaptation patterns of an increasing number of our children, youth and adults.

When Public Law 94-142 was implemented in 1976, it was estimated that 2% of the school age population would be served in special education programs in public schools for children designated as learning disabled. By the school year 1985-86, this percentage had increased to 4.7%, or approximately 2.1 million public school age youngsters served in the programs for the learning disabled. [According to U.S. Department of Education figures published in 1996, 10.43% percent of children aged 6-17 were served under the Individuals with Disabilities Education Act (IDEA), Part B for the 1994-95 school year; of these, approximately 51% were identified as having Specific Learning Disabilities. More information on special education statistics may be found in the chapter titled "Selected Special Education Statistics."]

This figure does not include, because no reliable data are available, the numbers or percentage of the learning disabled among the approximately 12 million students in private schools in this country.

"Some Reflections on Vulnerable Youth: Learning Disabilities and Substance Abuse," from *Their World* 1989, by John B. Sikorski, MD, National Center for Learning Disabilities, 381 Park Avenue South, Suite 1420, New York, NY 10016; reprinted with permission.

Reliable studies indicate that five to eighteen percent of the current school age population are effected. Parents, educational and clinical professionals, and the effected individuals themselves, express concern about the causes, symptomatic manifestations and consequences of the learning disability phenomenon.

Identifying Risk Factors

The past decade has seen an increase in school district and community agency efforts toward identifying the vulnerabilities and the risk factors, as well as the development of a wide variety of intervention programs to impact on the down stream consequences which many learning disabled youngsters may experience. In addition to the remedial academic focus, many such programs are designed to develop social and interpersonal skills, as well as special abilities and talents, which in turn impact on the self-esteem, sense of competence, and peer and authority relationships which may be problematic for many learning disabled youngsters.

Epidemioiogical as well as longitudinal studies during this past decade tend to confirm the individual and anecdotal experience of many concerned parents and professionals that learning disabled youth are at risk for the development of concomitant and subsequent psychological and social problems. These problems may range from a sense of isolation and depression, behavioral and conduct disorders, alcohol and drug abuse, involvement with the Juvenile Court because of delinquent behavior, as well as risk for truancy, school drop out and under-employability.

It must be emphasized that the learning disabled youth's risk for subsequent emotional and behavioral problems is not causally determined by the learning disability, but rather may be an increased statistical probability for its development in any given case—a risk factor.

Being at the Wrong Place at the Wrong Time

The vulnerability of a specific adolescent to manifest any of these risk factors may be increased by fortuitous circumstances, i.e., being at the wrong place at the wrong time. Or by adverse environmental conditions, i.e., the epidemic of alcohol and drug abuse sweeping the homes, schools and neighborhoods of every strata and group of our contemporary society.

Family Influence

The extent and severity of this substance abuse epidemic and its impact on the vulnerable and at risk individuals, as well as society, was highlighted by the 1988 report of the White House conference for a Drug-Free America. Its impact on families and the community was underscored by the National Council of Juvenile and Family Court Judges in its recent publication *Drugs   The American Family In Crisis: 39 Recommendations*. After reviewing the startling increase in substance abuse among the general population, the National Council estimated that substance abuse was a significant factor in 60 to 90% of all cases referred to their courts. Concerning the risk to youth, the publication states that:

> The major factors that lead youth into substance abuse are heavily influenced by the family. When the family is functioning effectively, these risks are reduced. When it is dysfunctional, they are greatly increased. A family history of alcoholism; family management problems; early child antisocial behavior; parental drug use and tolerant attitudes toward use; child failure in formal schooling; and alienation from society are some of the risk factors largely attributable to family environment. When present to any appreciable degree, they are precursors of child substance abuse.

In addition to family and environmental factors, the learning disabled youth may show an increased vulnerability because of their accumulated information processing and skill deficits, along with variable self-esteem and peer interaction problems. These factors make it more stressful and difficult to cope with the "normal" demands and expectations of contemporary adolescent transitions, let alone provide for the confidence and security which may be required to resist the peer pressure for the substance abusing experience.

There is no clear evidence that having a learning disability will cause a given youth to become a substance abuser. Further, there is no reliable medical evidence that a learning disabled child who may be appropriately treated for concomitant attention deficit disorder/hyperactivity with Ritalin or other appropriately prescribed medications necessarily has a higher risk for substance abuse.

Identification with a Caring Adult

Rather, the thrust of recent longitudinal studies indicates that vulnerable children with various combinations of learning disabilities, attention deficits/hyperactivity disorders, may be more successfully treated with multimodality programs. Such individualized comprehensive treatment programs may include special education, individual psychotherapy and/or family management and counseling and, where appropriate, specific prescription medication.

The outcome data from these individualized multimodality studies, particularly where a prosocial bonding or identification with a caring teacher or other adult professional occurs, indicates that the risk of subsequent conduct disorder, delinquency and school failure can be significantly diminished.

Herein lies the hope and direction for future programming . . . but it will require commitment and cost by all of us.

—by John B. Sikorski, M.D.

Part Seven

Special Information for Older Students and Adults with Learning Disabilities

Chapter 36

Adults with Learning Disabilities: Assessing the Problem

When adults suspect they may have a learning disability, they often begin a search for solutions. They may have difficulty in locating resources to diagnose the disability. For many individuals, obtaining a diagnosis can involve locating one or more professionals to select, perform, and interpret diagnostic tests.

Why Is Diagnostic Testing Necessary?

These tests are needed because:

* Obtaining accurate diagnostics is the first step in overcoming the effects of a learning disability.
* Learning with a learning disability requires different learning strategies.

What Is the Diagnostic Process for Adults?

The diagnostic process for adults with learning disabilities is different from diagnosis and testing for children. While diagnosis for children and youth is tied to the education process, diagnosis for adults is more directly related to problems in employment, life situations,

National Information Center for Children and Youth with Disabilities (NICHCY) *Briefing Paper* Update, January 1995, adapted from the HEATH Resource Center; and "A Learning Disabilities Checklist," from *National Resources for Adults with Learning Disabilities*, HEATH Resource Center, September 1995.

and education. An adult will need to find a diagnostician experienced in working with adults and who is oriented to adult school and work-related learning needs. The assessment process will include a diagnosis and an evaluation to decide on possible choices for treatment.

The diagnosis identifies the type of specific learning disability by showing strengths and weaknesses in the way an individual learns and uses information. Both informal and formal activities are used in this process. For example, information may be collected about the person's life and academic history and why there is a need for the testing. More formal activities would include measuring learning/work style, such as visual memory or memory for numbers.

An evaluation can then be offered, suggesting ways to overcome some of the effects of the disability. This may include strengthening skills by working with someone who takes into account the way the individual learns best. Until recently, it was not widely recognized that learning disabilities have influenced the lives of adults, especially those whose conditions were not diagnosed during school years. It is now clear that adults should be evaluated in a manner related to their age, experience, and career objectives.

How Do You Find Someone to Perform the Testing?

You may be wondering how to find a professional qualified to conduct adult assessments. Several local agencies can either perform the tests or refer you to diagnosticians for adults within the community. Agencies to contact for information include:

- The public school system—Ask about Adult Education programs conducted through the school system and the availability of testing;
- Adult Literacy Programs or Literacy Councils—These may be listed in your local telephone book.
- Learning Disability Association in your area, often listed in the telephone book with the name of the city or county first;
- Counseling or Study Skills Centers at a local community college;
- Guidance Counselors in high school;
- Orton Dyslexia Society;
- Special Education Programs at a local public school or university; and
- Vocational Rehabilitation Agency in your state or county.

These organizations or individuals may also be able to put you in touch with an educational therapist or learning specialist in private practice who can perform and interpret the tests you need.

Questions to Ask Evaluators

- Have you tested many adults with learning disabilities?
- What is the cost of the testing? What does this cost cover?
- Can insurance cover the costs? Are there other funding sources? Can a payment program be worked out?
- How long does the testing take?
- Will there be a written report of the assessment? Will I be able to meet with you to discuss the results?
- Will our discussion give me information regarding why I am having trouble with my school, job, or life at home?
- Will you also give me ideas on how to improve (remediate) my areas of disability and how to get around (compensate for) my disabilities?
- Will the report make recommendations about where to go for immediate help?
- If there are additional questions, are you available for more consultation? If so, what are the charges?

A Learning Disabilities Checklist

A checklist is a guide. It is a list of characteristics. It is difficult to provide a checklist of typical characteristics of adults with learning disabilities because their most common characteristics are their unique differences. In addition, most adults exhibit or have exhibited some of these characteristics. In other words, saying yes to any one item on this checklist does not mean you are a person with a learning disability. Even if a number of the following items sound familiar to you, you are not necessarily an individual with a learning disability. However, if you say "that's me" for most of the items, and if you experience these difficulties to such a degree that they cause problems in employment, education, and/or daily living, it might be useful for you to obtain an assessment by qualified professionals experienced in working with adults with learning disabilities.

There are many worthwhile checklists available from a number of organizations. The following checklist was adapted from lists of learning disabilities' characteristics developed by the following organizations: Learning Disabilities Association of America, *For Employers...A*

Look at Learning Disabilities, 1990; ERIC Clearinghouse on Disabilities and Gifted Education, *Examples of Learning Disability Characteristics*, 1991; The Orton Dyslexia Society's *Annals of Dyslexia*, Volume XLIII, 1993; and the Council for Learning Disabilities, *Infosheet*, October 1993.

While individuals with learning disabilities have average or above average intelligence, they do not excel in employment, education, and/or life situations at the same level as their peers. Identified characteristics are as follows:

- May perform similar tasks differently from day to day;
- May read well but not write well, or write well but not read well;
- May be able to learn information presented in one way, but not in another;
- May have a short attention span, be impulsive, and/or easily distracted;
- May have difficulty telling or understanding jokes;
- May misinterpret language, have poor comprehension of what is said;
- May have difficulty with social skills, may misinterpret social cues;
- May find it difficult to memorize information;
- May have difficulty following a schedule, being on time, or meeting deadlines;
- May get lost easily, either driving and/or in large buildings;
- May have trouble reading maps;
- May often misread or miscopy;
- May confuse similar letters or numbers, reverse them, or confuse their order;
- May have difficulty reading the newspaper, following small print, and/or following columns;
- May be able to explain things orally, but not in writing;
- May have difficulty writing ideas on paper;
- May reverse or omit letters, words, or phrases when writing;
- May have difficulty completing job applications correctly;
- May have persistent problems with sentence structure, writing mechanics, and organizing written work;
- May experience continuous problems with spelling the same word differently in one document;
- May have trouble dialing phone numbers and reading addresses;

- May have difficulty with math, math language, and math concepts;
- May reverse numbers in checkbook and have difficulty balancing a checkbook;
- May confuse right and left, up and down;
- May have difficulty following directions, especially multiple directions;
- May be poorly coordinated;
- May be unable to tell you what has just been said; and
- May hear sounds, words, or sentences imperfectly or incorrectly.

As mentioned previously, an adult with learning disabilities may exhibit some of these characteristics, but not necessarily all of them. If an individual exhibits several or many of these characteristics to such a degree that they cause problems in work, school, or everyday life, he or she might benefit from an assessment by qualified professionals.

Chapter 37

Getting Ready for College: Advising High School Students with Learning Disabilities

Increasing numbers of students with learning disabilities are enrolling in two- and four-year colleges and universities. Since 1985, among first-time, full-time freshmen who reported having any disability, the percentage of those with learning disabilities doubled from 15 percent to 32 percent. Currently nearly a third of all freshmen with disabilities report having learning disabilities.

Some of the most frequently asked questions of the HEATH staff are about students with learning disabilities who are preparing to make the transition from high school to college. In addition, HEATH staff are asked many questions by students with learning disabilities who plan to enroll in graduate school, including law school and medical school. Such questions indicate that students with learning disabilities can, and do have successful undergraduate experiences. High school students with learning disabilities who are considering going to college should be encouraged to pursue this goal.

Students should be aware that colleges and universities are not all alike. Their missions or purposes, entrance criteria, programs of study, and requirements for certifications, associate degrees, and baccalaureate degrees vary. Similarly, students with learning disabilities are not all alike. Their goals, strengths and weaknesses vary. Also, people change their minds—plans and goals change over time. The student who enrolls in a vocational certification program in a two-year

HEATH Resource Center/American Council on Education, Publication No. 92350R, 1995; reprinted with permission.

community college today may be the student who completes a baccalaureate degree program in a four-year university tomorrow.

Students with learning disabilities, who will choose to continue their formal education beyond high school, need to take a variety of preparatory steps to get ready for college while in high school. In addition, they need to make real choices regarding their goals after high school well before their senior years to maximize their options.

The information in this chapter was developed to help in that process by answering many of the questions that students have, and listing sources of additional information. While this chapter was designed for high school students with learning disabilities, this paper should also be useful to those who advise students in their college-search process, including parents, teachers, and guidance counselors. Unless otherwise specified, information in this chapter is based on the writers' participation in numerous workshops and national conferences, materials collected by HEATH staff, and conversations with successful college students with disabilities, as well as experienced campus Disability Support Services officers. Additional information can be obtained by contacting the organizations or consulting the publications included in the Selected Resources section of this chapter.

Developing Self Knowledge

Successful college students with learning disabilities, college advisors, as well as campus Disability Support Services staff agree that developing knowledge about one's self—the nature of one's learning disabilities as well as one's personal and academic strengths and weaknesses—is vital in getting ready for college.

Students need to become familiar with how they learn best. Many successful students with learning disabilities acquire compensatory learning strategies to help them use the knowledge they have accumulated, to plan, complete and evaluate projects, and to take an active role in shaping their environments. They need to learn how to apply strategies flexibly, and how to modify or create strategies fluently to fit new learning situations. For example, compensatory strategies may include:

- allowing more time to complete tests, papers, and other projects,
- listening to audio tapes of text books while reading,

- making up words to remind students to use the knowledge they have. For example:

  F.O.I.L. (First Outer Inner Last) to remember the sequence of steps in solving algebra problems when in school,

  P.A.L. (Practice Alert Listening) when talking with friends and family, at work, and in school, or

  U.S.E. (Use Strategies Every day).

All students learn from experience. Those with learning disabilities need to exercise their judgment, make mistakes, self-identify them, and correct them. Learning new information in a new setting, such as a college classroom or dormitory, can be frustrating. Set-backs are an inevitable part of the learning process, but can impair self-esteem, which is essential to taking responsibility for one's life. Self-esteem is built and rebuilt one day at a time. Students need explicit strategies to monitor and restore their self-esteem.

Some students have difficulty understanding or making themselves understood by their peers, families, and instructors. For example, some learning disabilities may affect timing in conversations, or decisions about when to study and when to socialize. Students need to really think about how motivated they are. They should ask themselves these questions:

- Do I really want to go to college and work harder than I ever did before?
- Am I really ready to manage my social life?

In order to gain self knowledge, HEATH staff suggest the following ideas:

Become familiar with one's own learning disability. Since the professional documentation of the learning disability is the vehicle for understanding one's strengths and weaknesses it is essential that each student has a full and frank discussion about that documentation with his or her parents as well as the psychologist or other expert who assessed the student. Students may want to ask questions such as:

- What is the extent of the disability?
- What are my strengths? How do I learn best?
- Are there strategies that I can use to learn despite these disabilities?

447

Learn to be "self-advocates" while still in high school! Self-advocates are people who can speak up in logical, clear and positive language to communicate about their needs. Self-advocates take responsibility for themselves. To be a self-advocate, each student must learn to understand his or her particular type of learning disability, and the resultant academic strengths and weaknesses. They must be aware of their own learning styles. Most importantly, high school students with learning disabilities need to become comfortable with describing to others both their disability and their academic-related needs. At the college level, the student alone will hold the responsibility for self-identification and advocacy.

Practice self-advocacy while still in high school. Many students with learning disabilities develop self-advocacy skills through participating in the discussions to determine the Individualized Education Program (IEP) and/or the Individualized Transition Plan (ITP). Armed with knowledge about learning strengths and weaknesses, the student can be a valued member of the planning team.

Develop strengths and learn about areas of interest. Students with learning disabilities, as do others, often participate in sports, music, or social activities after school. Others try working in a variety of jobs or community volunteer projects. Activities in which a student can excel can help to build the self-esteem necessary to succeed in other areas.

Understanding Legal Rights and Responsibilities

Recent legislation protects the rights of people with disabilities. In order to be effective self-advocates, students need to be informed about this legislation. It is especially important to know about the Rehabilitation Act of 1973 (especially Section 504), the Americans with Disabilities Act (ADA) of 1990 and how they differ from the Individuals with Disabilities Education Act (IDEA) of 1990. In addition the Family Educational Rights and Privilege Act (FERPA) of 1974 protects the confidentiality of student records, which is very important for students with learning disabilities and their families to understand.

IDEA, Section 504, and ADA: Understanding the Differences

High school students with learning disabilities must understand their rights under Section 504 of the Rehabilitation Act and the

Americans with Disabilities Act (ADA) (which guarantee the civil rights of persons with disabilities) and how these differ from the rights and services they received under the Individuals with Disabilities Education Act (IDEA).

Under IDEA, which is the legislation that guarantees a free appropriate public education and governs the provision of special education services to students with disabilities in elementary and secondary schools, the school is responsible for identifying students with disabilities, for providing all necessary assessments, and for monitoring the provision of special education services. These special education services, which are described in detail in a student's Individualized Education Program (IEP) and Individualized Transition Plan (ITP), could significantly alter the requirements of the "standard" high school academic program. Requirements for high school diplomas may be changed under IDEA, as well. For example, dependent on their particular disabilities, some students' programs of study under IDEA may not include certain language, mathematics, or science courses that are usually required courses for a diploma.

However, IDEA does not apply to higher education. Colleges and universities do not offer "special" education. Under Section 504 and the ADA, colleges and universities are prohibited from discriminating against a person because of disability. Institutions must provide reasonable modifications, accommodations, or auxiliary aids which will enable qualified students to have access to, participate in, and benefit from the full range of the educational programs and activities which are offered to all students on campus. Examples which may assist students with learning disabilities include, but are not limited to, the use of readers, note takers, extra time to complete exams, and/ or alternate test formats.

Decisions regarding the exact accommodations to be provided are made on an individualized basis, and the college or university has the flexibility to select the specific aid or service it provides, as long as it is effective. Colleges and universities are not required by law to provide aides, services, or devices for personal use or study.

Unlike elementary and secondary schools, postsecondary institutions are not required to design special academic programs for students with disabilities. Postsecondary institutions are required to provide accommodative services so that qualified students with disabilities will have equal access to the regular academic program. After equal access is provided, it is everyone's own responsibility to do well, or not do well. Section 504 and the ADA do not require postsecondary institutions to alter their requirements for either admissions or for graduation.

Understanding the Changes in Level of Responsibility

Students with learning disabilities need to know that the level of responsibility regarding the provision of services changes after high school. As mentioned, throughout the elementary and secondary years, it is the responsibility of the school system to identify students with disabilities and to initiate the delivery of special education services. However, while Section 504 and the ADA require postsecondary institutions to provide accommodative services to students with disabilities, once the student has been admitted to a college or university it is the student's responsibility to self-identify and provide documentation of the disability. The college or university will not provide any accommodation until a student takes the following two steps:

- Step 1. The enrolled student who needs accommodative services must "self-identify." That means he or she must go to the Office of Disability Support Services, or the office (or person) on campus responsible for providing services to students with disabilities, and request services.

- Step 2. He or she must provide documentation of his or her disability. For the student with a learning disability, such documentation is often a copy of his or her testing report and/or a copy of the IEP or ITP.

Understanding Your Rights to Privacy

Students and their families are often concerned about who will be able to see their educational records. They want to be sure that written records will be confidential and available only to those with a legitimate interest in them To protect the privacy of student records the Family Educational Rights and Privacy Act (FERPA) was passed in 1974 and later amended several times. FERPA is also known as the Buckley Amendment in recognition of Senator James Buckley of New York who introduced it.

FERPA gives students the right to have access to their educational records, consent to release a record to a third party, challenge information in those records, and be notified of their privacy rights. FERPA affects all colleges and universities which receive federal funds. FERPA rights belong to the student regardless of age (and to the parents of a dependent student as defined by the Internal Revenue Service). A "student" is a person who attends college or university and/or for whom the institution maintains educational records (former students and alumni, for example) but not applicants to the institution or those denied admission. The college must inform students of their FERPA rights, procedures to allow a student access to his or her record, and procedures to consent to release a record to a third party. Publishing this information in a catalogue or bulletin satisfies this requirement. FERPA protects a student's record from being shared (without the student's permission) with "curious" faculty, administrators, other students, the press, or anyone without a legitimate reason for seeing the record. According to Subpart E: The Impact of Section 504 on Postsecondary Education, a publication of the Association on Higher Education and Disability AHEAD (see Selected Resources section) the following information is provided about confidentiality.

> Any information regarding disability gained from medical examinations or appropriate post-admissions inquiry shall be considered confidential and shall be shared with others within the institution on a need-to-know basis only. In other words, other individuals shall have access to disability-related information only in-so-far as it impacts on their functioning or involvement with that individual...

> For example, faculty members do not have a right or a need to access diagnostic or other information regarding a student's disability. They only need to know what accommodations are necessary/appropriate to meet the student's disability-related needs, and then only with permission of the student...

> Disability-related information should be kept in separate files with access limited to appropriate personnel. Documentation of disability should be held by a single source within the institution in order to protect the confidentiality of persons with disabilities by assuring such limited access.

Transition Planning for College

Leaving high school is an eventuality that all students face. Under the IDEA preparing for this transition has been formalized by requiring that the IEP for each student receiving special education services include a statement of the transition services needed. In many locations the IEP be comes an Individualized Transition Plan, or ITP.

451

It documents the student's disabilities, describes specific courses for the student to take, accommodative services for the school to provide, notes post-high school plans, and identifies linkages with relevant community agencies, such as Vocational Rehabilitation Services. Students with learning disabilities planning to go to college are encouraged to take an active part in the transition planning process.

College Options

Students with learning disabilities who are planning to go to college should make themselves aware of the general categories of postsecondary educational institutions. Knowing the type of college one will attend affects the student's course selections while still in high school. There are over 3,000 colleges and universities in the United States. In addition to varying in size, scope of program offered, setting (urban, suburban, or rural), residential or commuter, and cost of attendance, there are several factors of special importance for students with learning disabilities.

Admissions Criteria:

Some colleges have open admissions. These colleges admit anyone over age 18 or with a high school diploma. At some colleges with open admissions, however, alternate diplomas or certificates of completion may not be acceptable for admission. Students must check with the college to be sure that the earned high school completion document will meet admissions criteria. Standardized college admissions testing is not required at open admissions colleges, nor is any particular high school course selection. Grades in high school are not relevant. Open admissions colleges may be two-year or four-year. They usually do require students to take a "placement exam" to determine at which level to begin college course work. Students who have not taken an academic preparatory program in high school may need to complete some high school level courses before taking college courses for credit toward a college degree. Such courses are usually available as remedial courses and may be taken at the college.

Other colleges have selective admissions requirements. Applicants to selective colleges must meet the criteria set by that particular college. Schools with selective criteria may look for students with high grade point averages, rigorous academic preparation, high scores on the standardized college admissions tests, and strong personal qualities and evidence of achievement. Some colleges are more selective than others. Some standard, commercially available college guides list colleges by the degree of selectivity, or "how hard it is to get in" —from "most difficult" to "minimally difficult." Selective colleges may require applicants to submit high school grade point average and rank in class, scores on standardized admissions tests (SAT or ACT), and letters of recommendation. Some may require a personal interview, and some may be particularly interested in the student's extracurricular activities.

Types of Institutions:

Two-year colleges are most frequently public community colleges located in urban, suburban, and rural areas across the United States. Most are open admissions institutions and are non-residential. Some are independent (private) junior colleges which encourage students to earn an Associate Degree. Community colleges attract students who choose to take either a few selected courses in their interest area, vocational courses to train for specific jobs, as well as those who pursue an undergraduate certificate (to study a specific field of training), or an Associate Degree, some of whom plan to transfer to a four-year institution.

Four-year colleges or universities may be open enrollment or selective. Most require students to pursue a degree, and many are residential. Four-year colleges are also located in various settings, and in small communities they may be the center of cultural life. Tuition, room, board, and books are generally more expensive per year than the cost of attendance at a community college.

Colleges with programs for students with learning disabilities. Hundreds of colleges and universities have comprehensive programs on campus specially designed for students with learning disabilities. Staffed by individuals trained in the area of learning disabilities, these programs offer—in addition to the standard services offered by the campus as a whole—services that go above and beyond making a program accessible. Examples include tutoring services, either in students' coursework or in general areas of deficit, such as study skills, organizational skills, or time management. Counseling services may also be provided—personal, academic, or vocational. As the services provided in such programs do go above and beyond those that the college or university is required to provide under Section 504 and ADA, many colleges and universities charge for these services above the tuition fee. (Services required by Section 504 and ADA are provided at no cost to the student).

It is also possible that such programs have their own separate admissions requirements. Students who wish to learn more about such programs should either call each of the colleges and universities that they are interested in and ask if such a program exists on campus, or check one of the many guidebooks found in public libraries and bookstores that contain listings of, and information about, such programs. (See the Selected Resources section for further information about such guidebooks.)

Documentation of a Learning Disability

A high school student with a learning disability is one who has been evaluated by professionals. Such professionals (a school psychologist or educational diagnostician), after reviewing the results of various tests and other evidence, provide for each student a written diagnosis that a learning disability exists. Recommendations for accommodative services and programs are also usually part of the written document. This document can serve as a vehicle for the student to understand his or her strengths and weaknesses, as well as a "ticket" to obtain the accommodative services necessary to participate in regular college programs. There are several points for a student planning to go to college to keep in mind concerning the documentation of a learning disability:

- IDEA requires reevaluations to be conducted at least every three years, therefore, students with learning disabilities may be wise to have a comprehensive reevaluation conducted close to high school graduation time. This will ensure, for students who are going directly into postsecondary education, that the documentation that they take with them will be timely.

- If the student is unable to be evaluated close to graduation from high school, it is possible that a college or university, after receiving documentation, may decide that the documentation is too old. This may occur if the college or university feels that the information does not adequately describe the student's current academic strengths and weaknesses, learning styles, etc. Such current information can be invaluable in determining the most appropriate accommodations for the student. While an agreed

454

upon definition does not exist within the postsecondary/disability community of "how old is too old," evidence from the field suggests a range of two-five years. While it is ultimately the student's responsibility to obtain necessary documentation, some colleges and universities do provide testing services. Students should ask about campus-based possibilities before going to a private diagnostician.

- Students and parents should study and discuss the documentation in order to fully understand what it conveys about the student's strengths, weaknesses, and recommended accommodative services. If the report is not clear, discuss it with the school psychologist or whoever has prepared it.

- Many high schools routinely destroy copies of student records after a predetermined number of years. As students with learning disabilities will need copies of select items in their records to show to the college or university as documentation of their disability, students should make sure that they have complete copies of all of their records upon leaving high school.

Course Selection and Accommodative Services

Students with learning disabilities should consider various college options as well as their academic strengths and weaknesses in planning their high school program. Students seeking admission to selective institutions MUST meet the criteria set by the college. Students planning to attend a non-selective college should check to see if the high school diploma or certificate of attendance meets the entrance criteria.

Successful college students with learning disabilities report that high school courses teaching keyboard skills and word processing are especially important. A high school transcript displaying successful completion of a wide array of courses (science, math, history, literature, foreign language, art, music) are attractive to selective college admissions staff. Involvement in school- or community-sponsored clubs, teams, or performances also enhance a college admission candidate's application.

Students interested in any of the emerging technical careers should explore the tech-prep programs available in many areas. Such tech-prep programs include a partnership between secondary vocational-technical schools and postsecondary institutions—most often community colleges. These tech-prep programs help people prepare for careers in such areas as engineering technology; applied science; mechanical, industrial, practical art, or trade; or agriculture; health; or business. They offer both classroom instruction and practical workbased experience.

Accommodative services are essential to the success of many students with learning disabilities. Prior to the ITP meeting at which the services will be listed, students should try out various accommodations which have proven successful to others. These may include:

- listening to a tape recording of written material while reading it,

- using extended time to complete exams (usually time and a half),

- using a computer to write out exams or papers,

- taking the exam in a quiet place without distraction of other students or intrusive noises.

In addition, students with learning disabilities may benefit from mini-courses in study skills, assertiveness training, and time management. The importance of listing the accommodative services for each student in the ITP cannot be emphasized strongly enough. The types of accommodations students may receive when taking standardized college admissions tests or licensing examinations may depend on the evidence of having received them in high school.

College Application Process

For students with learning disabilities to assume responsibility for college application processes, they need to have an accurate idea of what they have to offer colleges. They also need to have an accurate idea of the academic requirements and admission procedures of the colleges or universities in which they are interested. Successful college students with learning disabilities advise that the actual college application process should begin as early as possible—in one's high school junior year. That is the time to review the documentation of the learning disabilities and work on understanding strengths, weaknesses, learning styles, and accommodative services. In addition, the following activities are part of the process and will be discussed in this section.

Creating a Short List

The staff of the HEATH Resource Center are often asked for a list of colleges or universities that are best for students with learning disabilities. Our answer is always the same—HEATH does not compile such a list because different schools are better for different students for different reasons. HEATH staff do go on to suggest the following:

1. The student, parents, and anyone else that is important to the college-search process should make a short list of six to ten schools that the student is interested in. The key at this point is to temporarily set aside any disability-related concerns. Create the short-list according to all other factors that are important, just as any student going through the college-search process might. These factors may include: components of various academic programs offered, admissions-related requirements, cost, opportunities for financial aid, location, community resources, athletics, social activities, as well as others. The reason for putting disability-related concerns aside at this point is that, under Section 504 and the ADA, all schools are required to provide accommodative services to qualified students with disabilities, including students with learning disabilities.

2. After the first version of the short list is created, bring disability-related concerns back into the picture. Now work to refine the short list by becoming familiar with the services that are provided to students with learning disabilities at each of the colleges or universities on the list. Most colleges and universities today have a Disability Support Services Office (which may also be called Special Student Services, or Disability Resource Center, or a similar name) or a person designated by the college president to coordinate services for students with disabilities. Some schools have comprehensive learning disabilities programs.

3. Personally visit, preferably while classes are in session, so that you can get an impression of campus daily life, or talk by telephone with the staff of the Disability Support Services Office or the learning disabilities program. Campus staff may be able to give only general answers to questions of students who have not yet been admitted and for whom they have not reviewed any

documentation. Nevertheless, a student can get a good idea about the nature of the college by asking questions such as:

- Does this college require standardized college admissions test scores? If so, what is the range of scores for those admitted?

- For how many students with learning disabilities does the campus currently provide services?

- What are their major fields of study?

- What types of academic accommodations are typically provided to students with learning disabilities on your campus?

- Will this college provide the specific accommodations that I need?

- What records or documentation of a learning disability are necessary to arrange academic accommodations for admitted students?

- How is the confidentiality of applicants' records, as well as those of enrolled students, protected? Where does the college publish Family Education Rights and Privacy Act guidelines which I can review?

- How is information related to the documentation of a learning disability used? By whom?

- Does the college or university have someone available who is trained and understands the needs of adults with learning disabilities?

- What academic and personal characteristics have been found important for students with learning disabilities to succeed at this college?

- How many students with learning disabilities have graduated in the past five years?

- What is the tuition? Are there additional fees for learning disabilities-related services? If so, what services beyond those required by Section 504 and the ADA do you get for those fees?

In addition to talking with college staff, try to arrange a meeting with several college students with learning disabilities and talk with them about the services they receive and their experiences on campus. Such a meeting can be requested at the time of scheduling the interview with the college staff.

While you will certainly be interested in the answers to the questions, the impressions that you get during the conversations will be equally important and may serve as a way to make final refinements to the short list.

Caution about Course Waivers and Substitutions

Colleges and universities are not required to alter admissions requirements, nor are they required to alter programmatic requirements for students with learning disabilities once they have been admitted. Students should keep such factors in mind when creating their short lists. For example, a student with a math-related learning disability would be poorly advised to accept admission at a university on the assumption that the math requirements will be waived once that student is admitted. While colleges and universities need to give consideration to requests of students with learning disabilities for course waivers and substitutions, such waivers and substitutions are not often granted. If the campus academic committee, to whom a request for waiver is made, determines that the course in question is not an essential component of the student's course of study, it is possible that a waiver will be granted. Substitutions of other courses which convey the essential elements of the requirement (such as substituting a course in the culture of another country for a course in foreign language) are more readily granted than waivers, according to reports from the field. However, if the course in question is found to be an essential element to the student's course of study or the degree sought, it is unlikely that a waiver or a substitution would be granted. Therefore, passing such a course would continue to be a requirement for graduation. Remember, accommodative services, including the provision of course waivers and substitutions, are not to be used in a way that would lower academic standards established by the college or university.

Admissions Tests and Accommodations

If the colleges on the student's short list require standardized test scores, the following information is important to understand. With proper documentation, high school students with learning disabilities may take standardized college admissions tests, such as the PSAT, SAT, and ACT, with individually determined accommodations. Examples of such accommodations for students with learning disabilities may include:

- individual administration of the test,
- audio cassette tape or large print test editions,
- special answer sheets,
- extended testing time.

However, the rules and procedures for taking each of the standardized tests with accommodations varies, and students should contact the agency that administers each standardized test that he or she will need to take for specific information. Contact information for the testing agencies is provided in the Selected Resources section.

As is the case with each of the steps in the college search process, starting early is better than starting late. Do not wait until the last minute to contact these agencies. The tests are given across the country on specific dates only. It is the responsibility of the student to request information and accommodations in a timely fashion in order to meet the standard time lines and requirements of the agency.

Again, any accommodative service given by a testing agency to a student with a learning disability is solely meant to give that student equal footing in the testing environment. It is then every student's responsibility to do well, or not do well. Tests taken by students with disabilities are scored in the same fashion as those taken by students without disabilities. Scores of tests taken under a non-standard administration (that is, those taken with accommodations) are so noted when they are reported to the schools.

Application and Disclosure

Once students have decided on the final version of their short-list, it is time to begin the formal application process. To apply to any college, candidates must complete a form—usually one designed by the particular college—formally requesting admission. Such forms cover basic information about the prospective student. The form may not, however, require the student to disclose whether or not he or she has a disability. In addition, the student must usually supply the college with an official transcript of high school grades. Some colleges require the student to write and send a personal essay, and obtain letters of recommendation from teachers and others who can speak for the student's ability to succeed in college. Some colleges may be especially interested in evidence of a candidate's performance ability in sports, the arts, or other talents.

At this time the student will need to decide whether or not to "disclose" the fact that he or she has a disability. (Colleges and universities attempting to overcome past discrimination or wishing to voluntarily overcome past effects of limited participation by students with disabilities may invite applicants for admission to indicate the existence of disabilities on the application form, but may not require the applicant to respond to this pre-admission inquiry.) However, should a student decide to disclose his or her disability, this information in and of itself can not be used as a basis for denying admission. Colleges and universities can not discriminate solely on the basis of disability. On the other hand, colleges and universities are also under no obligation to alter their admissions requirements or standards. This means that having a learning disability, or any disability, does not entitle a student to admission at any college or university. Students with disabilities, like all other prospective applicants, must meet the admissions criteria established by the college or university.

College level admissions committees do, however, often maintain a degree of flexibility with regard to the particular qualifications that they look for in prospective students. As a result, HEATH staff often suggest that high school students with learning disabilities consider the option of disclosing their disability during the application process (either through a required essay and/or during the personal interview, if there is one). By disclosing the disability the student may explain possible discrepancies within various pieces of admissions documents. For example, a student with a learning disability may present a high school transcript with excellent grades, but may also submit SAT scores that are quite low. Or, another student may present high SAT scores, while transcript grades are varied. Such discrepancies are typical of a student with a learning disability. However, if an admissions committee is not aware that such discrepant information is being presented by a student with a learning disability, admission may be denied.

Disclosure of a learning disability does not guarantee admission. It can however, offer the student the opportunity to provide the admissions committee with additional insights. For example, within a required essay, the student may explain his or her learning disability, and how the disability accounts for any discrepancies in his or her academic record. Students might convey an understanding of their learning disability, and how academic strengths and weaknesses mesh with interests in specific courses and fields of study. Students may also go on to state plans for managing their learning disability at the college level, and describe how they would work with the Office of Disability Support Services, noting their understanding of the student's responsibilities in making his or her college career successful.

Making a College Choice

After understanding his or her particular academic strengths and weaknesses, narrowing down the short list, visiting campuses, taking standardized college admissions tests if necessary, and completing the applications, students will be faced with making a choice among those colleges which have offered admission. Students who have worked hard at getting ready for college will be able to identify the school which seems "right."

In the Meantime

In addition to becoming familiar with all of the tips and procedures discussed in this paper, there are a number of additional ways that high school students with learning disabilities can prepare for college. In order to make themselves more attractive candidates, students should consider the following:

- Take courses in high school that will help prepare for college. If appropriate, take foreign language credits and computer training while still in high school.

- Consider internships, or part-time jobs, or volunteer community service that will develop necessary skills.

- Consider enrolling in a summer pre-college program specifically designed for students with learning disabilities in either the summer before or after the high school senior year. Such short-term experiences (most programs are designed to last anywhere from one week to one month) have been shown to be incredibly helpful in giving students a feel for what college or university life will be like. (Each spring, HEATH produces Summer Pre-College Programs for Students with Learning Disabilities which is a listing of select programs across the country).

- Contact the local Vocational Rehabilitation (VR) agency and investigate eligibility requirements. VR agencies may offer a variety of services to eligible students with learning disabilities, including vocational assessment, tuition assistance, or testing services.

- Explore sources of financing the college education. Most families need financial assistance to pay the costs of attending college. While there is very little scholarship money specifically for students with learning disabilities, readers are encouraged to review the HEATH paper, Financial Aid for Students with Disabilities.

- Become familiar with, and practice using, the various compensatory strategies identified earlier in this chapter. For example, students may want to practice talking to their high school teachers and administrators about their academic strengths and weaknesses and the ways in which they compensate for their learning disabilities.

- Join one of the national organizations which provide support not only to students with learning disabilities, but also to parents and professionals, as well. Participation in the activities of such organizations is an excellent way to build confidence, to increase disability awareness and disability-related knowledge, and to get information about special programs and resources. (HEATH's Resource Directory and National Resources for Adults with Learning Disabilities provide brief descriptions of these national organizations as well as complete contact information.)

A Message to Students

Awareness of your strengths, your advocacy skills, and persistence are among the most important tools you can use to build your future through education. You can maximize the range of colleges that may admit you by playing an active role in high school, getting appropriate support, continually assessing your growth, and carefully planning. Students may be admitted only to colleges and universities to which they actually apply. More students who have learning disabilities than ever before are applying to, enrolling in, and graduating from

America's colleges and universities. You can join the growing number of undergraduates who have learning disabilities. Good luck in getting ready for college.

Selected Resources

Learning Disability Advocacy Organizations

Learning Disabilities Association of America (LDA)
4156 Library Road
Pittsburgh, PA 15234
(412) 341-1515
(412) 344-0224 (Fax)

LDA is a non-profit, 60,000 member national organization and referral service. It provides free information on learning disabilities and puts an inquirer in contact with one of 700 local chapters throughout the country. In addition to the quarterly newsletter, *Newsbriefs*, LDA produces the biannual *Learning Disabilities Multidisciplinary Journal*, and annually sponsors a professional, international conference. There is an annual membership fee, which includes a newsletter subscription.

National Center for Learning Disabilities (NCLD)
381 Park Avenue South, Suite 1420
New York, NY 10016
(212) 545-7510
(212) 545-9665 (Fax)

NCLD, established in 1977, is a national not-for-profit organization committed to improving the lives of individuals with learning disabilities. Its services include: raising public awareness and understanding, national information and referral, educational programs, and legislative advocacy. NCLD produces educational tools, including an annual magazine called *THEIR WORLD*, newsletters, and a five-part video series entitled *We Can Learn*. NCLD's referral, through a computerized database and trained volunteers and staff, links parents, professionals and others concerned with LD and those who can help them. Memberships are available to the public, which entitles individuals and organizations to receive a special packet of information on LD, as well as regular updates on LD.

464

National Network of Learning Disabled Adults (NNLDA)
800 N. 82nd Street
Scottsdale, AZ 85257
(602) 941-5112

NNLDA is an organization run by and for people who have learning disabilities. A free newsletter and list of self-help groups is available. Please send a stamped envelope for mail responses.

Orton Dyslexia Society
The Chester Building, Suite 382
8600 LaSalle Road
Baltimore, MD 21286-2044
(410) 296-0232; (800) 222-3123
(410) 321-5069 (Fax)

The Orton Dyslexia Society is an international non-profit organization concerned with the complex issues of dyslexia, a specific learning disability. The Society promotes effective teaching approaches and related clinical educational intervention strategies, supports and encourages interdisciplinary study and research, and is committed to dissemination of research through conferences, publications, and 43 volunteer branches staffed by professionals. Guidelines are available for the College Affiliate Program, a network of support groups for students with dyslexia on college campuses.

Standardized Test Administrators

College Board
SAT Services for Students with Disabilities
P.O. Box 6226
Princeton, NJ 08541-6226
(609) 771-7137; (609) 882-4118 (TT)
(609) 771-7681 (Fax)

Through its Admissions Testing Program, the College Board provides special arrangements to minimize the possible effects of disabilities on test performance. Two plans are available. Plan A (Special Accommodations) is for students with documented hearing, learning, physical, and/or visual disabilities. It permits special test editions, special answer sheets, extended testing time, aids, and flexible test dates. Plan B, which offers extended time only, is for those with documented learning disabilities. Plan B permits additional testing time for the SAT and TSWE (Test of Standard Written English). Call or write for Information for Students with Special Needs, or Information for Counselors and Admissions Officers.

ACT Test Administration
P.O. Box 4028
Iowa City, IA 52243-4028
(319) 337-1332; (319) 337-1701 (TT)
(319) 337-1285 (Fax)

ACT (American College Testing) will arrange for individual administration of assessments for students with physical or perceptual disabilities, given proper documentation of the disability. Individual administrations may be approved, for example, for those who can not take the tests within the allotted time using regular-type test booklets, or for those who need to use large-type or audio cassette versions of the tests. For further information, call or write for a Request for Special Testing.

Commercially Available Guides to College Programs for Students with Learning Disabilities

Peterson's Colleges with Programs for Students with Learning Disabilities (Fourth Edition, 1994), edited by Charles T. Mangrum II and Stephen S. Strichart, is a comprehensive guide to over 800 colleges and universities in the United States and Canada, including two-year, four-year, and graduate programs. Available for $31.95, plus $6.75 shipping and handling, from Peterson's Guides, P. O. Box 2123, Princeton, NJ 08543-2123. (800) 338-3282.

The K&W Guide to Colleges for the Learning Disabled (Third Edition, 1995), edited by Marybeth Kravets and Imy F. Wax, analyzes more than 200 colleges around the United States that offer programs and services specifically geared to students with learning disabilities. Available for $28.00, plus $3.00 shipping and handling, from Educators Publishing Service, Inc., 31 Smith Place, Cambridge, MA 021381000. (800) 225-5750.

The two guides listed above are often available in local bookstores and libraries.

Information about Tech Prep Programs

Tech Prep, by Bettina A Lankard (1991). Digest No. 108. ERIC Clearinghouse on Adult, Career, and Vocational Education.

centerfocus (number 5/June 1994) features *Emerging Tech Prep Models: Promising Approaches to Educational Reform*. This is a publication of the NCRVE, National Center for Research in Vocational Education at 2150 Shattuck Avenue, Suite 1250, Berkeley, CA 94704. (800) 762-4093.

Information about Legal Issues

The Family Educational Rights and Privacy Act of 1974 is monitored by the Family Policy Compliance Office, U.S. Department of Education, 600 Independence Avenue, SW, Washington, DC 20202-4605. (202) 260-3887 (voice) or (202) 260-8956 (TT).

The Association on Higher Education and Disability (AHEAD) has published a number of books about legal issues, including:

- *Subpart E: Impact of Section 504 on Postsecondary Education*, by Jane Jarrow;
- *Title by Title: The ADA and Its Impact on Postsecondary Education*, by Jane Jarrow; and
- *Issues in Higher Education and Disability Law*, by Jeanne Kincaid, Esq. and Jo Anne Simon, Esq.

Each book is available for $35 ($20 for AHEAD members). AHEAD, P.O. Box 21192, Columbus, OH 43221. (614) 488-4972 (voice and TT).

Additional Materials from HEATH

Please contact HEATH for a full *Publications List*. Selected relevant materials are listed below.

- Access to the Science and Engineering Lab and Classroom
- Financial Aid for Students with Disabilities
- How to Choose a College—Guide for the Student with a Disability
- Learning Disabled Adults in Postsecondary Education
- Measuring Student Progress in the Classroom
- National Resources for Adults with Learning Disabilities
- *Summer Pre-College Programs for Students with Learning Disabilities*

- "The ADA/Section 504—The Law and Its Impact on Postsecondary Education" (brochure)
- "Vocational Rehabilitation Services—A Postsecondary Student Consumer Guide" (brochure)

—by Vickie M. Barr,
Rhona C. Hartman,
Stephen A. Spillane, Ph. D.

Chapter 38

The Law and Its Impact on Postsecondary Education

What Is the Law?

Section 504 of the Rehabilitation Act of 1973 states that:

"No otherwise qualified person with a disability in the United States...shall, solely by reason of...disability, be denied the benefits of, be excluded from participation in, or be subjected to discrimination under any program or activity receiving federal financial assistance."

Who Is Protected Under the Law?

A "person with a disability" includes "any person who (a) has a physical or mental impairment which substantially limits one or more of such person's major life activities; (b) has a record of such an impairment, or (c) is regarded as having such an impairment."

A "qualified person with a disability" is defined as one who meets the requisite academic and technical standards required for admission or participation in the postsecondary institution's programs and activities. Section 504 protects the civil rights of individuals who are qualified to participate and who have disabilities such as, but not limited to, the following:

- Blindness or visual impairments
- Cerebral palsy

American Council on Education, 9th ptg 10M/12/95/92947G; 1995.

469

- Chronic illnesses, such as: AIDS, arthritis, cancer, cardiac diseases, diabetes, multiple sclerosis, muscular dystrophy or psychiatric disabilities
- Deafness or hearing impairments
- Drug or alcohol addiction (Section 504 covers former users and those in recovery programs and not currently using drugs or alcohol.)
- Epilepsy or seizure disorders
- Mental retardation
- Orthopedic impairment
- Specific learning disability
- Speech disorder
- Spinal cord or traumatic brain injury

What Is the Impact of the Law on Postsecondary Education?

Colleges and universities receiving federal financial assistance must not discriminate in the recruitment, admission, or treatment of students. Students with documented disabilities may request modifications, accommodations, or auxiliary aids which will enable them to participate in and benefit from all postsecondary educational programs and activities. Postsecondary institutions must make such changes to ensure that the academic program is accessible to the greatest extent possible by all students with disabilities.

Under the provisions of Section 504, universities and colleges may not:

- limit the number of students with disabilities admitted;
- make preadmission inquiries as to whether or not an applicant is disabled;
- use admissions tests or criteria that inadequately measure the academic qualifications of disabled students because special provisions were not made for them;
- exclude a qualified student with a disability from any course of study;
- limit eligibility to a student with a disability for financial assistance or otherwise discriminate in administering scholarships, fellowships, internships, or assistantships on the basis of disability;
- counsel a student with a disability toward a more restrictive career;

- measure student achievement using modes that adversely discriminate against a student with a disability; or
- establish rules and policies that may adversely affect students with disabilities.

What Can Colleges and Universities Do to Implement Program Modifications?

For college students with disabilities, academic adjustments may include adaptations in the way specific courses are conducted, the use of auxiliary equipment and support staff, and modifications in academic requirements. A college or university has the flexibility to select the specific aid or service it provides, as long as it is effective. Such aids or services should be selected in consultation with the student who will use them.

Postsecondary institutions can make modifications for students with disabilities such as:

- removing architectural barriers;

- providing services such as readers for blind or learning disabled individuals, qualified interpreters and notetakers for deaf and hard of hearing students, or notetakers for students with learning disabilities or mobility impairments. (Colleges and universities may, but need not, provide aids, devices, or services of a personal nature, such as personal assistants, wheelchairs, or specially certified tutors.);

- providing modifications, substitutions, or waivers of courses, major fields of study, or degree requirements on a case-by-case basis (Such accommodations need not be made if the institution can demonstrate that the changes requested would substantially alter essential elements of the course or program.);

- allowing extra time to complete exams;

- permitting examinations to be individually proctored, read orally, dictated, or typed;

- increasing the frequency of tests or examinations;

- changing test formats (e.g., from multiple choice to essay);

- using alternative forms for students to demonstrate course mastery (e.g., a narrative tape instead of a written journal);

- and permitting the use of computer software programs or other assistive technological devices to assist in test-taking and study skills.

Chapter 39

Educational Software and Adaptive Technology for Postsecondary Students with Learning Disabilities

The computer is often characterized as an impartial tutor, providing a risk-free, patient learning partner. It is also known as an interactive environment for creative and independent learning. Using a computer, learners may adjust and manipulate their own experiences by controlling the method of input (touch, voice), type of output (graphics, text, audio), and pace of instruction. Computer software accommodates different learning styles and thus can motivate the student to participate actively in learning. Individuals can learn to use a computer to maximize their strengths and accommodate for areas of weakness. A benefit of computer technology is its ability to help all learners participate equally.

In education at all levels there is a growing emphasis on integrating students with disabilities and those without disabilities. Computer equipment may be adapted to many learning styles to help a student with a disability participate in the same learning experience as a student without a disability.

Recent federal legislation has encouraged postsecondary students to assert their rights to nondiscriminatory access to any campus program or facility, including campus-sponsored computer labs. The Americans with Disabilities Act passed in 1990 and the Rehabilitation Act of 1973 (amended in 1992)—especially Section 504 of the Rehabilitation Act—mandate that qualified individuals with disabilities shall not be discriminated against solely by reason of disability.

Heath Resource Center/American Council on Education, Publication No. 86927R, 1994; reprinted with permission.

Students are becoming more proactive in asking for, or demanding, cost-effective adaptive technologies in higher education learning centers, work environments, and in career development and educational testing centers. Passage of the Technology-Related Assistance for Individuals with Disabilities Act of 1988 (Tech Act) and the 1994 amendments have increased access to technology for use in the home, at school, at work, and in recreation. Information and referral services under the Tech Act can help students as well as institutions choose the standard and adaptive technology most appropriate to the situation. As a result, technology is fast becoming an integral part of the everyday life of persons with disabilities.

According to a recent Research Brief, approximately 8 percent of community college students, 5 percent of undergraduates at four-year public institutions, and 6 percent of undergraduates at four-year independent postsecondary institutions have disabilities. (*Today's College Students: Varied Characteristics by Sector*, 1994. American Council on Education, One Dupont Circle, Washington, DC 20036.) Among full time/first time college freshmen, learning disabilities is the fastest growing disability group, having increased from 15 percent of those with disabilities in 1985 to 25 percent of those with disabilities in 1991. (*College Freshmen with Disabilities: A Statistical Profile*, 1992. American Council on Education/HEATH Resource Center. One Dupont Circle, Washington, DC 20036.) Disability support service providers at every type of institution report increasing numbers of students with learning disabilities seeking services each year. In attempting to meet this growing need, many colleges and universities have incorporated the use of technology into the support services they provide to students with learning disabilities. These support services may be provided through Offices of Disability Support Services, Learning Resource Centers, or Computer Labs. High-tech and low-tech solutions have enabled students with learning disabilities to compete equally with their non-disabled peers in the educational environment. Such solutions have included a variety of educational software, word processing applications, and adaptive technology.

Educational Software

Educational software is specifically written and used to teach, and provide training or information to increase the user's cognitive base in a particular academic, vocational, or skill area. Such software has many benefits over some of the more traditional skill-building methods.

Students with learning disabilities often need repetition in order to build skills and retain information.

Many postsecondary students with learning disabilities, especially those in need of developmental support, have experienced previous failures in their educational endeavors. Computer software programs offer a nonjudgmental forum for study and practice. Whether the student requires one exercise or one hundred, the computer remains neutral. Because repetition is, by nature, tedious for one who has already reached mastery, tutoring, although effective in many ways, may not be the method of choice for skill building. Moreover, practice worksheets, although a useful supplement to teaching, often mean "busy work." Educational software provides a fresh and dynamic means of skills reinforcement and application. The computer software can provide exercises to reinforce correct use of grammar, passages to build reading comprehension, and problems to practice mathematical skills, all with immediate feedback and explanation.

For those students whose learning disabilities affect the auditory and/or visual perception, format and presentation of material is critical. Thus, educational software programs which employ a multisensory approach: visual display techniques, such as color coding and an auditory feedback as well as manipulative activities, may enhance learning ability.

Word Processing

Word processing is a system of producing typewritten documents, such as reports, by use of automated equipment such as electronic typewriters and computers. Students who have access to word processing software report that they write more frequently than they did without the computer. The word processing (WP) software provides an approach and reduces difficulties of writing by hand, such as tedium and physical limitations of writing unreadable handwriting. WP software can also facilitate a sequential approach to writing when used with an accompanying outlining software package.

One of the most important areas in which WP software can help all students, including those with learning disabilities, is the revision process. By electronically reorganizing the information through moving text around, the student is able to write a draft and edit easily to make revisions. WP software also allows students to develop more sophisticated papers by including examples later by using the *insert text* function. WP helps the student reduce repetition and wordiness by enabling the him or her to use the delete key. It can also help the student improve spelling, and develop the student's vocabulary through the spell checker and the thesaurus functions.

Many students with learning disabilities who have used WP software have shown much pride in their finished paper and have gained a sense of accomplishment. As a result, they become more willing to share ideas and interact productively with other students than they were before. Once the student learns a basic WP software package, he or she is able to transfer many of the skills to other packages. Providing computer access to students with disabilities helps campuses to be in compliance with disability Civil Rights laws (Section 504 of the Rehabilitation Act of 1973, amended 1993 and the Americans with Disabilities Act of 1990). Many Disability Support Services personnel believe that the use of technology as both a teaching tool and as a means of access tends to increase student retention by facilitating independence and successful academic experiences for students with disabilities.

Adaptive Technology

Adaptive technology is any piece of technology to which alterations have been made that make its use possible or easier by individuals not previously afforded access. Many students who have learning disabilities are adequately served by standard word processors with spell checkers for composing papers. Some students with learning disabilities need additional assistance from adaptive technology which is now available in certain programs. (See Table 39.1 for complete information.) For example, students whose visual channel is compromised may benefit from using screen print enlargers, voice synthesizers, text scanner and/or speech recognition units. Many postsecondary institutions have established an adaptive technology laboratory or accessible computer stations which enable students with disabilities to access the full range of programs and services. Providing adaptive technology enables the institution to meet the individual needs of a wide range of students.

Examples of adaptive technology include on-screen print enlargers, voice synthesizers, voice recognizers as well as multi-sensory enhancements to computers. A program such as VISTA, which enlarges the on-screen print, offers students a clearer, more focused view of their writing as they compose and edit.

Readers should also be aware that with many computers (Macintosh and IBM) individuals are able to change the font size to something larger which in some instances is an appropriate size instead of purchasing an enlarger.

In addition, students reading back their own work often read what they intended to write, rather than what they actually wrote. Errors, such as word omissions and dropped endings, may go unnoticed during the editing phase. A voice synthesizer, such as Arctic Vision, and/ or a text scanner, such as the Kurzweil Personal Reader, facilitates auditory editing by featuring voice output provided by a neutral reader. The Kurzweil is particularly effective for students with a strong auditory channel; the voice synthesizer offers a multisensory experience of seeing the composition on the computer screen while hearing it read.

Soundproof, a product designed specifically for individuals with learning disabilities, consists of a voice synthesizer and several reading and writing applications. This hardware/software combination provides students with a comprehensive multi-sensory writing and editing experience. In addition, a voice recognition unit, such as Dragon Dictate or Dragon Dictate IBM Voice Type, for alternative input may be useful for the student with extremely poor eye/hand coordination. With the voice input, the student can "tell" the computer what to change instead of key-stroking the text.

Implementation on Campus

Access to information technology is vital to academic learning and research. But the standard information technology communication can stand between a person with a learning disability and equal educational opportunity. What is the obligation of educators and computing services professionals to provide access to information technology for students, faculty, and staff with learning disabilities? Do colleges and universities have mandated responsibilities to provide computer access? As noted at the beginning of this resource paper, the Americans with Disabilities Act and Section 504 of the Rehabilitation Act require nondiscriminatory access to any campus program or facility, including campus sponsored computing. Thus, the answer to the above question is yes.

Campuses around the country are now establishing computer support services for persons with disabilities. But many schools are not yet aware of the need for such services, nor of important federal legislation that makes providing these services a must. Following are selected examples of how a variety of campuses are providing computer access for students with disabilities.

Table 39.1a. Educational Software—Development English and Composition.

Program	Skill/Subject	Computer	Publisher
Evergreen Diagnostic	Pre & post Diagnostic Grammar tests	PC Compatible	Houghton Mifflin
Parts of Speech I	nouns, pronouns & verbs	Apple, PC Compatibles, Macintosh	Queue
Parts of Speech II	adjectives, adverbs, prepositions & conjunctions	Apple, PC Compatibles, Macintosh	Queue
Sentences	subjects & predicates	Apple, PC Compatibles	Queue
Sentence Patterns	types of sentences	Apple, PC Compatibles, Macintosh	Queue
Agreement	pronouns & antecedents	Apple, PC Compatibles, Macintosh	Queue
Agreement	subjects & verbs	Apple, PC Compatibles, Macintosh	Queue
Managing the Sentence	sentence errors	Apple, PC Compatibles, Macintosh	Queue
Improving Your Writing Series I	eliminating obscurity & wordiness	Apple, PC Compatibles, Macintosh	Queue
Writing This Way for Students with LD	phrases, clauses, sentence sense, fragment run-ons, combining sentences, quotes, punctuation, capitalization, spelling, parallelism, italics, pronoun reference, verb phrases, modifiers, agreement & concise writing	Apple, Macintosh	Interactive Learning Materials

Table 39.1b. Educational Software—Development English and Composition.

Program	Skill/Subject	Computer	Publisher
Composition III	modes of writing	Apple, PC Compatibles, Macintosh	Queue
Grammar Gremlins	sentence structure, possessives, punctuation, contractions, subject/verb agreement	Apple, PC Compatibles	Davidson & Associates
Writer's Helper State II	writing & revising	PC Compatibles	Conduit
Grammatik V	editing	PC Compatibles, Macintosh	Reference Software
Correct Grammar	editing	Macintosh	Writing Tool
Vocabulary Machine	vocabulary & spelling	Apple, PC Compatibles	Southwest Ed. Psych Services, Inc.

Publisher Resources

Conduit
University of Iowa
Oakdale Campus
Iowa City, IA 52242
(319) 335-4100

Davidson & Associates, Inc.
19840 Pioneer Avenue
Torrance, CA 90503
(800) 545-7677

Houghton Mifflin
One Memorial Drive
Cambridge, MA 02178
(800) 992-5121

Interactive Learning Materials
1109 E. Sunnyslope Street
Petaluma, CA 94952
(707) 778-8264

Queue Intellectual Software
338 Commerce Drive
Fairfield, CT 06430
(800) 232-2224

Reference Software
1555 N. Technology Lane
Orem, UT 54057
(801) 225-5000

Southwest Ed Psych Services, Inc.
2001 W. Silvergate Drive
Changler, AZ 85224-1201
(602) 253-6528

Writing Tool Group
P.O. Box 6113
Novato, CA 94948
(415) 382-8000

University of Nebraska-Lincoln

The Educational Center for Disabled Students (ECDS) was established in the 1980's as a three-year demonstration project funded by the U.S. Department of Education and the University of Nebraska Foundation. It has evolved into an integral part of the services for the Students with Disabilities Office, providing students with computer-based compensatory tools that allow them to participate fully in a broad range of tasks related to course demands.

The program focuses on integrating academic and technical support with the provision of disability related services. The students go through an intake procedure to determine technological and academic support needs, followed by training and support specific to their individual needs. The Nebraska State Department of Vocational Rehabilitation works with the University to provide adaptive equipment and training to students with disabilities.

The ECDS has helped students with learning disabilities to compete successfully in the postsecondary environment. In addition, the technology available in the ECDS has helped this small office provide services to a growing population of students with diverse disabilities. For more information contact Christy Horn, Director, Services for Students with Disabilities, 132 Administration Building, University of Nebraska-Lincoln, Lincoln, NE 68588-0401. (402) 472-3787 (Voice); (402) 472-3785 (TT); (402) 472-9440 (Fax).

California State University Northridge

The Computer Access Lab at California State University, Northridge (CSUN) now has a large inventory of equipment with over 40 Apple, Macintosh, IBM, Toshiba, Hewlett Packard and NeXt computers, fully-supported peripherals and software appropriate to the needs of students with disabilities. The Lab has encouraged the use of a number of exceptional technologies including speech recognition, Virtual Reality and robotics.

The primary goal of the Computer Access Lab is to provide computing access to students with disabilities and to prepare them for employment. Students are trained in the Lab and then encouraged to use computers in other labs scattered throughout the campus.

The Lab environment includes an administrator of the Lab/Learning Disabilities Program, other persons devoted to computer access, a learning disability specialist, and an engineer. Funding began under a State Department of Rehabilitation grant, along with equipment grants from a variety of manufacturers and distributors. The program is now fully-institutionalized within CSUN.

In addition to operating the Computer Access Lab, CSUN also sponsors an annual international conference on technology, technology training for rehabilitation counselors and employers. CSUN also possesses Universal Access System, a two-way infra-red system that makes computers accessible. For more information contact Harry J. Murphy, Director, Disability Support Services, 18111 Nordhoff Street, Northridge, CA 91330. (818)885-2869 (Voice). (818) 885-4929 (Fax).

Nassau Community College, NY

Nassau Community College provides all the students with disabilities attending the College with full access to computers as part of their educational experience. Called the Computer Access Project, the program provides a comprehensive array of adaptive devices which enable a student with a motor or visual disability to use the computer. In addition, students with writing and other language disabilities (such as those with learning disabilities and hearing impairments) have access to a variety of software designed to assist them in overcoming their language difficulties.

The goal of this program is to provide each student with a disability who needs adaptive devices, with accessible computers in any of the College's computer facilities, so that they can make full use of the institution's educational offerings. Students can then use the College computer centers either in connection with a classroom assignment or for their own work in the same way as their non-disabled classmates. In addition, instruction is provided in the fuller use of the computer for personal and vocational needs. Students are also assisted to acquire machines of their own whenever that may be possible. The adaptive aids chosen for campus were those which would assist the largest number of students. Nassau Community College tries to use off-the-shelf commercial equipment wherever possible to demonstrate the basic availability of adaptive devices, as well as to keep the cost down.

Telecommunication devices are used to permit students to access the mainframe computer in upper level computer courses and to use the College's library's computerized catalog system.

For more information contact Victor Margolis, Coordinator, Nassau Community College, Disability Support Services, Stewart Avenue, Garden City, NY 115306793. (516) 222-7138 (Voice); (516) 222-7617 (TT).

Montgomery Community College, MD

Disability Support Services (DSS) at Montgomery College is dedicated to assisting students with disabilities to accomplish their personal, scholastic, and career goals by teaching academic and advocacy skills and by eliminating the physical, technical and attitudinal barriers that limit their range of opportunities. DSS provides services to students with disabilities within an ecological/technological framework that focuses on modifying the environment to accommodate individual differences. Through a combination of funds received from The Maryland Division of Career, Technology and Adult Learning (Carl Perkins Funding) and the Montgomery College Foundation, DSS established the Adaptive Technology Lab within the Learning Center facility. The Adaptive Technology Laboratory houses IBM compatible networks, Macintosh workstations, and Apple IIe workstations. The Lab also houses adaptive technology used for alternative methods of input, output and adaptive peripherals. An array of audiovisual equipment is loaned to the students as needed. For more information contact Janet Merrick, Coordinator, Montgomery Community College, Disability Support Services, Rockville Campus, 51 Mannakee Street, Rockville, MD. 301-294-9672 (TT); 301-279-5058 (Voice); 301-279-5089 (Fax).

Postsecondary institutions have a mandate to provide equal opportunities in education to all students. By implementing adaptive computer technology and services, institutions are taking steps to fulfill that responsibility.

While the large number of students with disabilities are seeking services reflect improvement in meeting the needs of this population, it also highlights the fact that there is still a great deal of work to do. With planning and the effective use of technology, equal education promised to all students, can be provided and students can be better prepared to take their productive places in the workforce and society.

Selected Resources

National Computer Resources

American Association for Higher Education
Project EASI
One Dupont Circle, Suite 360
Washington, DC 20036
(310) 640-3193
Internet: csmiclc@oac.ucla.edu

Apple Computer, Inc.
National Special Education Alliance
Worldwide Disability Solutions Group
20525 Mariani Avenue, 36SE
Cupertino, CA 95014
(408) 974-7910

Clearinghouse on Computer Accommodation
General Services Administration
KGDO, 18th and F Street, NW
Room 2022
Washington, DC 20405
(202) 501-4906

Closing The Gap, Inc
P.O. Box 68
Henderson, MN 56044
(612) 248-3294

IBM Special Needs Information Referral Center
IBM Educational Systems
P.O. Box 1328 - Internal Zip 5432
Boca Raton, FL 33432
(800) 426-2133

RESNA Technical Assistance Project
1700 North Moore Street, Suite 1540
Arlington, VA 22209
(703) 524-6686

Chapter 40

Social Skills: The Bottom Line for Adult LD Success

Learning disabilities are school-related problems, closely tied to the old "3 R's—Reading, 'Riting, and 'Rithmetic"—yet the byword with parents often seems to be "social skills—that's the bottom line!" Indeed, adults with learning disabilities find, too, that their successes or failures in their personal lives or jobs are often more affected by their social skills than by their academic learning.

Adults with learning disabilities who are beginning to share their successes (and their failures) in life have indicated repeatedly that many of the problems they have had are related to social skills generally taken for granted by others without learning problems. They have had to learn these skills, often completely on their own, after very painful social and vocational experiences of failure.

These areas of learning are usually considered to be chiefly social, because although they are not exclusively so, all of them have certain social implications. All seem to be related either to the learning disabilities of the individual, or to some of the characteristics of Attention Deficit Hyperactivity Disorder (AD/HD), a frequent accompanying problem.

In most of the literature, the focus is on the deficit side of these problems as they affect children's relationships and self-esteem as

"Social Skills: The Bottom Line for Adult Learning Disabilities Success," by Marnell L. Hayes in *Their World*, National Center for Learning Disabilities, 381 Park Avenue South, Suite 1420, New York, NY 10016; reprinted with permission.

children, rather than on the positive learning which might help children and adults with learning disabilities avoid the social and vocational penalties they might otherwise suffer.

Social Skills Deficits

Social skills deficits may be related to impulsivity, both verbal and motor, poor visual perception of facial and body language cues, poor auditory perception of vocal cues, invasion of the personal space of others, inappropriate touching, untidiness, disorganization, and a number of other such problems. Mood swings, overreaction, and depression may also provide problems for the individual with learning disabilities.

For example, Roger is a brilliant designer. Some of his learning disability and AD/HD problems were overlooked because society generally is more tolerant of quirky behavior in creative artists. But Roger often failed to get important contracts in projects for which his talent and creativity seemed to make him a clear choice. It seems that among Roger's LD-AD/HD related problems was great difficulty in reading social signals and body language. He was unable to interpret the signals given in an interview or during a design presentation which signaled that the interview was over, and that he should thank the interviewer for his time and leave. In other words, Roger overstayed his welcome and often talked himself out of a job.

Importance of Early Intervention

Parents and teachers can help children with learning disabilities learn to deal with some of the common problems they experience in such a way that these problems do not hit home in adulthood for the first time. Early intervention can help teach the skills other children learn almost automatically, and provide plenty of practice in developing strategies which will help in ensuring greater social acceptance in childhood and adolescence as well as greater social and vocational competence in adulthood.

Strategies for Early Intervention at Home

Some of the most useful techniques, ideal for parents to use on a day-to-day basis, combine self-talk, role-playing, and reinforcement. Self-talk is simply describing your own techniques for dealing with particular situations so that the learning disabled child becomes aware of what the parent is doing and why.

Self-Talk

For example, a parent might say, "Since I know that I want to look nice when I go out, I'm going to go look in the mirror and see if I look all right. Oops! I think I need to comb my hair before I go."

Certainly, most adults would take a quick glance in the mirror before going out. Few, however, would make a point of describing to a child what is happening, or why. This is exactly the sort of behavior the child with a learning disability might not notice, but the non-LD child would pick up without instruction.

Reinforcement

Parents might lead the child with learning disabilities to perform the same action, and then reinforce (praise or reward) good observation. "Let's see what you might need to do before we go to grandmother's. Oh, your shirt is dirty? Good for you for noticing! Let's get a clean one on."

Role-Playing

Role-playing can be useful in helping children learn many of the social conventions with which learning disabled adults have difficulty, but which most non-LD children learn easily through simple exposure. For example, parents might play "What is the thing to do if" or "What is the thing to say if" as a good car trip game or even a dinner table game. "What is the thing to do if you are at your friend's to play, and her mother says 'My, it's getting late. It will be time for supper soon'?"

"What is the thing to say if someone calls and you answer the telephone while Mother and Daddy are having an argument?"

In role-playing, parent and child might take turns in the roles. Part of the time, the child should make up the situation, and the parent should play the role of the child giving the answer. This gives the child the opportunity to think of social situations which require good social skills, and lets the parent model appropriate responses without "preaching."

Types of Social Skills Affecting Adult LD Success

Some of the common adult problems related to learning disability or AD/HD which may cause social or vocational difficulties are listed below, along with early intervention strategies which parents and teachers may find helpful.

Perception of Facial Expression and Vocal Cues

Adults with visual perception problems often miss the messages that people send and receive through facial expression. Such common expressions as a frown, narrowed eyes, or pursed lips, which might signal that what is being heard is inappropriate in some way, are often missed. Parents and teachers can help by using role-playing often, or by simply asking for feedback in day-to-day situations: "David, what do you think my face is saying to you? Do I look like I am pleased about what you are doing, or not?"

Difficulty with auditory perception more often results in problems in interpreting vocal tone. Practice with the child in noticing and responding to such vocal cues as rising volume, sounds of exasperation and anger, or tones of impatience or boredom.

Language and Social Conventions

A common problem for some learning disabled adults is not recognizing the language conventions people use daily. Perhaps the most common is the recitation of physical woes which may follow the innocuous "Hi, there, how are you?" or "How's it going?" Lots of practice with such common expressions, including what the expected reply might be, can be helpful.

Vocal Monitoring

Knowing just how loudly one is speaking, and how closely that loudness level approaches the right level for a particular situation, is difficult for some adults and children with learning disabilities. Parents can use particular cues, such as hand signals or cue phrases ("use your indoor voice" or "your almost-whisper voice") to help the child reach the right level. When the child is speaking appropriate level, provide praise: "That was good—you used your indoor voice the whole time at dinner tonight!"

Skills in Asking for Help in Receiving Information

Sue is a secretary with learning disabilities. Her charming "I know this message is important, so I need to write it down. Would you say your name again for me, please?" disarms even the most impatient caller to the office where she works, and gives her time to get the written messages she needs to supplement her memory problems. She had to learn by trial and error, rather than by direct instruction, how to get both the time and the repetition she needs to be the top-notch secretary she is.

Students with learning disabilities are rarely taught how to get their regular classroom teachers to give them information in a way they can best use it. The parent or special teacher can help the child learn to say, "I want to remember—can you say it again for me?" instead of "Huh?" or to say "I have to write it down—can you give me more time?" or even "I want to get a good grade—please explain the directions to me one more time."

Body Awareness Skills

Poor body image and lack of awareness of the position of body parts can make adults with learning disabilities appear awkward or even provocative. Role-playing, sitting in various chairs or couches, getting out of cars, sitting or standing up, walking up or down stairs, or performing a variety of ordinary physical activities, with the parent and the child taking turns observing and practicing the moves, can be helpful. Parents with camcorders can use them while youngsters act out their own skits and then view themselves.

Mealtime behavior, too, is often difficult for adults and children who lack ease and grace. Too much tolerance of poor table manners in children can be socially crippling for the adult who must be able to manage social conversation and table manners simultaneously. One or two "table manner practice" meals a week can be ideal training time for the whole family, including the non-learning disabled siblings. Restaurant practice, with discussion of what foods are easiest to eat in public social situations can be useful as well.

Organizational Skills

Not exclusively a problem of people with learning disabilities, disorganization builds upon itself to further complicate life. For the individual with learning disabilities, however, its complications are many. Disorganization leads to visual distraction, time-consuming backtracking to find things or do something that would have been easier done earlier. Well-meaning parents of learning disabled children often keep the child's environment organized, instead of helping the child learn the skills for himself or herself.

Parents or teachers can work with the child to organize things in a way that is personally helpful by having the child be a part of the process: "Where would be a good place for you to put all the things you need to take to school each morning? If you find a place that is easy for you to remember, I'll help you get things there each night before bedtime" or "How can you arrange your desk so that you have room to work, and still have all the things close that you might need?"

Personal Space Awareness

Personal space, that invisibly-defined area surrounding a person which varies in extent according to culture and personality, can be invaded by a person who doesn't easily observe body language or facial cues as to how much closeness a person can tolerate. Learning disabled people who also have spacial discrimination problems may move too close or touch inappropriately, and not be aware of the other person's backing away or negative response.

Children with learning disabilities may stand too close and miss visual cues, and they may touch the other person often and inappropriately, but they may also touch or handle other objects in the environment, such as items on the teacher's desk or decorative objects in a living room. Adults with this problem often find themselves misunderstood. Men may be thought fresh or pushy, and women may be thought to be inviting physical attention they do not want if they stand too close to others or touch inappropriately. Both men and women may be thought too forward or even threatening.

Mood Swings, Overreaction, and Depression

A variety of emotional difficulties may accompany the social skills problems of children and adults with learning disabilities. While social skills training is a natural area for direct help by parents, more severe social and emotional problems can best be treated by those with special training. Parents can look to the school for help in locating school-based or community-based counseling services. Parents of adults with learning disabilities can encourage their adult children to seek assistance as well.

Conclusion

Whether or not social skills are the "bottom line" for individuals with learning disabilities, it is certainly true that children with good social skills have more opportunities for positive interactions with their peers, and enhanced ability to benefit from academic and prevocational training. For help with children's social skills deficits, parents may wish to seek the assistance of their child's teacher. Social skills training may be written into the IEP, just as other skill training might be. Helping your child learn those things he or she needs to achieve this goal can be time well spent, and seeing your child achieve success both vocationally and professionally is more than ample reward.

— by Marnell L. Hayes

Chapter 41

Employing Persons with Learning Disabilities: Legal Implications and Management Strategies

Currently, as a result of a long period of declining birth rates, the United States is facing a substantial and worsening skilled labor shortage. Demographers and other analysts identify individuals with disabilities as a primary resource with which to address the current labor shortage. If the United States is to remain competitive in the international marketplace, we must have a well trained, well educated and highly motivated work force. Millions of Americans with disabilities who have been denied access to the workplace are well educated and well trained; others can easily be trained. What is more, these citizens are some of the most highly motivated people in our society today.

To meet their labor force requirements employers will increasingly need to draw upon all members of the working-age population, including those who are underemployed or not employed at all. Persons with learning disabilities are frequently found in both these categories: they are a valuable and underutilized resource, willing to meet tough workplace challenges if employers give them the opportunity.

It is estimated that there are currently some 6 million persons with learning disabilities in the work force. They occupy positions at every level from chief executive officer of corporations to messengers. Overall they have proved themselves to be loyal, willing, and productive employees. People with learning disabilities who are not employed

Produced by the Harold McGraw Learning Disabilities Clinic of the International Center for the Disabled, © ICD 1992; reprinted with permission. International Center for the Disabled (ICD), 340 East 24th Street, New York, NY 10010-4097; (212) 679-0100.

lack only one thing: opportunity. Employers who provide that opportunity will benefit not only those whom they hire; they will also benefit their businesses, the economy, and society as a whole.

Types of Learning Disabilities

Mary has a learning disability. Therefore, she.... Completing the sentence isn't easy. Learning disabilities have many different causes, produce a wide variety of behaviors, occur in numerous combinations, and may be mild to severe. Subtle abnormalities in the brain or central nervous system are thought to cause these disorders. In some families, more than one person has a learning disability, which suggests that these conditions may be hereditary. In other cases, injury to the nervous system shortly before or after birth is suspected. Intrauterine chemical imbalance, oxygen deprivation shortly after birth, postnatal high fevers or concussions and nutrition may be involved, but much more research needs to be done before cause and effect are established.

Learning disabilities became a field of study when Samuel Kirk coined the term in 1963 in a speech that helped launch a broad-based movement that brought together parents, psychologists, educators, speech pathologists and other professionals. Initially the movement focused on the educational needs of children with learning disabilities and on securing special programs to help youngsters overcome the effects of these disorders. As the children and the field matured, the problems of adults with learning disabilities also came to be recognized.

Some common manifestations of learning disabilities in adult are described below.

Reading. Easily the best known learning disability is dyslexia, difficulty in learning to read. Dyslexia becomes apparent when a child begins learning to read. He or she may reverse letters or words, seeing "saw" for "was" or "6" for "9" or may have difficulty discriminating between sounds. Reading difficulties are frequently addressed in school or through tutoring with reading specialists or learning disability specialists. With proper help, dyslexics will learn to read, but as working adults most likely will have problems with speed of reading or reading for sustained periods of time. They may have poor comprehension or retention of what they have read. Confusion between similar words may persist as well as difficulty in reading unfamiliar words. Word and letter reversals may re-appear in adulthood under conditions of stress.

Nina is a dyslexic: she is a high school graduate who completed a college program in fashion design. Her designs are outstanding, but her correspondence must be carefully proofread by her secretary; Nina always mixes up look-alike words like "through," "thought" and "though."

Handwriting. Henry is a highly recommended engineer. Yet his employment application has a mixture of capital and block letters that look as though they were scrawled by a 6-year-old in the kind of script hurried doctors use on prescriptions. The penmanship is barely readable and words are misspelled. Today, with the widespread use of word processors, Henry's difficulty with handwriting need not be a problem.

Written Language. Grammar, syntax and punctuation are a hard code to crack for some people with written language disorders. Others find it hard to present well-organized written work, and express themselves much better orally. John has an I.Q. of 114. He has superior mathematical ability and appears to compensate well for his reading difficulty. In addition, he is a lucid and persuasive speaker. However, he has difficulty in organizing written work. In preparing presentations for clients, he works best in a team context. As his colleagues are grateful for the skill and comfort he has in making presentations, they are willing to do the writing.

Oral Language. The importance of humor in the workplace is underscored by the popularity of television comedies based on everyday life in police stations, hospitals, newspaper offices, television and radio networks and other places of employment. Some people with learning disabilities can't tell a joke; they may not laugh when someone else tells a joke if they lack the language skills to understand humor based upon verbal ability—such as use of words with double meanings.

Mathematics. Lois is a highly valued accountant. Yet she has never mastered such basic math functions as 7 x 8 or 42 divided by 6. Fortunately for her, in high school and college she was permitted to use a calculator during math tests. She always uses a calculator in the office. Her work, even when she is not using computer-based systems, is therefore always accurate.

Some difficulties with math are related to the same problems causing dyslexia. For example, the individual will reverse numbers (e.g.,

451 for 154) or confuse operational symbols, especially + and x. People with this type of difficulty will have learned to proofread their work carefully to find any errors of this type; they may need help from a co-worker for proofreading.

Sometimes an individual may have other types of difficulties which appear to be math-related, but which in fact are not. For example, the new assistant regularly made mistakes in adding up columns of numbers. She was able to add accurately but she had a visual tracking problem that caused her to lose her place in a column or row of numbers and therefore make mistakes. Using the simple strategy of covering part of the work with a sheet of paper enabled her to keep her place and improve her accuracy.

Memory. A supervisor tells a clerk to pick up a package from a particular vendor in the mail room. The clerk starts to go to the mail room, but pauses to take a telephone call. Afterwards he can't remember the particular vendor's name. A short-term memory deficit has caused him to forget the supervisor's instructions. Memory deficits can impair long- or short-term memory for information as simple as daily routines, directions and assigned tasks. The clerk would have no trouble if given written directions or if he trained himself to jot down notes in situations in which he knows he will not be able to depend upon his memory.

Time. In the late 20th century, being late can be a social and economic disaster. The clock rules the age of faxes, modems and fast results, much to the discomfort of those people with a learning disability that leads to difficulty in organizing time. Arriving at work on time is only the first challenge they face each day. They can solve that with a digital alarm clock set to an hour they know will allow them enough time to dress, eat breakfast, and travel to work. If an early morning meeting is scheduled at another location, however, extra planning is needed. A person with this difficulty may have problems determining how long it will take to travel by foot, car, or public transportation from one point to another.

Ever spend too much time on a task? Engrossed in one task, some workers whose learning disabilities manifest themselves in time management difficulties won't think to hurry up or put a task aside because two other tasks must be done that day. And they will be unable to organize five tasks that require different lengths of time to complete and have different deadlines so that all are done on time. In most cases, training in time management will greatly help.

Space. For some people with learning disabilities, comprehending spatial relationships is extremely difficult. They can't read maps and they rely heavily on familiar landmarks to find their way—not only to and from work, but also within the workplace. Clear signage will help solve an in-the-building problem, and a reasonable accommodation for external problems (e.g., a first sales call to a new client in an unfamiliar location) may be to have other employees go along who can later advise on the easiest route to take.

Attention. Attentional difficulties often occur in individuals with learning disabilities. These difficulties include hyperactivity (e.g., being unable to sit still without tapping the feet or playing with paper clips), impulsivity (e.g., rushing to answer a question or do a task before thinking it through), and disinhibition (acting without thinking, sometimes inappropriately). Seating that is positioned to minimize distracting stimuli and well-timed breaks can help persons with attentional difficulties. Greater self-awareness may decrease (but probably will not fully control) the effects of this disability.

Sequencing. A buzz saw must be turned on before the worker places a piece of wood in front of it. If the task is done backwards, the saw can throw the wood in the worker's face. To take a second situation: an administrative assistant is told to make up a guest list, order invitations, keep track of responses, and order refreshments for an event. Doing these activities in order is crucial to planning how many invitations and how much food to order.

For some people with learning disabilities, learning the sequence of routine tasks such as working a buzz saw or organizing an event is difficult. These individuals don't automatically process information in sequence. The worker may watch or listen very attentively to a trainer or supervisor but have difficulty in properly sequencing a task. The supervisor may simply tell the employee to accomplish a task he or she had done before and assume the employee knows how to put all the pieces together again. In some sequencing situations, demonstration and modeling are of great help; in others, visual cues (e.g., numbering or color matching) and the ordering and placement of tools and materials are valuable.

Some employees with a learning disability can do the job in these situations, but literally don't know where to begin. For a glimpse at an individual's discomfort, imagine all the notes in a Mozart symphony played not as he wrote them but in random order. They're all there and the orchestra knows how to play each one, but all you hear is noise. Written instructions are invaluable in minimizing sequencing problems.

Social and Emotional. Letters and numbers aren't the only symbols that people with learning disabilities have difficulty reading. Depending on the source of their disability, they may be unable to read visual cues such as anger or concern in a coworker's face—or hear the message in a supervisor's tone of voice. As a consequence, they won't recognize when they are causing friction in the work place, or they may feel they are being criticized when no criticism is intended. Role-playing, modeling and direct instruction in social skills usually improve matters. Self-cueing strategies to prevent impulsivity or inappropriate responses are also effective.

Some people with learning disabilities have difficulty in communicating. While they grope for the right words to respond to a question, the supervisor can interpret their behavior as indifference or lack of sensitivity. Others may stand too close to people, not understanding the unspoken rules of personal space. Yet others may seem stand-offish, not participating in the give-and-take workplace culture that their co-workers take for granted. If colleagues and co-workers are sensitive and understanding, the impact of these difficulties is lessened.

Employers should note that persons with learning disabilities may have more than one problem, but if so, their problems are usually related. For example, a person with poor fine motor skills may have illegible handwriting and not be able to operate complex machinery on an assembly line; however, that same person may be an excellent reader and good at mathematical calculations.

Let's consider another example: James is a dyslexic. He also graduated from law school and passed the bar exam. He requires more time to prepare his work than other lawyers since he reads at a very slow rate. Owing to related difficulties, his spelling is poor and consequently any documents he writes must be carefully proofread.

Employing People with Learning Disabilities: It's in Your Best Interest

The Committee for Economic Development surveyed nearly 1,000 large and small companies in the National Federation of Independent Businesses. According to the responses, "learning how to learn" is one of the most important keys to success for the entry-level employee and the employee who wants to advance. The businesses reported difficulty in finding young applicants who could turn this key and unlock their potential.

People with learning disabilities can learn. Most strive to do their work well—another top attribute identified in the survey. They constitute a large, untapped pool of able workers, many with extraordinary talents and skills. Some are unemployed; many are underemployed. That they are poorly used in the workplace is a loss to American enterprise—public, private and nonprofit.

A Shortage of Workers

The United States is now beginning to face labor shortages as the baby boomers move through the work force. Never before have people with learning disabilities been as needed by employers as at present. People with disabilities offer a pool of talented workers whom the nation simply cannot afford to ignore, especially in connection with the high-tech growth industries of the future. [Former] President Bush identifies Americans with disabilities as a valuable source upon which to draw to help meet projected labor shortages.

Jay Rochlin, past Executive Director of the President's Committee on Employment of People with Disabilities, emphasized and expanded on the President's views. Testifying before Congress in favor of The Americans with Disabilities Act, he stated that the Department of Labor's major report, Opportunity 2000, also concluded that businesses will be able to satisfy their labor needs only if they successfully confront barriers to employment and empower individuals at present outside the economic mainstream to take advantage of meaningful employment opportunities. Comprehensive civil rights legislation provides protections from employment discrimination for persons with disabilities and also enhances the private sector's access to an additional resource of human capital—specifically, qualified individuals with disabilities who at present lack the opportunities they seek.

Recent studies suggest that most individuals with learning disabilities generally are able to meet the demands of the workplace. If diagnosed early, these individuals will have received appropriate assistance during their school years and will have learned the compensatory and coping strategies they need. Many who were not identified and did not learn standard compensatory and coping strategies frequently have developed personal strategies that work well in meeting their needs at work and at home.

Clearly, hiring and training persons with learning disabilities is a vital enterprise for American employers, though it naturally gives rise to concern because popular wisdom tends greatly to overstate the obstacles. In fact, the potential gain for employers is considerable: five to ten million adults are believed to have learning disabilities, and the great majority of them have valuable contributions to make.

Uncommon Strengths

Aside from individual vocational strengths (e.g., clerical abilities, graphic skills, or analytical powers), people with learning disabilities often develop strengths of character in response to their disabilities. These can be of great value to their employers.

Dale Brown, the learning disabilities specialist on the President's Committee on Employment of Persons with Disabilities, cites three attributes as typical:

- **Overcompensation.** A particular disability can make a person better suited for a job. For example, a non-ambulatory person may prove excellent in tedious desk-top work while a hyperactive security guard might walk rounds more often than his or her co-workers.

- **Self-discipline.** Overcoming a disability takes hard work by the individual. Imagine the self-motivation and commitment involved in learning to read despite a natural tendency to confuse letters.

- **Creativity.** Seeing the word differently can be an asset if a person is looking for new solutions to problems, new ways of doing things, or new products. For some people, having a learning disability means having to figure everything out for themselves. Sometimes they figure out a better way.

Add to Dale Brown's list loyalty and drive to succeed. If learning disabilities had brought a person several bad experiences in the workplace, if he or she had been fired from a job or jobs, wouldn't that person be loyal to an employer who offered an opportunity for success? Perhaps the employee received more time in training, individual lessons, or a job accommodation that relieved him or her of the one task the disability made difficult to do. Finding another job, having to start over and face new problems, might not be that appealing.

Likewise, having failed before, wouldn't an employee consider success on the job to be very desirable? Consider Ned, an exceptionally bright young man whose SAT scores were high enough to rank him as a "Commended Scholar." Due to a learning disability, his spelling and handwriting were so poor that he had great difficulty taking essay tests and writing research papers. College became a painful experience; he dropped out.

Ned was determined to prove he could succeed. He registered with a temporary employment agency and wound up doing manual labor at a construction site. Ned worked so diligently that he finished his job ahead of schedule, and his employer voluntarily gave him a bonus. The agency assured Ned that because he was such a good worker it would find him another, higher skilled position.

Real success for Ned will be to secure a job that challenges him to the upper limits of his potential, a job in which he can effectively apply compensatory and coping strategies with the support of an aware and sympathetic employer. People with disabilities, just like anyone else, realize when they are underemployed—and are not likely to feel fulfilled.

For employers, finding the most effective and productive way to use a worker with a learning disability will not be difficult if the employee is open and forthcoming and the employer is positive and pragmatic. Willingness on the part of the employer to make job accommodations (if needed) and readiness on the part of the employee to identify and discuss any problems will lead to on-the-job success. Whereas a professional-level employee with a learning disability might be a self-advocate and at ease in meeting with supervisors, lower-level or blue-collar workers or those in unskilled or supported employment might need more active intervention from the human resources department. In all cases, however, when employers and employees work together and succeed in achieving their goals, the effort can be very rewarding for all concerned.

Employing Persons with Learning Disabilities: It's the Law

"I'm going to do whatever it takes to make sure that Americans with disabilities are included in the mainstream.... They're not going to be left out anymore."

—*President George Bush*

On July 26, 1990, President Bush signed into law The Americans with Disabilities Act (ADA), which prohibits discrimination against

Americans with disabilities. The new law affirms that these Americans—like women, minorities, the aged, and Americans without disabilities—have a right to fair treatment in employment, public services, public accommodations and telecommunications.

Based on the Civil Rights Act of 1964 and Title V of the Rehabilitation Act of 1973, ADA bars bias against Americans with disabilities by employers, employment agencies, labor organizations, and joint labor-management committees. The provisions designed to ensure equal employment opportunities and fully accessible workplaces will be phased in over five years: July 26, 1992 for employers with 25 or more workers, and July 26, 1994 for employers with 15 or more workers.

As of these dates, discrimination against "a qualified individual with a disability" will be illegal in regard to job application procedures, the hiring or discharge of employees, employee compensation, advancement, job training, and other conditions of employment.

The federal agencies responsible for carrying out Congress' mandate are now writing the regulations for implementing The Americans with Disabilities Act. The full impact of the law and the extent of the rights of persons with disabilities will become clearer as the regulations go into effect. In addition, Americans with learning disabilities are also protected by Section 504 of the Rehabilitation Act of 1973, which forbids discrimination on the basis of a disability in all programs that receive federal funds.

In summary, employers can expect to experience greater and more insistent demands upon them to expand and maximize opportunities for persons with disabilities. The recent legislation is an important thrust, but concurrently advocacy, media attention and deeply held public concerns for social and economic justice must continue to play an effective role.

Hiring Practices

Some commonly asked questions include:

Who is a "qualified individual with a disability?" A qualified individual with a disability is a person who meets legitimate skill, experience, education, or other requirements of a job that he or she holds or seeks, and who can perform the "essential functions" of the position with or without reasonable accommodation. Requiring the ability to perform "essential" functions ensures that a person will not be considered unqualified simply because of inability to perform marginal or incidental job functions. If the person is qualified to perform essential job functions except for limitations caused by a disability, the employer must consider whether the individual could perform these functions with a reasonable accommodation.

Can an employer inquire as to whether a prospective employee is disabled? An employer may not make a pre-employment inquiry on an application form or in an interview as to whether, or to what extent, an individual is disabled. The employer may ask a job applicant whether he or she can perform particular job functions. If the applicant has a disability known to the employer, the employer may ask how he or she can perform job functions that the employer considers difficult or impossible to perform because of the disability, and whether a job accommodation would be needed. A job offer may be conditioned on the results of a medical examination, provided that the examination is required for all entering employees in the same job category regardless of disability, and that the information obtained is handled according to the confidentiality requirements specified in the Act.

Must an employer select a qualified applicant with a disability over other applicants? No. An employer is free to select the most qualified applicant available and to make decisions based on reasons unrelated to the existence or consequence of a disability. For example, if two persons apply for a job opening as a typist, one a person with a disability who accurately types 50 words per minute, the other a person without a disability who accurately types 75 words per minute, the employer may hire the applicant with the higher typing speed, if typing speed is needed for successful performance of the job.

May employers give tests to prospective employees who disclose that they have a learning disability? Can persons with learning disabilities be expected to pass the same tests as other employees have to take for purposes of selection? Employment tests and other types of selection criteria may not be used to screen out a person with a learning disability unless that standard can be shown to be a business necessity. For example, many employers require an employee to have a driver's license in order to qualify for a job—even though the job does not involve driving. The employer may believe that an employee who drives will be on time for work, or may be able to do an occasional errand. This requirement, however, would be marginal and should not be used to exclude persons with disabilities who can perform essential job functions that do not include driving.

The ADA protects persons with disabilities from discrimination by requiring that job criteria actually measure abilities required in doing a job. Two important rules designed to ensure a fit between job criteria and an applicant's actual ability to do the job are:

1. A person with a learning disability cannot be disqualified simply because of an inability to perform nonessential or marginal functions of the job; for example, a person applying for the job of heavy equipment operator cannot be denied the job simply because he or she could not pass a written test used by the employer for entering a training program.

2. A selection criterion may be used to screen out individuals with learning disabilities only if it can be shown that the criterion is consistent with business necessity. For instance, the employer is permitted to require that employees qualify for a training program. If the person with a learning disability could not be trained, the employer would be permitted to deny him or her the job.

More information on the important topic of accommodations is provided later in this chapter.

Identification

How does an employer know whether an employee has a learning disability? The employer may never learn if the employee does not choose to announce it. Learning disabilities are rightly called the "invisible handicap." Many outstanding employees have learned to compensate for or to conceal learning disabilities and offer consistently good job performance. Nothing adverse or out of the ordinary comes to the employer's attention. Other adults with learning disabilities have never been diagnosed; instinctively they have developed strategies that help them function without professional help. Sometimes people who have a learning disability are reluctant to admit to it, fearing they might be discriminated against. If an employee self-identifies as having a learning disability, or if it is recognized that one exists, then the employer can take a proactive approach. Basic questions that are helpful include: "How do you learn best?"; "What kind of supervision is most useful?"; and "Do you need, or could you benefit from, any particular accommodations or assistance within the workplace?"

Can an employer inquire as to whether an employee is disabled? After an employee is hired, all medical examinations and inquiries must be job related and necessary for the conduct of the employer's business. The employer is required to post notice in accessible format of the employer's obligation to provide reasonable accommodation, to state who is entitled to an accommodation, when the duty to provide a reasonable accommodation is triggered, and the process of determining the appropriate accommodation.

Accommodations

"Accommodation is key to assuring that individuals with learning disabilities are provided an opportunity to contribute productively and to receive meaningful training."

> — *Interagency Committee on Handicapped Employees,*
> *U.S. Equal Opportunity Commission*

An accommodation is any change in a job or work environment that enables a disabled person to do the job. Craig A. Michaels, a senior coordinator for learning disability projects at the National Center on Employment and Disability, divides accommodations into three basic categories:

1. environmental modifications—removal of architectural barriers;
2. equipment modifications—assistive devices and special tools; and
3. procedural modifications—restructuring tasks, altering work methods, and changing work schedules.

One obvious accommodation is providing wheelchair access to a building and bathrooms so that an employee who uses a wheelchair can enter the workplace and can use needed facilities. Most equipment and procedural modification needs are simple and practical and can be met with few problems and modest expense. Accommodations for persons with learning disabilities will consist primarily of procedural modifications, e.g., restructuring a job. Other accommodations discussed later in this chapter are less obvious, but just as important in opening many jobs to them.

We noted previously that The Americans with Disabilities Act requires employers to make "reasonable accommodation" for disabled employees in the workplace.

What is a "reasonable" accommodation? Sometimes a person with a learning disability has difficulty with part of a job. The employer must determine whether that part is an essential element of the job. A lawyer, for example, is hired for legal expertise, not for the ability to spell. Likewise, an actuary needs to be adept in using probability formulas; good penmanship is desirable but hardly crucial to figuring out complex statistical problems. When a "qualified" individual's learning disability interferes with performance on the job, the law requires that the employer make "reasonable accommodation" unless to do so would cause an undue hardship. Reasonable accommodation might include a secretary who can proofread for the lawyer and a word processor for the actuary.

Employers must provide reasonable accommodations to assist people with disabilities to meet legitimate criteria. If a training program is necessary for a lathe operator who has a reading disability to operate a lathe, then it is incumbent upon the employer to modify methods for training and testing to permit the operator to participate. For example, a reader could be provided to assist the operator with the training program's reading requirements, or the lathe operator could be required to exhibit mastery of information learned in ways other than through a written test.

How can an employer tell if an employee is truly learning disabled or just trying to get off easy? In order to be eligible for accommodations, an employee with disabilities must provide documentation of his or her disability. This usually consists of diagnostic reports of evaluations conducted by licensed professionals, usually a psychologist and often a learning disabilities specialist. While the average supervisor may not feel qualified to receive or interpret these reports, the human resources department is likely to have an individual (perhaps the affirmative action officer) designated to review this documentation. It is unlikely that an individual with a learning disability will request accommodations that are not truly needed. Research indicates that individuals with disabilities are less likely than their nondisabled peers to request needed accommodations, in many cases failing to request accommodations that would make their work easier.

Is the employer responsible for eliciting from employees information about needed accommodations? Many persons with disabilities do not require any accommodation. In the cases of those who do need accommodations, an employer is only required to accommodate a "known" disability of a qualified applicant or employee; if the employee has not disclosed the disability, the employer is not responsible for accommodations. Also, if a person with a "known" disability does not request an accommodation, the employer is not obligated to provide one.

If a person with a known disability is having difficulty performing his or her job, it would be permissible for the employer to discuss the possibility of a reasonable accommodation with the employee. However, in the absence of a request, it would be inappropriate to provide an accommodation, especially where it could have an adverse effect on the employee.

If an employee with a disability requests, but cannot suggest, an appropriate accommodation, the employer and the individual should work together to identify one. Individual supervisors within a company may be assisted in this matter through referral to human resources personnel or to employee assistance programs (EAPs). Also, there are a variety of public and private resources that can provide consultation on this matter.

Some examples of accommodations for persons with learning disabilities follow; the list is not exhaustive, but suggests the kinds of solutions employers and employees can develop.

Remember Nina, the fashion designer with dyslexia? Her story was told above. Nina's employers were interested in having her attend a series of management training seminars. Although Nina and her trainer were initially concerned about her ability to keep up with the outside reading, they discovered that audio tapes for the training materials could be ordered from the National Library Service for the Blind and Physically Handicapped.

Remember Henry, the engineer? His handwriting problem made it impossible for him to hand-letter engineering documents. His employers valued his engineering leadership and found it reciprocally beneficial to restructure his job—depending on designers and draftsmen under Henry's supervision for hand lettering. Henry has a related problem of determining the orientation of parts he designs; sometimes he designs a left-oriented part where a right-oriented part is needed. Henry has learned to check his designs for orientation errors and to have others check them as well.

507

A clerical employee with a learning disability may be an excellent typist, but have spelling problems that interfere with reading. The office manager can give another clerk responsibility for proofreading this worker's typing. Alternatively, the employee can use a word processor with a spell check.

A salesperson with a learning disability may be very good at cultivating customers, but have difficulty computing the final sale and end-of-month reports. The store could devise a system whereby another salesperson would finish the sale—with equitable distribution of any commission that might be involved. An employee who has difficulty judging time may be helped in several ways. Make sure the office has at least one digital clock that can easily be seen from the employee's desk. Schedule planning meetings to assist with time management problems.

An employer can make sure the immediate work environment of an employee with a learning disability does not interfere with work. For example, an employee who has attentional difficulties should be given a quiet non-distracting work area, not next to an open window, a noisy air conditioner, or a hallway used by other workers on their way to the rest rooms. Make sure he or she is seated in the most orderly part of the office with the least traffic.

Computer software is available to help persons with learning disabilities use computers. These programs include "talking" word-processing programs, text editors, spell checkers, and aids for people who have difficulty using computer keyboards that require two keys to be depressed simultaneously.

For Severe Problems. Supported employment is an employment model developed to help persons with severe disabilities work at real jobs with workers who do not have disabilities. Usually the person with the disability is placed in the job by a vocational rehabilitation agency from which a staff member continues to provide services at the job site. A job coach trains the person at the place of employment and helps him or her form good working relationships with co-workers. The coach provides periodic assessment and support for many years after the original placement. Follow-up services are designed to troubleshoot potential problems that can be caused by a change in supervisors, a new work assignment, or other changes in the person's life at home or at work. Full- and part-time jobs are eligible for inclusion in supported employment programs. Approximately 20 percent of the population of persons with learning disabilities have disabilities severe enough to warrant supported employment.

Training Persons with Learning Disabilities

As of 1990, American employers were spending $30 billion annually on employee training programs—and they are expected spend as much as $15 billion more each year in the new decade. The amount represents a substantial investment in remedial courses teach Johnny and Jenny how read, or write, or do arithmetic, and in advanced courses teach them new skills essential the ever-changing modern workplace.

The stakes have risen considerably, but employers still would do well answer the first question—"Why Can't Johnny Read? Or Write? Or Do Arithmetic?"—before placing an employee in a generic training program. An educational deficit can be the result of many causes, ranging from inadequate schooling to a mental impairment to a learning disability.

If the cause is a learning disability, traditional methods may need adaptation achieve the desired results. Yes, even with a history of failure, Johnny and Jenny can learn if training is adapted compensate for the disability. When this happens, everyone profits: the employee has a job and the employer's investment is returned with good work.

The most important aspect of training an employee with a learning disability and using job-related testing is understanding. The employer and employee both need understand: (1) what is being taught or tested, (2) which is the best way for the employee learn, and (3) whether the employee is learning.

They also need be understanding of each other. No employer wants waste money or resources on a useless educational program. No employee wants feel useless. Success is a shared interest.

Here are some strategies for ensuring success.

Content. What is the purpose of training? What does the employer want the employee learn? Make sure the testing or training focuses on skills or information the employee will need do the job and not extraneous information or abilities, such as being a good test taker.

Teaching Techniques. How does this employee learn? Regardless of whether trainees have learning disabilities or not, don't rely on extensive lecturing. Make sure there are plenty of visuals—graphs, charts, and text—for illustration. With dyslexics, put more emphasis on speech, audio and video; minimize or eliminate printed materials and charts that will only confuse the learner.

Notes: For some people with learning disabilities taking notes while listening is an exceedingly difficult task. Provide class notes or find a good note taker in the course who will share notes. Always provide detailed outlines that can help the learner follow how the course is organized.

Distractions. Make sure the training environment and the materials used for training are free of distractions. Background noises such as a loud air conditioner can distract someone with a learning disability. Similarly, an all-purpose diagram that contains too much information can be a minefield for some learners. They won't be able sort out what they need know and what they can ignore.

Feedback. Don't wait until the course is over find out that the employee hasn't mastered Step A. Take time throughout the program ask questions and make sure the learner is learning. Review regularly.

Time. Unless speed is crucial job performance, give the employee a generous amount of time for learning and test taking. For some people finding the words to answer a question takes longer than finding the answer. They can do the job—but not the test—in a reasonable amount of time.

Encouragement. Whenever possible, praise your employees' accomplishments and let them know you believe they can succeed.

Supervision

One of the most important areas for accommodation is in the daily supervision of employees with learning disabilities. The relationship between supervisors and employees is based on a continuing exchange of information. No matter how simple or complex the job, the supervisor communicates instructions the employee and the employee responds by doing the job or explaining why the job can't be done as ordered.

When a learning disability interferes with the responsive exchange of information, everyone has a problem. The employer's work isn't completed on schedule. The supervisor's leadership is in question. The employee with the learning disability believes his or her job is in jeopardy.

Few factors are as crucial to the success or failure of an employee with a learning disability as the relationship the immediate supervisor. Not only can good supervision help prevent stand-offs, but more important, it can lead a productive relationship that will benefit employer, boss, and worker. Here are some tips on supervising these employees.

Communication Style. What is the best way communicate with the employee? Some people with learning disabilities do well with oral instructions. Others have trouble remembering spoken instructions and work better with a written list or memo. If you run into a problem, ask whether the employee has a preference and then note which works better. For employees who have difficulty with oral directions, observe the following guidelines:

- Beware of information overload. Don't talk about work you're thinking about assigning next month when you want something else done today.

- Be sure that the employee understands what you are saying. If you have any doubt, ask the worker repeat your instructions.

- Make sure your meaning is clear. Does the employee misinterpret the tone of your instructions? Remember, sometimes a person with a learning disability will take correction as criticism.

- Provide visual aids (e.g., written directions, diagrams) whenever possible.

- Don't assume an employee with a learning disability will pick up indirect cues about what is expected. You won't get your message across by dropping hints if the employee has difficulty reading faces or understanding tones of voice.

Organization. If you want a multi-step job done, make sure the employee has a list of all the steps in the order in which they are be done. Don't assume the employee can figure out how organize a complex task—even when the task is repeated from time to time.

For example, if the administrative assistant has to organize a staff meeting once a month, have the employee keep a standing checklist of everything that has be done from mailing memos to ensuring that minutes are completed and distributed.

Patience. A person with a learning disability may need more time learn a new task or accommodate to change. Pressure will not speed up the process. It may delay or make impossible the acquisition of a new skill. Let the employee know you want him or her take whatever time is necessary—your concern is that he or she learns or adapts well.

Flexibility. Is your new short-order cook putting the mayo on the bread before putting the lettuce on the other half of the sandwich? Do you like to do the lettuce first? Does it matter which goes on the sandwich first? Often people with learning disabilities will find their own ways to do things. If they can do the job, can you find it in you to accept their adaptations?

Feedback. Create opportunities for the employee tell you about any problems he or she may be having on the job. You can't solve them until you know what they are.

Encouragement. Most of us respond well praise. Finding something positive to say can provide a big boost an employee with a learning disability who is struggling with a new task or a change in the work environment.

After You're Gone. Have you left a record of the employee's accomplishments and special needs in the files? If you know your successor, tell the new boss that the worker has a learning disability and does excellent work. You will save the supervisor and the employee a great deal of frustration if you share what you've learned about working successfully with this person.

Employee Assistance Programs

Many companies subscribe to an employee assistance program. These programs, usually called EAPs, can be a valuable source of help to employees with learning disabilities. They are formal programs designed to help troubled employees recognize, identify, and solve personal problems before they result in termination from the job and loss of income. EAPs provide confidential support services to employees who are experiencing problems that interfere with their job performance and productivity. Program staff typically provide an assessment and some counseling, while referring the employee to appropriate specialists.

Supervisors may suggest that an employee who has problems avail him- or herself of EAP services or an employee may make an entirely private, personal contact with the EAP. An employee's problem could be discussed only between the employee and the EAP counselor, or a referral could be made to a selected specialist, or, at the employee's request, an appropriate EAP staff member might act as an intermediary, speaking to a supervisor on an employee's behalf.

Employee unions generally participate in an EAP retained by an employer, or participate in a member assistance program (MAP), developed for union members.

Employees have every reason to have confidence in EAPs and MAPs and their services; the programs are confidential, voluntary, and entirely non-punitive: they operate from the assumption that it is normal for people have problems. A company's willingness pay for EAP services reflects the contemporary management view that workers' private and work lives are not totally separate and that personal problems affect job performance. Unions hold similar views. And, of course, once personal problems have been solved, job performance and productivity normally improve and fear of or cause for termination usually end.

Getting Help: Resources and Referrals

Have a problem accommodating an employee's learning disability? Need an idea?

The Job Accommodation Network (JAN) is a free database service offered by the President's Committee on Employment of People with Disabilities. Write or call JAN to consult with an expert who will provide information on solutions that other employers have found useful in similar circumstances.

IBM has a National Support Center for Persons with Disabilities that can help employers locate software that will help persons with learning disabilities enhance their performance. Resource guides are available to anyone who calls.

Professional services are available throughout the United States and Canada. If you don't know a clinician who treats learning disabilities, you can call one of the following for a referral or suggestion:

- Special education department of a college or university in your area
- Any state or local vocational rehabilitation office in your area
- Any local organization that provides services people with disabilities
- Any of the national organizations listed below.

Americans with Disabilities Act (ADA)
U.S. Department of Justice
P.O. Box 66118
Washington,D.C. 20035-6118
(202) 514-0301
(202) 514-0381 (TDD)

**Association of Handicapped Student Service Programs
in Postsecondary Education**
P.O. Box 21192
Columbus, OH 43221

HEATH Resource Center
One Dupont Circle, Suite 800
Washington, DC 20036-1193
(202) 939-9320; (800) 544-3284

ICD (International Center for the Disabled)
340 East 24th Street
New York, NY 10010-4097
(212) 679-0100
(212) 889-2440 fax
(212) 889-0372 TTY

IBM National Support Center for Persons with Disabilities
P.O. Box 2150
Atlanta, GA 30301-2150
(800) 426-2133

Job Accommodation Network
809 Allen Hall
West Virginia University
P.O. Box 6122
Morgantown, WV 26506-6122
(800) 526-2262 (Canada)
(800) 526-7232 (U.S., except West Virginia)
(800) 526-4698 (West Virginia)

Learning Disabilities Association
4156 Library Road
Pittsburgh, PA 15234
(412) 341-1515 or 241-8077

National Center for Disability Services
201 I.U. Willets Road
Albertson, NY 11507
(516) 747-5400

National Center for Learning Disabilities
99 Park Avenue
NewYork, NY 10016
(212) 687-7211

National Network of Learning Disabled Adults
800 North 82nd Street, Suite F2
Scottsdale, AZ 85257
(602) 941-5112

Orton Dyslexia Society
Chester Building, Suite 382
8600 LaSalle Road
Baltimore, MD 21286-2044
(410) 296-0232

President's Committee on Employment of People with Disabilities
1331 F Street, N.W., Suite 300
Washington, D.C. 20004-1107
(202) 376-6200
(202) 376-6205 (TDD)

U.S. Department of Justice, Civil Rights Section, Washington, D.C.:

The Americans with Disabilities Act
Americans with Disabilities Act Requirements Fact Sheet
Americans with Disabilities Act Requirements in Public Accommodations Fact Sheet
Americans with Disabilities Act Statutory Deadlines
Americans with Disabilities: Questions and Answers

U.S. Equal Employment Opportunity Commission
1801 L Street NW
Washington, D.C.
(800) 669-EEOC (voice)

Chapter 42

National Resources for Adults with Learning Disabilities

National Resource Centers

American Association for Adult and Continuing Education (AAACE)
1101 Connecticut Avenue, NW Suite 700
Washington, DC 20036
(202) 429-5131

The AAACE is a professional association for practitioners concerned with enhancing the quality of adult learning. The organization fosters the development and sharing of information, theory, research, and best practices with its members.

Association on Higher Education and Disability (AHEAD)
P.O. Box 21192
Columbus, OH, 43221
(614) 488-4972
(614) 488-1174 (Fax)

HEATH Resource Center, American Council on Education and National Adult Literacy and Learning Disabilities Center, September 1995. Additional copies of this publication are available from HEATH Resource Center, One Dupont Circle, Suite 800, Washington, DC 20036, telephone (800) 544-3284 or within the Washington DC area (202) 939-9320; or National Adult Literacy and Learning Disabilities Center, Academy for Educational Development, 1875 Connecticut Avenue, NW, Washington, DC 20009, telephone (202) 844-8185 or (800) 953-ALLD.

AHEAD, formerly the Association on Handicapped Student Service Programs in Postsecondary Education, is an international, multicultural organization of professionals committed to full participation in higher education for persons with disabilities. The Association has numerous training programs, workshops, publications, and conferences.

Career College Association (CCA)
750 First Street, NE, Suite 900
Washington, DC 20002-4242
(202) 336-6749
(202) 336-6828 (Fax)

CCA is an educational association with approximately 600 members from independent, nonprofit, and taxpaying colleges/schools. All of these accredited institutions prepare people for careers in business. CCA publishes an annual *Directory of Private Accredited Career Schools and Colleges of Technology*, which provides general information about accredited institutions in a variety of business career fields.

Division of Adult Education and Literacy Clearinghouse
U.S. Department of Education
Office of Vocational and Adult Education
400 Maryland Avenue, SW
Washington, DC 20202
(202) 205-9996
(202) 205-8973 (Fax)

This clearinghouse links the adult education community with existing resources in adult education and provides information which deals with programs funded under the Adult Education Act (P.L. 100-297). The clearinghouse provides a number of free publications, fact sheets, bibliographies, directories, abstracts, etc. available for the adult with special learning needs.

ERIC Clearinghouse on Adult, Career, and Vocational Education
1900 Kenny Road
Columbus, OH 43210-1090
(614) 292-4353
(800) 848-4815

Part of the ERIC System, this clearinghouse offers publications, information, and referrals to those working with adults who are learning disabled. It does not provide direct services, but it disseminates materials through the ERIC database and clearinghouse publications. Two examples of available publications are: *Adults with Learning Disabilities: An Overview for the Adult Educator*, by Jovita Ross-Gordon (IN337 $7), and *Teaching Adults with Learning Disabilities* (ERIC Digest #99, no cost).

HEATH Resource Center

National Clearinghouse on Postsecondary Education for Individuals with Disabilities
American Council on Education
One Dupont Circle, NW, Suite 800
Washington, DC 20036
(202) 939-9320
(800) 544-3284
(202) 833-4760 (Fax)

The HEATH Resource Center operates the national clearinghouse on postsecondary education for individuals with disabilities. A program of the American Council on Education, HEATH serves as an information exchange for the educational support services, policies, procedures, adaptations, and opportunities of American campuses, vocational-technical schools, adult education programs, and other training entities after high school. The Center collects and disseminates this information so that people with disabilities can develop their full potential through postsecondary education and training.

Learning Disabilities Research and Training Center

The University of Georgia
534 Aderhold Hall
Athens, GA 30602
(706) 542-1300
(706) 542-4532 (Fax)

The Learning Disabilities Research and Training Center focuses on four research strands: policy and funding; functional assessment; employment/transition; and consumer empowerment. Training activities include a series of teleconference distance learning programs, field-based internships, train-the-trainer courses, and technical assistance for transition personnel and consumers. Contact the Center to receive the free newsletter and additional information.

Materials Development Center
Stout Vocational Rehabilitation
Institute University of Wisconsin-Stout
Menomonie, WI 54751
(715) 232-1342

The Center develops and disseminates information to professionals about vocational rehabilitation and training of students with disabilities. Materials include information on vocational evaluation, work adjustment, job placement, and independent living.

National Adult Literacy and Learning Disabilities Center (National ALLD Center)
Academy for Educational Development
1875 Connecticut Avenue, NW Suite 800
Washington, DC 20009-1202
(202) 884-8185
(202) 884-8422 (Fax)

The Center, established in October 1993, is a national resource for information exchange regarding learning disabilities and their impact on the provision of literacy services. Funded by the National Institute for Literacy, the Center provides technical assistance in current best practices in learning disabilities to literacy providers and practitioners. In addition to sharing information, the Center develops and refines knowledge on effective practices for serving adults with learning disabilities.

National Association for Adults with Special Learning Needs (NAASLN)
P.O. Box 716
Bryn Mawr, PA 19010
(610) 525-8336
(610) 525-8337 (Fax)

NAASLN is a non-profit organization designed to organize, establish, and promote an effective national and international coalition of professionals, advocates, and consumers of lifelong learning for the purpose of educating adults with special learning needs.

National Association of Vocational Education Special Needs Personnel (NAVESNP)

Special Needs Division American Vocational Association
2020 14th Street
Arlington, VA 22201
(703) 522-6121

NAVESNP is a national association of vocational education professionals concerned with the education of disabled, disadvantaged, and other special needs students.

National Center for Research in Vocational Education (NCRVE)

University of California at Berkeley
2150 Shattuck Avenue, Suite 1250
Berkeley, CA 24704
(510) 642-4004
(510) 642-2124
(800) 762-4093

The Center provides a wide range of materials for professionals about curriculum development, technical education, career planning, and preparation for employment.

National Clearinghouse on ESL Literacy Education (NCLE)

Center for Applied Linguistics
1118 22nd Street, NW
Washington, DC 20037
(202) 429-9292
(202) 659-5641 (Fax)

NCLE's objective is to provide timely information to practitioners and others interested in adult ESL literacy education.

Recording for the Blind (RFB)

20 Roszel Road
Princeton, NJ 20542
(609) 452-0606
(800) 221-4792

RFB is a national non-profit organization that provides taped educational books free on loan, books on diskette, library services, and other educational and professional resources to individuals who cannot read standard print because of a visual, physical, or perceptual disability.

General Education

Contact Center Inc.
National Literacy Hotline
P.O. Box 81826
Lincoln, NE 68501
(800) 228-8813
(402) 464-5931 (Fax)

This national toll-free hotline refers callers to the literacy program in their local area.

General Educational Development Testing Service (GEDTS)
Center for Adult Learning and Educational Credentials
American Council on Education
One Dupont Circle
Washington, DC 20036
(202) 939-9490
(800) 626-9433
(202) 775-8578 (Fax)

GEDTS administers the GED Tests and provides information on disability-related adaptations/accommodations for the GED Tests to prospective examinees and instructors. Successful GED Test takers earn a high school equivalency diploma. The tests are available in audio, Braille, and large print editions. GEDTS also publishes *GED Items*, a bimonthly newsletter for examiners and adult education instructors.

Institute for the Study of Adult Literacy
The Pennsylvania State University
204 Calder Way, Suite 209
University Park, PA 16801-4756
(814) 863-3777
(814) 863-6108 (Fax)

This organization creates high-technology learning tools such as computer-aided instruction in adult basic education, workplace literacy, and family literacy.

Laubach Literacy Action (LLA)

P.O. Box 131
Syracuse, NY 13210
(315) 422-9121
(315) 422-6369 (Fax)

Laubach Literacy Action is the nation's largest network of adult literacy programs providing basic literacy and ESL instruction through trained volunteers. LLA affiliates in the United States serve more than 950 communities in 45 states.

Learning Resources Network

1554 Hayes
Manhattan, KS 66502
(913) 539-5376

This network for educators provides resources to adult education and adult basic education service providers.

Literacy Volunteers of America (LVA)

5795 Widewaters Parkway
Syracuse, NY 13214
(315) 445-8000
(315) 445-8006 (Fax)

LVA is a national non-profit organization with more than 400 affiliate programs in 40 states. LVA is the exclusive distributor of PULL: Project for Unique Learners in Literacy. It was developed to answer questions on teaching adult learners who appear to have the ability to learn to read, but who may not be experiencing success with the traditional methods.

National Center on Adult Literacy (NCAL)

University of Pennsylvania
3910 Chestnut Street
Philadelphia, PA 19104-3111
(215) 898-2100
(215) 898-9804 (Fax)

The National Center on Adult Literacy (NCAL) was established in 1990 by the Office of Educational Research and Improvement at the U.S. Department of Education, with co-funding from the U.S. Departments of Labor and Health and Human Services. The mission of

NCAL addresses three primary challenges: to enhance the knowledge base about adult literacy; to improve the quality of research and development in the field; and to ensure a strong, two-way relationship between research and practice. Dissemination efforts include a newsletter, publication of reports on a broad range of topics relevant to adult literacy, Internet usage, and more.

National Institute for Literacy (NIFL)
800 Connecticut Avenue, NW, Suite 200
Washington, DC 20202-7560
(202) 632-1500
(202) 632-1512 (Fax)

The Institute's work focuses on four key priorities: providing leadership in the literacy field through national and state advocacy activities; creating and gathering knowledge and information that can improve the quality of literacy services; collaborating to build national, state, and local capacity for effective service delivery; and facilitating communication in the literacy community through a national information and communication system.

Rural Clearinghouse for Lifelong Education and Development
Kansas State College
111 College Court Building
Manhattan, KS 66506-6001
(913) 532-5560
(913) 532-5637 (Fax)

The Rural Clearinghouse for Lifelong Education and Development is a national effort to improve rural access to continuing education. The Clearinghouse serves the complete range of educational providers including colleges and universities, community colleges, cooperative extension programs, libraries, community-based organizations, and community/economic development corporations in a variety of ways.

Learning Disabilities Organizations

Council for Learning Disabilities (CLD)
P.O. Box 40303
Overland Park, KS 66204
(913) 492-8755
(913) 492-2546 (Fax)

CLD is a national professional organization dedicated solely to professionals working with individuals who have learning disabilities. Mission: Committed to enhance the education and life span development of individuals with learning disabilities. CLD establishes standards of excellence and promotes innovative strategies on research and practice through interdisciplinary collegiality, collaboration, and advocacy. CLD's publication, *Learning Disability Quarterly*, focuses on the latest research in the field of learning disabilities with an applied focus.

LAUNCH, INC.
Department of Special Education—ETSA
Commerce, TX 75428
(214) 886-5932

LAUNCH provides resources for learning disabled individuals, coordinates efforts of other local, state, and national LD organizations, acts as a communication channel for people with learning disabilities through a monthly newsletter, and provides programs to enhance social interaction.

Learning Disabilities Association of America, Inc. (LDA)
4156 Library Road
Pittsburgh, PA 15234
(412) 341-1515
(412) 344-0224 (Fax)

LDA (formerly ACLD), a non-profit volunteer advocacy organization, provides information and referral for parents, professionals, and consumers involved with or in search of support groups and networking opportunities through local LDA Youth and Adult Section Chapters. A publication list is available. The Association also prints *LDA Newsbriefs*, a bi-monthly newsletter for parents, professionals, and adults with LD. Available for $13.50/year by contacting LDA.

National Center for Learning Disabilities (NCLD)
381 Park Avenue South, Suite 1420
New York, NY 10016
(212) 545-7510
(212) 545-9665 (Fax)

NCLD is an organization committed to improving the lives of those affected by learning disabilities (LD). NCLD provides services and conducts programs nationwide, benefiting children and adults with LD, their families, teachers, and other professionals. NCLD provides the latest information on learning disabilities and local resources to parents, professionals, employers, and others dealing with learning disabilities. NCLD's annual publication is *Their World*.

National Network of Learning Disabled Adults (NNLDA)
808 N. 82nd Street, Suite F2
Scottsdale, AZ 85257
(602) 941-5112

The NNLDA provides information and referral for LD adults involved with or in search of support groups and networking opportunities. A list of support groups for LD adults is available by request. The Network publishes a quarterly newsletter and holds an annual general assembly in conjunction with the annual meeting of the President's Committee on Employment of People with Disabilities.

Orton Dyslexia Society
8600 LaSalle Road
Chester Building, Suite 382
Baltimore, MD 21286-2044
(410) 296-0232
(800) 222-3123

The Society is an international scientific and educational association concerned with the widespread problem of the specific language disability of developmental dyslexia. Local and state chapters serve as literacy resources for dyslexic adults and those who teach or advise them.

Rebus Institute
1499 Bayshore Blvd, Suite 146
Burlingame, CA 94010
(415) 697-7424
(415) 697-3734 (Fax)

The Rebus Institute is a national non-profit organization devoted to the study and dissemination of information on adult issues related to Specific Learning Disabilities (LD) and Attention Deficit Disorders (ADD). Its goal is to promote public awareness of the abilities, strengths, and methods that lead to success for adults with LD/ADD.

Attention Deficit Disorder Organizations

Adults with learning disabilities and adults with attention deficit disorder (ADD) often share some of the same characteristics. An adult with a learning disability may also have an attention deficit disorder. Information about national organizations that serve individuals with attention deficit disorder is provided for those adults who have both a learning disability and an attention deficit disorder, as determined by qualified professionals.

ADDult Support Network
2620 Ivy Place
Toledo, OH 43613

The ADDult Support Network is a volunteer organization affiliated with the Attention Deficit Disorder Association (ADDA). The Network keeps a running list of local ADD support groups across the country and can refer individuals to the group closest to them. Those interested in obtaining such a referral are asked to send a self-addressed stamped envelope. The Network publishes a quarterly newsletter, *ADDult News* ($8.00/year), and also makes available an ADDult Information Packet on adults with ADD ($3.00).

Children and Adults with Attention Deficit Disorder (CHADD)
499 Northwest 70th Avenue, Suite 308
Plantation, FL 33317
(305) 587-3700
(305) 587-4599 (Fax)

CHADD is a non-profit, parent-based organization that disseminates information on ADD and coordinates more than 460 parent support groups. It also publishes a semi-annual magazine, *CHADDER*, and a newsletter, *Chadderbox*.

The Attention Deficit Information Network, Inc. (AD-IN)
475 Hillside Avenue
Needham, MA 02194
(617) 455-9895

AD-IN is a non-profit volunteer organization that offers support and information to families of children with attention deficit disorder (ADD), adults with ADD, and professionals through an international network of 60 parent and adult chapters. Contact AD-IN for a

527

list of chapters, as well as to receive cost information for information packets specifically designed for adults with ADD, parents, or educators. AD-IN also provides information to those interested in starting a new local chapter, and serves as a resource for information on training programs and speakers for those who work with individuals with ADD.

Challenge Inc.
P.O. Box 488
Westbury, MA 01985
(508) 462-0495 (Phone/Fax)

Provides referrals to parent support groups nationally. Responds to information requests and refers appropriate requests to their professional advisors.

Employment

Job Accommodation Network (JAN)
West Virginia University
809 Allen Hall
Morgantown, WV 26506
(304) 293-7186
(800) ADA-WORK

JAN is an international information network and consulting resource that provides information about employment issues to employers, rehabilitation professionals, and persons with disabilities. Callers should be prepared to explain their specific problem and job circumstances. Sponsored by the President's Committee on Employment of People with Disabilities, the Network is operated by West Virginia University's Rehabilitation Research and Training Center. Brochures, printed materials, and a newsletter are available free of charge.

Mainstream, Inc.
3 Bethesda Metro Center, Suite 830
Bethesda, MD 20814
(301) 654-2400
(301) 654-2403 (Fax)

Established in 1975, this non-profit organization works with employers and service providers around the country to increase employment opportunities for persons with disabilities. Mainstream produces publications and videos and provides in-house training, seminars, and technical assistance on compliance with the Americans with Disabilities Act (ADA). Mainstream operates its own placement program, Project LINK, in Washington, DC and Dallas, TX.

President's Committee on the Employment of People with Disabilities
1331 F Street, NW
Washington, DC 20036
(202) 376-6200
(202) 376-6205
(202) 376-6859 (Fax)

The President's Committee on the Employment of People with Disabilities is an independent federal agency. The committee's mission is to facilitate the communication, coordination, and promotion of public and private efforts to empower Americans with disabilities through employment. The committee offers several publications that address aspects of employment for LD adults including *Pathways to Employment for People with Learning Disabilities* and *Employment Considerations for Learning Disabled Adults*. Both are free.

The Dole Foundation for the Employment of People with Disabilities
1819 H Street, NW
Washington, DC 20006-3603
(202) 457-0318
(202) 457-0473 (Fax)

The Dole Foundation is the nation's leading grant maker in the field of employment for people with disabilities. Grant funds of $500 to $100,000 are available to non-profit organizations conducting innovative projects related to employment and disability. Foundation funding priorities include under served populations, minorities, women, rural programs, older workers, career advancement, and programs stressing placement with small employers.

Technology

ABLEDATA-REHAB DATA
Alliance for Technology Access (ATA)
2173 E. Francisco Blvd
San Rafael, CA 94901
(415) 455-4575

The Alliance for Technology Access is a national organization dedicated to providing access to technology for people with disabilities through its coalition of 45 community-based resource centers in 34 states and the Virgin Islands. Each center provides information, awareness, and training for professionals, and provides guided problem solving and technical assistance for individuals with disabilities and family members.

Apple Computer Inc., Worldwide Disability Solutions Group (WDSG)
Apple Technologies
1 Infinite Loop
Cupertino, CA 95014
(800) 776-2333

The Worldwide Disability Solutions Group at Apple works with key education, rehabilitation, and advocacy organizations nationwide to identify the computer-related needs of individuals with disabilities and to assist in the development of responsive programs. WDSG is involved with Apple's research and development to ensure that Apple computers have built-in accessibility features.

IBM Special Needs Information Referral Center
IBM Educational Systems
P.O. Box 1328
Internal Zip 5432
Boca Raton, FL 33432
(407) 982-9099
(800) 426-2133

The Center responds to requests for information on how IBM products can help people with a wide range of disabilities use personal computers. While the Center is unable to diagnose or prescribe an assistive device or software, free information is provided on what is available and where one can go for more details.

National Rehabilitation Information Center (NARIC)
8455 Colesville Road, Suite 935
Silver Spring, MD 20910
(301) 588-9284
(800) 322-0956

The ABLEDATA database contains descriptions of more than 17,000 commercially available products for rehabilitation and independent living.

RESNA Technical Assistance Project
1700 North Moore Street, Suite 1540
Arlington, VA 22209
(703) 524-6686
(703) 524-6630 (Fax)

Provides technical assistance to states on the development and implementation of consumer responsive statewide programs of technology related assistance under the Technology-Related Assistance for Individuals with Disabilities Act of 1988.

Life Management

In the Life Management section, programs have been selected that not only provide postsecondary training, but also provide residential housing for their enrolled students.

Berkshire Center
18 Park Street, Box 160
Lee, MA 01238
(413) 243-2576

A postseconary program for young adults with learning disabilities ages 18–26. Half of the students attend Berkshire Community College part-time while the others go directly into the world of work. Services include: Vocational/Academic preparation, tutoring, college liaison, life skills instruction, driver's education, money management, psychotherapy and more. The program is year-round with two years being the average stay.

Center for Adaptive Learning
3350 Clayton Road, Suite A
Concord, CA 94519
(510) 827-3863
(510) 827-4080 (Fax)

Adults 18–40 years of age learn the essentials of independent living in a program that offers residential living, social skills training, sensory motor training, counseling, roommate peer counseling, cognitive retraining, and job placement. Students either work or attend local community colleges, and job coaching and tutoring are available. Apartments in the community are available, and most are clients of Vocational Rehabilitation.

Chapel Haven, Inc.
1040 Whalley Avenue
New Haven, CT 06515
(203) 397-1714
(203) 397-8004 (Fax)

Chapel Haven is an individualized, year-round, transitional independent living program for young adults with a wide range of learning disabilities. The program includes life skills training in an apartment setting, pre-vocational training, vocational placement and support, and practical academics. Participants learn all of the skills necessary to make a smooth entry into independent community living. Comprehensive non-residential, community-based independent living services are also available. These include life skills follow-ups, vocational assistance, social/recreational programs, and adult education classes, as well as benefits coordination.

Creative Community Services (CCS)
1720 Peachtree Road, Suite 127
Atlanta, GA 30309
(404) 872-6818

Serving young adults 20–35 years of age, this organization creates living arrangements for people with a range of learning disabilities who want to lead adult lifestyles but still need some support and assistance. CCS helps locate housing; provides a live-in counselor, if needed; helps develop a plan for each participant's future development; provides one-to-one training in necessary areas; and offers ongoing support for participants and their families.

Getting Ready for the Outside World
Riverview School
Route 6A
East Sandwich, MA 02537
(508) 888-0489
(508) 888-1315 (Fax)

This is a transitional program for high school graduates who would like to continue in an academically based postsecondary school, but need to develop academic skills or independent living skills.

Horizon Program
University of Alabama
Education Bldg., Room 157
901 South 13th Street
Birmingham, AL 35294-1250
(205) 975-6770
(800) 822-6242
(205) 975-6764 (Fax)

The Horizons Program is a college-based, non-degree program for students with specific learning disabilities and other mild learning problems. This specially designed, two-year program prepares individuals for successful transitions to the community.

Independence Center
3640 S. Sepulveda Boulevard, #102
Los Angeles, CA 90034
(310) 202-7102
(310) 398-3776 (Fax)

Independence Center provides a supportive program in which young adults with learning disabilities learn the skills necessary to live independently. These include job skills, apartment care, social skills, and adult decision making. Vocational training is accomplished through apprenticeships and/or enrollment in vocational schools or community college programs.

National Council of Independent Living Programs (NCIL)
2111 Wilson Blvd, Suite 40
Arlington, VA 22201
(703) 525-3406
(703) 525-3409 (Fax)

NCIL is the national membership association of local not-for-profit corporations known as Independent Living Centers (ILC). NCIL focuses its attention on national policy issues and the independent living movement, while local centers focus much of their attention on local and state policy issues. NCIL provides technical assistance and leadership to its membership.

New Lifestyles, Inc.
5975 W. Sunrise Boulevard, Suite 208A
Sunrise, FL 33130
(305) 797-6313
(305) 797-2813 (Fax)

New Lifestyles specializes in the provision of psychological and educational services to individuals with learning difficulties. It provides admission, program management, and clinical support services for the Foundation for Independent Living, a not-for-profit independent living program developed by parents to meet the lifelong needs of their children. It provides administrative and clinical support services for the College Living Experience, an independent living, academic, and career support program for individuals of average intelligence with learning disabilities.

Life Development Institute
P.O. Box 15112
Phoenix, AZ 85060
(602) 955-2920

The Life Development Institute conducts a variety of programs designed to enable participants to obtain employment and independent living status commensurate with individual capabilities. Vocational assessment and training is provided through community based programs or direct job placements.

Professional Assistance Center for Education (PACE)
National-Louis University
2840 Sheridan Road
Evanston, IL 60201-1796
(708) 475-1100
(708) 256-1057 (Fax)

PACE is a non-credit, non-degree, two-year postsecondary program for students with learning disabilities. The program prepares young adults for careers as aides in preschools or human service agencies. In addition to professional preparation coursework, the curriculum also focuses on social skills and independent living skills. Students receive a certificate of completion at the conclusion of the program. College residential life is an integral part of the program.

Threshold Program
Lesley College
29 Everett Street
Cambridge, MA 02138
(617) 349-8181
(617) 349-8189 (Fax)

Threshold is a two- to three-year non-degree, college based pro gram that helps young adults develop the academic, vocational, social, and independent living skills necessary for independence. Students prepare for paraprofessional roles in offices, early childhood settings, or settings that serve elderly or disabled consumers. Most graduates participate in Threshold's third-year Transition Program, which provides support as they venture into apartment living and paid employment.

Vista Program of Westbrook
1356 Old Clinton Road
Westbrook, CT 06498
(203) 399-8080
(203) 399-4097 (Fax)

Vista offers an individualized program for young adults in transition to work and independent living. Through work experiences, individual and group counseling, seminars, and coursework, students develop skills and behaviors necessary for success in adulthood. Among the skills addressed are interpersonal relationships, positive self-esteem, and time management.

Vocational Independence Program (VIP)
New York Institute of Technology
Independence Hall
Central Islip, NY 11722
(516) 348-3354
(516) 348-0437

The Vocational Independence Program at New York Institute of Technology is a three-year certificate program for students with moderate to severe learning disabilities. The VIP curriculum emphasizes independent living, social and vocational skills, as well as individual academic support.

Publications

Adult Basic Education and General Educational Development Programs for Disabled Adults: A Handbook for Literacy Tutors and Instructors
Free Library of Philadelphia
Library for the Blind and Physically Handicapped (LBPH)
919 Walnut Street
Philadelphia, PA 19107
(800) 222-1754
(215) 925-3213

This publication was funded by the Division of Adult Basic Education of the Pennsylvania Department of Education and the U.S. Department of Education. It represents the experiences gained from the teaching of two GED classes for adults with disabilities. It contains a section on learning disabilities.

A.L.L. Points Bulletin
U.S. Department of Education
Division of Adult Education and Literacy
400 Maryland Avenue, SW
Washington, DC 20202-7240
(202) 205-8959

This bi-monthly newsletter of the Division of Adult Education and Literacy focuses on selected areas of interest in the field of adult education, current research, new publications, and upcoming events. Free of charge.

Campus Opportunities for Students with Learning Differences
Octameron Associates
P.O. Box 3437
Alexandria, VA 22302
(703) 836-5480

Campus Opportunities for Students with Learning Differences— 4th Edition (1994), by Judith M. Crooker, addresses high school students with learning disabilities and their parents as they take the necessary steps in secondary school years to be ready to apply for college. It is available by prepaying $3.

Centergram
Center on Education and Training
Ohio State University
1900 Kenny Road
Columbus, OH 43210
(800) 848-4815

Centergram provides information on education and training issues. Free of charge.

Challenge
P.O. Box 488
West Newbury, MA 01985
(508) 462-0495

The *Challenge* newsletter focuses on Attention Deficit Disorder. Available for $20/year.

Closing The Gap (CTG)
Box 68
Henderson, MN 56044
(612) 248-3294

CTG—Closing The Gap, a bi-monthly newsletter, provides in-depth coverage of computers and disabilities for basic education. Available for $21/year.

College Students with Learning Disabilities: A Handbook
LDA Bookstore
4156 Library Road
Pittsburgh, PA 15234
(412) 341-1515

Written by Susan A. Vogel, this publication is designed for students with learning disabilities, admissions officers, faculty and staff, and/ or administrators. The handbook discusses Section 504 in regard to college admissions, program accessibility, teaching and testing accommodations, test taking, and self-confidence building strategies. Available for $5.80.

Computer Disability News
National Easter Seal Society
230 W. Monroe Street
Chicago, IL 60606
(312) 726-6200
(312) 726-1491 (Fax)

Computer Disability News provides general information about computers and disability in education, the workplace, and independent living. Available for $15/year.

Learning (dis)Abilities
Learning Disabilities Consultants
P.O. Box 716
Bryn Mawr, PA 19010
(215) 525-8336

Learning (dis)Abilities contains a mixture of national and Pennsylvania news and resources. Available for $10/year.

Learning Disabilities, Graduate School, and Careers: The Student's Perspective
Learning Opportunities Program
Barat College
700 Westleigh Road
Lake Forest, IL 60045
(708) 234-3000

This publication informs the reader about the transition from college to graduate school or a career. In addition, a pamphlet called *Employers Guide to Learning Disabilities*, by Susan Little (Illinois Department of Human Rights), is available to assist employers who wish to comply with the Americans with Disabilities Act (ADA). Both are available for $3.

National Networker
National Network of Learning Disabled Adults
808 N. 82nd Street, Suite F2
Scottsdale, AZ 85257
(602) 941-5112

The *National Networker* is the quarterly newsletter for adults with learning disabilities.

OSERS News in Print
Office of Special Education and Rehabilitative Services
U.S. Department of Education
400 Maryland Avenue, SW, Switzer Building
Washington, DC 20202-3583
(202) 205-8241

OSERS provides information, research, and resources in the area of special learning needs. Published quarterly. Free.

Peterson's Guide to Colleges with Programs for Learning Disabled Students
Book Ordering Department
P.O. Box 2123
Princeton, NJ 08543-2123
(800) 338-3282

Peterson's Guide to Colleges with Programs for Learning Disabled Students, by Charles T. Mangrum II, Ed.D. and Stephen S. Strichart, Ph.D., is a comprehensive guide to more than 900 two-year colleges and universities offering special services for students with dyslexia and other learning disabilities. Peterson's Guide is available for $19.95, plus $4.75 shipping and handling.

PIP College "HELPS"
Partners in Publishing (PIP)
1419 West First
Tulsa, OK 74127
(918) 835-8258

PIP has available a wide variety of materials and publications on adults with learning disabilities. *PIP College "HELPS"* is a publication of Partners in Publishing. Written for adults with LD, parents, and service providers, it includes timely information and "first person" articles. Available for $33/year.

Postsecondary LD Network News
University of Connecticut
U-64, 249 Glenbrook Road
Storrs, CT 06269-2064
(202) 486-2020

Postsecondary LD Network News is published three times a year. It focuses on a variety of topics concerning adults with learning disabilities, service delivery, legal issues, and the latest resources in the field. Subscriptions are $20/year for individuals, and $30/year for schools. Contact Pat Anderson.

Promoting Postsecondary Education for Students with Learning Disabilities — A Handbook for Practitioners
PRO-ED
8700 Shoal Creek Boulevard
Austin, TX 78757
(512) 451-3246
(512) 451-8542 (Fax)

This Handbook is made up of comprehensive and practical chapters designed for the service provider. The Handbook also contains a comprehensive reference section, as well as 18 useful appendices.

Schoolsearch Guide to Colleges with Programs and Services for Students with Learning Disabilities
Schoolsearch Press
127 Marsh Street
Belmont, MA 02178
(617) 489-5785

This Guide lists more than 600 colleges and universities that offer programs and services to high school graduates with learning disabilities. *Schoolsearch Guide* is available for $29.95 from Schoolsearch Press.

Succeeding Against the Odds — Strategies and Insights from the Learning Disabled
Jeremy P. Tarcher, Inc.
5858 Wilshire Blvd.
Los Angeles, CA 90036
(213) 935-9980/9800

Succeeding Against the Odds, by Sally L. Smith, is filled with information on adults with learning disabilities. The author discusses the hidden handicaps, defines learning disabilities, and provides characteristics of individuals with learning disabilities. The book looks at the responsibility of preparing for adulthood. It also includes information for parents and teachers. Available for $12.95.

Understanding Your Learning Disability
The Ohio State University at Newark
University Drive
Newark, OH 43055
(614) 366-9246

Understanding Your Learning Disability (1988), by Cheri Warner, provides tips for students based on the author's experience as a Learning Disability Specialist. It offers definitions, characteristics, and suggestions related to reading, math, notetaking, test taking, social interactions, and organizational strategies. Available for $1.

Unlocking Potential: College and Other Choices for Learning Disabled People: A Step by Step Guide
Woodbine House
5615 Fishers Lane
Rockville, MD 20852
(800) 843-7323

Unlocking Potential, by Barbara Schieber and Jeanne Talpers, Adler & Adler (1987), is a comprehensive resource for considering, locating, and selecting postsecondary resources. The award winning book teaches and assists readers throughout the entire postsecondary selection process. Available for $ 12.95 (paperback).

Toll-Free Numbers

American Association for Vocational
Instructional Materials .... (800) 228-4689
Center for Adult Literacy & Learning .... (800) 642-2670
ERIC Clearinghouse on Adult, Career, and
Vocational Education .... (800) 848-4815
Equal Employment Opportunity Commission ... (800) 669-3362
Federal Financial Aid Hot Line .... (800) 433-3243
HEATH Resource Center .... (800) 544-3284
Job Accommodation Network .... (800) 526-7234
Learning Resources Network .... (800) 678-5376
Literacy Hot Line .... (800) 228-8813
National Center for Research in Vocational
Education .... (800) 762-4093
National Library Services for the Blind and
Physically Handicapped .... (800) 424-8567

Orton Dyslexia Society .... (800) 222-3123
Recording for the Blind .... (800) 221-4792
Social Security Administration .... (800) 772-1213
U.S. Office of Educational Research and
Improvement .... (800) 424-1616

Appendix

Sources of Help and Information on the Internet

Appendix

Sources of Help and Information on the Internet

General Resources

Internet Resources for Special Children
http://www.irsc.org/

Learning Disabilities Association of America
http://205.164.116.200/LDA/index.html

Learning Disabilities Online: "the interactive guide to learning disabilities for parents, teachers, and students"
http://www.ldonline.org/index.html

Special Needs Education Network
http://www.schoolnet.ca/sne/snenews/volume1/issue8/index.html

U.S. Department of Education
http://www.ed.gov/

PART I—Introduction to Learning Disabilities

LD in General
http://www.ldonline.org/ld_indepth/general_info/general.html

Learning Disabilities
http://gopher.nimh.nih.gov/publicat/learndis.htm

Learning Disabilities
http://www.irsc.org/learn_db.htm

PART II—Assessment

Assessment
http://www.ldonline.org/ld_indepth/assessment/assessment.html

ERIC Digest 530:
Connecting Performance Assessment to Instruction
gopher://ericir.syr.edu:70/00/Clearinghouses/16houses/ERIC_EC/
Instruction_Management/Digest_530

Intervention Techniques
http://curry.edschool.Virginia.EDU/go/cise/ose/information/
interventions.html

SNE News:
"The Politics of Inclusion" and "Moving from Testing to Assessment
http://www.schoolnet.ca/sne/snenews/volume1/issue8/index.html

PART III—Dyslexia and Other Academic Skills Disorders

Dyslexia and Learning Disabilities Resource
http://www.greenwood.org/respar.html

The Dyspraxia Foundation
http://www.emmbrook.demon.co.uk/dysprax/homepage.htm

The International Dyslexia Foundation
http://www.interdys.org/

PART IV—Sensory and Communication Disorders

American Speech-Language-Hearing Association
http://www.asha.org/

Deaf Resources
http://curry.edschool.virginia.edu/go/cise/ose/categories/hi.html

Processing Deficits
http://www.ldonline.org/ld_indepth/process_deficit/pro_deficits.html

Resources for the Visually Impaired
http://curry.edschool.virginia.edu/go/cise/ose/categories/vi.html

Speech and Language
http://www.ldonline.org/ld_indepth/speech-language/speech-
language.html

Web Resources On Communication Disorders
http://curry.edschool.virginia.edu/go/cise/ose/categories/cd.html

PART V—Other Neurological Disorders That Impede Learning

ADD and ADHD
http://www.ldonline.org/ld_indepth/add_adhd/add-adhd.html

ADD/ADHD
http://www.irsc.org/add.htm

Autism
http://www.irsc.org/autism.htm

The Autism Society of America
http://www.autism-society.org/

Children and Adults with Attention Deficit Disorders
http://chadd.org/

PART VI—Legal and Social Information for Parents of Learning Disabled Children

The Disability Activist
http://www.teleport.com/~abarhydt/

ERIC Digest 509:
Juvenile Correction and the Exceptional Student
gopher://ericir.syr.edu:70/00/Clearinghouses/16houses/ERIC_EC/
Instruction_Management/Digest509

Legal and Legislative
http://www.ldonline.org/ld_indepth/legal_legislative/
legal_legislative.html

Parenting and Support Resources
http://www.irsc.org/parents.htm

Self-Esteem
http://www.ldonline.org/ld_indepth/self_esteem/self_esteem.html

Social Skills
http://www.ldonline.org/ld_indepth/social_skills/soc-skills.html

PART VII—Special Information for Older Students and Adults with Learning Disabilities

Eric Digest 466:
College Planning for Students with Learning Disabilities
gopher://ericir.syr.edu:70/00/Clearinghouses/16houses/ERIC_EC/
Learning_Disabilities/Digest466

ERIC Special Ed/Technology Resources
http://www.cec.sped.org/minibibs/techreso.htm

National Institute On Life Planning Home Page
http://www.sonic.net/nilp/

Parent Pals Assistive Technology Special Education Links
http://www.parentpals.com/1.0Specialed/1.1geninfo/1.1.7Tech.html

Resources About Learning Disabilities:
 Employment and Related Issues
http://ncld.org/resources4.html

Post Secondary Education
http://www.ldonline.org/ld_indepth/postsecondary/index.html

Transition
http://www.ldonline.org/ld_indepth/transition/transition.html

Index

Index

NOTE: Italicized "n" after page number indicates a note; page numbers in italics indicate tables or figures.

A

551

569

Diabetes Sourcebook, 2nd Edition

Basic Information about Insulin-Dependent Diabetes, Noninsulin-Dependent Diabetes, Gestational Diabetes, and Related Disorders, Including Diabetes Prevalence Data, Management Issues, the Role of Diet and Exercise in Controlling Diabetes, Insulin and Other Diabetes Medicines, and Complications of Diabetes Such as Eye Diseases, Digestive Disorders, Periodontal Disease, Amputation, and End-Stage Renal Disease; Along with Reports on Current Research Initiatives, a Glossary, and Resource Listings for Further Help and Information

Edited by Karen Bellenir. 800 pages. 1998. 0-7808-0224-1. $78.

Diet & Nutrition Sourcebook, 1st Edition

Basic Information about Nutrition, Including the Dietary Guidelines for Americans, the Food Guide Pyramid, and Their Applications in Daily Diet, Nutritional Advice for Specific Age Groups, Current Nutritional Issues and Controversies, the New Food Label and How to Use It to Promote Healthy Eating, and Recent Developments in Nutritional Research

Edited by Dan R. Harris. 662 pages. 1996. 0-7808-0084-2. $78.

"Useful reference as a food and nutrition sourcebook for the general consumer."
— *Booklist Health Sciences Supplement, Oct '97*

"Recommended for public libraries and medical libraries that receive general information requests on nutrition. It is readable and will appeal to those interested in learning more about healthy dietary practices."
— *Medical Reference Services Quarterly, Fall '97*

"An abundance of medical and social statistics is translated into readable information geared toward the general reader." — *Bookwatch, Mar '97*

"With dozens of questionable diet books on the market, it is so refreshing to find a reliable and factual reference book. Recommended to aspiring professionals, librarians, and others seeking and giving reliable dietary advice. An excellent compilation." — *Choice, Feb '97*

Diet & Nutrition Sourcebook, 2nd Edition

Basic Information about Nutrition, Including General Nutritional Recommendations, Recommendations for People with Specific Medical Concerns, Dieting for Weight Control, Nutritional Supplements, Food Safety Issues, the Relationship between Nutrition and Disease Development, and Other Nutritional Research Reports; Along with Statistical and Demographic Data, Lifestyle Modification Recommendations, and Sources of Additional Help and Information

Edited by Karen Bellenir. 600 pages. 1998. 0-7808-0228-4. $78.

Ear, Nose & Throat Disorders Sourcebook

Basic Information about Disorders of the Ears, Nose, Sinus Cavities, Pharynx, and Larynx, Including Ear Infections, Tinnitus, Vestibular Disorders, Allergic and Non-Allergic Rhinitis, Sore Throats, Tonsillitis, and Cancers That Affect the Ears, Nose, Sinuses, and Throat, Along with Reports on Current Research Initiatives, a Glossary of Related Medical Terms, and a Directory of Sources for Further Help and Information

Edited by Karen Bellenir and Linda M. Shin. 592 pages. 1998. 0-7808-0206-3. $78.

Endocrine & Metabolic Disorders Sourcebook

Basic Information for the Layperson about Pancreatic and Insulin-Related Disorders Such as Pancreatitis, Diabetes, and Hypoglycemia; Adrenal Gland Disorders Such as Cushing's Syndrome, Addison's Disease, and Congenital Adrenal Hyperplasia; Pituitary Gland Disorders Such as Growth Hormone Deficiency, Acromegaly, and Pituitary Tumors; Thyroid Disorders Such as Hypothyroidism, Graves' Disease, Hashimoto's Disease, and Goiter; Hyperparathyroidism; and Other Diseases and Syndromes of Hormone Imbalance or Metabolic Dysfunction, Along with Reports on Current Research Initiatives

Edited by Linda M. Shin. 632 pages. 1998. 0-7808-0207-1. $78.

Environmentally Induced Disorders Sourcebook

Basic Information about Diseases and Syndromes Linked to Exposure to Pollutants and Other Substances in Outdoor and Indoor Environments Such as Lead, Asbestos, Formaldehyde, Mercury, Emissions, Noise, and More

Edited by Allan R. Cook. 620 pages. 1997. 0-7808-0083-4. $78.

". . . a good survey of numerous environmentally induced physical disorders . . . a useful addition to anyone's library ."
— *Doody's Health Science Book Reviews, Jan '98*

". . . provide[s] introductory information from the best authorities around. Since this volume covers topics that potentially affect everyone, it will surely be one of the most frequently consulted volumes in the *Health Reference Series*." — *Rettig on Reference, Nov '97*

"Recommended reference source."
— *Booklist, Oct '97*

Fitness & Exercise Sourcebook

Basic Information on Fitness and Exercise, Including Fitness Activities for Specific Age Groups, Exercise for People with Specific Medical Conditions, How to Begin a Fitness Program in Running, Walking, Swimming, Cycling, and Other Athletic Activities, and Recent Research in Fitness and Exercise

Edited by Dan R. Harris. 663 pages. 1996. 0-7808-0186-5. $78.

"A good resource for general readers."
— *Choice, Nov '97*

"The perennial popularity of the topic . . . make this an appealing selection for public libraries."
— *Rettig on Reference, Jun/Jul '97*

Food & Animal Borne Diseases Sourcebook

Basic Information about Diseases That Can Be Spread to Humans through the Ingestion of Contaminated Food or Water or by Contact with Infected Animals and Insects, Such as Botulism, E. Coli, Hepatitis A, Trichinosis, Lyme Disease, and Rabies, Along with Information Regarding Prevention and Treatment Methods, and a Special Section for International Travelers Describing Diseases Such as Cholera, Malaria, Travelers' Diarrhea, and Yellow Fever, and Offering Recommendations for Avoiding Illness

Edited by Karen Bellenir and Peter D. Dresser. 535 pages. 1995. 0-7808-0033-8. $78.

"Targeting general readers and providing them with a single, comprehensive source of information on selected topics, this book continues, with the excellent caliber of its predecessors, to catalog topical information on health matters of general interest. Readable and thorough, this valuable resource is highly recommended for all libraries."
— *Academic Library Book Review, Summer '96*

"A comprehensive collection of authoritative information."
— *Emergency Medical Services, Oct '95*

Gastrointestinal Diseases & Disorders Sourcebook

Basic Information about Gastroesophageal Reflux Disease (Heartburn), Ulcers, Diverticulosis, Irritable Bowel Syndrome, Crohn's Disease, Ulcerative Colitis, Diarrhea, Constipation, Lactose Intolerance, Hemorrhoids, Hepatitis, Cirrhosis, and Other Digestive Problems, Featuring Statistics, Descriptions of Symptoms, and Current Treatment Methods of Interest for Persons Living with Upper and Lower Gastrointestinal Maladies

Edited by Linda M. Ross. 413 pages. 1996. 0-7808-0078-8. $78.

". . . very readable form. The successful editorial work that brought this material together into a useful and understandable reference makes accessible to all readers information that can help them more effectively understand and obtain help for digestive tract problems."
— *Choice, Feb '97*

Genetic Disorders Sourcebook

Basic Information about Heritable Diseases and Disorders Such as Down Syndrome, PKU, Hemophilia, Von Willebrand Disease, Gaucher Disease, Tay-Sachs Disease, and Sickle-Cell Disease, Along with Information about Genetic Screening, Gene Therapy, Home Care, and Including Source Listings for Further Help and Information on More Than 300 Disorders

Edited by Karen Bellenir. 642 pages. 1996. 0-7808-0034-6. $78.

"Provides essential medical information to both the general public and those diagnosed with a serious or fatal genetic disease or disorder." — *Choice, Jan '97*

". . . geared toward the lay public. It would be well placed in all public libraries and in those hospital and medical libraries in which access to genetic references is limited."
— *Doody's Health Sciences Book Review, Oct '96*

Head Trauma Sourcebook

Basic Information for the Layperson about Open-Head and Closed-Head Injuries, Treatment Advances, Recovery, and Rehabilitation, Along with Reports on Current Research Initiatives

Edited by Karen Bellenir. 414 pages. 1997. 0-7808-0208-X. $78.

Health Insurance Sourcebook

Basic Information about Managed Care Organizations, Traditional Fee-for-Service Insurance, Insurance Portability and Pre-Existing Conditions Clauses, Medicare, Medicaid, Social Security, and Military Health Care, Along with Information about Insurance Fraud

Edited by Wendy Wilcox. 530 pages. 1997. 0-7808-0222-5. $78.

"The layout of the book is particularly helpful as it provides easy access to reference material. A most useful addition to the vast amount of information about health insurance. The use of data from U.S. government agencies is most commendable. Useful in a library or learning center for healthcare professional students."
— *Doody's Health Sciences Book Reviews, Nov '97*

Immune System Disorders Sourcebook

Basic Information about Lupus, Multiple Sclerosis, Guillain-Barré Syndrome, Chronic Granulomatous Disease, and More, Along with Statistical and Demographic Data and Reports on Current Research Initiatives

Edited by Allan R. Cook. 608 pages. 1997. 0-7808-0209-8. $78.

Kidney & Urinary Tract Diseases & Disorders Sourcebook

Basic Information about Kidney Stones, Urinary Incontinence, Bladder Disease, End Stage Renal Disease, Dialysis, and More, Along with Statistical and Demographic Data and Reports on Current Research Initiatives

Edited by Linda M. Ross. 602 pages. 1997. 0-7808-0079-6. $78.

Learning Disabilities Sourcebook

Basic Information about Disorders Such as Dyslexia, Visual and Auditory Processing Deficits, Attention Deficit/Hyperactivity Disorder, and Autism, Along with Statistical and Demographic Data, Reports on Current Research Initiatives, an Explanation of the Assessment Process, and a Special Section for Adults with Learning Disabilities

Edited by Linda M. Shin. 579 pages. 1998. 0-7808-0210-1. $78.

Men's Health Concerns Sourcebook

Basic Information about Health Issues That Affect Men, Featuring Facts about the Top Causes of Death in Men, Including Heart Disease, Stroke, Cancers, Prostate Disorders, Chronic Obstructive Pulmonary Disease, Pneumonia and Influenza, Human Immunodeficiency Virus and Acquired Immune Deficiency Syndrome, Diabetes Mellitus, Stress, Suicide, Accidents and Homicides; and Facts about Common Concerns for Men, Including Impotence, Contraception, Circumcision, Sleep Disorders, Snoring, Hair Loss, Diet, Nutrition, Exercise, Kidney and Urological Disorders, and Backaches

Edited by Allan R. Cook. 760 pages. 1998. 0-7808-0212-8. $78.

Mental Health Disorders Sourcebook

Basic Information about Schizophrenia, Depression, Bipolar Disorder, Panic Disorder, Obsessive-Compulsive Disorder, Phobias and Other Anxiety Disorders, Paranoia and Other Personality Disorders, Eating Disorders, and Sleep Disorders, Along with Information about Treatment and Therapies

Edited by Karen Bellenir. 548 pages. 1996. 0-7808-0040-0. $78.

"This is an excellent new book . . . written in easy-to-understand language."
— *Booklist Health Science Supplement, Oct '97*

". . . useful for public and academic libraries and consumer health collections."
— *Medical Reference Services Quarterly, Spring '97*

"The great strengths of the book are its readability and its inclusion of places to find more information. Especially recommended." — *RQ, Winter '96*

". . . a good resource for a consumer health library."
— *Bulletin of the MLA, Oct '96*

"The information is data-based and couched in brief, concise language that avoids jargon. . . . a useful reference source." — *Readings, Sept '96*

"The text is well organized and adequately written for its target audience." — *Choice, Jun '96*

". . . provides information on a wide range of mental disorders, presented in nontechnical language."
— *Exceptional Child Education Resources, Spring '96*

"Recommended for public and academic libraries."
— *Reference Book Review, '96*

Ophthalmic Disorders Sourcebook

Basic Information about Glaucoma, Cataracts, Macular Degeneration, Strabismus, Refractive Disorders, and More, Along with Statistical and Demographic Data and Reports on Current Research Initiatives

Edited by Linda M. Ross. 631 pages. 1996. 0-7808-0081-8. $78.

Oral Health Sourcebook

Basic Information about Diseases and Conditions Affecting Oral Health, Including Cavities, Gum Disease, Dry Mouth, Oral Cancers, Fever Blisters, Canker Sores, Oral Thrush, Bad Breath, Temporomandibular Disorders, and other Craniofacial Syndromes, Along with Statistical Data on the Oral Health of Americans, Oral Hygiene, Emergency First Aid, Information on Treatment Procedures and Methods of Replacing Lost Teeth

Edited by Allan R. Cook. 558 pages. 1997. 0-7808-0082-6. $78.

"Recommended reference source." — *Booklist, Dec '97*

Pain Sourcebook

Basic Information about Specific Forms of Acute and Chronic Pain, Including Headaches, Back Pain, Muscular Pain, Neuralgia, Surgical Pain, and Cancer Pain, Along with Pain Relief Options Such as Analgesics, Narcotics, Nerve Blocks, Transcutaneous Nerve Stimulation, and Alternative Forms of Pain Control, Including Biofeedback, Imaging, Behavior Modification, and Relaxation Techniques

Edited by Allan R. Cook. 667 pages. 1997. 0-7808-0213-6. $78.

"The information is basic in terms of scholarship and is appropriate for general readers. Written in journalistic style . . . intended for non-professionals. Quite thorough in its coverage of different pain conditions and summarizes the latest clinical information regarding pain treatment." — *Choice, Jun '98*

"Recommended reference source."
— *Booklist, Mar '98*

Pregnancy & Birth Sourcebook

Basic Information about Planning for Pregnancy, Maternal Health, Fetal Growth and Development, Labor and Delivery, Postpartum and Perinatal Care, Pregnancy in Mothers with Special Concerns, and Disorders of Pregnancy, Including Genetic Counseling, Nutrition and Exercise, Obstetrical Tests, Pregnancy Discomfort, Multiple Births, Cesarean Sections, Medical Testing of Newborns, Breastfeeding, Gestational Diabetes, and Ectopic Pregnancy

Edited by Heather E. Aldred. 737 pages. 1997. 0-7808-0216-0. $78.

". . . for the layperson. A well-organized handbook. Recommended for college libraries . . . general readers."
— *Choice, Apr '98*

"Recommended reference source."
— *Booklist, Mar '98*

"This resource is recommended for public libraries to have on hand."
— *American Reference Books Annual, '98*

Public Health Sourcebook

Basic Information about Government Health Agencies, Including National Health Statistics and Trends, Healthy People 2000 Program Goals and Objectives, the Centers for Disease Control and Prevention, the Food and Drug Administration, and the National Institutes of Health, Along with Full Contact Information for Each Agency

Edited by Wendy Wilcox. 698 pages. 1998. 0-7808-0220-9. $78.

Rehabilitation Sourcebook

Basic Information for the Layperson about Physical Medicine (Physiatry) and Rehabilitative Therapies, Including Physical, Occupational, Recreational, Speech, and Vocational Therapy; Along with Descriptions of Devices and Equipment Such as Orthotics, Gait Aids, Prostheses, and Adaptive Systems Used during Rehabilitation and for Activities of Daily Living, and Featuring a Glossary and Source Listings for Further Help and Information

Edited by Theresa K. Murray. 600 pages. 1998. 0-7808-0236-5. $78.

Respiratory Diseases & Disorders Sourcebook

Basic Information about Respiratory Diseases and Disorders, Including Asthma, Cystic Fibrosis, Pneumonia, the Common Cold, Influenza, and Others, Featuring Facts about the Respiratory System, Statistical and Demographic Data, Treatments, Self-Help Management Suggestions, and Current Research Initiatives

Edited by Allan R. Cook and Peter D. Dresser. 771 pages. 1995. 0-7808-0037-0. $78.

"Designed for the layperson and for patients and their families coping with respiratory illness. . . . an extensive array of information on diagnosis, treatment, management, and prevention of respiratory illnesses for the general reader."
— *Choice, Jun '96*

"A highly recommended text for all collections. It is a comforting reminder of the power of knowledge that good books carry between their covers."
— *Academic Library Book Review, Spring '96*

"This sourcebook offers a comprehensive collection of authoritative information presented in a nontechnical, humanitarian style for patients, families, and caregivers."
— *Association of Operating Room Nurses, Sept/Oct '95*

Sexually Transmitted Diseases Sourcebook

Basic Information about Herpes, Chlamydia, Gonorrhea, Hepatitis, Nongonoccocal Urethritis, Pelvic Inflammatory Disease, Syphilis, AIDS, and More, Along with Current Data on Treatments and Preventions

Edited by Linda M. Ross. 550 pages. 1997. 0-7808-0217-9. $78.